Housing Conditions

tenants' rights

Jan Luba QC is a circuit judge. He was formerly a barrister in the housing team at Garden Court Chambers in London. He was called to the Bar in 1980 and was made Queen's Counsel in 2000. Jan is co-author of *Defending Possession Proceedings* (LAG) and *Housing Allocation and Homelessness* (Jordans). He writes, with Sam Madge-Wyld, the monthly series: 'Housing: recent developments' in *Legal Action*. At the time of writing, Jan was a resident judge at the County Court at Central London and the acting Designated Civil Judge for the London Region.

Catherine O'Donnell is a barrister at Garden Court Chambers in London. Catherine practices in all areas of housing law and has a particular interest in disrepair and housing conditions. She is ranked as a leading junior in social housing in Legal 500 (2019). Prior to coming to the bar Catherine worked in the voluntary sector. Catherine writes the housing repairs update in *Legal Action*.

Giles Peaker is a partner in the housing team at Anthony Gold solicitors, with a wide ranging housing practice. He is the founder and editor of the Nearly Legal housing law website and a former chair of the Housing Law Practitioners Association. Giles worked with Karen Buck MP on the Homes (Fitness for Human Habitation) Act 2018 from its conception in 2015. Giles was the housing Legal Aid Lawyer of the Year in 2018.

The purpose of Legal Action Group is to promote equal access to justice for all members of society who are socially, economically or otherwise disadvantaged. To this end, it seeks to improve law and practice, the administration of justice and legal services.

Housing Conditions

tenants' rights

SIXTH EDITION

by HHJ Jan Luba QC, Catherine O'Donnell

and Giles Peaker

LAG the access to justice charity

Legal Action Group
2019

This edition published in Great Britain 2019
by LAG Education and Service Trust Limited
National Pro Bono Centre, 48 Chancery Lane, London WC2A 1JF
www.lag.org.uk

British Library Cataloguing in Publication Data
a CIP catalogue record for this book is available from the British Library.

FSC
www.fsc.org
MIX
Paper | Supporting responsible forestry
FSC® C020438

This book has been produced using Forest Stewardship Council (FSC) certified paper. The wood used to produce FSC certified products with a 'Mixed Sources' label comes from FSC certified well-managed forests, controlled sources and/or recycled material.

print ISBN 978 1 912273 42 3
ebook ISBN 978 1 912273 43 0
print / ebook bundle ISBN 978 1 912273 44 7

Typeset by Refinecatch Limited, Bungay, Suffolk
Printed in Great Britain by Hobbs the Printers, Totton, Hampshire

Author's note

This book is intended to be of help to tenants and their advisers in getting to grips with law and practice relating to poor housing conditions in rented housing.

Our own work on it has been greatly strengthened by the contributions of others. In particular, Mel Cairns of the Health and Housing Group drafted appendix D for us, Stephen Gilchrist of Clarke Barnes solicitors provided invaluable assistance with chapter 6 (on Environmental Protection Act prosecutions), and Eleanor Solomon of Anthony Gold solicitors gave substantial help with the section on legal aid funding. Other professional colleagues who have provided helpful advice include: Deirdre Forster, Jane Grant, Pam Griffiths, Sara Stephens and Jacqueline Everett.

More generally, we owe a debt of gratitude and pay our respects to all legal aid housing lawyers and advisers who work so hard to improve housing conditions for their clients.

We pay particular tribute to Karen Buck MP and Justin Bates, without whom there would have been considerably less need for this new edition.

We recognise that our work builds on that of contributors to earlier editions of this work under its previous title *Repairs: tenants' rights*. They include Stephen Knafler QC, Beatrice Prevatt and Deirdre Forster.

We would also like to thank the following family members and friends for their unstinting support: Adriana Luba, Phil Taylor and Beth Peaker.

The excellent-as-ever Esther Pilger at LAG has tried to iron out our mistakes but any that remain are entirely down to us.

The text reflects our understanding of the law of England as at 20 March 2019.

Jan Luba
Catherine O'Donnell
Giles Peaker
April 2019

Contents

Table of cases

Cody v Philps December 2005 *Legal Action* 28, *Housing Law Casebook* 7th edn paras R19.1, R19.11, West London County Court	2.11, 3.13, 3.218
Collins v Hopkins [1923] 2 KB 617, [1923] 6 WLUK 78, 34 ALR 703, KBD	2.146
Collins v Northern Ireland Housing Executive [1987] 1 WLUK 75, [1987] 2 NIJB 27, CA (NI)	2.157
Commissioner of Police of the Metropolis v Brown [2018] EWHC 2046 (Admin), [2018] 7 WLUK 747, [2018] 4 Costs LR 897	3.77
Connaught Restaurants Ltd v Indoor Leisure Ltd [1994] 1 WLR 501, [1994] 4 All ER 834, [1993] 7 WLUK 217, [1993] 46 EG 184, [1993] EG 143 (CS), (1993) 143 NLJ 1188, [1993] NPC 118, (1993) *Times*, July 27, CA	3.13
Conroy v Hire Token Ltd [2001] 5 WLUK 706, February 2002 *Legal Action* 22, *Housing Law Casebook* 7th edn para R18.40, Manchester County Court	7.119
Coventry City Council v Cartwright [1975] 1 WLR 845, [1975] 2 All ER 99, [1975] 1 WLUK 730, 73 LGR 218, (1975) 119 SJ 235, DC	6.17, 6.23
Coventry City Council v Doyle [1981] 1 WLR 1325, [1981] 2 All ER 184, [1980] 12 WLUK 168, [1981] JPL 666, QBD	6.10, 6.81, 6.105
Credit Suisse v Beegas Nominees Ltd [1994] 4 All ER 803, [1993] 9 WLUK 9, (1995) 69 P & CR 177, [1994] 1 EGLR 76, [1994] 12 EG 189, [1994] 11 EG 151, [1993] EG 157 (CS), [1993] NPC 123, (1993) *Independent*, September 15, ChD	7.26, 7.39
Cunningham v Birmingham City Council [1997] 5 WLUK 71, [1998] Env LR 1, (1998) 30 HLR 158, [1998] JPL 147, [1997] COD 448, (1997) *Times*, June 9, (1997) *Independent*, May 19, QBD	6.16
D&F Estates Ltd v Church Commissioners for England [1989] AC 177, [1988] 3 WLR 368, [1988] 2 All ER 992, [1988] 7 WLUK 197, 41 BLR 1, 15 Con LR 35, [1988] 2 EGLR 213, (1988) 4 Const LJ 100, [1988] EG 113 (CS), (1988) 85(33) LSG 46, (1988) 138 NLJ Rep 210, (1988) 132 SJ 1092, HL	2.173, 2.174
DR v Southwark LBC December 2014 *Legal Action* 26, Lambeth County Court	2.72
DR v Southwark LBC December 2015 *Legal Action* 41, *Housing Law Casebook* 7th edn para R18.42, Central London County Court	2.72, 3.46, 7.94
Dadd v Christian Action (Enfield) Housing Association December 1994 *Legal Action* 18	7.126
Dame Margaret Hungerford Charity Trustees v Beazeley [1993] 4 WLUK 217, (1994) 26 HLR 269, [1993] 29 EG 100, [1993] EG 90 (CS), [1993] NPC 71, (1993) *Times*, May 17, CA	2.89, 2.259
Darlington BC v Munnelly December 2015 *Legal Action* 42	6.37
Dashwood v Dashwood [1927] WN 276, 64 LJNC 431, ChD	3.178

Table of statutes

Table of statutory instruments

Civil Legal Aid (Procedure) Regulations (Procedure Regs) 2012 SI No 3098–	
reg 9	4.41
reg 22(1)(b)(ii)	4.26
reg 38	4.68
Pt 5 (regs 50–53)	4.53
Civil Legal Aid (Remuneration) Regulations 2013 SI No 422–	
Sch 1 Pt 1 Table 1	4.35
Civil Legal Aid (Statutory Charge) Regulations 2013 SI No 503	4.71
reg 4(1)	4.72
reg 4(2)	4.73
Civil Procedure Rules 1998 (CPR) SI No 3132	3.88, 3.116
r1.1(2)(c)	3.88
r3.14	3.156
PD3E	3.156
r7.4(1)(b)	3.114
r7.4(2)	3.114
r7.5(1)	3.113
r7.6(3)	3.113
r12.4(1)	3.143
r12.4(2)(a)	3.143
r12.7	3.143
r16.3	3.110
r16.3(4)	3.111
r16.4(2)(a)(ii)	3.115
PD16 para 4.2	3.116
PD16 para 4.3	3.116
PD16 para 7.3	3.116
Pt 18	3.119
r19.3	3.47
r20.4	4.11
r20.7(3)(b)	3.227
r20.42	3.217
r21.5(3)	3.106
Pt 23	3.143, 3.201
r24.2	3.144
PD24 para 7	3.143
PD24 para 9.2	3.146
r25.1(1)(b)	3.195
r25.1(1)(f)	3.204
r25.6	3.142, 7.11
r25.7	3.142
PD25A para 4.3	3.129
r26.3	3.147
r26.6(1)(a)	3.149
r26.6(1)(b)	3.149, 4.50
r26.6(4)	3.150
r31.6	3.160
r31.10(6)	3.161

Table of abbreviations

ADR	alternative dispute resolution
AST	assured shorthold tenancy
ATE	after-the-event
CCICA Regs 2013	Consumer Contracts (Information, Cancellation and Additional Charges) Regulations 2013
CCMS	Client and Cost Management System
CFA	conditional fee agreement
CJA 1967	Criminal Justice Act 1967
CPR	Civil Procedure Rules
CRA 2015	Consumer Rights Act 2015
Crim PR	Criminal Procedure Rules
C(RTP)A 1999	Contracts (Rights of Third Parties) Act 1999
DA 2015	Deregulation Act 2015
DCLG	Department for Communities and Local Government
DQ	directions questionnaire
DWP	Department for Work and Pensions
DA 2015	Deregulation Act 2015
DPA 1972	Defective Premises Act 1972
ECF	Exceptional Case Funding
EHO	environmental health officer
ELR	Emergency Legal Representation
EPA 1990	Environmental Protection Act 1990
FR Regs 2013	Civil Legal Aid (Financial Resources and Payment for Services) Regulations 2013
HA 1961	Housing Act 1961
HA 1985	Housing Act 1985
HA 1988	Housing Act 1988
HA 1996	Housing Act 1996
HA 2004	Housing Act 2004
HHSRS	Housing Health and Safety Rating System
HHSRS Regs 2005	Housing Health and Safety Rating System Regulations 2005
HMO	house in multiple occupation
HRA 1998	Human Rights Act 1998
HPA 2016	Housing and Planning Act 2016
JC	Judicial College

LA 1980	Limitation Act 1980
LAA	Legal Aid Agency
LASPO 2012	Legal Aid, Sentencing and Punishment of Offenders Act 2012
LCG	Lord Chancellor's Guidance
LGHA 1989	Local Government and Housing Act 1989
LOC	letter of claim
LTA 1985	Landlord and Tenant Act 1985
LTA 1987	Landlord and Tenant Act 1987
MCOL	Money Claims Online
Merits Regs 2013	Civil Legal Aid (Merits Criteria) Regulations 2013
MHCLG	Ministry of Housing, Communities and Local Government
OFT	Office of Fair Trading
OLA 1957	Occupiers Liability Act 1957
PCCSA 2000	Powers of Criminal Courts (Sentencing) Act 2000
PD	Practice Direction
PHA 1936	Public Health Act 1936
Procedure Regs 2012	Civil Legal Aid (Procedure) Regulations 2012
QOCS	Qualified One-way Costs Shifting
RA 1977	Rent Act 1977
RICS	Royal Institution of Chartered Surveyors
RSH	Regulator of Social Housing
SCCO	Senior Courts Cost Office
SRA	Solicitors Regulation Authority
TCC	Technology and Construction Court
UCTA 1977	Unfair Contract Terms Act 1977
UTCC Regs 1999	Unfair Terms in Consumer Contracts Regulations 1999

CHAPTER 1

Introduction

This book

1.1 This book is about bad housing conditions in rented accommodation in England.[1] It is primarily written for the assistance of the *occupiers* of that housing and their advisers, but it will also be useful to landlords and to those who advise them.

1.2 The book covers the private rented sector, council housing and homes let by housing associations or other social landlords. It deals with all rented accommodation, whether a house, maisonette, flat or simply a room. Although the title would suggest it is exclusively about the rights of 'tenants', much of the text will be of help to other occupiers of rented housing (the family members of tenants, their lodgers, sub-tenants, guests and visitors) and to those who live near poor quality rented housing and are affected by its condition.

1.3 Earlier editions of this book have focussed heavily on problems with housing conditions related to 'repair' and 'disrepair'. This new edition takes a broader approach in the light of recent legal developments.[2] The changed approach is reflected not only in the book's new title[3] – there has also been considerable revision and restructuring of the content. The text of the book is now concerned more generally with problems arising from the poor condition of much rented housing. It therefore deals with fitness for human habitation and with health and safety issues going well beyond the traditional concern of lawyers and other advisers with the topic of repair/disrepair (while also dealing with those issues).

1.4 The book not only tackles what tenants can do to obtain better conditions themselves, but also what local councils, responsible for housing conditions in their areas, can do to help them achieve improved conditions. The structure of the book follows that approach. Early chapters focus on the individual rights of tenants (and the responsibilities of landlords), how they might enforce their rights in the civil courts, how they can fund the costs of their legal advice and representation, and what remedies they can obtain. The later chapters consider the broader statutory schemes by which local councils can take action to help tenants and tackle bad housing conditions. They also explain how to trigger intervention by councils, and how tenants

1 Housing is a topic devolved to the governments of Northern Ireland, Scotland and Wales. Each of those countries has its own laws and procedures governing the condition of rented housing.

2 In particular, the recent Homes (Fitness for Human Habitation) Act 2018.

3 Previous editions were titled *Repairs: tenants' rights*.

might get help from the criminal courts to address the unhealthiest homes. The final chapter deals with compensation for victims of poor housing conditions.

1.5 The relevant law is often complex and hard to access. We have therefore reproduced the most relevant statutory provisions in the appendices. The terminology used to describe particular problems with housing can also be complex, so we have an appendix explaining, with diagrams, the main technical features found in rented accommodation. Even the paperwork involved in pursuing a claim for a remedy can be complex, so the appendices include worked examples of the documentation used in all the main stages of enforcement of rights using the legal system.

1.6 The book is light on legal theory and heavy on practicalities – and deliberately so. There is no expectation that the reader will digest the book from start to finish. It is intended to be practitioner-friendly and to be a resource to be dipped into, as and when necessary. The hope is that the detailed contents lists at the start of each chapter and the detailed index at the back will lead the reader to the most helpful point in the text.

1.7 Sadly, as the text demonstrates, most of the relevant law is not simple. Housing conditions have been the subject of much legislation and numerous court decisions over many decades – as the footnotes and tables indicate. To keep matters as simple as possible, we have only referred in the footnotes to a maximum of two reference points to each court case. Where there are further sources for that case, they are given in the table of cases. Any reader who wishes to obtain the full text of any modern decision of the higher courts will find that available, free of charge, on the excellent website of the British and Irish Legal Information Institute.[4]

1.8 Although this is the sixth edition, it may not be the last. Feedback and comment from readers, particularly on suggestions for improvement or addition, would be warmly welcomed by the authors.

1.9 Readers may find it helpful to keep up to date with the matters covered in this book by consulting the annual *Housing repairs: update* in *Legal Action*.

The law about housing conditions

1.10 The law about housing conditions in England is to be found in a myriad of statutes, regulations and in the judge-made common law.

4 www.bailii.org.

There is much that could and should be done to codify, simplify and improve the law relating to housing conditions. Too often the complexity of the underlying law, and the absence of the resources needed to enforce it, have together proved too daunting a challenge both to tenants and their advisers. Likewise to busy local housing authorities which should be enforcing minimum housing conditions but are weighed down with other priorities and starved of resources.

1.11 It is now more than two decades since Lord Woolf, having been invited to review the way the courts handled civil housing cases, reported that 'reform of the substantive law on housing could do more than anything to reduce delay'.[5] There has been ample time for successive governments to digest the comprehensive and compelling case he made for a simplification of the law on housing.

1.12 In 1996, the law reform body, the Law Commission, set out the problems that the state of the law on housing conditions was causing and the need for change. It produced a draft Landlord and Tenant Bill suitable for swift introduction in, and passage through, Parliament.[6] However, that course was not adopted.

1.13 The Law Commission subsequently took on the challenge of reviewing and codifying the whole law relating to rented accommodation. That huge task was completed in the Spring of 2006. In its final report, *Renting homes*,[7] the Law Commission not only called for implementation of the recommendations about repairs that it had made ten years earlier,[8] but also offered a new charter of clear rights and obligations relating to repair in rented housing[9] and, again, a draft bill containing the necessary legislation. Again, nothing has happened to make those changes to the law in England.

1.14 However, the position on legislation and law reform relating to housing conditions in England has not been wholly bleak.

1.15 The Housing Act (HA) 2004 was designed to reform the law relating to the way in which local councils could secure decent housing conditions in their areas. Since coming into force in 2006, it has given councils powers and duties to tackle adverse housing conditions through the broader medium of addressing housing hazards, rather than fitness or disrepair and through a landlord's licence conditions.

5 *Access to Justice: final report*, July 1996, para 16.2.

6 Law Com 238 *Landlord and tenant: responsibility for state and condition of property*, 19 March 1996.

7 Law Com 297 *Renting homes: the final report*, Cm 6781, 2006.

8 *Renting homes: the final report*, Part 2 para 2.28.

9 *Renting homes: the final report*, Part 8.

Although (as chapter 5 of this book describes) the assessment process is complex and enforcement is by no means straightforward, there has been much recent progress in inspection and enforcement.[10] However, the HA 2004 did little to address the need for legislative improvements in tenants' individual rights to address housing conditions.

1.16 When the Localism Act 2011 was passing through Parliament, amendments were put forward to change the law for the better. The amendments sought, among other things, to widen the scope of tenant's rights to cover rectification of design defects and/or to make landlords liable to keep their premises fit for purpose. The proposed amendments were not accepted by the government on the basis that the then division of responsibilities and obligations between landlord and tenant was the right one and that a mechanism existed already to take action against landlords who fail to provide safe accommodation, namely, the housing health and safety rating system under the HA 2004.[11]

1.17 The more recent Consumer Rights Act 2015 simplified and codified the law relating to unfair terms in tenancy agreements and the Deregulation Act 2015 enacted some measures to prevent tenants who raise issues about housing conditions from being subject to 'retaliatory eviction' for doing so. Yet further legislation has brought some modest change – not least through the assembly of a national database of 'rogue' landlords who are convicted of offences relating to poor housing conditions.[12]

1.18 A more ambitious attempt was made in the Homes (Fitness for Human Habitation) Bill 2015 to require that residential rented accommodation be provided and maintained in a state of fitness for human habitation. The private member's bill, introduced by Karen Buck MP, was deliberately talked-out by an opponent at its Commons Second Reading on 16 October 2015.

1.19 Those campaigning for change were not to be deflected. The bill was re-introduced and, with some modification, achieved UK Government and cross-party support. The Homes (Fitness for Human Habitation) Act 2018 was passed in December 2018. It was written by one of our authors, Giles Peaker, with fellow housing specialist Justin Bates. It represents the biggest advance in tenant's rights relating to housing conditions for a generation. Initially, from

10 In 2018–19, the UK Government announced that the operation of the system in England would be subject to consultation and review. See too *HHSRS – 11 years on* (Chartered Institution of Environmental Health, December 2017).

11 See further, December 2011 *Legal Action* 21.

12 Housing and Planning Act 2016 ss30–31.

20 March 2019, it will require all new lettings to be of homes fit for habitation and require that they be kept fit. In due course, it will come to apply to virtually all residential tenancies whenever granted. The change it brings was the prompt for the new edition of this work. Its detailed ramifications are set out in chapter 2.

1.20 However, the job is not yet done. There is still more, much more, that can be done to simplify and codify the law so as to bring a single comprehensive set of legal standards into force. Those seeking to achieve that are to be commended for their continuing efforts.

Rented housing in England

1.21 A decade or two ago, this book would have been used most often by advisers helping tenants to address problems with the housing let to them by *social* landlords, ie local housing authorities and (less commonly) housing associations. They were then by far the most common forms of letting.

1.22 However, times have changed. Within the social landlord sector itself, housing association tenancies are now more numerous than council tenancies. Also, yet more significantly, there has been an explosion in the growth of the private rented sector.[13] These developments require separate consideration of what are now the two distinct halves of the rented housing sector: private rented accommodation and social housing.

Private rented sector

1.23 In recent years, the extent of private renting in England has grown dramatically. There are now over four million privately rented homes.[14] Happily, surveys of tenant satisfaction suggest that the majority of homes are provided and maintained in good condition.[15]

13 In 2017–18, 19 per cent (4.5 million) of households were renting privately, up from 10 per cent in 2002. The proportion of households renting social housing remained steady at 17 per cent (4.0 million): *English Housing Survey Headline Report 2017–18* (MHCLG, January 2019).

14 In 2017–18, 19 per cent (4.5 million) of households were renting privately, up from 10 per cent in 2003. The proportion of households renting social housing remained steady at 17 per cent (4.0 million): *English Housing Survey Headline Report 2017–18* (MHCLG, January 2019).

15 84 per cent of private tenants were satisfied with their current accommodation in the last national survey: *English Housing Survey Private Rented Sector, 2016–17* (MHCLG, July 2018).

1.24 The finance and political energy put into the *Decent Homes* initiative in the social rented sector (see below), was never matched in the private rented sector and has left standards in the sector scarcely altered. The private rented sector in England had the highest proportion of non-decent homes (25 per cent) in 2017.[16] That equates to more than a million homes. However, a Private Rented Sector (Decent Homes Standard) Bill intended to apply the decent homes standard as a legal requirement for the private sector did not get beyond a Commons first reading stage in 2015.[17]

1.25 While there has been a decrease in the proportion of private rented sector homes which were labelled 'non-decent' (from 47 per cent to 25 per cent), the absolute number of non-decent dwellings has not fallen due to the general increase in size of the sector. The most serious problems – Category 1 hazards – are much more prevalent in the private sector, with 14 per cent of private rented sector dwellings failing the minimum safety standard under the Housing Act 2004 (see chapter 5), compared with six per cent of social housing homes.[18]

1.26 As a result, there has been, and remains, significant concern about housing standards at the (relatively) lower-rent end of the market. 'Rogue' private landlords are letting poor quality, unhealthy and sometimes dangerous homes and ignoring their repairing obligations. Recent policy initiatives in England, have been directed at driving those landlords to either improve their performance or leave the sector.

1.27 In September 2014, the Royal Institution of Chartered Surveyors (RICS) published the *Private rented sector code of practice*[19] drawn up by organisations representing landlords, letting agents and property managers. It was intended to promote best practice in the letting and management of the private rented sector and aims to ensure good quality homes are available for rent. It includes a section on repairs and maintenance, which reminds landlords that they should be aware of repairing obligations imposed by statute and common law.[20] It also states: i) that matters of disrepair should be dealt with promptly and in a timely manner appropriate to their urgency; ii) that landlords should ensure that tenants know how to report repair and maintenance issues and have an established procedure for dealing

16 *English Housing Survey Headline Report 2017–18* (MHCLG, January 2019).

17 Private Rented Sector (Decent Homes Standard) Bill moved by Laura Sandys MP (South Thanet) (Con): Hansard, 28 January 2015, col 874.

18 *English Housing Survey Headline Report 2017–28* at 2.16 (MHCLG, January 2019).

19 *Private rented sector code of practice* (1st edn 2014, updated July 2015).

20 Para 4.3.4.

with urgent requests for repair work, particularly for out-of-office hours; and iii) that tenants must never be evicted for simply requesting repairs to the property.

1.28 The Code also stresses that when arranging repair and maintenance work on a let property, landlords must be aware that tenants are entitled to quiet enjoyment of their homes and must seek to minimise disruption. They should consult tenants on the details and programme for carrying out such works, unless urgency or the tenancy agreement dictates otherwise. Works must be carried out to a reasonable minimum standard so that they do not need to be repeated within a short period of time relative to their nature and reasonable expectations. Landlords are also expected to maintain accurate and complete records of all maintenance and insurance of the property and to inspect the property at appropriate intervals to identify whether or not there are any hazards or repairs that require attention, with records kept of the inspections and any action required and taken.[21] Members of any of the professional organisations that have signed up to the Code agree to abide by its contents.

1.29 While useful, the Code is less prescriptive than the draft that was circulated for consultation in April 2014, which included specific time limits of 24 hours for emergency repairs and 28 days for non-urgent repairs. Also, the Code does not have the force of law (in line with the then UK government's stated commitment to minimise excessive regulation of the sector). A real practical difficulty is that the worst landlords in the private sector are unlikely to be members of the landlord organisations that have signed up to the code.

1.30 Given those difficulties, recent UK Governments have taken a range of initiatives to tackle the 'rogue' end of the private rented sector in England including publication of a guide[22] for local authorities on the powers available to them to force up conditions and the distribution of additional financial resources to support action to enforce minimum standards.[23]

1.31 By the end of 2015, the UK Government was saying:

> The government wants to support good landlords who provide decent well maintained homes, and avoid further regulation on them ... However, a small number of rogue or criminal landlords knowingly rent out unsafe and substandard accommodation. We are determined

21 Paras 4.3.4–4.3.5.

22 *Rogue landlord enforcement: guidance for local authorities* (MHCLG, April 2019).

23 For example, '*£ 2 million for councils to crackdown on rogue landlords*' (MHCLG Press Release, 8 November 2018).

to crack down on these landlords so that they either improve the service they provide or leave the sector.[24]

1.32 The real issue is whether all local authorities will have the resources available to them to utilise the provisions described in this book to 'clear up' the rogue end of the private sector.[25] Experience has shown that whether a private tenant will get effective council help to tackle poor housing conditions is a 'postcode lottery', entirely determined by the willingness and resources of the particular local council.[26]

Social housing

1.33 In 2017–18, there were 4 million households in social rented housing: 2.4 million rented from housing associations, and 1.6 million from local housing authorities.[27] Until the latter part of the 20th century, some of the worst housing conditions in tenanted housing were to be found on social housing estates and in individual council properties neglected by cash-starved local authority landlords and housing associations unable to invest in repair and improvement of them.

1.34 In the new century, unprecedented investment was made in England, through both central government and private finance, in improving the condition of social sector rented housing. Literally billions of pounds were poured into the *Decent Homes Programme* designed to ensure that every home let by a social landlord in England was a 'decent' home by 2010. Before that target date had expired, debate had already begun on what would follow in 2010 and beyond.[28]

1.35 No 'decent home' standard was ever enacted in legislation,[29] but from 2001 onwards central government in England was determined to drive up the quality of the social housing stock by pumping-in, or

24 *Tackling rogue landlords and improving the private rental sector: Government's Response* (DCLG, November 2015).

25 See, *Rogue landlords have little to fear from cash-strapped councils* [2015] *Guardian Housing Network*, 26 August and *Rogue landlords in London: a survey of local authority enforcement in the private rented sector* (Caroline Pidgeon LAM, October 2016).

26 For more detail see *Private Rented Sector: Fourth Report of Session 2017–2019* (House of Commons, Housing, Communities and Local Government Committee, HC 440, April 2018).

27 *English Housing Survey Headline Report 2017–18* at 1.9 (MHCLG, January 2019).

28 See, for example, *Beyond Decent Homes: decent housing standards post-2010*, Chartered Institute of Housing, August 2009.

29 The non-statutory details of the standard for England are in *A Decent Home: definition and guidance for Implementation June 2006 – update* (DCLG, 2006).

levering-in, new investment. For local authority landlords, it often came at a high price – disposal of the entire housing stock to a new breed of social landlord: the large-scale voluntary transfer housing association. However, for hundreds of thousands of tenants, it has meant repaired or improved homes – albeit often at significantly higher rents.

1.36 Sadly, not all social housing was brought up to the desired standard. A National Audit Office report on the programme in England published in 2010 found that:

> Hundreds of thousands of families are still living in properties which are not warm, weather tight, or in a reasonable state of repair. The [responsible central government] Department's efforts have been undermined by weaknesses in the information it holds.[30]

At the beginning of April 2011, there were still 217,000 council houses that were in such a poor state of repair that they didn't meet the decent standard.[31]

1.37 The last UK coalition government provided £1.6 billion to the Decent Homes programme in England for the period 2011 to 2015. A further £160 million was allocated for 2015 to 2016.[32] In London, policy and funding responsibility lies with the Mayor.[33] Outside London, the programme is run by the Homes and Communities Agency on the government's behalf.

1.38 The policy intention of the UK Government is now that: 1) following changes to the Housing Revenue Account (self-financing) system, local councils should have – or be able to borrow – the resources they need to keep all their social housing at a decent level; and 2) housing associations should be able to raise the funds they need on the open market. However, by 2017, 13 per cent of social rented homes still failed the Decent Homes Standard.[34]

1.39 No tenant of social housing has been able to directly enforce the Decent Homes Standard in respect of their own home, otherwise

30 *The Decent Homes Programme* (National Audit Office, Report by the Comptroller and Auditor General HC 212 Session 2009–2010, 21 January 2010). See too, *Beyond Decent Homes (*House of Commons Communities and Local Government Committee, Fourth Report of Session 2009–10, Volume I Report, together with formal minutes, 8 March 2010).

31 *Local Authority Housing Statistics, England 2010–2011* (CLG, November 2011).

32 *2010 to 2015 government policy: rented housing sector* Policy paper May 2015.

33 For his Decent Homes Programme details, see *Existing Housing Stock:* www.london.gov.uk/priorities/housing-land/improving-quality/existing-housing-stock.

34 *English Housing Survey Headline Report 2017–18* at 2.13 (MHCLG, January 2019).

than by insisting on their other existing legal rights described in this book. However, new avenues for *indirect* enforcement of minimum standards in the social housing sector have sprung up, not least as a result of the establishment of new regulators of social landlords.

1.40 In statutory directions made in November 2009, the then secretary of state required the social housing regulator for England to include the Decent Homes Standard in the new national quality standards that all social housing providers had to meet from April 2010.[35] Those requirements now form part of the Consumer Standards enforced by the current social landlord regulator for England, the Regulator of Social Housing (RSH). The Home Standard[36] requires that registered providers of social housing shall:

- ensure that tenants' homes meet the standard set out in section five of the government's Decent Homes Guidance and continue to maintain their homes to at least this standard;
- provide a cost-effective repairs and maintenance service to homes and communal areas that responds to the needs of, and offers choices to, tenants, and has the objective of completing repairs and improvements right first time; and
- meet all applicable statutory requirements that provide for the health and safety of the occupants in their homes.

1.41 The RSH publishes an annual consumer regulation review, setting out examples of the cases which it has investigated in detail under the Consumer Standards.[37] Where it decides that there are reasonable grounds to conclude that a breach of a consumer standard has resulted in, or risked, serious detriment to tenants, it publishes a regulatory notice setting out its findings.

1.42 From the perspective of individual tenants, the failure of social landlords to deal with their responsibilities for the condition of rented homes should not need to be addressed by litigation or by involving the regulator. The use of internal complaints procedures, and ultimately recourse to an ombudsman, ought to be sufficient to stimulate the necessary action.

35 *Directions to the Tenant Services Authority: Summary of responses and Government response*, Communities and Local Government, November 2009.

36 *Home Standard* (Homes and Communities Agency, April 2012).

37 See: *Consumer regulation review 2017–18* (RSH, July 2018).

1.43 The Local Government and Social Care Ombudsmen certainly took a firm line in respect of default by council landlords.[38] However, since April 2013, complaints about housing management issues – such as repairs – in relation to all forms of social landlord have fallen within the jurisdiction of the Housing Ombudsman Service (HOS).[39] Complaints about housing conditions are consistently the biggest category of complaints the HOS deals with, accounting for over one third of all complaints dealt with each year. It has published a report identifying the main causes of such complaints and giving good practice guidance.[40]

1.44 The underlying improvement in the condition of the social rented housing stock[41] has not been the only reason for a decline in the number of legal claims brought against social landlords about housing conditions. Many such landlords have done much to improve their responses to reports of repair and to react promptly and effectively to responsibly made claims. The process was spurred-on and assisted by helpful Good Practice Guidance issued by central government[42] and thereafter by the adoption and enforcement of the *Pre-action protocol for housing disrepair cases*.[43]

1.45 Again, there is no room for complacency. Many social housing tenants are still living in poor conditions. This book is applicable to them just as much as it is to their private sector counterparts.

38 See, for example, *Guidance on good practice: Remedies* (April 2018). Note that this document replaces the previous LGO guidance and key principles document of the same name issued in July 2011 when the LGO still dealt with housing repair complaints.

39 *Property Condition Factsheet* (Housing Ombudsman Service).

40 *Room for Improvement: spotlight an complaints about repairs* (HOS, March 2019).

41 While housing conditions improved in all tenures between 2006 and 2013, the greatest improvement occurred in the social rented sector where the number of non-decent homes almost halved from 1.1 million (29 per cent) in 2006 to 593,000 (15 per cent) in 2013. *English Housing Survey Headline Report 2013–14* (DCLG, February 2015). However, year-on-year improvement stalled in 2014 and has not recovered: *English Housing Survey Headline Report 2017–18* (MHCLG, January 2019).

42 *Housing Disrepair: Legal Obligations, Good Practice Guidance,* Department for Transport Local Government and the Regions, January 2002.

43 Reproduced in appendix B of this book.

CHAPTER 2

The tenant's rights and the landlord's obligations

continued

The sources of rights

The tenancy agreement

2.1 A tenant occupies premises under the terms of a contract of letting, ie a tenancy agreement. This contract may be made orally or in writing, or may even be inferred from the circumstances (for example, where a person occupies premises with exclusive possession and the landlord accepts money as rent).[1]

2.2 The terms of the contract or 'tenancy agreement' may be:

- expressly incorporated into the agreement either orally or in writing; or
- implied into the tenancy agreement either by statute or by the operation of the common law.

2.3 Whether express or implied, these terms may impose obligations on the landlord relating to the condition of the property, which the landlord is then contractually bound to perform.

Express terms and unfair terms

2.4 The common law (the judge-made law developed by the system of precedent) concerning housing conditions in rented property, was formulated in the 18th and 19th centuries, and rested on the fundamental principle of *caveat emptor*, ie let the buyer beware the bargain. In dealings with land and houses (as with other property) the onus was placed on the person intending to take the premises to have inspected them, assessed their quality, and then freely negotiated an appropriate contract or tenancy agreement accordingly.

2.5 It followed from the application of this principle that, once property had been accepted by the tenant, the landlord had almost complete immunity from obligations about the condition of the property other than those imposed by the contract (if any). The landlord was bound only by the express terms of the agreement. Clearly, a strict application of the principle *caveat emptor* in today's society is wholly inappropriate and artificial, since the landlord and incoming tenant no longer (if they ever did in the past) bargain as equals over the letting of property. Protection of the interests of tenants has come not from the common law, but from statute.

1 *Street v Mountford* [1985] AC 809, [1985] 2 WLR 877, HL; *AG Securities Ltd v Vaughan* [1990] 1 AC 417, [1988] 3 WLR 1205, HL.

2.6 Where repairing and fitness obligations are now imposed by law on landlords (eg by the Landlord and Tenant Act (LTA) 1985 s9A or s11),[2] the statutes generally provide that these obligations cannot be transferred to tenants by way of express contractual terms and any attempt to do so is void.[3]

2.7 The Unfair Contract Terms Act (UCTA) 1977 did not apply to leases but the Unfair Terms in Consumer Contracts Regulations (UTCC Regs) 1999[4] did where the tenant was a consumer and the landlord let on standard terms.[5] These regulations could be used to render unenforceable written tenancy terms which are unfair,[6] where the tenancy was entered into after 30 June 1995 but before 1 October 2015 and the term was not individually negotiated. The regulations could therefore assist tenants by preventing landlords from relying on unfair contractual terms by which they might seek to qualify or undermine their own obligations.

2.8 From 1 October 2015, the UCTA 1977 and the UTCC Regs 1999 were replaced by Part 2 of the Consumer Rights Act (CRA) 2015 in respect of tenancies commencing after 1 October 2015. Part 2 of the Act applies to all consumer contracts regardless of whether they have been individually negotiated with the consumer.[7] There is also a requirement for the court to consider whether a term is unfair even if the issue is not raised by any of the parties.[8] Unfair terms are rendered unenforceable.[9] Part 1 of Schedule 2 to the CRA 2015 contains an indicative and non-exhaustive list of terms of consumer contracts that may be regarded as unfair for the purposes of this Part.[10]

2.9 In *Peabody Trust v Reeve*[11] it was held that if a standard tenancy agreement allowed a landlord to vary the terms unilaterally, such a

2 See paras 2.24–2.59 and 2.60–2.93.

3 LTA 1985 ss9A(4) and 11(4); and *Islington LBC v Keane*, December 2005 *Legal Action* 28, *Housing Law Casebook* 7th edn, paras R1.6 and R19.12, Clerkenwell County Court.

4 1999 SI No 2083.

5 *R (Khatun) v Newham LBC* [2004] EWCA Civ 55, [2004] HLR 29, CA.

6 See UTCC Regs 1999 reg 5; *Rochdale BC v Dixon* [2011] EWCA Civ 1173, [2012] HLR 6.

7 CRA 2015 s61.

8 CRA 2015 s71, implementing the European Court of Justice ruling in *Pannon GSM Zrt v Erzsébet Sustikné Győrfi* (Case C-243/08), [2010] 1 All ER (Comm), [2009] ECR 1-4713.

9 CRA 2015 s62.

10 CRA 2015 s63.

11 [2008] EWHC 1432 (Ch), [2009] L&TR 6.

term would be unfair (albeit this is permitted by statute in respect of secure tenancies[12]).

2.10 For general guidance on the correct approach in determining whether terms on housing conditions are fair, reference may usefully be made to the Competition & Markets Authority (CMA) *Unfair contract terms guidance: Guidance on the unfair terms provisions in the Consumer Rights Act 2015.*[13] The guidance suggests, for example, that a term excluding a tenant's right to set off the cost of repairs against rent would be unfair.[14]

2.11 In *Cody v Philps,*[15] a district judge struck out a term which prevented any set-off or deduction whatsoever against the rent, thereby enabling the tenant to defend a possession claim for rent arrears on the basis of a disrepair counterclaim. Such a clause now falls within the list of contractual terms which may be regarded as unfair.[16]

2.12 Advisers may also wish to refer to the Office of Fair Trading's (OFT) investigations of tenancy terms in Newham and Wandsworth in London in 2005.[17]

2.13 If the tenancy agreement contains an express term imposing an obligation on the landlord, the adviser should consider whether the term covers the housing conditions in question. This involves asking:

- what activity has the landlord contracted to perform? and
- on which parts of the dwelling has the landlord contracted to perform this activity?

2.14 Secure tenancy agreements can be varied unilaterally by the landlord under the Housing Act (HA) 1985.[18] Other tenancy agreements can be varied by agreement between the parties. The adviser should therefore ascertain whether the original terms about housing conditions have been varied.

2.15 Various different formulations of wording, such as 'put in repair', 'keep in repair', 'good and substantial repair and condition' and many others, are used in express obligations, and the meanings of the

12 Housing Act (HA) 1985 ss102 and 103.

13 Unfair contract terms: CMA37, CMA July 2017.

14 *CMA37 Annex A: Historic examples of fair and unfair terms.* p27–29.

15 December 2005 *Legal Action* 28; *Housing Law Casebook* 7th edn paras R19.1 and R19.11, West London County Court.

16 CRA 2015 Sch 2 Part 1 para 2.

17 See: http://webarchive.nationalarchives.gov.uk/20140402142426/http://www.oft.gov.uk/news-and-updates/press/2005/163-05 re Newham.

18 HA 1985 ss102(1) and 103(1); *Palmer v Sandwell MBC* (1988) 20 HLR 74, CA; *R v Brent LBC ex p Blatt* (1992) 24 HLR 319, DC; and *Rochdale BC v Dixon* [2011] EWCA Civ 1173, [2012] HLR 6.

various permutations are examined in detail in the traditional legal textbooks.[19] Whatever the wording of an express term, a covenant on housing conditions will never be construed to require the landlord to renew the whole property, ie, to turn an old and decaying house into a new and sound one.[20] Nor will it be construed to require the landlord to remove all potential hazards.[21] Accordingly, a covenant is to be construed having regard to the condition of the property as it was at the date of letting.[22]

2.16 In *Holding & Barnes plc v Hill House Hammond Ltd*,[23] the Court of Appeal reviewed the authorities on the proper approach to the construction of contracts. It held that, in construing express repairing obligations, a common sense approach was required, having regard to the background factual matrix in which the contract was produced and disregarding the 'old intellectual baggage of "legal" interpretation'. This was applied in *Petersson v Pitt Place (Epsom) Ltd*,[24] where a judge's decision that both a landlord and tenant were obliged to repair a roof terrace was overturned. The Court of Appeal held that leases have to be construed so as to avoid overlapping repairing obligations. In *Daejan Properties Ltd v Campbell*[25] the Court of Appeal overturned the judge's decision that a tenant's obligation in a lease (to contribute 40 per cent to the cost of repair and exterior decoration of the tenant's flat) should be construed as an obligation to contribute 40 per cent to the cost of repair and external decorations for the whole building. In restricting the tenant's liability to 40 per cent of the costs of the exterior of the tenant's flat only, the Court of Appeal held that the repairing obligation should be construed as meaning what it said, as it was not possible to say that there had been a clear mistake nor was it commercially nonsensical.

2.17 The High Court judgment in *Hunt v Optima (Cambridge) Ltd*[26] sets out a useful review of the law relating to a landlord's obligations

19 See Woodfall, *Landlord and Tenant*, Sweet & Maxwell, Volume 1–13.048; Hill and Redman's *Law of Landlord and Tenant*, Volume 1-A3285, LexisNexis; Dowding and Reynolds, *Dilapidations the Modern Law and Practice*, 6th edn, Sweet & Maxwell, 2017.

20 *Lister v Lane* [1893] 2 QB 212, CA; and *Pembery v Lamdin* [1940] 2 All ER 434, CA.

21 *Alker v Collingwood Housing Association* [2007] EWCA Civ 343, [2007] HLR 29.

22 *Proudfoot v Hart* (1890) 25 QBD 42, CA.

23 [2001] EWCA Civ 1334, [2002] L&TR 7.

24 [2001] EWCA Civ 86, [2002] HLR 52.

25 [2012] EWCA Civ 1503, [2013] HLR 6.

26 [2013] EWHC 681 (TCC).

under an express covenant. The obligation under the lease was to 'maintain, repair renew and amend the main structure of the building'. It was held that:

> These words are not simply synonyms for each other although they may well overlap in relation to any individual item of work that needs to be done. Thus maintaining a gutter may involve clearing leaves out of it and checking that the brackets are still supporting the gutter; if the support has corroded a new support will have to be provided and that work overall may all be said to be maintenance repair and renewal. However, an inadequate roof may be or become incapable of maintenance as such or even repair; it may need to be wholly replaced and as necessary a different type of roof provided; there will then be renewal by amendment.

2.18 It is common for landlords of residential property to: (a) contract to carry out repairs (but not to carry out improvements, or to keep the premises in as good a state as when let, or to ensure that the dwelling remains suitable for human habitation); and (b) contract to repair only the structural or external parts of the dwelling (but not the internal, non-structural parts, eg, internal doors, kitchen fittings, decorations and so forth).

2.19 The adviser must check carefully whether the tenancy agreement contains obligations which are more extensive. For example, in *Welsh v Greenwich LBC*,[27] the tenancy agreement provided that the landlord would 'maintain the dwelling in good condition and repair'. The landlord was held liable in civil proceedings for severe condensation and mould growth not involving structural or external disrepair. The Court of Appeal accepted that the phrase 'good condition' was intended to mark a separate concept and to make a significant addition to what was conveyed by the word 'repair'. Liability for condensation dampness was also established in *Johnson v Sheffield CC*,[28] where the tenancy agreement provided that the landlord would keep the dwelling 'fit to live in'. (But see LTA 1985 s9A implied term at para 2.32 below.)

2.20 Many tenancy agreements, particularly those drafted by social landlords, contain express repairing obligations dealing with common parts. In *Southwark LBC v Long*,[29] the tenancy agreement provided that the landlord would 'take reasonable steps to keep the estate and common parts clean and tidy'. The landlord was held

27 (2001) 33 HLR 40, (2001) 81 P&CR 12, CA.

28 August 1994 *Legal Action* 16, Sheffield County Court.

29 [2002] EWCA Civ 403, [2002] HLR 56.

liable for rubbish left outside the rubbish chute, which, although in working order, was inadequate in size. It was not sufficient that the landlord had instructed contractors to clean the rubbish chute and bin chamber because it did not have an adequate system for monitoring the contractors' performance.

2.21 Many social landlords also include lengthy definitions of exactly what is covered by their repairing obligations, which may be wider than the obligations implied by statute. For example, many social landlords agree that they are obliged to keep parts of the interior in repair, such as internal doors, or to keep fittings in repair and working order. The message for all tenants and their advisers is: always check first exactly what the tenancy agreement says.

Rights given by Parliament

2.22 As just explained, the basic rule at common law is that the landlord is not liable for housing conditions except insofar as expressly made liable in the tenancy agreement. The common law exceptions to this rule, described below (see para 2.142), are piecemeal and limited in scope. As a result, Parliament has legislated to create rights for tenants and occupiers and to impose obligations on landlords.

2.23 There are two main types of legislation: first, there are those provisions that imply limited obligations into certain kinds of tenancy, see LTA 1985 s9A and s11; and second, those that then add liability for defects by way of a tortious 'duty to take care', eg Occupiers' Liability Act (OLA) 1957 ss1 and 4, Defective Premises Act (DPA) 1972 and a minor statutory duty under HA 1985.

Terms implied into tenancy agreements

Fitness for human habitation – LTA 1985 s9A

2.24 Until 2018, there was no statutory implied term that a property should be fit for habitation that had any effect. LTA 1985 s8 remained on the statute books, but subject to rent limits that had not been updated since 1957, so it had no application in practice. As long ago as 1996, the Law Commission proposed the enactment of a general implied term about fitness.[30] However, its proposals were not taken up for many years (see para 1.12). In 2002, in *Lee v Leeds CC*,[31] the

30 Law Commission, *Landlord and Tenant: Responsibility for State and Condition of Property* LC238, HMSO, 1996.

31 [2002] EWCA Civ 6, [2002] 1 WLR 1488.

Court of Appeal held that there was no basis for implying into tenancies of social housing let by public authorities an obligation to keep a dwelling in good condition or to remedy defects which make it unfit for human habitation and called for legislation. A private members bill – the Homes (Fitness for Human Habitation) Bill[32] – which would have required that residential rented accommodation is provided and maintained in a state of fitness for human habitation, was introduced in 2015 but failed to complete its second reading in the House of Commons after being talked out (see para 1.18).

2.25 In 2017, the Homes (Fitness for Human Habitation) Bill was again brought forward by Karen Buck MP. This time, the bill gained cross-party and UK Government support. Royal Assent for the Homes (Fitness for Human Habitation) Act 2018 was given on 20 December 2018.[33]

2.26 The 2018 Act amends LTA 1985 to introduce a new section 9A, section 9B and section 9C and amends section 10, for England. The existing sections 8 and 9 continue in force in Wales, pending the entry into force of Renting Homes (Wales) Act 2016 and implementing regulations. What follows is concerned with England only. For the full text of LTA 1985 ss9A–10, see appendix A.

2.27 The amended LTA 1985 provisions will, over an implementation period, imply a new term into all tenancies of less than seven years, into all currently existing periodic tenancies, and into new secure and some assured tenancies with a fixed term of seven years or more.[34] Lettings for longer periods are also covered where the landlord has an option to end the letting within seven years of commencement. However, by section 13(2), lettings for less than seven years may fall outside section 9A if the tenant can renew for a further term, making more than seven years in total. These provisions, together with those relating to renewed lettings, are somewhat complex and an adviser should pay close attention to the terms of LTA 1985 ss12–15 before giving a conclusive opinion.

2.28 The obligation is non-excludable and cannot be limited by agreement.[35] Any provision of a lease or agreement is void to the extent

32 www.publications.parliament.uk/pa/bills/cbill/2015/0015/150015%20.pdf.

33 www.legislation.gov.uk/ukpga/2018/34/contents/enacted/data.htm.

34 LTA 1985 s9B(1) as inserted by the Homes (Fitness for Human Habitation) Act 2018 and s13(1A) as inserted by Localism Act 2011 s166. Section 9A is only implied into assured tenancies which are granted by a private registered provider of social housing which are not shared ownership leases.

35 LTA 1985 s9A(4) as inserted by Homes (Fitness for Human Habitation) Act 2018.

that it purports to exclude or limit the obligation, or impose a penalty on the tenant in the event of the tenant relying on the obligation.

Dates in force and implementation period

2.29 The Homes (Fitness for Human Habitation) Act 2018 entered into force three months after Royal Assent, on 20 March 2019. At that date, the amendments to Landlord and Tenant Act 1985 came into effect.

2.30 LTA 1985 s9B provides that section 9A, the implied term, applies to:

a) all new tenancies of the kind to which it applies granted on or after 20 March 2019;[36]
b) all periodic tenancies that are in existence on 20 March 2019 after a period of 12 months, so from 20 March 2020;[37]
c) all tenancies that come into existence as periodic tenancies after 20 March 2019 on the expiry of a fixed term granted before 20 March 2019[38] (this would include statutory periodic tenancies arising at the end of a fixed term assured shorthold, or assured tenancies granted after a fixed term 'starter' tenancy, or a secure tenancy coming into existence at the end of an introductory tenancy. The position on 'contractual periodic' tenancies is less certain[39]); and
d) all 'replacement' or renewal fixed term tenancies granted after 20 March 2019 on the expiry of a fixed term granted before 20 March 2019.[40]

2.31 So, with the exception of fixed term tenancies of two or more years granted before 20 March 2019, the LTA 1985 s9A implied term

36 LTA 1985 s9B(3) as inserted by Homes (Fitness for Human Habitation) Act 2018.

37 LTA 1985 s9B(4) as inserted by Homes (Fitness for Human Habitation) Act 2018.

38 LTA 1985 s9B(5) as inserted by Homes (Fitness for Human Habitation) Act 2018.

39 A 'contractual periodic' tenancy is an assured shorthold where the tenancy agreement is for a stated fixed term and thereafter on a periodic basis. See *Leeds City Council v Broadley* (Rev 1) [2016] EWCA Civ 1213, [2017] 1 WLR 738. The Court of Appeal agreed that this was a single tenancy, but did not definitively decide whether it was one tenancy with two distinct terms (fixed and periodic) – in which case, the start of the periodic would mean LTA 1985 s9A applied – or a single term – in which case it may be arguable that s9A does not apply to any contractual periodic where the overall tenancy began pre 20 March 2019.

40 LTA 1985 s9B(6) as inserted by Homes (Fitness for Human Habitation) Act 2018.

should apply to the majority of applicable tenancies by 20 March 2020.

The fitness obligation – LTA 1985 s9A

2.32 LTA 1985 s9A implies into all relevant tenancies the following:

> (1) In a lease to which this section applies of a dwelling in England (see section 9B), there is implied a covenant by the lessor that the dwelling–
> (a) is fit for human habitation at the time the lease is granted or otherwise created or,
> if later, at the beginning of the term of the lease, and
> (b) will remain fit for human habitation during the term of the lease.

The extent of this obligation beyond the limits of the let dwelling is set out in section 9A(6):

> (6) Where a lease to which this section applies of a dwelling in England forms part only of a building, the implied covenant has effect as if the reference to the dwelling in subsection (1) included a reference to any common parts of the building in which the lessor has an estate or interest.

There are a number of exceptions to the obligation to let and keep the dwelling in a condition fit for habitation set out at section 9A(2) and (3):

> (2) The implied covenant is not to be taken as requiring the lessor–
> (a) to carry out works or repairs for which the lessee is liable by virtue of–
> (i) the duty of the lessee to use the premises in a tenant-like manner, or
> (ii) an express covenant of the lessee of substantially the same effect as that duty;
> (b) to rebuild or reinstate the dwelling in the case of destruction or damage by fire, storm, flood or other inevitable accident;
> (c) to keep in repair or maintain anything which the lessee is entitled to remove from the dwelling;
> (d) to carry out works or repairs which, if carried out, would put the lessor in breach of any obligation imposed by any enactment (whenever passed or made);
> (e) to carry out works or repairs requiring the consent of a superior landlord or other third party in circumstances where consent has not been obtained following reasonable endeavours to obtain it.
>
> (3) The implied covenant is also not to be taken as imposing on the lessor any liability in respect of the dwelling being unfit

for human habitation if the unfitness is wholly or mainly attributable to–

(a) the lessee's own breach of covenant, or
(b) disrepair which the lessor is not obliged to make good because of an exclusion or modification under section 12 (power of county court to authorise exclusions or modifications in leases in respect of repairing obligations under section 11).

2.33 In determining whether a house is fit for human habitation, regard is to be had to its condition in respect of a number of factors set out in LTA 1985 s10(1). These factors include the list from the old section 8: repair, stability, freedom from damp, internal arrangement, natural lighting, ventilation, water supply, drainage/sanitary conveniences, facilities for the preparation and cooking of food, and facilities for the disposal of waste water.

2.34 In addition, the amended section 10 adds to that list:

> in relation to a dwelling in England, any prescribed hazard;

2.35 A 'prescribed hazard' is defined at section 10(2):

> 'prescribed hazard' means any matter or circumstance amounting to a hazard for the time being prescribed in regulations made by the Secretary of State under section 2 of the Housing Act 2004.

2.36 The current list of hazards prescribed in regulations made under Housing Act (HA) 2004 s2 is the Housing Health and Safety Rating System (HHSRS) hazard list. This contains 29 hazards, as listed in the Housing Health and Safety Rating System (England) Regulations 2005 Sch 1:[41]

> Damp and mould growth
> Asbestos and manufactured mineral fibres
> Biocides
> Carbon monoxide and fuel combustion products
> Lead
> Radiation
> Uncombusted fuel gas
> Volatile organic compounds
> Electrical hazards
> Excess cold
> Excess heat
> Crowding and space
> Entry by intruders
> Lighting (including natural)
> Noise
> Domestic hygiene, pests and refuse

41 SI No 3208.

Food safety
Personal hygiene, sanitation and drainage
Water supply for domestic purposes
Falls associated with baths etc.
Falls on the level
Falls associated with stairs and steps
Falls between levels
Fire
Hot surfaces and materials
Collision and entrapment
Explosions
Position and operability of amenities
Structural collapse and falling elements

2.37 The meaning of 'hazard' is as defined at HA 2004 s2(1), with the reference to a potential occupier omitted.[42] With that omission, the definition reads:

> 'hazard' means any risk of harm to the health or safety of an actual occupier of a dwelling or HMO [house in multiple occupation] which arises from a deficiency in the dwelling or HMO or in any building or land in the vicinity (whether the deficiency arises as a result of the construction of any building, an absence of maintenance or repair, or otherwise).

2.38 In applying the list of hazards, there is no restriction to any specific category of hazard under the HHSRS system. Any deficiency to the dwelling or building which would fall under an HHSRS category and gives rise to a risk of harm to the health and safety of an occupier (not necessarily the tenant) would be a factor of the condition of the building to which regard should be had in determining whether the dwelling is fit for habitation.

2.39 As such, there is no requirement for an HHSRS assessment, or a finding of an HHSRS category 1 or 2 hazard in order to establish unfitness, although such an assessment and finding in respect of the current occupiers would be strong evidence of unfitness.

2.40 The dwelling will be unfit for human habitation if, and only if, it is so far defective in one or more of these matters (the section 10(1) list) that it is not reasonably suitable for occupation in that condition.

Interpreting sections 9A and section 10

2.41 Since LTA 1985 s8 fell into disuse by reason of the prescribed rent levels many years ago, there is as yet no recent case-law on the

42 LTA 1985 s10(3) as amended by Homes (Fitness for Human Habitation) Act 2018.

meaning of sections 9A and 10 (as amended). However, the wording of the implied terms and of the 'test' for unfitness parallels that of section 8 and the unamended section 10, such that prior case law will still be relevant to some degree. It should be noted, however, that section 8 did not extend to the building of which the dwelling forms part, unlike section 9A.

2.42 Breaches of the terms implied in relation to fitness for habitation have been successfully established in a wide range of cases. For example:

- a small house in which the sole window in a main room could not be safely opened;[43]
- premises where plaster had fallen from the ceiling;[44]
- the complete collapse of a ceiling;[45] and
- accommodation in which a sanitary convenience was defective and serious dampness had accrued from defective guttering.[46]

2.43 A 'rule of thumb' guide to the standards required by section 8 was set out by Atkin LJ in 1926:

> If the state of repair of a house is such that by ordinary use damage may naturally be caused to the occupier, either in respect of personal injury to life or limb or injury to health, then the house is not in all respects reasonably fit for human habitation.[47]

2.44 The courts had, however, developed a serious limitation to the usefulness of section 8 by confining its application to premises which could be made fit by the landlord at reasonable expense.[48] This controversial decision rests on a concession made in argument and has no foundation within the LTA 1985 itself. It stood unchallenged for over four decades. It is ripe for review if it is sought to apply it to section 9A. It is worth noting that there is no such 'reasonable expense' defence or excuse where remedial works have been ordered to remedy an HHSRS hazard by way of Improvement Notice, or Emergency Remedial Action, under HA 2004 s5.

43 *Summers v Salford Corporation* [1943] AC 283, [1943] 1 All ER 68, HL.

44 *Walker v Hobbs & Co* (1889) 23 QBD 458.

45 *Fisher v Walters* [1926] 2 KB 315, KBD.

46 *Horrex v Pidwell* [1958] CLY 1461.

47 *Morgan v Liverpool Corporation* [1927] 2 KB 131, CA, approved in *Summers v Salford Corporation*.

48 *Buswell v Goodwin* [1971] 1 WLR 92, [1971] 1 All ER 418, CA.

2.45 More recent judicial approaches to 'fitness for habitation' can be found in cases on HA 1985 s604 (repealed in England by HA 2004 Sch 16, with effect from 6 April 2006) and DPA 1972 s1.[49]

2.46 In *Rendlesham Estates plc and others v Barr Ltd*[50] Edwards-Stuart J set out a definition of fitness for the purposes of DPA 1972 s1. The dwelling must:

(a) be capable of occupation for a reasonable time without risk to the health or safety of the occupants: where a dwelling is or is part of a newly constructed building, what is a reasonable time will be a question of fact (it may or may not be as long as the design life of the building); and
(b) be capable of occupation for a reasonable time without undue inconvenience or discomfort to the occupants.[51]

2.47 In further passages, Edwards-Stuart J set out examples of what may amount to unfitness, including:

- defective foundations;
- a lift that broke down with 'monotonous regularity (subject to the degree of inconvenience)';
- no safe means of access or escape from a dwelling;
- hazards to the common parts;
- interior doors or partition walls that did not meet building regulation fire safety requirements at the time of construction; and
- mould and damp in living rooms and bedrooms.[52]

2.48 In *Bole and another v Huntsbuild Ltd*,[53] Dyson LJ held that the assessment of whether a dwelling was unfit was not a matter of 'considering each defect individually and asking whether that defect, or indeed that defect taken in conjunction with other individual defects, rendered the dwelling unfit for habitation'. Rather, the question should be approached by asking 'whether the dwelling as a whole was unfit for habitation'.[54]

49 See case-law on HA 1985 s604 (repealed in England by HA 2004 Sch 16, with effect from 6 April 2006) and DPA 1972 s1, eg *McMinn v Bole & Van den Haak v Huntsbuild Ltd & Money* [2009] EWHC 483 (TCC), *Harrison and others v (1) Shepherd Homes Ltd (2) National Housing Building Council and (3) NHBC Building Control Services* [2011] EWHC 1811 (TCC), and *Rendlesham Estates plc and others v Barr Ltd* [2014] EWHC 3968 (TCC), [2015] 1 WLR 3663.

50 [2014] EWHC 3968 (TCC).

51 *Rendlesham Estates plc and others v Barr Ltd* [2014] EWHC 3968 (TCC), [2015] 1 WLR 3663 at 68.

52 *Rendlesham Estates plc* at 70, 71, 72, and 79.

53 [2009] EWCA Civ 1146.

54 *Bole and another v Huntsbuild Ltd* [2009] EWCA Civ 1146 at 34.

2.49 The High Court recently heard an appeal concerning an express term on 'fit for habitation' in *Baillie v Savage*.[55] The risk of collapse of a further part of a garden retaining wall adjacent to the house made the property unfit for habitation. *Summers v Salford Corp*[56] on the risk of a window sash falling and injuring a tenant was cited.

2.50 In *Johnson v Sheffield CC*,[57] the landlord's liability for condensation dampness was established where the tenancy agreement provided that the landlord would keep the dwelling 'fit to live in'.

Extending the duty to the building of which the dwelling forms part

2.51 LTA 1985 s9A(6) parallels the wording of section 11(1A). The interpretation of this section should follow the interpretation of section 11(1A) as set out at para 2.78 below. The effect is that any defect to the common parts (including the structure) of a building of which the dwelling forms part – such as a flat in a block, or a room in a house in multiple occupation (HMO) – that is capable of rendering the dwelling unfit will fall under the implied term where the landlord has an estate or interest in the part with the defect. For example, deficiencies in the fire safety of the common parts or structure of the building could render the dwelling unfit, even if there were no relevant defects inside the dwelling itself.

2.52 In *Edwards v Kumarasamy*[58] the Supreme Court held that a leaseholder's right of way over the entrance hall of a block of flats owned by a separate freeholder was an interest in land sufficient to make the leaseholder liable to their subtenant for disrepair to the entrance hall under section 11(1A).[59] The same should apply to defects or hazards to the common parts that would make the dwelling unfit.

2.53 However, note should be taken of section 9A(2)(e), under which the landlord is not required to carry out works or repairs which require the consent of a superior landlord or other third party, where the consent has not been obtained following reasonable endeavours to obtain it. Where the landlord is a leaseholder of a flat and the relevant defect is to the common parts, it is possible (though not certain) that the landlord will not have sufficient rights to carry out repairs without the consent of the freeholder.

55 [2018] EWHC 3035 (Ch).

56 [1943] AC 283, HL.

57 August 1994 *Legal Action* 16, Sheffield County Court.

58 [2016] UKSC 40, [2016] AC 1334.

59 *Edwards v Kumarasamy* [2016] UKSC 40 at 23–27.

Limitations of section 9A

2.54 The operation of section 9A has limitations.

2.55 Common law provisions on notice to the landlord of the defects will apply. Notice requirements are set out in detail at paras 2.311–2.321 below. Where the unfitness is to the dwelling, no liability arises until the landlord has been put on notice and has had a reasonable time to rectify the defects. However, where the defect is outside the dwelling, to common parts or other parts under the landlord's control, the landlord is taken to have immediate knowledge of the defect regardless of actual knowledge.

2.56 The landlord is not required to carry out works (nor will be liable for damages) where:

i) The works are the obligation of the tenant under the duty to use the premises in a tenant-like manner. (It is likely that this will be the basis for arguments over liability for condensation and mould.)
ii) Works entail repairing or maintaining anything the tenant is entitled to remove from the premises. (Effectively, the tenant's or their household's belongings, possibly including white goods, heaters etc.)
iii) Works would be to rebuild or reinstate the dwelling after destruction or damage by act of God (fire, flood, storm) or inevitable accident.
iv) The works or repairs would be in breach of any obligation imposed by an enactment. (This would include works that would be in breach of planning permission, or listed building restrictions, or conservation area restrictions.) This limitation only extends to the specific works which would be in breach.
v) The works require the consent of a superior landlord or third party, reasonable endeavours have been made by the landlord to obtain that consent, but it has not been given. (This may include works to common parts or the building where the landlord is a leaseholder and a separate freeholder retains the common parts or structure, or where the works require access to an adjoining property owned by another party, or where council permission is required.) 'Reasonable endeavours' will not extend to the landlord bringing legal proceedings against the other party.
vi) Where the unfitness is wholly or mainly attributable to the tenant's own breach of covenant. (Again, this is likely to be raised in condensation and mould cases.)

2.57 The provision only applies to new tenancies starting on or after 20 March 2019, or to existing tenancies as set out at para 2.30 above. There is no liability in damages for unfitness existing prior to the implied term being of application to the tenancy involved, but once the term is implied into the tenancy, there will be liability to remedy pre-existing unfitness thereafter.

2.58 The provision only applies to tenancies of under seven years (with certain exceptions at section 9B(1)(b)).

2.59 The provision does not apply to certain properties let to local authorities and other public bodies (LTA 1985 s14(4)) or to a lease granted to the Crown or government departments (LTA 1985 s14(5)).

The repairing obligation – Landlord and Tenant Act 1985 s11

2.60 This is the main statutory repairing obligation which is implied into all tenancies of less than seven years beginning on or after 24 October 1961. It is also implied into secure and some assured tenancies granted after 1 April 2012 with a fixed term of seven years or more.[60] Lettings for longer periods are also covered where the landlord has an option to end the letting within seven years of commencement. However, by section 13(2), lettings for less than seven years may fall outside section 11 if the tenant can renew for a further term, making more than seven years in total. These provisions, together with those relating to renewed lettings, are somewhat complex and an adviser should pay close attention to the terms of LTA 1985 ss12–15 before giving a conclusive opinion.

2.61 Nowadays, most tenants can rely on this repairing obligation, even if their tenancy agreement contains no express repairing obligations.

2.62 LTA 1985 s11 implies into tenancy agreements an obligation on landlords to effect certain repairs which is both absolute and non-excludable. Section 11 replaced HA 1961 s32. For the full text of LTA 1985 ss11–17 see appendix A.

2.63 The obligation is as follows (as amended by the HA 1988 in respect of tenancies entered into on or after 15 January 1989):

> 11(1) In a lease to which this section applies . . . there is implied a covenant by the lessor–
>
> (a) to keep in repair the structure and exterior of the dwelling-house (including drains, gutters and external pipes),

60 LTA 1985 s13(1A) as inserted by Localism Act 2011 s166. Section 11 is only implied into assured tenancies which are granted by a private registered provider of social housing which are not shared ownership leases.

(b) to keep in repair and proper working order the installations in the dwelling-house for the supply of water, gas and electricity and for sanitation (including basins, sinks, baths and sanitary conveniences but not other fixtures, fittings and appliances for making use of the supply of water, gas or electricity), and

(c) to keep in repair and proper working order the installations in the dwelling-house for space heating and heating water.

(1A) If a lease to which this section applies is a lease of a dwelling-house which forms part only of a building, then subject to subsection (1B), the covenant implied by sub-section (1) shall have effect as if–

(a) the reference in paragraph (a) of that subsection to the dwelling-house included a reference to any part of the building in which the lessor has an estate or interest; and

(b) any references in paragraphs (b) and (c) of that subsection to an installation in the dwelling-house included a reference to an installation which, directly or indirectly, serves the dwelling-house and which either–

(i) forms part of any part of a building in which the lessor has an estate or interest; or

(ii) is owned by the lessor or under his control.

(1B) Nothing in subsection (1A) shall be construed as requiring the lessor to carry out any works or repairs unless the disrepair (or failure to maintain in working order) is such as to affect the lessee's enjoyment of the dwelling-house or of any common parts, as defined in section 60(1) of the Landlord and Tenant Act 1987, which the lessee, as such, is entitled to use.

2.64 Tenancies that pre-date 15 January 1989 do not have the benefit of section 11(1A) and (1B), so the obligation to repair for those tenants is limited to the structure and exterior of the dwelling and the installations therein. However pre-1989 tenants not covered by the amendments to section 11, may be able to rely on the common law implied terms described in paras 2.142–2.162, or from 20 March 2020, on the provisions of LTA 1985 s9A.

2.65 The landlord cannot exclude the obligation imposed by section 11 by the use of express contractual terms. Any term purporting to exclude liability (section 12(1)(a)) or transfer it to the tenant (section 11(4)) is void.[61]

2.66 The landlord or the landlord's agent is given a statutory right to enter premises for the purpose of viewing the condition and state of repair on giving the tenant 24 hours' notice in writing: section 11(6).

61 *Irvine's Estate v Moran* (1991) 24 HLR 1, QBD; *Islington LBC v Keane* December 2005 *Legal Action* 28, *Housing Law Casebook* 7th Edn, para R1.6, Clerkenwell County Court.

Interpreting section 11

2.67 Owing to the breadth of the implied terms contained in section 11, the component parts have been subject to close scrutiny.

2.68 **'keep in repair'** The covenant to keep in repair is a continuing obligation to keep up the standard of repair in the dwelling throughout the duration of the tenancy. Moreover, it also requires the landlord to put the premises into repair if they were not in good repair at the outset of the tenancy.[62]

2.69 For the scope of works covered by the term 'repair' see paras 2.236–2.260 below.[63]

2.70 **'the structure and exterior'** For section 11(1)(a) or (1A)(a) to apply, it must be shown that there is actually some part of the structure or exterior which is in a state of disrepair and therefore requires 'repair', ie, 'the covenant will only come into operation where there has been damage to the structure and exterior which requires to be made good'.[64] Evidence of damage to decoration, clothing, bedding, curtains, etc is all to no avail unless some part of the structure or exterior can be shown to require repair.

2.71 The **structure** is less than the whole dwelling but more than just the load-bearing elements. It is usually taken to refer to:

> . . . those elements of the overall dwelling-house which give it its essential appearance, stability and shape. The expression does not extend to the many and various ways in which the dwelling-house will be fitted out, equipped, decorated and generally made to be habitable . . . in order to be part of the structure of the dwelling-house a particular element must be a material or significant element in the overall construction . . .
>
> . . . to some extent, in every case there will be a degree of fact to be gone into to decide whether or not something is or is not part of the structure of the dwelling-house.[65]

2.72 It is now clear that (contrary to previous authority) internal wall plaster is part of the structure. In *Grand v Gill*[66] the Court of Appeal overturned the earlier decision in *Irvine's Estate v Moran* that plaster was not part of the structure for the purposes of LTA 1985 s11, but more in the nature of a decorative finish.[67] It found that plaster was

62 *Proudfoot v Hart* (1890) 25 QBD 42, CA.

63 See too *Brunskill v Mulcahy* [2009] EWCA Civ 686.

64 *Quick v Taff Ely BC* [1986] QB 809, [1985] 3 WLR 981, CA, at 818E.

65 *Irvine's Estate v Moran* (1992) 24 HLR 1, QBD, at 5. See also *Pearlman v Governors of Harrow School* [1979] QB 56, [1978] 3 WLR 736, CA.

66 [2011] EWCA Civ 554, [2011] 1 WLR 2253.

67 *Irvine's Estate v Moran* (1992) 24 HLR 1, QBD.

'a smooth constructional finish to walls and ceilings to which decoration can then be applied rather than a decorative finish in itself'. Liability has subsequently been established in respect of saturated plaster which was apparently caused by condensation dampness with the trial judge finding that 'it cannot be said that with that level of humidity or moisture retention, whatever the cause may be, that it has not reached a stage of being in disrepair'.[68] Liability was upheld on appeal by HHJ Lochrane who found that 'hygroscopic plaster is damaged beyond recovery'.[69]

2.73 The **exterior** is the outside or external part of the dwelling-house. The liability under the covenant extends to all outside parts of the dwelling that has been let.

2.74 The interpretation of the words 'structure' and 'exterior' may be illustrated as follows:

- A partition wall between the dwelling and another house or flat is part of the structure or exterior.[70]
- Floor joists in a dwelling are part of the structure; the structure is not limited to items in the ownership of the landlord.[71]
- In relation to a house, the path and steps which are the immediate and ordinary means of access are within the 'exterior'[72] but the paving of the backyard is not.[73]
- The roof (if any) is part of the structure of a house as is any skylight it contains (see para 2.78 for roofs of flats).[74]
- The walls are part of the structure, together with any cement rendering.[75] However, a plasterboard false wall which had been nailed to the wall surface was not: it was affixed to the structural wall; it had not become part of it.[76]
- Plaster is part of the structure.[77]

68 *DR v Southwark LBC* December 2014 *Legal Action* 26, Lambeth County Court.

69 *DR v Southwark LBC* December 2015 *Legal Action* 40, *Housing Law Casebook* 7th edn, R18.42, Central London County Court.

70 *Green v Eales* (1841) 2 QB 225, 114 ER 88.

71 *Marlborough Park Services Ltd v Rowe and another* [2006] EWCA Civ 436, [2006] HLR 30, CA.

72 *Brown v Liverpool Corporation* [1969] 3 All ER 1345, [1984] 13 HLR 1, CA.

73 *Hopwood v Cannock Chase DC* [1975] 1 WLR 373, [1975] 1 All ER 796, CA.

74 *Taylor v Webb* [1937] 2 KB 283, [1937] 1 All ER 590, CA.

75 *Granada Theatres Ltd v Freehold Investment (Leytonstone) Ltd* [1959] Ch 592, [1959] 1 WLR 570, CA.

76 *Fincar SRL v 109/113 Mount Street Management Co Ltd* [1999] L&TR 161, [1998] EGCS 173, CA. This case might now be decided differently in respect of the plasterboard wall in the light of the reasoning in *Grand v Gill*.

77 *Grand v Gill* [2011] EWCA Civ 554, [2011] 1 WLR 2253.

- External joinery will usually be part of the structure, and failure to paint it so as to protect it from rot will be a failure to repair.[78]
- Windows will be part of the structure if they are a substantial and integral part of the wall.[79]
- The ordinary windows in a house or flat are part of the exterior of the dwelling.[80] External windows will usually be both part of the structure and part of the exterior.[81]
- Banisters are part of the structure: a staircase is an essential feature of a house which is necessary to complete its intended appearance, stability, shape and identity and banisters are an integral part of the staircase.[82] However, this depends on whether banisters were originally installed.[83]
- An extractor fan is part of the structure.[84]

2.75 Where the dwelling-house is a flat, 'structure and exterior' has been held to extend to: the outside wall(s) of the flat, the outside of the inner party wall of the flat, the outer sides of the horizontal divisions between the flat and the flats above and below, and ceilings and walls of the flat,[85] and the whole of the roof terraces of flats except for their tiled surface areas.[86] Where the ceiling and roof of a top-floor flat form an inseparable structural unit, the roof will be within the structure or exterior of the flat. In the case of other flats, whether a common roof is within the covenant will be a question of fact according to the particular circumstances.[87]

78 *Irvine's Estate v Moran* (1991) 24 HLR 1, QBD.

79 *Boswell v Crucible Steel Co of America* [1925] 1 KB 119, CA; and *Holiday Fellowship v Hereford* [1959] 1 WLR 211, [1959] 1 All ER 433, CA.

80 *Ball v Plummer* (1879) 23 SJ 656, CA.

81 *Sheffield CC v Oliver* Lands Tribunal LRX/146/2007, December 2008 *Legal Action* 31.

82 *Hannon v Hillingdon Homes Ltd* [2012] EWHC 1437 (QB).

83 See *Sternbaum v Dhesi* [2016] EWCA Civ 155 and *Dodd v Raebarn Estates Ltd and others* [2016] EWHC 262 (QB), [2016] HLR 12, both DPA 1972 claims where an absence of banisters to communal stairs was held not fall under repairing obligations where the banisters had not previously existed.

84 *Aden v Birmingham CC* December 2013 *Legal Action* 16, *Housing Law Casebook* 7th edn, para R18.25, Birmingham County Court.

85 *Campden Hill Towers Ltd v Gardner* [1977] QB 823, [1977] 2 WLR 159, CA.

86 *Ibrahim v Dovecorn Reversions Ltd* (2001) 82 P&CR 362, ChD.

87 *Douglas-Scott v Scorgie* [1984] 1 WLR 716, [1984] 1 All ER 1086, CA; *Rapid Results College v Angell* [1986] 1 EGLR 53, CA; *Straudley Investments v Barpress Ltd* [1987] 1 EGLR 69, CA; *Hatfield v Moss* [1988] 2 EGLR 58, CA.

2.76 **'the dwelling-house'** This means the building or part of a building which is let to the tenant wholly or mainly as a private residence: LTA 1985 s16(b).

2.77 The 'structure and exterior' with which section 11(1)(a) is concerned, then, is the 'structure and exterior of the dwelling-house' let to the tenant, ie, the tenant's own house or flat. Usually, therefore, the provision could not be used by the tenant of the lower of two flats to get the roof over the upper flat repaired, even if the disrepair was causing damage to the lower flat, since on any view the roof would not be part of the structure or exterior of the lower flat.

2.78 The position is different for tenancies entered into on or after 15 January 1989. In these tenancies, the term implied by section 11 is extended to include not only the structure and exterior of the let dwelling but also the remaining parts of the building in which the landlord retains an estate or interest (section 11(1A)), providing the disrepair is in fact affecting the tenant's enjoyment of his or her own dwelling-house or the common parts. So in the example above, if water was penetrating into the lower flat owing to defects in the roof above the upper flat, the tenant of the lower flat could use section 11(1A) to get the roof over the upper flat repaired, (even though it was not part of the structure or exterior of the lower flat), provided that the landlord of the lower flat owned or had some other interest in the roof above the upper flat as well.

2.79 In *Edwards v Kumarasamy*[88] a landlord of a second floor flat was held not to be liable under section 11(1A) for an injury caused to his tenant when he tripped on a broken paving slab on a path leading from the front entrance door of the block across a courtyard to the communal rubbish bins. The Court of Appeal had found that the path was part of the exterior of the front hall and that the landlord's right (under his lease) to use the front hall, the car parking spaces and bin store took effect as legal easements so that the landlord had an estate or interest in the paved area where the tenant sustained his accident. However, the Supreme Court held that while that a leaseholder's right of way over the entrance hall of a block of flats owned by a separate freeholder was an interest in land sufficient to make the leaseholder liable to their subtenant for disrepair to the entrance hall under section 11(1A), the paved path was not part of the exterior of the building. Further (strictly obiter), as the path was not in the possession or either the landlord or the tenant, notice to the landlord of the want of repair was required for liability.

88 *Edwards v Kumarasamy* [2016] UKSC 40, [2016] AC 1334.

2.80 **'keep in . . . proper working order'** These words necessarily presuppose that at the start of the tenancy the relevant installations were in proper working order, so that, if by reason of disrepair or design fault an installation has never been in proper working order, a landlord with knowledge of the defect will be in continuing breach of the implied term.[89]

2.81 However, what if an installation for the supply of water, gas or electricity has been in proper working order but ceases to work properly owing to changes in supply? In *O'Connor v Old Etonians Housing Association Ltd*,[90] the Court of Appeal held that an installation would be in proper working order if it was able to function under those conditions of supply that it was reasonable to anticipate would prevail. If a variation to the supply occurred which could not have been reasonably anticipated, the landlord's duty to keep an installation in proper working order might require him or her to make modifications to the installation depending on the circumstances of the case, including the duration of the variation and the cost of modification.

2.82 **'the installations in the dwelling-house'** The landlord is obliged to keep in repair and in working order the installations specifically mentioned in section 11(1)(b) and (c). The provision also extends to other installations for the supply of water, gas, electricity, sanitation, heating and hot water. Water or gas pipes, electrical wiring, water tanks,[91] boilers, radiators and other space heating installations, such as vents for underfloor heating, will be within the repairing obligation.

2.83 The installations must usually be *in* the tenant's dwelling. However, some tenants (and particularly those in high-rise flats) experience major problems as a result of the failure of installations serving blocks or estates but sited outside their homes, for example, central heating boilers. Historically, the courts declined to extend the benefit of the repairing covenant to such tenants. In the *Campden Hill Towers* case,[92] Megaw LJ said:

> . . . .the installations in the physical confines of the flat must be kept in repair and capable, so far as their own structural and mechanical condition is concerned, of working properly. But no more than that.

89 *Liverpool CC v Irwin* [1977] AC 239, [1976] 2 WLR 562, HL.

90 [2002] EWCA Civ 150, [2002] Ch 295.

91 *Sheldon v West Bromwich Corporation* (1984) 13 HLR 23, (1973) 25 P&CR, 360, CA.

92 *Campden Hill Towers v Gardner* [1977] QB 823, [1977] 2 WLR 159, CA at 835H.

2.84 The requirement that the defective installations must be in the dwelling has been lifted for more recent tenants. If the tenancy was granted on or after 15 January 1989, the obligation to repair and keep in proper working order is extended to any installation which (a) either directly or indirectly serves the dwelling *and* (b) is either owned by or under the control of the landlord or forms part of any part of a building in which the landlord has an estate of interest, providing that the defect is in fact 'such as to affect the lessee's enjoyment of the dwelling-house or of any common parts' (LTA 1985 s11(1A)(b)). This provision effectively overcomes the restrictions of the *Campden Hill Towers* decision. It gives more recent tenants' rights to require repairs to, for example, the communal heating boiler, the pump in the district heating system and the water tank on the roof of the tower block. However, it does not assist tenants where the defect is to an installation which is not owned by the landlord or under his control or where it is in a part of a building in which the landlord has no estate or interest. In *Niazi Services Ltd v Van der Loo*,[93] the landlord of a flat above a restaurant was held not liable for poor water pressure in the flat where this was because of works in the restaurant below, in which the landlord had no estate or interest.

2.85 Apart from the installations specifically mentioned in the section, the repairing obligation does not extend to fixtures, fittings, and appliances for making use of water, gas or electricity: section 11(1)(b).

2.86 In *Wycombe Area Health Authority v Barnett*,[94] the Court of Appeal held that the obligation in section 11(1)(b) and (c) to keep the installations in the premises in proper working order did not impose a duty on the landlord to lag water tanks and pipes so as to avoid damage in exceptionally severe cold weather. The court did indicate, however, that a landlord would be liable if the pipes were prone to burst within the normal temperature range, and that since there was in any event no liability on the part of the tenant to do so, any prudent landlord would insulate the pipes to avoid damage being caused to his or her property.

2.87 Even though the landlord will be presumed to know of the disrepair in the parts of the property that he or she retains (so that there is no need for actual notice of such disrepair to be given), it is not certain that the courts will presume that the landlord knows of the effect on the individual tenants. It may, therefore, be advisable to ensure that the landlord has actual knowledge (preferably by notice)

93 [2004] EWCA Civ 53, [2004] 1 WLR 1254.

94 (1982) 5 HLR 84, (1984) 47 P&CR 394, CA.

of both the defect and effect before proceeding for breach of section 11(1A). It is a defence for the landlord to show in such proceedings that, despite using reasonable endeavours, he or she was unable to obtain the right to carry out the works to the particular part of the building concerned (eg, where the disrepair emanates from a flat of which the landlord is the freeholder but where the leaseholder is exercising a right to refuse access): section 11(3A).

Standard for section 11 repairs

2.88 The repairing obligations implied into tenancy agreements by section 11 are subject to the important qualification that, in determining the standard of repair to be required, regard is to be had to the age, character, and prospective life of the dwelling-house and the locality in which it is situated: section 11(3). Reference to age, character and locality does no more than re-state the position which applies in any event at common law: see para 2.15. This is an area in which expert evidence may be required. In *Montoya v Hackney LBC*,[95] a finding that twisting of the doors and windows amounted to disrepair was overturned in the light of evidence from the single joint expert that the defects were commensurate with the age and type of property and so they did not amount to disrepair. The trial judge should not have departed from the only expert evidence in the case.

2.89 At least where disrepair is materially affecting the tenant's comfortable enjoyment of the dwelling-house, its 'prospective life' is only relevant if demolition is imminent.[96] On the other hand, the fact that complete reconstruction is envisaged is a good reason for patch repairing the roof in the meantime, even though ordinarily replacement would have been required.[97]

2.90 A landlord is entitled to perform his repairing obligations in the manner which is least onerous to him, provided that he chooses a reasonable method of repair. The paying party can choose the cheapest option where there are two ways in which the covenant can be performed.[98]

2.91 Where there is an obligation to repair which requires the replacement of installations or fittings which are beyond economic repair,

95 December 2005 *Legal Action* 28, QBD.

96 *Newham LBC v Patel* [1978] 13 HLR 77, [1979] JPL 303, CA; cf *McClean v Liverpool CC* (1988) 20 HLR 25, CA.

97 *Dame Margaret Hungerford Charity Trustees v Beazeley* (1994) 26 HLR 269, CA.

98 *Gibson Investments Ltd v Chesterton Plc* [2002] EWHC 19 (Ch), [2002] 2 P&CR 494; *Riverside Property Investments Ltd v Blackhawk Automotive* [2004] EWHC 3052 (TCC).

the obligation is to replace them on a like for like or nearest equivalent basis. There is no requirement to upgrade fittings or bring them in line with current standards (unless required to do so by law or to comply with any necessary regulations).[99]

2.92 The standard of repair is no higher for a social landlord than it is in the private rented sector.[100]

Limitations of section 11

2.93 The operation of section 11 is circumscribed in a number of ways:

- No liability can be imposed on the landlord for breach of section 11 until the landlord has knowledge of the defects complained of and fails to effect repairs within a reasonable period of time thereafter (but see paras 2.311–2.321).
- The provision applies only to tenancies commencing on or after the passage of the HA 1961, ie, 24 October 1961: section 13(1).
- It applies to periodic and fixed-term leases of less than seven years. It does not usually apply to lettings for more than seven years but there are exceptions, see para 2.27 above.
- Section 11 does not apply to certain agricultural tenancies within the Agricultural Holdings Act 1948: section 14(3).
- In pre-15 January 1989 tenancies, it does not extend to common parts of the building containing the accommodation let to the tenant, nor to parts of the premises retained by the landlord but which the tenant is permitted to use.
- Section 11 does not extend to any item which the tenant is entitled to remove from the premises, for example, a tenant's own electric fire (although the position would be different if the fire was provided by the landlord). Nor does it relieve the tenant of the obligation to use the premises in a tenant-like manner (see paras 2.330–2.333). Nor does it require the landlord to re-instate premises destroyed by Act of God or inevitable accident etc: section 11(2).
- Section 11 does not assist most business tenants: section 32(2).
- Section 11 does not apply to certain properties let *to* local authorities and other public bodies: section 14(4).
- Section 11 does not bind the Crown. It cannot therefore be relied on by the tenants of most government departments and

99 See *Sunlife Europe Properties Ltd v Tiger Aspect Holdings Ltd* [2013] EWHC 463 (TCC), [2013] P&CR 4. This case concerns the repairing obligations on a tenant in a commercial lease but the principle would be equally applicable to a landlord of a residential tenancy.

100 *Wainwright v Leeds CC* (1984) 13 HLR 117, CA.

agencies.[101] However, this may be discriminatory in breach of Article 14 of the Human Rights Act (HRA) 1998 Sch 1.[102]

Important note for pre-1961 tenancies

2.94 Tenancies which would otherwise be outside section 11 because they started before 24 October 1961 may nevertheless gain the benefit of the provision. For example, where a fair rent has been registered on the basis that the tenancy is subject to section 11 and the landlord has accepted rent following that registration, the landlord will be bound by the repairing obligation.[103] Alternatively, a pre-1961 tenant may be able to show that he or she is covered by section 11 because the earlier tenancy has been determined and replaced by one commencing after 1961. This will be the case for all local authority tenants because in the 1960s and 1970s council rent increases were achieved by a process of notice to quit and re-grant. Pre-1961 tenants not covered by section 11 may be able to rely on one of the common law implied terms described above.

Outside the tenancy agreement

Occupiers' Liability Act 1957

2.95 Under the OLA 1957, the 'occupier' of land or premises owes a 'common duty of care' to all visitors except to the extent that he or she lawfully restricts liability: OLA 1957 s2(1). The 'common duty of care' is a duty to take such care as is reasonable in all the circumstances to ensure that the visitor will be reasonably safe when on the premises for the purpose for which he or she was invited: OLA 1957 s2(2). The test to be applied is an objective one; it does not depend upon the standards of safety a landlord may set for itself as a matter of policy.[104] These provisions can impose duties on landlords who are the legal 'occupiers' of all or part of a building. The landlord remains the occupier of the common parts of any building which he or she owns. [105]

101 *Department of Transport v Egoroff* (1986) 18 HLR 326, CA. The Crown Tenancies Bill 2016–17 would have amended this position, but the Bill fell at the 2017 General Election and there has been no further legislation.

102 *Larkos v Cyprus* (1999) 7 BHRC 244, [1998] EHRLR 653; *Nicholas v Secretary of State for Defence* [2015] EWCA Civ 53, [2015] HLR 25, CA.

103 *Brikom Investments v Seaford* [1981] 1 WLR 863, [1981] 2 All ER 783, CA; *Johnstone v Charlton and Taylor*, May 1998 *Legal Action* 21, *Housing Law Casebook*, 7th edn, para R8.2, Sunderland County Court.

104 *Esdale v Dover DC* [2010] EWCA Civ 409.

105 *Wheat v E Lacon & Co Ltd* [1966] AC 552, [1966] 2 WLR 581, HL; *Dear v Newham LBC* (1987) 19 HLR 391, QBD; *Jordan v Achara* (1988) 20 HLR 607, CA.

2.96 The duty is a personal duty on a landlord so that a landlord can be liable for the acts of an independent contractor. In *Alexander v Freshwater Properties Ltd and Christopher Place*[106] both the landlord and the builder were held equally liable for the removal of a self-closing device and door handle on a communal front entrance door, which resulted in a tenant catching her finger in the door.

2.97 The statute prohibits any attempt by a landlord to exclude or reduce his or her obligations to people not party to the contract who are visitors under the terms of the tenancy agreement: OLA 1957 s3(1).

2.98 Although the OLA 1957 imposes a liability on the landlord for injury caused by defects in the part of a building 'occupied' by the landlord, it does not provide a mechanism by which the landlord may be forced to repair such defects in the common parts in advance of an accident.

2.99 A landlord will owe no duty under the OLA 1957 in respect of premises which are let to tenants. In *Drysdale v Hedges*[107] it was held that Parliament could not have intended landlords to have duties under both the OLA 1957 and the DPA 1972; OLA 1957 s2 was replaced by DPA 1972 s4 which therefore defined the extent of a landlord's duty.

Defective Premises Act 1972

Defective Premises Act 1972 s1

2.100 DPA 1972 s1 imposes a duty on all those, including landlords, who undertake work for or in connection with the provision of a dwelling to:

(a) do the work in a professional or workmanlike manner;
(b) use proper materials; and
(c) ensure that the dwelling is fit for human habitation when completed.[108]

For the full text of DPA 1972 s1, see appendix A.

2.101 The origins of the statute lie in a Law Commission report, *Civil Liabilities of Vendors and Lessors of Defective Premises*,[109] that may usefully be referred to when interpreting or construing the Act.[110]

106 [2012] EWCA Civ 1048.

107 [2012] EWHC 4131 (QB).

108 See, eg, *McMinn Bole & Van den Haak v Huntsbuild Ltd & Money* [2009] EWCA Civ 1146.

109 Law Com No 40.

110 *Alker v Collingwood Housing Association* [2007] EWCA Civ 343, [2007] HLR 29, per Carnwath LJ at para 20.

The duty is owed by builders as well as by architects, surveyors, specialist sub-contractors and any others taking on work in connection with the provision of a dwelling. The mere enlargement of an existing dwelling does not fall within the scope of DPA 1972 s1. Work must produce a new dwelling in terms of the identity of the dwelling being changed.[111] The common parts of an apartment block are not part of a dwelling but work done to the common parts is work done in connection with the provision of a dwelling and therefore within the definition in DPA 1972 s1.[112]

2.102 The duty is also owed by the employer, eg the local authority or property development company, which engages the builder to do the work: DPA 1972 s1(4). The duty is owed to the person for whom the dwelling is initially provided and to all persons subsequently acquiring a legal or equitable interest in it. The duty is owed in respect of work which commenced after 1 January 1974 and can apply to a failure to undertake necessary works.[113]

2.103 Whether a dwelling is 'unfit for habitation' will always depend upon the facts of the particular case. A judge is not obliged to consider each defect individually but is entitled to ask whether the dwelling as a whole is unfit.[114]

2.104 The scope of DPA 1972 s1 is technically restricted by section 2, which excludes all dwellings covered by 'an approved scheme'. NHBC was such an approved scheme but the approval lapsed before 1992. There has subsequently been no approved scheme, so, given the limitation period for claims, section 2 is of no current application.

2.105 Damages recoverable for breach of section 1 may include damages for economic loss and damages for the loss of enjoyment of the premises.[115]

2.106 The cause of action is treated as accruing when the work (or any post-completion remedial work) is completed: DPA 1972 s1(5).[116] The limitation period will be six years under Limitation Act 1980 s2, since liability

111 *Jenson v Faux* [2011] EWCA Civ 423, [2011] 1 WLR 3038.

112 *Rendlesham Estates Plc v Barr Ltd* [2014] EWHC 3968 (TCC), [2015] 1 WLR 3663.

113 *Andrews v Schooling* [1991] 1 WLR 783, [1991] 3 All ER 723, CA.

114 *McMinn Bole & Van den Haak v Huntsbuild Ltd & Money* [2009] EWCA Civ 1146, see also *Harrison & Others v (1) Shepherd Homes Ltd (2) National Housing Building Council and (3) NHBC Building Control Services* [2011] EWHC 1811 (TCC) and *Bole and another v Huntsbuild Ltd* [2009] EWCA Civ 1146.

115 *Murphy v Brentwood DC* [1991] 1 AC 398, [1990] 3 WLR 414, HL per Lord Bridge at 480H–B; *Bayoumi v Protim Services Ltd* (1986) 30 HLR 785, CA.

116 *Alexander v Mercouris* [1979] 1 WLR 1270, [1979] 3 All ER 305, CA; *Alderson v Beetham Organisation* [2003] EWCA Civ 408, [2003] 1 WLR 1686.

is strict. As a claim under the DPA 1972 s1 is a claim for breach of statutory duty rather than a claim in common law negligence, no advantage can be taken of any possible extension of time under Limitation Act 1980 s14A which would allow a court to extend the limitation period to three years from the date of knowledge. If the action includes a claim for personal injuries, Limitation Act 1980 s11 should apply.

2.107 The duty under DPA 1972 s1 is not extinguished by any disposal of the reversion: DPA 1972 s3. DPA 1972 s3 therefore abolishes the immunity of landlords in respect of work carried out before the letting and provides that, in respect of such work, the landlord is liable to any person who might be reasonably expected to be affected by negligent work, eg, the tenant's family and visitors as well as the tenant him or herself. The full text of section 3 is in appendix A.

Defective Premises Act 1972 s4

2.108 DPA 1972 s4 serves two distinct purposes, which can be broadly summarised as follows: (1) in some circumstances it makes landlords liable for personal injury or property damage caused by disrepair, even though the landlord did not have knowledge of the need for repair; and (2) in some circumstances, it creates new obligations to prevent the condition of the dwelling causing personal injury or property damage. The full text of DPA 1972 s4 is in appendix A.

The basic duty

2.109 The DPA 1972 applies from 1 January 1974, whether or not the tenancy began before that date: DPA 1972 s4(3). It applies to all of the land let, not just the dwelling-house. For example, it applied to the patio at the rear of the dwelling-house in *Smith v Bradford MBC*[117] and to a front garden in *Rogerson v Bolsover DC*.[118] It does not apply to land which is not let, eg, the common parts.

2.110 The duty is owed to 'all persons who might reasonably be expected to be affected by defects in the state of the premises': that includes the tenant as well as the tenant's family members and visitors,[119] and workmen sent by the landlord's contractors.[120]

2.111 The duty is a duty to 'take such care as is reasonable in all the circumstances' to see that the persons owed the duty are reasonably safe from personal injury or property damage caused by a 'relevant defect' of which the landlord knew or 'ought . . . to have known'.

117 (1982) 4 HLR 86, (1982) 44 P&CR 171, CA.

118 [2019] EWCA Civ 226.

119 *Smith v Bradford MBC* (1982) 4 HLR 86, (1982) 44 P&CR 171 CA.

120 *Hannon v Hillingdon Homes Ltd* [2012] EWHC 1437 (QB).

2.112 A 'relevant defect' is a defect which the landlord is either:

- bound to repair or maintain under the express or implied terms of the contract including LTA 1985 s11; or
- bound to repair or maintain under DPA 1972 s4(4) (see para 2.122).

2.113 The definition of a relevant defect does not embrace a consideration of whose fault it was that the defect came into existence. Accordingly, in *Hannon v Hillingdon Homes Ltd*[121] the landlord was held liable for the injury caused to a workman when he slipped on a staircase, where the bannister had been removed by the tenant after the tenancy commenced.

2.114 A landlord's obligation under a tenancy agreement to repair and maintain the property or to keep it in good condition does not impose an obligation to put it in a safe condition and a defect is not a relevant defect simply because it is hazardous.[122] DPA 1972 s4 does not impose a statutory warranty that premises are reasonably safe.

2.115 A tenant of one property can rely on section 4 in relation to relevant defects in other properties owned by the same landlord where the landlord has repairing obligations in relation to the defect in the other property or has reserved a right to enter and repair in default. In *Wadsworth v Nagle*,[123] the tenant of a lower flat affected by water penetration from the flat above claimed damages from the landlord who was also the landlord of the flat above. The claim failed because the upper flat was let on a long lease with the repairing obligation for internal repair falling on the tenant and the landlord had no express or implied right to enter the upper flat to repair the defective bath sealant which caused the water penetration.

2.116 The landlord cannot exclude or modify the duty: DPA 1972 s6(3).

The duty where the landlord ought to have known of the defect

2.117 DPA 1972 s4(1), (2) and (3) create no new repairing or maintaining obligations,[124] but they do superimpose a 'duty to take care' on top of existing repairing obligations in such a way that the landlord can be liable for personal injury or damage to property when he or she 'ought . . . to have known' of the likelihood of such injury or damage. This goes beyond the usual requirement that the landlord has actual knowledge of the defect (see paras 2.311–2.318).

121 [2012] EWHC 1437 (QB).

122 *Alker v Collingwood Housing Association* [2007] EWCA Civ 343, [2007] HLR 29.

123 [2005] EWHC 26 (QB).

124 *McNerny v Lambeth LBC* (1989) 21 HLR 188, CA; *Boldack v East Lindsey DC* (1999) 31 HLR 41, CA.

2.118 DPA 1972 s4(2) provides that:

> The said duty is owed if the landlord knows (whether as a result of being notified by the tenant or otherwise) or if he ought in all the circumstances to have known of the relevant defect.

2.119 The courts expect landlords to take positive steps to inspect for latent defects when the landlord is aware that a problem might exist, but not to inspect for unforeseeable dangers.[125] However, there is no duty to have a system of inspection.[126]

2.120 Cases in which, on special facts, the landlord ought to have known of the risk of personal injury are:

- *Clarke v Taff Ely BC*[127] – failure to undertake simple routine inspection of the floor in an older house prone to floorboard rot;
- *Smith v Bradford MBC* [128] – failure to undertake proper pre-letting inspection of void premises in which a former tenant had built a defective patio;
- *Sykes v Harry*[129] – failure to service a gas heater; and
- *Hannon v Hillingdon Homes Ltd*[130] – failure to notice the removal of a banister by the tenant, despite home visits having been undertaken by the landlord's staff and agents.

2.121 In the case of gas installations, the Gas Safety (Installation and Use) Regulations 1998[131] require landlords to inspect gas appliances annually. Failure to inspect is likely to result in the court holding that a landlord 'ought to have known' of any defect causing personal injury or property damage for the purposes of DPA 1972 s4.

Additional obligations

2.122 DPA 1972 s4(4) provides:

> Where premises are let under a tenancy which expressly or impliedly gives the landlord the right to enter the premises to carry out any description of maintenance or repairs of the premises, then, as from the time when he first is, or by notice, or otherwise can put himself, in a position to exercise the right and for so long as he is or can put himself in that position, he shall be treated for the purposes of

125 *Morley v Knowsley BC*, May 1988 *Legal Action* 22, *Housing Law Casebook* 7th edn, para R16.2, CA.

126 *Rogerson v Bolsover DC* [2019] EWCA Civ 226.

127 (1980) 10 HLR 44, QBD.

128 (1982) 4 HLR 86, (1982) 44 P&CR 171, CA.

129 [2001] EWCA Civ 167, [2001] QB 1014.

130 [2012] EWHC 1437 (QB).

131 SI No 2451.

> subsections (1) to (3) above (but for not other purposes) as if he were under an obligation to the tenant for that description of maintenance or repair of the premises; but the landlord shall not owe the tenant any duty by virtue of this subsection in respect of any defect in the state of the premises arising from, or continuing because of, a failure to carry out an obligation expressly imposed on the tenant by the tenancy.

2.123 This section has the result that, where a landlord is expressly or impliedly permitted to enter the premises let, to carry out work of repair or maintenance, the landlord comes under a positive duty to ensure that his or her failure to carry out that type of repair or maintenance does not cause personal injury or property damage. This section has no application to parts which are not let, for example, exterior paths.[132]

2.124 Advisers should therefore consider carefully what rights to enter the premises have been granted to the landlord by the tenancy agreement. Usually, express rights of entry are limited to inspection and carrying out repairs. This was the case in *Boldack v East Lindsey DC*,[133] where another right of entry granted by the tenancy agreement was the right to remove any articles left on the premises at the end of the tenancy, but this did not provide a relevant right of entry because it only arose at the end of the tenancy when the council was entitled to possession of the premises. Accordingly, there was no duty to remove the paving slab which had caused injury to the tenant's sons, because it was neither work of repair nor work of maintenance.

2.125 However, in *Dunn v Bradford MDC*,[134] there was an express term that tenants would permit their landlord to enter the premises for the purpose of executing 'repairs or improvements'. It was claimed that this gave the landlord the right to carry out improvements and that the landlord therefore had a duty to carry out such improvements as were necessary to eradicate condensation dampness. The court held that DPA 1972 s4(4) could not be used to compel a landlord to remedy design defects or to impose a duty on a landlord to carry out works of improvement going beyond such repair and maintenance as was necessary to maintain the house in the condition in which it was first let.

2.126 The scope of DPA 1972 s4(4) is potentially quite wide because the Court of Appeal held in *McAuley v Bristol CC*[135] that the landlord of a council house let on a periodic tenancy had an implied right to enter the house to carry out any works of repair which were necessary to

132 *King v South Northamptonshire DC* (1992) 24 HLR 284, (1992) 64 P&CR 35, CA.

133 *Boldack v East Lindsey DC* (1999) 31 HLR 41, CA.

134 [2002] EWCA Civ 1137, [2003] HLR 154.

135 [1992] QB 134, (1991) 23 HLR 586, CA.

remove a 'significant risk' of personal injury to the tenant, his or her family or visitors. By virtue of DPA 1972 s4(4), that right was converted into a duty, breach of which resulted in the landlord being held liable for personal injury to one of the tenants. This does not, however, impose any obligation on a landlord to remedy a design defect which poses a danger to health unless the works necessary to remedy that defect are works of maintenance or repair. The fact that a landlord may be entitled to enter to abate a statutory nuisance[136] does not give rise to a deemed obligation on the landlord to remedy the statutory nuisance, unless the works necessary to do so are works of maintenance or repair. This is because the duty under DPA 1972 s4(4) is limited to works of maintenance or repair.[137]

2.127 The duty under DPA 1972 s4 does not give rise to a strict liability.[138] Latent or undetectable defects do not give rise to liability.

2.128 The duty under DPA 1972 s4 can be enforced proactively by an application for an injunction to cure the defect, before it causes harm.[139]

Housing Act 1985

2.129 Where a secure tenant claims to exercise a right to buy, the landlord is obliged to serve on the tenant a notice which shall include a description of any structural defect known to the landlord, affecting the dwelling-house or building in which it is situated.[140] Any failure to notify such a defect can give rise to a claim for breach of statutory duty. In *Begum v Birmingham CC*[141] the tenant, who bought her house in 2003, successfully sued the council which had failed to disclose a history of structural movement and cracking. Although the defects were not apparent when the house sale inspection report was completed, the court found that the council had been aware of structural defects in 1990 and that this knowledge remained vested in the council even though it had kept no records.

Environmental Protection Act 1990

2.130 Unhealthy housing can be the subject of a criminal prosecution of the landlord under the Environmental Protection Act (EPA) 1990.

136 *Lee v Leeds CC* [2002] EWCA Civ 6, [2002] 1 WLR 1488.

137 *Alker v Collingwood Housing Association* [2007] EWCA Civ 343, [2007] HLR 29.

138 *Lafferty v Newark & Sherwood District Council* [2016] EWHC 320 (QB), [2016] HLR 13.

139 *Barrett v Lounova (1982) Ltd* [1990] 1 QB 348, [1989] 2 WLR 137, CA.

140 HA 1985 s125(4A).

141 [2015] EWCA Civ 386, December 2015 *Legal Action* 40.

See chapter 6 for a full account of the EPA 1990 rights and the procedure for bringing a prosecution.

Human Rights Act 1998

2.131 HRA 1998 s6(1) provides that it is unlawful for a public authority to act in a way which is incompatible with the Convention rights set out in HRA 1998 Sch 1.

2.132 Article 8 of HRA 1998 Sch 1 provides that:

> 1 Everyone has the right to respect for his private and family life, his home and correspondence.
> 2 There shall be no interference by a public authority with the exercise of this right except such as is in accordance with the law and is necessary in a democratic society in the interests of national security, public safety or the economic well-being of the country, for the prevention of disorder or crime or for the protection of the rights and freedoms of others.

2.133 Attempts, so far, to extend a landlord's liability for housing conditions by virtue of the HRA 1998 have been unsuccessful. In *Lee v Leeds CC*,[142] it was held that LTA 1985 s11, as construed in *Quick v Taff Ely BC*[143] (namely that the obligation to keep in repair the structure did not extend to the rectification of design faults), was not incompatible with Article 8 and that the HRA 1998 did not require that LTA 1985 s11 be reinterpreted. The amendments to LTA 1985 by the Homes (Fitness for Human Habitation) Act 2018 will increasingly make this issue redundant in the future.

2.134 HRA 1998 s6 imposes on a public authority (which may now include registered social landlords and private registered providers as well as local authorities[144]) an obligation to take steps to ensure that the condition of a dwelling-house which is let for social housing is such that the tenant's Convention rights under Article 8 are not infringed, but such an obligation is not unqualified. The steps which a public authority must take to ensure compliance with Article 8 must be determined in each case, by having due regard to the needs and resources of the community and of individuals.[145]

142 [2002] EWCA Civ 6, [2002] 1 WLR 1488.

143 [1986] QB 809, [1985] 3 WLR 981, CA.

144 *R (Weaver) v London & Quadrant Housing Trust* [2009] EWCA Civ 587, [2010] 1 WLR 363.

145 *Lee v Leeds CC* [2002] EWCA Civ 6, [2002] 1 WLR 1488 at paras 48–49.

2.135 Therefore, it is possible that, in exceptional circumstances, a landlord which is a public authority could be in breach of an occupier's right to respect for his or her home under Article 8 where it allowed a property to deteriorate into very poor condition. Conditions were not considered to be sufficiently bad for there to be a breach of Article 8 in either *Lee v Leeds CC*[146] (where the premises had been found to be prejudicial to health by reason of condensation dampness) or *Thornton and Jarrett v Birmingham CC*[147] (where there was major dampness but the premises were no longer prejudicial to health at the relevant time).

2.136 In a number of cases, the European Court of Human Rights has held that severe environmental pollution may prevent individuals from enjoying their homes to such a degree as to affect their private and family life adversely and that there may be positive obligations, inherent in effective respect for private and family life, to take action to stop such harm.[148]

2.137 However, in *Fadeyeva v Russia*[149] the European Court of Human Rights held that that, although an applicant had no medical evidence directly linking her ill health to toxins produced by the steel plant near her home, the applicant's prolonged exposure to the toxins 'inevitably made her more vulnerable to various diseases' and 'adversely affected the quality of her life at home'. On that basis, the actual detriment to the applicant's health and well-being reached a level sufficient to bring it within the scope of Article 8. This would suggest that the threshold for a claim under Article 8 may not be as high as previously thought and could well be attained by a tenant adversely affected by condensation dampness.

2.138 Although there has yet to be a successful claim brought for housing defects under the HRA 1998, a positive result was achieved in the field of nuisance in *Marcic v Thames Water Utilities Ltd*,[150] where the Court of Appeal found Thames Water liable in common law nuisance to an owner-occupier, for the recurrent flooding of his property by overflowing sewage, and on the basis that the water authority's failure to act was a breach of the owner's Convention rights under Article 8 and Protocol 1 of Article 1. However, the House

146 [2002] EWCA Civ 6, [2002] 1 WLR 1488.

147 November 2004 *Legal Action* 27, *Housing Law Casebook*, 7th edn, para R18.89, Birmingham County Court.

148 *Lopez Ostra v Spain* (1994) 20 EHRR 277, ECtHR; *Guerra v Italy* (1998) 26 EHRR 357, ECtHR.

149 October 2005 *Legal Action* 18, *Housing Law Casebook* 7th edn, para A7.4, ECtHR.

150 [2002] EWCA Civ 64, [2002] QB 929.

of Lords subsequently rejected all the claims in that case on the basis that liability in nuisance would be inconsistent with the statutory scheme for regulation of water and sewage undertakers which also provided a fair balancing mechanism for the assessment of priority and enforcement, so there was no breach of the Convention.[151]

2.139 More recently, in *Dobson v Thames Water Utilities Ltd and another*,[152] it was held as a preliminary issue that the principle in *Marcic* did not preclude claims in nuisance involving allegations of negligence or claims under the HRA 1998 where the exercise of adjudicating on those causes of action was not inconsistent with, and did not involve conflicts with, the statutory process under the Water Industry Act 1991. The Court of Appeal considered the principles for the award of damages in nuisance claims and under the HRA 1998 and held that it was unlikely that any further award for damages under the HRA 1998 would be made where there had already been an award of damages for nuisance.

Common law rights (judge-made)

2.140 Beyond the contractual rights conferred expressly or impliedly by the terms of a tenancy agreement, English law has been extremely slow to impose any further obligations on landlords, or even to give tenants remedies for injury sustained as a result of the condition of rented premises. Indeed, landlords letting premises have long had a very broad exemption from any liability to repair or to prevent injury to occupiers. However, progress has been made, through both the common law and statute, in piercing the landlord's 'cloak of immunity from responsibility' in respect of shoddy housing.

2.141 The courts have implied various terms into certain tenancy agreements, and the common law torts in negligence and in nuisance can impose liability in respect of certain defects and interference with the tenant's enjoyment of the premises.

Common law implied terms

2.142 At common law, the landlord has no duty to repair or to ensure that the dwelling is habitable.[153] Nor is the landlord under a common law duty of care to take reasonable steps to ensure that any occupier of the rented premises does not suffer personal injury or damage to his or

151 *Marcic v Thames Water Utilities Ltd* [2003] UKHL 66, [2004] 2 AC 42.

152 [2009] EWCA Civ 28, [2009] 3 All ER 319.

153 *Cavalier v Pope* [1906] AC 428, HL; *Robbins v Jones* (1863) 15 CB (NS) 221.

her property as the result of defects to the premises.[154] This is historically why the terms of the contract are of such importance to a tenant with problems relating to housing conditions. There are, however, a number of exceptions to the common law immunity of the landlord achieved by implying terms which impose obligations on landlords.

Lettings of furnished dwellings

2.143 Where the landlord lets a furnished dwelling for immediate occupation, it will be an implied term of the contract of letting that the premises are fit for human habitation at the start of the tenancy.[155]

2.144 The term does not apply to lettings of unfurnished dwellings.[156] Furthermore, the obligation is strictly an initial one, ie, that the premises were fit when they were let.[157] However, the term will be broken if the dwelling is initially unfit but the lack of fitness becomes obvious only at a later stage of the tenancy.[158]

2.145 Guidance on whether the premises are unfit for habitation is as set out at paras 2.42–2.50 above.

2.146 The courts have held that dwelling-houses are unfit for human habitation at common law if they are heavily infested by bugs,[159] have a defective drainage[160] or sewerage system,[161] or carry an infection,[162] or if there is a lack of safety,[163] or an insufficiency of water supply.[164] The obligation is confined to fitness for habitation and the implied term does not require the landlord to ensure that the premises are in structural repair when let, eg cracked ceiling plaster will not be covered.

2.147 This common law provision will be effectively superseded by the introduction of LTA 1985 s9A by the Homes (Fitness for Human Habitation) Act 2018.[165]

2.148 Generally, common law implied terms can be excluded from any letting by an express term to the contrary. However, previous OFT

154 *McNerny v Lambeth LBC* (1989) 21 HLR 188, CA.
155 *Smith v Marrable* (1843) 11 M&W 5; *Hart v Windsor* (1844) 12 M & W 68; *Wilson v Finch-Hatton* (1877) 2 Ex D 336.
156 *McNerny v Lambeth LBC* (1989) 21 HLR 188, CA.
157 *Sarson v Roberts* [1895] 2 QB 395.
158 *Harrison v Malet* (1886) 3 TLR 58.
159 *Smith v Marrable* (1843) 11 M&W 5.
160 *Wilson v Finch-Hatton* (1877) 2 Ex D 336.
161 *Harrison v Malet* (1886) 3 TLR 58.
162 *Bird v Greville* (1884) C&E 317; *Collins v Hopkins* [1923] 2 KB 617.
163 *Edwards v Etherington* (1825) Ry&M 268.
164 *Chester v Powell* (1885) 52 LT 722.
165 See para 2.24 onwards.

guidance suggests that it would be unfair for a landlord to use an express term to avoid this implied term in lettings to which the UTCC Regs 1999 and now CRA 2015 Part 2 apply.[166]

Dwelling-houses held under a licence

2.149 Where there is a licence and not a tenancy, a term may be implied in the licence requiring the licensor to take reasonable care to ensure that the condition of the dwelling does not cause personal injury to any of the occupiers or damage their property,[167] or that the premises are of sound construction and reasonably suitable for the purposes required by the licensee.[168]

Means of access and communal facilities

2.150 It is an implied term for most tenancies of residential accommodation that the landlord is obliged to take reasonable care to keep means of access and communal facilities (eg, shared rubbish chutes or lifts) in repair and proper working order, if that is not already required by an express term.[169]

Ancillary property owned by the landlord

2.151 The courts will generally imply a term imposing a duty on the landlord to take reasonable care to ensure that the condition of ancillary property retained in his or her ownership (eg, the roof of a block of flats, common hall, water tanks, heating plant or drains) does not deteriorate so as to cause personal injury to the tenant or damage to his or her property.[170]

2.152 There will, however, be no grounds for implying a term about repair of the common parts where provision is comprehensively made for such repairs in a written tenancy agreement.[171]

166 *Guidance on unfair terms in tenancy agreements* OFT356, para 3.14. This Guidance was withdrawn by the CMA in July 2017 and has not been replaced in detail. For current CMA guidance on unfair contract terms see CMA37, CMA July 2017.

167 *Greene v Chelsea BC* [1954] 2 QB 127, CA.

168 *Wettern Electric Ltd v Welsh Development Agency* [1983] 1 QB 796, [1983] 2 WLR 897, QBD; cf *Morris-Thomas v Petticoat Lane Rentals* (1987) 53 P&CR 238, CA.

169 *Miller v Emcer Products* [1956] Ch 304, [1956] 1 All ER 237, CA; *Liverpool CC v Irwin* [1977] AC 239, [1976] 2 WLR 562, HL; *King v South Northamptonshire DC* (1992) 24 HLR 284, (1992) 64 P&CR 35, CA; cf *Duke of Westminster v Guild* [1985] QB 688, [1984] 3 WLR 630, CA.

170 *Dunster v Hollis* [1918] 2 KB 795, KBD; *Cockburn v Smith* [1924] 2 KB 119, CA; *Duke of Westminster v Guild* [1985] QB 688, [1984] 3 WLR 630, CA.

171 *Gordon v Selico Ltd* (1986) 18 HLR 219, CA.

Quiet enjoyment/derogation from grant

2.153 A landlord either expressly, or by necessary implication, contracts to give the tenant 'quiet enjoyment' of the rented premises for the duration of the letting. This may be breached in circumstances of poor housing conditions, for example by a landlord failing to keep watertight the building containing the tenant's flat, thereby allowing the flat to be penetrated by rain-water or dampness,[172] or by carrying out work on other parts of the building, causing noise and nuisance to the tenants.[173]

2.154 The covenant of quiet enjoyment is prospective in nature and does not apply to things done before the grant of the tenancy even though they may have continuing consequences.[174] Accordingly, in *Southwark LBC v Mills*,[175] the landlord did not breach the covenant by failing to install effective soundproofing. The doctrine of *caveat lessee*[176] applied: the tenant took the premises in the state in which they were let and could not complain about any pre-existing defect.

2.155 The covenant does not create new obligations about housing conditions. However, if the landlord fails to perform his or her obligations or carries out those obligations so as to interfere unreasonably with the tenant's occupation there will be a breach of the covenant of quiet enjoyment in addition to other causes of action.[177] In *Goldmile Properties v Lechouritis*,[178] the Court of Appeal held that a lease containing a landlord's repairing obligation and a covenant for quiet enjoyment had to be construed to give effect to both provisions. Accordingly, a landlord had to take all reasonable precautions to prevent disturbance being caused by repairs but could not be required to take every possible precaution. In *Thornton and Jarrett v Birmingham CC*,[179] HHJ McKenna found that the council had breached the covenant of quiet enjoyment when it had failed to rehouse the tenant while repair works were carried out, even though she had not asked to be rehoused; not all reasonable steps to minimise the risks had been taken having regard to the tenant's children, aged eight and ten.

172 *Booth v Thomas* [1926] Ch 397, CA; *Gordon v Selico Ltd* (1986) 18 HLR 219, CA.

173 *Mira v Aylmer Square Investments Ltd* (1990) 22 HLR 182, CA; *Sampson v Wilson* [1996] Ch 39, CA.

174 *Southwark LBC v Mills* [2001] 1 AC 1, [1999] 3 WLR 939, HL.

175 [2001] 1 AC 1, [1999] 3 WLR 939, HL.

176 See paras 2.4–2.5 above.

177 *Duke of Westminster v Guild* [1985] 1 QB 688, [1984] 3 WLR 630, CA.

178 [2003] EWCA Civ 49, [2003] 2 P&CR 1, CA.

179 November 2004 *Legal Action* 27; *Housing Law Casebook* 7th edn, para R18.89, Birmingham County Court.

2.156 A landlord shall not 'derogate from his grant' of a tenancy to the tenant. This implied term may be breached by poor housing conditions or fitness, if a landlord allows premises retained in his or her ownership or occupation to be in such a state as to interfere with the tenant's tenancy. The principle of non-derogation from grant cannot be used to create new obligations about housing conditions.[180]

Correlative obligations

2.157 If the tenancy agreement requires the tenant to pay for certain works or services, it will usually be implied that the landlord will actually perform those works or services.[181] In *Edmonton Corporation v Knowles*,[182] the tenant was obliged to pay to the landlord the cost of redecorating the exterior in every third year of the term. It was held that there was a correlative obligation on the landlord to carry out the redecoration. Similarly, in *Collins v Northern Ireland Housing Executive*,[183] tenants were obliged to pay standing charges and amounts for consumption of heating and hot water provided through a central system. It was held that it was an implied term of a collateral contract, which existed between the parties, that the landlord authority would provide and maintain the heating system.

2.158 Other tenants' obligations can also result in correlative terms being implied which are binding on the landlord. In general, a term will be implied into a contract where the implication of the term is necessary to give business efficacy to a transaction and where both parties would have agreed to its insertion had its absence been pointed out to them when they made the contract.[184]

2.159 In *Barrett v Lounova (1982) Ltd*,[185] the tenant was contractually bound to carry out all inside repairs and leave the inside of the premises in good repair and condition. There were no express repairing obligations binding on the landlord and LTA 1985 s11 (see paras 2.60–2.94) did not apply because the tenancy began before 24 October 1961. The dwelling was in a poor state of repair, suffering from severe

180 *Duke of Westminster v Guild* [1985] 1 QB 688, [1984] 3 WLR 630, CA.

181 *Edmonton Corporation v Knowles* (1962) 60 LGR 124.

182 (1962) 60 LGR 124.

183 [1987] 2 NIJB 27 CA(NI).

184 *Liverpool CC v Irwin* [1977] AC 239, [1976] 2 WLR 562, HL; see also *Gavin and another v One Housing Group Ltd* [2013] EWCA Civ 580, [2013] 2 P&CR 17 for a more recent example where the Court of Appeal refused to imply a term into a commercial lease that the landlord was obliged to keep the retained parts in repair on the basis that there was no reason to do so based on necessity or business efficacy.

185 [1990] 1 QB 348, [1989] 2 WLR 137, CA.

rain-water penetration as the result of roof defects. The Court of Appeal held that it was an implied term of the agreement that the landlord would keep the exterior of the dwelling in repair:

> It is obvious, as shown by this case itself, that sooner or later the covenant imposed on the tenant in respect of the inside can no longer be complied with unless the outside has been kept in repair . . . In my view, it is therefore necessary, as a matter of business efficacy, to make this agreement workable, that an obligation to keep the outside in repair must be imposed on someone.[186]

2.160 The extent to which correlative obligations such as this may be more widely imposed remains unclear,[187] but the modern trend is against the implication of new implied terms. In *Adami v Lincoln Grange Management Ltd*[188] (a long leaseholder case), it was held that the decision in *Barrett v Lounova*[189] should be confined to its own facts. More recently, in *Lee v Leeds CC*,[190] the Court of Appeal declined to imply a term that the landlord remedy design defects or keep the dwelling in a condition which enabled the tenant to perform her obligations under the tenancy, namely to keep the inside of her home clean and in a reasonable state of decoration. The court relied on the fact that the landlord was already liable to repair the exterior, whereas in *Barrett v Lounova*[191] there was no exterior repairing covenant.

Implied term on quality of repair work

2.161 It has been held at county court level that there is an implied term to do repairs with reasonable care and skill and proper materials.[192] In *Biligi v Paddington Churches Housing Association*,[193] the landlord was held liable for condensation caused by the replacement of a kitchen window, which contained a spinner vent, by a sealed glazed unit with no vent, on the basis of a breach of the admitted covenant to carry out repairs in a proper workmanlike manner. In refusing permission to appeal, the Court of Appeal held that:

> . . . a kitchen window which is acknowledged to require ventilation and so has a spinner vent in it, has not been properly repaired if it is

186 *Barrett v Lounova* (1982) Ltd [1990] 1 QB 348, [1989] 2 WLR 137, CA, per Kerr LJ at 358C.

187 *Demetriou v Poolaction Ltd* [1991] 25 EG 113, CA.

188 (1998) 30 HLR 982, CA.

189 [1990] 1 QB 348, [1989] 2 WLR 137, CA.

190 [2002] EWCA Civ 6, [2002] 1 WLR 1488.

191 [1990] 1 QB 348, [1989] 2 WLR 137, CA.

192 *Walton v Lewisham LBC* May 1997 *Legal Action* 20, Tunbridge Wells County Court.

193 [2010] EWCA Civ 1341.

replaced with a sealed window that has neither a means of opening nor any form of ventilation.

2.162 The Supply of Goods and Services Act 1982 also creates a duty on those providing goods to ensure that they are of satisfactory quality and fit for purpose and on those providing services to do so with reasonable care and skill.[194] For contracts starting on or after 1 October 2015, the CRA 2015 contains similar provisions.[195]

Other common law rights

Negligence

2.163 The major developments made at common law in relation to liability for housing conditions have taken place in the field of negligence. The English common law of tort provides that a person injured physically or materially by the negligence of another can recover recompense from that other if: a duty of care is owed; the damage was foreseeable; and the wrongdoer failed to take reasonable care. Throughout its development, the common law avoided including tenants and their families among the class of persons to whom a landlord owed a duty of care. It is only relatively recently that case-law has made significant changes to this approach.

2.164 A landlord who lets a defective, dangerous or unsafe property on which he or she has done no work is immune from any action in negligence.[196] In *Rimmer v Liverpool CC*,[197] the Court of Appeal expressed the view that the immunity of the landlord, although questionable, is still 'too deeply entrenched in our law for any court below the highest to disturb or destroy it' and that to do so would possibly be 'so great a change in the law as to require legislation'. More recently in *McNerny v Lambeth LBC*,[198] an attempt to show that the immunity of the landlord had been overtaken by developments in case-law failed. In that case, the landlord had not negligently constructed the building but it was unable to cope with modern usage and was prone to chronic condensation dampness. The Court of Appeal held that the fundamental immunity of the landlord in the law of negligence

194 See Supply of Goods and Services Act 1982 ss4(2), (5) and 13 and *Harrison and others v Shepherd Homes, (2) National House Building Council, (3) NHBC Building Control Services Ltd* [2011] EWHC 1811 (TCC).

195 CRA 2015, see ss9, 10 and 49.

196 *Cavalier v Pope* [1906] AC 428, HL.

197 [1985] QB 1, [1984] 2 WLR 426, CA.

198 (1989) 21 HLR 188, CA.

had survived into the modern age and could be removed only by a change in law made by statute. No such change has yet been made.

2.165 Although the general immunity of a bare landlord in negligence still survives today, there are now a number of ways in which a landlord can be held liable in negligence in special circumstances.

The landlord builder

2.166 If the landlord designed or built the dwelling, he or she owes subsequent occupiers the same duty of care as is owed by builders who do not subsequently become the landlord of the dwelling, that is, a duty to take reasonable care to ensure that the dwelling does not contain any latent defects which cause personal injury or property damage.[199]

2.167 A tenant's knowledge of, or the opportunity for inspection of, a defect may negative the duty of care or break the chain of causation but only where it is reasonable to expect a tenant to remove or avoid the danger and unreasonable for the tenant to run the risk of being injured by the danger. This will not usually be the case.[200]

2.168 The duty of care will not be breached where works were carried out according to the standards of reasonably skilled workmen at the time the works were done.[201] This common law duty of care has largely been overtaken by the statutory duty imposed by the DPA 1972 s1 (see paras 2.100–2.107).

Works after letting

2.169 The landlord who carries out work after the tenancy begins will also probably be held to owe to his or her tenant the same duty of care that any contractor would owe to the occupier, that is, a duty to take reasonable care to ensure that defective workmanship or materials do not cause personal injury or property damage.[202] The duty extends to using reasonable material to ensure that the work is effective. So, for example, where a landlord tries to treat an infestation of bugs with inadequate materials, the landlord will be liable to the tenant for subsequent damage caused.[203]

199 *Rimmer v Liverpool CC* [1985] QB 1, [1984] 2 WLR 426, CA; *Murphy v Brentwood DC* [1991] 1 AC 398, [1990] 3 WLR 414, HL; *Targett v Torfaen BC*, [1992] 3 All ER 27, (1992) 24 HLR 164, CA.

200 *Rimmer v Liverpool CC* [1985] QB 1, [1984] 2 WLR 426, CA; *Targett v Torfaen BC*, [1992] 3 All ER 27, (1992) 24 HLR 164, CA.

201 *Adams v Rhymer Valley DC* (2001) 33 HLR 41, CA.

202 *AC Billings & Sons v Riden* [1958] AC 240, [1958] AC 240, HL.

203 *Sharpe v Manchester CC* (1981–82) 5 HLR 71, CA.

Works before letting

2.170 The common law has not yet expressly imposed on landlords who did not construct or design the dwelling any liability in tort to tenants or others for defective work carried out before the letting. However, any such remaining immunity has been removed by statute (DPA 1972 s3, see para 2.107). A landlord who does work before letting a property owes a duty to take reasonable care not to create an unnecessary risk of injury.[204] However, this duty was not breached where a tenant slipped on steps up to a house which were wet after rain, suffering a serious injury. Although the landlady had painted the steps with semi-gloss paint, there was no breach of duty as the paint was for exterior use and the container gave no warning not to use it on steps.[205]

Common parts

2.171 The general immunity of landlords in negligence does not extend to protect a landlord who negligently fails to repair or maintain the common parts of a property with the result that a tenant or others using the common parts are injured or their property is damaged.[206] There is a general duty on landlords in relation to hazards occurring on their land to do whatever is reasonable in the circumstances having regard to their capacity to act and their ability to abate or deal with the hazard. In *Stockley v Knowsley MBC*,[207] a landlord was held liable in negligence for failing to prevent frozen water pipes in the roof from bursting and flooding a tenant's flat. The council owed the tenant a duty of care to prevent flooding because in the circumstances it had been reasonable for them to abate or deal with the potential hazard. Simply telling a tenant to turn off the stopcock, without advising her where it was or how to do so, was insufficient to discharge the duty.

2.172 However, in *Stevens v Blaenau Gwent CBC*[208] there was held to be no duty to install safety locks to windows as there was no emergency or external threat which imposed a duty on the council to act. Given that the windows were part of the premises let, it would not appear that the council would have owed a duty of care, even if this had been the case, although this was not the reason given by the Court of Appeal for rejecting liability.

204 *Drysdale v Hedges* [2012] EWHC 4131 (QB).

205 *Drysdale v Hedges* [2012] EWHC 4131 (QB).

206 *Cockburn v Smith* [1924] 2 KB 119, CA; *Duke of Westminster v Guild* [1985] QB 688, [1984] 3 WLR 630, CA; *Lips v Older* [2004] EWHC 1686 (QB), [2005] PIQR P14.

207 [1986] 2 EGLR 141, CA.

208 [2004] EWCA Civ 715, [2004] HLR 54.

Limits on actions in negligence

2.173 There is no liability in negligence at common law unless and until harm is caused to the person or property of a victim. The duty will extend only to personal injury or property damage, not to pure economic loss or defects to the dwelling itself which might make occupation uncomfortable or distressing.[209]

2.174 A landlord will not be liable in negligence for the acts of an independent subcontractor.[210]

Nuisance

2.175 At common law, a private nuisance is an activity or state of affairs existing on land or premises which unduly interferes with the use or enjoyment of neighbouring land or premises.

2.176 A landlord will be liable for any common law nuisance arising on ancillary property owned by him or her and impinging on the tenant's dwelling-house.[211]

2.177 Tenants most commonly bring claims in nuisance against their landlords in respect of pest infestations. In *Sharpe v Manchester CC*,[212] the landlord was held liable in nuisance for a cockroach infestation which probably entered a tenant's flat through the service ducts in the common parts of the block of flats. However, there was no such liability in *Habinteg Housing Association v James*,[213] where there were no common parts retained by the landlord and the reserved rights of entry over the other tenanted flats did not give the landlord sufficient control over them for it to be liable for failure to treat any infestation emanating from them. More recently in *Siveter v Wandsworth LBC*,[214] the council was held liable for an infestation of poultry mites which had spread from pigeons nesting in a cupboard outside the tenant's flat into her flat. Overturning the trial judge, the Court of Appeal held

209 *Murphy v Brentwood DC* [1991] 1 AC 398, [1990] 3 WLR 414, HL; *D&F Estates v Church Commissioners* [1989] AC 177, [1988] 3 WLR 368, HL; *Department of the Environment v Thomas Bates & Sons Ltd* [1991] 1 AC 499, [1990] 3 WLR 457, HL.

210 *D&F Estates v Church Commissioners* [1989] AC 177, [1988] 3 WLR 368, HL.

211 *Sharpe v Manchester CC* (1981–82) 5 HLR 71, CA (cockroach infestation); *Sampson v Hodson-Pressinger* [1981] 3 All ER 710, (1984) 12 HLR 40, CA; cf *Southwark LBC v Mills* [2001] 1 AC 1, [1999] 3 WLR 939, HL (noise); *Guppy's (Bridport) Ltd v Brookling* (1984) 14 HLR 1, CA (major building works); *Gordon v Selico Co Ltd* (1986) 18 HLR 219, CA (water penetration); *Tennant Radiant Heat Ltd v Warrington Development Corporation* (1988) 11 EG 71, CA (water penetration).

212 (1981–82) 5 HLR 71, CA.

213 (1995) 27 HLR 299, CA.

214 [2012] EWCA Civ 351, [2012] HLR 26.

that it was not sufficient for the council simply to remove the nest and spray the area; in accordance with expert evidence, they should at least have inspected and probably treated the cupboard.

2.178 A landlord may be liable if he or she causes a nuisance by creating it or continues a nuisance by failing to take steps to abate the nuisance when he or she is aware or ought to be aware of its existence.[215] A landlord will not be liable where the defect causing the nuisance predates the grant of the tenancy because the principle of *caveat lessee* will be held to apply, ie, that the lessee takes subject to any defects existing at the date of the lease.[216] In *Jackson v J H Watson Property Investment Ltd*,[217] the landlord was not liable in nuisance for water penetration caused by faulty construction work to common parts by his predecessor in title because it pre-dated the grant of the lease.

2.179 A landlord may also be liable for a nuisance caused by disrepair within demised premises which arises after the grant of a lease and affects another tenant's property, but only where the landlord has an obligation to repair or has reserved the right to enter and repair, either expressly or by implication.[218] Accordingly, a landlord will be liable in nuisance for water penetration to a tenant's flat caused by plumbing leaks in the flat above which he or she has failed to remedy, where the landlord has an obligation or right to repair the plumbing leaks in the flat above.

2.180 Only persons with exclusive possession of land can bring an action in private nuisance.[219] Accordingly, no claim in nuisance can be brought by the children of a tenant,[220] but they may be able to bring a claim under the HRA 1998.[221]

Rights in practice – common issues with housing conditions

2.181 There is substantial overlap between the various rights in relation to housing conditions. Very often a problem or issue will be covered by

215 *Sedleigh-Denfield v O'Callaghan* [1940] AC 880, [1940] 3 All ER 349, HL at 897.

216 See *Southwark LBC v Mills* [2001] 1 AC 1, [1999] 3 WLR 939, HL.

217 [2008] EWHC 14 (Ch), December 2008 *Legal Action* 31.

218 *Nelson v Liverpool Brewery Co* (1877) 2 CPD 311; *Mint v Good* [1951] 1 KB 517, [1950] 2 All ER 1159, CA.

219 *Hunter v Canary Wharf Ltd* [1997] AC 655, [1997] 2 WLR 684, HL.

220 *Murphy and Peers v Stockport MBC* August 2002 *Legal Action* 27, *Housing Law Casebook* 7th edn, para R1.8, Stockport County Court.

221 See *Dobson and others v Thames Water Utilities Ltd and another* [2009] EWCA Civ 28.

two, or possibly more, of the statutory, contractual or common law rights. There are also issues which will only fall under one of the rights, depending on its nature or severity.

2.182 There are also statutory requirements in terms of elements of tenants' safety which are not enforceable by tenants themselves but which should be reported to, and may be enforceable by the local authority (see chapter 5).

2.183 Some of the most common issues encountered by tenants and advisers are examined below, with the applicable legal rights highlighted.

Right to a home fit to live in

2.184 As a result of the entry into force of the Homes (Fitness for Human Habitation) Act 2018, by March 2020, most tenants will have the right, as a minimum, to a home fit for habitation, by way of LTA 1985 ss9A and 10.

2.185 Given the substantial period of time since LTA 1985 s8 had any practical effect, and the very recent coming into force of LTA 1985 ss9A and 10, case-law is both limited and, to some extent, of uncertain applicability. Some general points are set out at paras 2.42–2.50 above.

2.186 However, it is clear from the amended section 10 that the factors that are to be considered in deciding whether a dwelling is unfit for habitation include the current list of 29 types of hazard under the HHRS.

2.187 Notably, these include:

- damp and mould growth;
- excess cold;
- excess heat;
- exposure to asbestos;
- carbon monoxide;
- gas exposure;
- crowding;
- security of the property;
- noise;
- arrangements for domestic hygiene;
- water supply;
- electrical hazards; and
- structural collapse.

The significance of this is that issues with the condition of the property that do not necessarily arise from disrepair but that do potentially impact on the health and safety of the tenants and their household may be actionable by the tenant. Examples of such issues are set out below.

2.188 There will often be an overlap with repair issues, for example excess cold due to a malfunctioning heating system, electrical hazards due to damage or fault, or damp due to leaks or a defective damp-proof course. In these cases, both LTA 1985 s9A and s11 (and other contractual or common law repairing obligations) will be engaged.

Lack of heating

2.189 An absence of a heating installation, or an inadequate heating installation not capable of bringing the dwelling to a reasonable temperature but which is otherwise functioning in its original state, would not be a matter of disrepair, but could amount to unfitness for the purposes of LTA 1985 ss9A and 10, with regard to there being a risk to the health and safety of the occupiers through excessive cold.

2.190 If the heating installation is in disrepair or otherwise not functioning to its original standard, the defect would fall under LTA 1985 s11 (as well as section 9A if it applies to the tenancy). See para 2.82.

2.191 Excessive cold due to lack of heating or inadequate heating may also give rise to a 'hazard' for the purposes of HA 2004 Part 1. The action that may be taken in such circumstances is described in chapter 5.

Condensation dampness and mould

2.192 In very basic terms, condensation dampness arises when a dwelling is incapable of dealing with the levels of water vapour being generated within it. This may be due to excessive production of vapour, inadequate insulation, lack of ventilation, insufficient heat input, or a combination of such factors. The presence of condensation is observed as condensed water on cool surfaces, mould spores, damp wall coverings and plaster, consequent infestation by house mites and (in severe cases) destruction of soft furnishings and/or wood and plaster fittings. The presence of acute condensation dampness brings with it conditions of mould growth, excessive humidity and, often, insect infestation. The grave effects of these conditions on the health and well-being of tenants have now been extensively documented as the references, set out in the resources below at para 2.217, indicate.

2.193 Even relatively recently constructed homes can be prone to the generation of condensation dampness and associated mould growth.[222]

2.194 For some time, tenants and their advisers have been using legal remedies to seek redress in such circumstances. For tenancies to which the Homes (Fitness for Human Habitation) Act 2018 amendments to LTA 1985 apply, section 9A may provide the most effective route to a remedy. The following short summary deals with various legal remedies to a condensation dampness problem.

2.195 Defects in the design or construction of a dwelling can lead to the dwelling being prone to condensation and consequential mould growth, even in normal use by the occupiers, for example:

- lack of adequate ventilation (for example, windows with no vents, or that don't open;
- lack of extraction in closed moist areas like internal bathrooms or kitchens);
- lack of insulation or cold bridging to external walls or ceilings.

2.196 Where such issues cause mould growth in normal use by the occupiers, mould growth can present a risk to the health and safety of the occupiers such that the dwelling is unfit for habitation. A claim under LTA 1985 s9A could require the remedying of the defects to the dwelling that give rise to the unfitness. This may have advantages over taking action using the EPA 1990 because an EPA prosecution can be forestalled simply by the removal of the immediate nuisance, eg by wiping away the mould before proceedings start.

Express or implied terms of the tenancy

Express terms

2.197 If the landlord has agreed to keep the premises 'fit to live in' or 'in good condition', or used similar general wording in a tenancy agreement, those express terms may be broken where dampness and mould growth arise from condensation and cause the premises to be in a poor condition or render them unfit to live in (see para 2.50).[223]

2.198 If the premises were let at a very low rent, let furnished or provided under licence, the fact that they were 'doomed' to suffer from

222 *Rendlesham Estates plc and others v Barr Ltd* [2014] EWHC 3968 (TCC), [2015] 1 WLR 3663 and *Hunt and others v Optima (Cambridge) Ltd and others* [2013] EWHC 681 (TCC).

223 *Welsh v Greenwich LBC* (2001) 33 HLR 40, (2001) 81 P&CR 12, CA; *Johnson v Sheffield CC* August 1994 *Legal Action* 16, Sheffield County Court; *Arnold v Greenwich LBC*, May 1998 *Legal Action* 21, Woolwich County Court.

condensation dampness from the outset may amount to breach of the implied warranty of fitness (see paras 2.143–2.148).

Implied terms – Landlord and Tenant Act 1985 s9A

2.199 A claim for breach of LTA 1985 s9A (where it applies to the tenancy) can be brought where such mould growth can present a risk to the health and safety of the occupiers such that the dwelling is unfit for habitation. See for example *Rendlesham Estates plc and others v Barr Ltd*[224] and also *Summers v Salford Corporation*,[225] in the latter inadequate ventilation due to a window that could not be opened was an element of the dwelling being unfit for habitation.

2.200 A central issue in any claim and remedy under LTA 1985 s9A will be the extent to which the condensation is caused by the tenant's use of the dwelling. If the use could be described as 'un-tenant like', the landlord is not liable to rectify the issue by reason of section 9A(2)(a). If the use could be described as in breach of any tenant covenant, the landlord is not liable for any unfitness wholly or mainly caused by that use under section 9A(3)(a). It is therefore likely that evidence of tenant use, and expert evidence as to defects in design and construction, will be required in any case which is not straightforward.

2.201 It is also likely that a similar approach will be applied as that adopted in *Dover DC v Farrar*,[226] an EPA 1990 case, in which the landlord was found not guilty as adequate facilities for heating and ventilation had been provided, but rising fuel prices had meant that the tenant could not afford to use the heating sufficiently (see para 2.209).

2.202 Other contractual and common law remedies for condensation dampness and mould are available.

2.203 The landlord will be liable for the effects of condensation dampness under LTA 1985 s11 where its presence is a *consequence* of disrepair for which the landlord is liable (eg, where disrepair to the structure has allowed the incursion of excess moisture or prevents normal ventilation).[227]

2.204 The landlord will also be liable for the effects of condensation dampness where those effects cause actual damage to the structure, exterior or other parts of the property which the landlord is liable to keep in repair.

224 [2014] EWHC 3968 (TCC), [2015] 1 WLR 3663, at 79.

225 [1943] AC 283, HL.

226 (1982) 2 HLR 32, DC.

227 *Lloyd v Rees* [1996] CLY 3725, Pontypridd County Court.

2.205 In *Quick v Taff Ely BC*[228] the Court of Appeal decided that LTA 1985 s11 cannot provide a remedy for a tenant suffering the effects of condensation dampness unless there is actual disrepair to the structure or exterior of the dwelling. Where such disrepair *can* be shown (eg, because the condensation has corrupted woodwork or caused plaster to crumble or to become hygroscopic) it will become actionable.[229] As the Court of Appeal has recently stated:

> Quick's case shows . . . that liability under repairing covenants . . . for conditions caused by condensation resulting from a design defect does not arise unless they result in physical damage covered by the landlord's covenant, when the repairing obligation will apply. In this case, however, the judge found (or ought to have found) that there was physical damage, resulting in disrepair, to what is said to have been part of the structure of the property, namely the plasterwork in the living room (front wall and ceiling) and in the kitchen (ceiling).[230]

2.206 Because the duty in DPA 1972 s4 springs from an obligation to repair or maintain the property, it too is of limited usefulness in a condensation case in the absence of actual damage to the structure or 'fabric' of the property.[231]

2.207 If work to rectify condensation fails to eradicate it, a claim might be brought for breach of DPA 1972 s1 in relation to that work. If the dwelling was negligently designed or constructed so as to generate condensation in ordinary use, a claim might be brought in negligence against the landlord or designer or builder (see paras 2.100–2.107).

2.208 Public health and environmental protection legislation has been long recognised as a satisfactory means of securing redress, because acute condensation dampness invariably gives rise to conditions which are 'prejudicial to health' and a statutory nuisance (see chapter 6).

2.209 However, in order to bring a successful prosecution under EPA 1990 s82, the tenant must be able to show that the conditions are the responsibility of the landlord. In *Dover DC v Farrar*[232] a conviction was quashed on appeal where the local authority landlord successfully established that dwellings had been constructed by it in accordance with prevailing standards and that, with sufficient use of the

228 [1986] QB 809, [1985] 3 WLR 981, CA.

229 *Staves v Leeds CC* (1991) 23 HLR 107, CA; *Switzer v Law* [1998] 7 CL 380, *Housing Law Casebook* 7th edn, para R18.85, Southport County Court.

230 *Grand v Gill* [2011] EWCA Civ 554, [2011] 1 WLR 2253 at [17].

231 *Abdullah v South Tyneside BC* September 1987 *Legal Action* 12, South Shields County Court.

232 (1982) 2 HLR 32, DC.

supplied heating system, the provision made for ventilation and insulation was adequate to avoid condensation. The fact that fuel price increases subsequent to construction meant that the tenants were unable to use the heating system was held not to be the responsibility of the landlord.

2.210 Regrettably, the *Dover* case has been used by local authorities and other landlords to persuade tenants, their advisers and magistrates that EPA 1990 s82 proceedings cannot successfully be founded on condensation dampness. In fact, the contrary is the case. The *Dover* decision is clear authority for the proposition that landlords can be prosecuted in relation to condensation dampness. Later cases have shown that, with the careful use of specialist written evidence and expert witnesses (especially independent environmental health officers (EHOs)), it is possible to prove in most condensation cases that the dampness does arise from the landlord's failure to get the condensation equation (heat/moisture/ventilation/insulation) right.[233]

2.211 In *Tower Hamlets LBC v Greater London Council*,[234] the Divisional Court dismissed an appeal against a conviction in relation to condensation dampness. The tenants and prosecuting authority claimed that the dwellings were insufficiently ventilated and insulated and that the inability of the flats to cope with normal moisture led to condensation for which the landlord was responsible. Considering the *Dover* case, Griffiths LJ said he did not read it as authority for the proposition that tenants should be required to use abnormal quantities of fuel to avert condensation. The court held that:

> ... a landlord is required to apply his mind to the necessity of ventilation and, if need be, to insulation and heating. The landlord must provide a combination of these factors to make a house habitable for the tenant.

2.212 Applying these authorities, the Divisional Court in *Birmingham DC v Kelly and others*[235] was able to uphold convictions even though the landlord was not in breach of any contractual or other obligation to repair. Liability for the condensation dampness was established from the evidence that there was some default by the council in relation to

233 *Lawton v East Devon DC* (1982) unreported, noted at *Roof* July/August 1982 p28; *McGourlick v Renfrew DC* (1982) unreported, noted at [1982] *Scolag* 182 and [1986] *Scolag* 83, Paisley Sheriff Court.

234 (1984) 15 HLR 54, DC, applied in *Law v Hillingdon LBC*, December 1989 *Legal Action* 16, Isleworth Crown Court.

235 (1985) 17 HLR 572, DC.

the design of the premises which caused the condensation difficulties and thus the mould.

2.213 Condensation dampness (or indeed any other form of dampness) may give rise to a 'hazard' for the purposes of HA 2004 Part 1. The action that may be taken in such circumstances is described in chapter 5.

Ombudsmen

2.214 The Local Government and Social Care Ombudsman[236] regularly accepted that failures to investigate properly or to resolve complaints of condensation dampness amounted to maladministration. The reports frequently contain not only recommendations for significant compensatory payments but also useful guidance on the proper approach to be adopted by councils in condensation cases. See, for example, the report on Investigation 746/1/84.[237]

2.215 In a more recent *Complaint concerning Bristol City Council*, the Local Government Ombudsman found that the council had failed, over a very long period, to carry out proper investigations in response to a tenant's complaints about her housing conditions. As a result, the family suffered damp and cold conditions for around seven years. The ombudsman said:

> The reality is that between 2001 and 2007 the only work completed by the council to mitigate the problems caused by damp/condensation was to install two extractor fans. Given the circumstances, that was wholly unacceptable.

He recommended over £8,000 compensation.[238]

2.216 Since April 2013, the Housing Ombudsman has responsibility for complaints about housing management matters, including disrepair and unfitness issues, relating to both housing association tenancies and council tenancies (see para 1.43).

Resources (chronological order)

2.217
- *Condensation in dwellings Part 1: Design guide*, Ministry of Public Buildings and Works, HMSO, 1970
- *Condensation in dwellings Part 2: Remedial measures*, Department of the Environment, HMSO, 1971
- 'Condensation', *Building Research Establishment (BRE) Digest* 110, 1972 edition

236 See para 1.43.
237 Noted at March 1986 *Legal Action* 33.
238 *Investigation Report 06B05370*, December 2007.

- D Watkinson, 'Legal remedies for condensation damp in the home', November 1985 *Legal Action* 153 and April 1986 *Legal Action* 49
- 'Surface condensation and mould growth in traditionally-built dwellings', *BRE Digest* 297, 1990 edition
- *Tackling condensation: a guide to the causes of, and remedies for, surface condensation and mould in traditional housing*, Building Research Establishment, 1991
- T Markus, 'Cold, Condensation and Housing Poverty' in R Burridge and D Ormandy (eds), *Unhealthy Housing: Research, Remedies and Reform*, Routledge & Chapman, 1993
- M Pawlowski, 'Tenant's remedies for condensation dampness' [1993] *Estates Gazette*, 4 September
- 'Moisture transfer and condensation', *IBSE Guide* section A10, 1999, Chartered Institution of Buildings Services Engineers
- *Code of Practice for the control of condensation in buildings*, British Standards Institution BS 5250, 2002
- T Hutton, 'Condensation' in *The Building Conservation Directory*, 2004
- J David Miller, 'Health effects from mold and dampness in housing in western societies: early epidemiology studies and barriers to further progress' in *Fundamentals of mold growth in indoor environments and strategies for healthy living* p183, 2011
- *Condensation risk – impact of improvements to Part L and robust details on Part C*, Department of Communities and Local Government, 2011
- *Recognition and Causes of Condensation*, Property Care Association, 2013

Dampness (other than condensation)

2.218 Dampness is a common problem, but its causes can take many forms. It may take the form of penetrating dampness, construction damp, rising damp,[239] condensation (see above) or traumatic damp (eg from floods).

2.219 Where dampness is caused by or is the result of disrepair, the tenant may have a legal remedy under contractual and implied repairing covenants, including LTA 1985 s11, as well as LTA 1985 s9A where that applies to the tenancy and the damp is such as to make

239 As in *Uddin v Islington LBC* [2015] EWCA Civ 369, [2015] HLR 28.

the dwelling unfit for habitation. It is not sufficient simply to establish 'dampness' in order to succeed in a legal claim.[240]

2.220 However, other sources of damp will fall outside the repairing obligations. Damp due to a defective or breached damp-proof course is disrepair, damp due to the absence of a damp-proof course in the first place is not, for example (although see *Uddin v Islington LBC*[241] on situations where installing a damp proof course may be the required remedy for other disrepair).

2.221 Where the damp conditions are due to defects in the design or construction of the property, such as a lack of damp-proof course, or inadequate ventilation, for example, these would still fall under the 'fitness' obligation in LTA 1985 s9A, where it applies to the tenancy.

2.222 If the damp conditions are caused wholly or mainly by the tenant, eg by obstructing ventilation, or as the result of a one-off flooding from a neighbour, there will be no liability on the landlord under LTA 1985 s9A, or under the repairing obligations.

2.223 The enforcement of statutory obligations under the EPA 1990 and/or the HA 2004 (see chapters 5 and 6) is not so much concerned with the reason for the presence of dampness but with the effect of it on the occupiers, although tenant causation will still be a factor.

2.224 A Parliamentary review of the dampness problem carried out 30 years ago by the Scottish Grand Committee[242] contains much information still useful today.

Resources (chronological order)

2.225
- *Dampness: one week's complaints in five local authority areas,* HMSO, Building Research Establishment (BRE), 1982
- SD Platt et al, 'Damp Housing, mould growth and symptomatic health state' *British Medical Journal,* 24 June 1989
- S Hunt, 'Damp and Mouldy Housing: an holistic approach' in R Burridge and D Ormandy (eds), *Unhealthy Housing: Research, Remedies and Reform,* Routledge & Chapman, 1993
- EG Gobert and TA Oxley, *Dampness in Buildings: Diagnosis, Treatment, Instruments,* Butterworth, second edition, 1994
- A Oliver, *Dampness in buildings,* Blackwell Publishing, second edition, 1996

240 *Southwark LBC v McIntosh* [2002] 08 EG 164, ChD; February 2002 *Legal Action* 22, *Housing Law Casebook* 7th edn, para R4.14; *Ball v Plymouth CC* [2004] EWHC 134 (QB).

241 [2015] EWCA Civ 369, [2015] HLR 28.

242 Report of the Scottish Grand Committee, House of Commons *Dampness in housing* (papers 206i and 206ii, session 1983/4).

- 'Rising damp in walls: diagnosis and treatment', *BRE Digest* 245, revised October 2007
- J Hetreed, *The Damp House: A Guide to the Causes and Treatment of Dampness*, Crowood Press, 2008
- D Ormandy (ed), 'Damp Mould and Health' in *Housing and health in Europe*, Routledge, 2009, chapter 7
- *Children living in homes with problems of damp* ENHIS fact sheet 3.5, December 2009
- A Hashemi, C Liyanage, K Hadjri, N Khatami, *Assessing the risks of dampness and mould growth in renovated properties*, (2014), Mass Customisation and Sustainability in Housing, ZEMCH 2014 international conference, June 2014, Londrina, Brazil, 30–44

Pest and vermin infestation

2.226 Infestation by pests or vermin is a common problem and one of the most unpleasant. Frequent issues include infestation with rats, mice, cockroaches, ants, fleas, mites, bedbugs and pigeons.

2.227 The *Housing Health and Safety Rating System Operating Guidance* recognises infestations by cockroaches, rodents, flies and pigeons as health risks.[243] Fleas and bed bugs are also acknowledged as causes of health problems.

2.228 Liability for a pest or vermin infestation, and with it the tenant's rights to have the infestation dealt with, is not straightforward. Unless there are express tenancy terms, the tenant's options are as follows.

2.229 For a tenancy to which LTA 1985 s9A applied at the start, an infestation present at the start of the tenancy may mean the dwelling is unfit, so that the tenant could bring a claim under sections 9A and 10. For furnished lettings, a similar common law implied term applies at the commencement of the tenancy (see paras 2.143–2.148 above).

2.230 However, if the infestation arises in the course of the tenancy, how the infestation has arisen is an essential question for liability. If the infestation has entered the dwelling from the common parts of a building, then the landlord is likely to be liable under LTA 1985 s9A and also in common law nuisance. If not, then it is likely that the landlord would assert that the infestation is due to the tenant's conduct.

2.231 If the dwelling is a house, the infestation cannot have arisen through parts retained by the landlord and under his or her control.

243 Office of the Deputy Prime Minister, February 2006.

In that instance, the question is whether the pests or vermin have accessed the property by way of disrepair for which the landlord is liable under the tenancy agreement or LTA 1985 s11 (eg holes in walls, or broken drain pipes, or holes in the roof).

2.232 If the infestation has no cause for which the landlord would be liable, or is the result of the actions of the tenant or their household, the landlord will not be responsible for the infestation under the tenancy agreement.

2.233 Local authorities have extensive powers to take action in cases of pest infestation (Prevention of Damage by Pests Act 1949 and Public Health Act 1936 Part 2). An infestation may also be a hazard under the HHSRS, so a local authority may serve notices under HA 2004 s5 (see chapter 5). Depending on the cause of the infestation, local authority action may result in a charge to the tenant by either the local authority or the landlord.

2.234 Premises infested with vermin are very likely to constitute a 'statutory nuisance' (see chapter 6) because they are prejudicial to health. If it can be shown that the incursion or infestation is caused by the 'act, default or sufferance' of the landlord, the tenant may rely on the processes of the EPA 1990 and, where necessary, prosecute the landlord using section 82.[244]

Resources

2.235 • A Arden and M Partington, *Housing Law*, Sweet & Maxwell, para 8–90, 'Vermin'

Right to a home in repair

2.236 Many contractual and statutory provisions impose obligations on landlords to 'repair' or 'keep in repair' the homes they let. Tenants will have corresponding rights to enforce these obligations. The following paragraphs explain the application of these obligations and rights.

Meaning of 'repair' and 'disrepair'

2.237 What exactly does the word 'repair' cover and how is it to be applied? Ultimately, the question of whether a disputed item of required work is repair or renewal or maintenance or improvement will be one for the courts, based on the facts of the individual case, but some

244 As in *White v Hackney LBC* March 1989 *Legal Action* 24, Highbury Corner Magistrates' Court.

decisions give a useful indication of the principles to be applied. For example, in *Lurcott v Wakeley*[245] it was said that repair means the restoration by renewal or replacement of subsidiary parts of the whole; whereas renewal, as distinguished from repair, means the reconstruction of the whole. In *Lurcott*, 'repair' was held to cover the replacement of a deteriorated wall, since the wall was only a subsidiary part of the whole.

2.238 Denning LJ has also given guidance on the test to be applied:

> If the work which is done is the provision of something new for the benefit of the occupier, that is, properly speaking an improvement; but if it is only the replacement of something already there which has become dilapidated or worn out, then, albeit that it is a replacement by its modern equivalent, it comes within the category of repairs not improvements.[246]

2.239 Sachs LJ said that the correct approach is to:

> . . . look at the particular building, look at the state which it is in at the date of the lease, look at the precise terms of the lease, and then come to a conclusion whether, on a fair interpretation of those terms in relation to that state, the requisite work can fairly be called repair.[247]

2.240 It is clear that repair is the converse of disrepair. There must be disrepair before the landlord is liable to repair. Disrepair occurs when there is deterioration, ie, when part of the building is in a worse condition than it was at some earlier time.[248]

2.241 For an examination of what 'structure and exterior' incorporates, for both LTA 1985 s11 and any similar express contractual term, see paras 2.70 to 2.75.

Inherent defects

2.242 It follows from the approach to the meaning of 'repair' and 'disrepair' described above, that the landlord is not liable under a repairing obligation simply because part of the dwelling was designed or constructed badly. If the dwelling has always had the defect in question, there has been no deterioration. In *Stent v Monmouth DC*[249] the front door did not have weatherboarding and permitted rain-water to penetrate into the dwelling. The landlord was not liable simply on

245 [1911] 1 KB 905, CA.

246 *Morcom v Campbell-Johnson* [1956] 1 QB 106, [1955] 3 WLR 497, CA.

247 *Brew Bros Ltd v Snax* [1970] 1 QB 612, [1969] 3 WLR 657, CA.

248 *Post Office v Aquarius Properties Ltd* [1987] 1 All ER 1055, (1987) 54 P&CR 61, CA; *Quick v Taff-Ely BC* [1986] 1 QB 809, [1985] 3 WLR 981, CA.

249 (1987) 19 HLR 269, CA.

this basis because the door had always been defective in that respect.[250] In *Post Office Properties Ltd v Aquarius Properties Ltd*[251] a defective kicker joint allowed ground water to penetrate laterally into a basement but the landlord was similarly not liable because the joint had always been defective.

2.243 It would, however, be going much too far to say that landlords are never liable to put right building defects which are 'inherent', ie, which have been present since construction. In *Stent v Monmouth DC*[252] the rain-water penetration eventually caused the door itself to rot, ie, deteriorate. Because the landlord was obliged under the terms of the tenancy agreement to keep the door in repair, it was required to repair the door. It was not relevant that the deterioration had been caused by an inherent defect. Furthermore, the court ordered the landlord to repair the door in such a way that future rain-water penetration and future disrepair to the door would not occur: by installing a proper, weather-proof door. In effect, the court ordered the landlord to rectify an inherent defect in order to remedy current disrepair and prevent future disrepair.

2.244 If the inherent defect causes disrepair to other parts of the building for which the landlord is responsible, the court will usually require the landlord to remedy that damage.[253] If it would be practical and sensible to remedy the underlying defect to prevent it from causing the same disrepair over and over again, then the courts will order the landlord to remedy the inherent defect.[254] The only exception occurs when the work involved is disproportionately extensive and/or costly.

Disproportionately extensive or costly work

2.245 It is always a question of degree whether that which the landlord is being asked to do can properly be described as a repair, or whether, on the contrary, it would involve producing a wholly different thing from that which was let: *Stent v Monmouth DC*.[255] Examples of work which has been held to be too extensive or costly to be a 'repair' are:

250 Subsequently the door deteriorated and there was liability.

251 [1987] 1 All ER 1055, CA.

252 (1987) 19 HLR 269, CA.

253 *Staves and Staves v Leeds CC* (1991) 23 HLR 107, CA.

254 *Ravenseft Properties v Davstone (Holdings) Ltd* [1980] QB 12, [1979] 2 WLR 897, QBD; *Elmcroft Developments Ltd v Tankersley-Sawyer* (1984) 15 HLR 63, CA; *Uddin and another v Islington LBC* [2015] EWCA Civ 369, [2015] HLR 28 and cf *Quick v Taff-Ely BC* [1986] QB 809. [1985] 3 WLR 981, CA.

255 (1987) 19 HLR 269, CA.

complete replacement of foundations;[256] complete replacement of cladding to a high-rise building;[257] the replacement of the whole of a steel frame;[258] and the installation of a damp-proof course.[259] Whether or not the work required is too extensive or costly in any given case will depend on exactly what work is required, what it is likely to cost, how long it will prolong the life of the dwelling and what the terms of the tenancy agreement are.[260]

2.246 The most recent guidance is given in *McDougall v Easington DC*,[261] where Mustill LJ said:

> It is my opinion that three different tests may be discerned, which may be applied separately or concurrently as the circumstances of the individual case may demand, but all to be approached in the light of the nature and age of the premises, their condition when the tenant went into occupation, and the other express terms of the tenancy:
> (i) whether the alterations went to the whole or substantially the whole of the structure or only to a subsidiary part;
> (ii) whether the effect of the alterations was to produce a building of a wholly different character than that which had been let;
> (iii) was the cost of the works in relation to the previous value of the building and what was their effect on the value and lifespan of the building?

2.247 In *McDougall v Easington DC*,[262] considerable work had been undertaken to a council house of system-built, concrete panel construction, namely the removal of the whole of the front and rear elevations, the replacement of the roof structure, and rain-water system, the replacement of windows and doors, and the stripping out of the interior fittings. These works were held to constitute an improvement rather than a repair, as the house 'not only looked different but was different ... The outcome was a house with a substantially longer life and worth nearly twice as much as before.' The works had given the house 'a new life in a different form'.[263]

256 *Lister v Lane* [1893] 2 QB 212, CA.

257 *Holding & Management Ltd v Property Holding & Investment Trust plc* (1989) 21 HLR 596, CA.

258 *Plough Investments Ltd v Manchester CC* [1989] 1 EGLR 244, ChD.

259 *Eyre v McCracken* (2001) 33 HLR 169, (2000) 80 P&CR 220, CA.

260 *Holding & Management Ltd v Property Holding & Investment Trust plc* [1989] 1 WLR 1313, (1989) 21 HLR 596, CA.

261 (1989) 21 HLR 310, (1989) 58 P&CR 201, CA.

262 (1989) 21 HLR 310, (1989) 58 P&CR 201, CA.

263 *McDougall v Easington DC* (1989) 21 HLR 310, (1989) 58 P&CR 201, CA, per Mustill LJ at 316.

2.248 A similar view was taken in *Eyre v McCracken*,[264] where the Court of Appeal reviewed the authorities on the installation of damp-proof courses and found that to require a Rent Act protected tenant to insert a damp-proof course into a property in 2001 would be to require him to give back to the landlord a different thing from that let to him in 1976 and would therefore be an improvement rather than a repair. This case is not, however, authority for the proposition that a landlord will not be obliged to insert a damp-proof course under the landlord's repairing obligations because the court held that 'the circumstances are very different from those involved in the consideration of the landlord's covenant in *Elmcroft Developments*'[265] (see para 2.255), where the installation of a damp proof course, to correct one which was ineffective because it had been positioned below ground, was held to be a repair.

2.249 Most recently, in *Uddin v Islington LBC*[266] the Court of Appeal approved the decision in *Elmcroft Developments* and also accepted that there was no sensible distinction between that case and one where no damp proof course had been installed to begin with.

Small defects

2.250 Conversely, small defects such as nail holes and minor cracking (to plaster or rendering) are in many cases not considered to be sufficiently serious to amount to disrepair.

2.251 The reason is that the courts have qualified the meaning of disrepair. It does not mean any degree of deterioration, but deterioration which as a matter of fact and degree is unacceptable after taking into account, and making allowances for, the age of the premises, their character, the local area and the type of tenants likely to want to rent them.[267]

Repair and decoration

2.252 An obligation to repair includes, if necessary, an obligation to carry out decoration required to preserve whatever is to be repaired.[268] The requirement to 'repair' carries with it an obligation on the landlord to make good or redecorate on completion of repair works.[269] On the

264 (2001) 33 HLR 16, CA.

265 *Eyre v McCracken* (2001) 33 HLR 16, (2000) 80 P&CR 220, CA, per Pill LJ at para 46.

266 [2015] EWCA Civ 369, [2015] HLR 28, CA.

267 *Anstruther-Gough-Calthorpe v McOscar* [1924] 1 KB 716, CA.

268 *Irvine's Estate v Moran* (1992) 24 HLR 1, QBD.

269 *McGreal v Wake* (1984) 13 HLR 107, CA; *Bradley v Chorley BC* (1985) 17 HLR 305, CA.

extent of a landlord's obligation to redecorate, see *Vukelic v Hammersmith and Fulham LBC*.[270] There is no liability to redecorate after improvement works (which are not considered to be works of repair) save where such redecoration is negotiated as a condition for granting a landlord permission to do improvement works.[271]

Prevention of future damage

2.253 An obligation to repair can include an obligation to prevent future damage.[272]

Patch repairs or complete renewal

2.254 The obligation to repair can sometimes require the landlord completely to renew or to replace part of a dwelling instead of carrying out a temporary or patch repair.

2.255 In *Elmcroft Developments Ltd v Tankersley-Sawyer*,[273] for example, the landlords conceded that their obligation to repair the structure required them to hack off and replace wall plaster each time it became damp but denied that it required them to tackle the source of the dampness (rising damp) by installing a damp-proof course. Ackner LJ said:

> The patching work would have to go on and on, because as the plaster absorbed (as it would) the rising damp, it would have to be renewed and the cost to the [landlords] in constantly being involved in this sort of work, one would have thought, would have outweighed easily the cost in doing the job properly. I have no hesitation in rejecting the submission that the appellant's obligation was repetitively to carry out futile work instead of doing the job properly once and for all.

2.256 The notion that patch repairing was sufficient to discharge the duty was similarly rejected in *Stent v Monmouth DC*.[274] In that case there had been a problem for over 30 years of rot to a wooden front door and frame. The landlords had repeatedly cut out and repaired parts of the door and frame and from time to time replaced the rotten wooden door with another wooden door which then rotted. The Court of Appeal had no hesitation in holding that, on the facts, the obligation to 'repair' was not discharged by these patch

270 [2003] EWHC 188 (TCC), November 2003 *Legal Action* 13.

271 *McDougall v Easington DC* (1989) 21 HLR 310, CA.

272 *Holding & Management Ltd v Property Holding & Investment Trust plc* (1989) 21 HLR 596, CA; *McDougall v Easington DC* [1989] 1 WLR 1313, (1989) 21 HLR 310, CA.

273 (1984) 15 HLR 63, CA.

274 (1987) 19 HLR 269, CA.

repairs. The council 'had the obligation to make good the design defect which caused the collection of water which occasioned the rotting'.[275] This was achieved by installing a self-sealing aluminium door.

2.257 Temporary repairs were found not be sufficient to avoid liability in disrepair in *Blue Manchester Ltd v North West Ground Rents Ltd*.[276] 'Stitch' repairs to glass windows on a 22-storey tower in Manchester were intended to last for three years, pending a permanent solution. The freeholder argued that there was no actionable disrepair in the interim. The court found that while it was not sufficient for the claimant simply to point to the temporary nature of the patch repairs, those repairs could only be regarded as structurally safe at the present if the landlord had or was in the process of commissioning a full expert report with recommendations that it intended to follow for the future structural safety of the building, so as to give confidence in the current arrangement for the future. This had not been done, so there was a current breach of the repairing covenant.

2.258 *Quick v Taff Ely BC*[277] does not fit happily with this line of authority. In that case a window sill and wall plaster required replacement because of damage caused by acute condensation dampness. That in turn could be cured by double glazing, insulation, etc. However, insufficient findings of fact had been made in the county court to show that the only 'proper' way of tackling the limited disrepair which had been proved was the major work urged by the tenant.

2.259 In summary, the test of whether patch repairs will suffice is whether tackling the root cause would be a 'mode of repair which a sensible person would have adopted; and the same reasoning applies if for the word "sensible" there is substituted some such word as "practicable" or "necessary" '.[278] The burden is on the tenant to lead the evidence which shows that further patch repairs will not suffice and that a more radical repair or replacement is necessary.[279] The tenant was unable to discharge this burden in *Dame Margaret Hungerford Charity Trustees v Beazeley*[280] where it was held that, since the property was to be completed reconstructed in the near future,

275 *Stent v Monmouth DC* (1987) 19 HLR 269, CA, per Sir John Arnold at 286.

276 [2019] EWHC 142 (TCC).

277 [1986] 1 QB 809, CA.

278 *Stent v Monmouth DC* (1987) 19 HLR 269, CA, per Stocker LJ at 284–5; see also *Carmel Southend Ltd v Strachan and Henshaw Ltd* [2007] EWHC 1289 (TCC).

279 *Murray v Birmingham CC* (1988) 20 HLR 39, CA.

280 (1994) 26 HLR 269, CA.

further patch repairs were sufficient, even though ordinarily the replacement of the roof would have been required.

Blocked conduits

2.260 Gutters and flues which are blocked are in disrepair.[281]

Right to installations that work properly

Sanitary installations

2.261 Where a landlord has permitted sanitary installations to remain in disrepair or out of proper working order the tenant may take action under contractual or common law repairing obligations. If conditions have become prejudicial to health or a nuisance, tenants should involve the Environmental Health Officers from the local housing authority to take action under the EPA 1990 (see chapter 6) or, if the conditions amount to a health and safety hazard, the HA 2004 (see chapter 5), or if LTA 1985 s9A applies to the tenancy, the tenant can also take action for breach of the implied term of fitness.

2.262 Additional powers are given to local housing authorities to deal with situations where there are insufficient sanitary conveniences in a dwelling or the existing ones require replacement. Enforcement, which is mandatory, is by notice from the council to the landlord followed, where necessary, by works in default of compliance and recovery of costs. For example, if it appears to a local authority that any water closets provided for or in connection with a building are in such a state as to be prejudicial to health or a nuisance, but that they can, without reconstruction, be put into a satisfactory condition, the authority must by notice require the owner or the occupier of the building to execute such works, or to take such steps by cleansing the closets or otherwise, as may be necessary for that purpose.[282] Again, in such a situation, there may well also be a breach of LTA 1985 s9A, although if the tenant has overcrowded the dwelling beyond the numbers allowed under any tenancy agreement, this would exempt the landlord from having to address any resulting insufficiency of sanitary facilities.

281 *Melles & Co v Holme* [1918] 2 KB 100, KBD; *Bishop v Consolidated London Properties Ltd* (1933) 102 LJKB 257; *Greg v Planque* [1936] 1 KB 669, CA; *Passley v Wandsworth LBC* (1998) 30 HLR 165, CA.

282 Public Health Act 1936 s45.

Resources

2.263 • A Arden and M Partington, *Housing Law*, Sweet & Maxwell, paras 8–55–8–65 'Sanitary accommodation'

Services (gas, water and electricity)

2.264 Under the covenant implied in most tenancies by LTA 1985 s11, a landlord is required to keep in repair and proper working order the installations in the dwelling for the supply of gas, electricity and water (section 11(1)(b)–(c)), or, in respect of certain tenancies, the installations serving the dwelling, wherever situated (see para 2.84). A failure to do so may cause unfitness and so a breach of LTA 1985 s9A where this applies to the tenancy (see paras 2.33–2.36).

2.265 However, problems commonly arise where, although the installations themselves are in good order, the landlord has caused loss of supply of the services themselves, eg, by failing to pay fuel or water services bills. In these circumstances, upon receipt of a complaint from the occupiers, a local housing authority can make the necessary arrangements with the relevant providers to ensure reconnection of the supply.

2.266 Most local authorities have delegated the power to carry out this service to EHOs or tenancy relations officers. Once supply is re-established the authority can recover any necessary costs from the landlord.[283] Such a loss of supply may also amount to unfitness and so a breach of LTA 1985 s9A, where applicable.

Drains and sewers

2.267 A 'drain' means a pipeline used for the drainage of one building, while a 'sewer' means a pipeline used for the drainage of more than one building. The law does not distinguish between foul and surface water sewers. A 'public' sewer is a sewer vested in the local water authority.[284]

2.268 Tenants may be caused serious inconvenience by the blockage, disrepair or overflow of drains as a result of landlord failure to repair or maintain them. Indeed, where the landlord is a 'public' authority (registered social landlord or local authority) or a water authority, the tenant may have a claim under LTA 1985 s9A (where applicable and the landlord is responsible for the sewer or drain), or in nuisance, negligence or possibly under the HRA 1998 if their home is flooded

283 Local Government (Miscellaneous Provisions) Act 1976 s33.

284 *Dear v Thames Water* (1994) 33 Con LR 43, QBD.

by water or sewage from drains or sewers (see para 2.139). The water authority or housing authority might also be responsible in nuisance or negligence even if it is not the landlord.[285]

2.269 LTA 1985 s11 makes landlords responsible for keeping the structure and exterior of the dwelling in repair, expressly including 'drains': see para 2.63. It seems logical to assume that the draftsman meant that a drain forms part of a dwelling up to the point at which it enters the public sewer, but it is likely that section 11(1A) would also apply to include drains up to the public sewer as part of the building.

2.270 Local authorities have extensive powers to require owners (and occupiers) to take remedial action where a drain or sewer is prejudicial to health or a nuisance (Building Act 1984 ss21 and 59). In default, the council may carry out the necessary work and recover its costs thereafter. Similarly, a local housing authority may, by notice, secure the performance of small repairs if a drain or sewer is insufficiently maintained or repaired and may undertake works (Public Health Act 1961 ss17 and 22).[286]

Resources

2.271
- S H Bailey *Garner's Laws of sewers and drains*, 10th edn, 2010
- *A simple guide to pipes, drains and sewers*, United Utilities, 2015

Right to a safe home

Gas safety

2.272 One of the most potentially dangerous aspects of tenanted residential accommodation is the gas supply and the condition of facilities for using that supply (gas fires, gas boilers, gas cookers, etc).

2.273 Depending upon the terms of a tenancy agreement, a landlord may be under an express contractual obligation to keep the gas supply maintained and safe and the facilities for its use in good repair and working order. If not, the provisions of LTA 1985 s11 will usually apply (para 2.63). They require the landlord to keep the installations for the supply of gas in repair and proper working order and also the installations for space heating and heating water (which may also depend on a gas supply).

2.274 Any failure to ensure that the gas installation and facilities are safe would be a breach of LTA 1985 s9A, where that applies to the

285 *Dear v Thames Water* (1994) 33 Con LR 43, QBD.

286 *Rotherham BC v Dodds* [1986] 1 WLR 1367, [1986] 2 All ER 867, CA.

tenancy, as it presents a clear risk to the health and safety of the occupiers of the dwelling.

2.275 Other legislation imposes obligations on landlords which are not directly enforceable by tenants and which go beyond the requirements of any contract. Under Gas Safety (Installation and Use) Regulations 1998[287] reg 36, a landlord is responsible for making sure that any gas appliances, gas piping and flues are well maintained and safe. The obligation arises from the granting of: any periodic tenancy; any statutory tenancy; any tenancy of a fixed term less than seven years; and any licence to occupy. It requires that at least an annual safety inspection is carried out by a qualified gas servicing engineer. The regulations are accompanied by an approved Code of Practice and Guidance.[288] Since 2009, the approved registration organisation has been 'Gas Safe Register'.

2.276 Failure by the landlord to arrange an inspection is likely to result, in a tenant's subsequent claim for damages, in a finding that the landlord 'ought to have known' (for the purposes of DPA 1972 s4) of any defect which would have been picked up on an annual inspection: see para 2.121. For an example of the application of LTA 1985 s11 and DPA 1972 in a carbon monoxide poisoning case arising from a faulty gas appliance see *Sykes v Harry*.[289]

2.277 Although the regulations are enforced by the Health and Safety Executive (which may prosecute the landlord), the tenant may also want to involve the EHOs of the local housing authority, who may be satisfied that the state of any defect relating to gas is such as to render the premises a 'hazard' requiring action under HA 2004 (see chapter 5).

A particular danger of poorly installed or defective gas fittings and appliances is the production of carbon monoxide gas. See further 'Carbon monoxide' below.

References

2.278
- *Landlords – A guide to landlords' duties: Gas Safety (Installation and Use) Regulations 1998*, Health and Safety Executive (HSE), March 2009
- *Gas safety FAQs – tenants*, HSE, available at: www.hse.gov.uk/gas/domestic/faqtenant.htm

287 SI No 2451.

288 *Safety in the installation and use of gas systems and appliances Gas Safety (Installation and Use) Regulations 1998 Approved Code of Practice and guidance* (HSE, 2018).

289 [2001] EWCA Civ 167, [2001] QB 1014.

- *Gas safety FAQs – landlords and letting agents,* HSE, available at: www.hse.gov.uk/gas/domestic/faqlandlord.htm

Electricity

2.279 Installations for supply of electricity in dwellings are *not* yet subject to the same annual inspection and certification obligations on landlords which apply in relation to gas installations.[290] On 19 July 2018, the Secretary of State for Housing, Communities and Local Government announced that regulations will be laid subject to the affirmative procedure to make electrical installation and safety testing compulsory every five years for private sector landlords.[291] A consultation on whether the same requirements should apply to the social housing sector closed in November 2018. The consultation response was published on 29 January 2019.[292] The response stated:

> Regulations requiring landlords to have electrical installations in privately rented homes checked every five years will be introduced as soon as parliamentary time allows. They will include a requirement on landlords to ensure that they must also have regard to new guidance in determining who is competent to carry out an electrical safety inspection.

2.280 Installations for the supply of electricity in a dwelling and to a dwelling must be kept in repair and proper working order by the landlord under the covenant implied by LTA 1985 s11 (para 2.63). But that covenant does not require the landlord to provide any electrical supply to a property where there is none at the outset of the tenancy, nor to provide a minimum number of sockets, light fittings, or other installations for making use of the electrical supply.

2.281 Where LTA 1985 s9A applies to a tenancy, an electrical installation that presents a risk to the health and safety of the occupiers, even if in its original condition, would potentially make the dwelling unfit. It may be arguable that a lack of an electrical supply also renders the dwelling unfit, given the safety element of lighting, or the food hygiene related ability to store food in a fridge.

290 Except in relation to houses in multiple occupation (HMOs) for which a statutory electrical safety inspection and certification is required every five years under the Management of Houses in Multiple Occupation (England) Regulations 2006 SI No 372.

291 As referenced at: http://data.parliament.uk/DepositedPapers/files/DEP2018-1267/Lord_Bourne_to_Peers.pdf.

292 Electrical safety in the private rented sector. Government response, MHCLG January 2019.

2.282 The Royal Institution of Chartered Surveyors (RICS) Code gives this advice to landlords and their agents:[293]

> You should ensure that a competent electrician undertakes a full-fixed wiring test within 10 years of installation, for new properties/full installations and it is recommended every five years thereafter. For HMOs the test must be undertaken every five years or as recommended by an electrician.
>
> On any change of tenancy, you should check the fixed wiring installation for defects that are visually obvious to a non-qualified layman, including checking leads and plugs (unless the plug is of the moulded type). You should provide an appropriate electrical certificate to the tenant.
>
> You must ensure that all alterations/repairs/improvements to the fixed electrical system comply with the latest edition of Part P of the Building Regulations and the latest Institution of Engineering and Technology (IET) Wiring Regulations.
>
> A competent person should undertake a portable appliance test (PAT) of all moveable electrical items or equipment provided by the landlord; for example, kettles, fridges, etc. as recommended in the HSE publication *Maintaining portable electrical equipment in low-risk environments*, or at more frequent periods recommended by a competent person or as a result of a risk assessment.
>
> If you are informed of a fault that could compromise safety, this should be dealt with immediately.

Resources

2.283
- Electrical Safety First (the charity and campaigning name of the Electrical Safety Council): www.electricalsafetyfirst.org.uk
- *Protect yourself in your rented home*, Electrical Safety First, March 2014
- *Landlords' guide to electrical safety*, Electrical Safety First, September 2015

Furniture and furnishings

2.284 Regulations impose obligations on landlords in relation to the fire safety of furniture and fittings.[294] While these obligations are not directly enforceable by tenants, in a furnished tenancy, it may be arguable that furniture and fittings that do not meet the requirements of the regulations amount to a risk to the tenant's health and safety sufficient to make the dwelling unfit and so in breach of LTA

293 RICS Private Rented Sector Code of Practice, July 2015 update at para 4.3.6.3.

294 Furniture and Furnishings (Fire) (Safety) Regulations 1988 SI No 1324.

1985 s9A unless remedied, or in breach of the common law fitness requirement for furnished lets (see para 2.143).

Fire and smoke

2.285 Prior to the entry into force of LTA 1985 s9A, introduced by Homes (Fitness for Human Habitation) Act on 20 March 2019, the legal powers available to individual tenants to require landlords to take fire precautions were poor (and remain so for those tenancies to which section 9A does not yet apply – see para 2.30). Although contractual and common law rights will usually require a landlord to maintain an existing fire escape or stairway, retained in his or her possession, they cannot be used to compel the landlord to provide such facilities or to bring existing facilities up to fire safety standards where they are not out of repair.

2.286 LTA 1985 s9A, however, extends to risks such as inadequate fire safety arrangements. For example, a breach of section 9A may from communal parts not having adequate fire doors, or failures of compartmentalisation between flats, or potentially unsafe cladding material, where these present a risk to the health and safety of occupiers of the dwelling. A building which did not meet fire safety requirements in its fabric, common parts, or installations could result in it being so defective that dwelling within it would not be fit for habitation. See for example *Rendlesham Estates plc and others v Barr Ltd.*[295] It is very likely that expert evidence would be required to establish the nature and extent of the fire hazard, but section 9A could provide a potential remedy for tenants not only in respect of the dwelling but of the building of which it is part.

2.287 If LTA 1985 s9A is not of immediate application, the tenant may need to rely on the willingness of the local fire authority and/or local housing authority to intervene to deal with inadequate fire safety measures. The law relating to their respective responsibilities is well beyond the scope of this book. A good starting point is provided by the omnibus Regulatory Reform (Fire Safety) Order 2005.[296] That has produced some overlap between the responsibilities of fire authorities and of local housing authorities (under their HA 2004 powers discussed in

295 [2014] EWHC 3968 (TCC), [2015] 1 WLR 3363 at 72.

296 SI No 1541. For examples of high-profile prosecutions for offences under those regulations, see *R v Wilson* [2013] EWCA Crim 1780, [2014] QB 704 (in respect of a fire at an hotel) and *New Look Retailers Ltd v London Fire & Emergency Planning Authority* [2010] EWCA Crim 1268, [2011] 1 Cr App R (S) 57 (in respect of a fire in a shop).

chapter 5). The resulting landscape of powers and duties in relation to fire safety is well mapped out in *Housing – fire safety: Guidance on fire safety provisions for certain types of existing housing.*[297]

2.288 Local councils still have power to require fire precautions to be taken in certain flats and tenements of more than two storeys (Building Act 1984 s72).

2.289 Legislation has been enacted specifically to address the dangers that smoke from fires represents in tenanted properties. The measures were introduced to require action from the 'small minority of private rented sector landlords who have proved resistant to non-regulatory approaches [to protect tenants] from preventable death or injury from fire'.[298]

2.290 The Smoke and Carbon Monoxide Alarm (England) Regulations 2015[299] came into force on 1 October 2015.[300] They require private landlords to ensure that during any period when premises are occupied under a tenancy: (1) each storey of the premises on which there is a room used wholly or partly as living accommodation is equipped with a working smoke alarm; and (2) checks are made by or on behalf of the landlord to ensure that each prescribed alarm is in proper working order on the day any new tenancy begins. 'Room' for these purposes includes a bathroom, lavatory, hall or landing. The 2015 regulations also require private landlords to install carbon monoxide detectors in every room containing a solid fuel appliance (but not a gas appliance).

2.291 The local authority's enforcement powers and penalties are the same as for carbon monoxide detectors as at para 2.302 below.

2.292 In March 2015, the UK Government announced £3 million funding to provide around 445,000 smoke alarms to be made available free from fire and rescue authorities to private sector landlords whose properties did not have alarms.[301]

2.293 It remains to be seen whether a tenant can establish any legal remedy if injured or likely to be injured as a result of a landlord's

297 Local Authority Co-ordinators of Regulatory Services (LACORS), 2008. There is a March 2009 update available at: www.cieh.org/library/Policy/Publications_and_information_services/Policy_publications/Publications/Guidance_on_fire_safety_provisions_for_certain_types_of_existing_housing_-_March_2009_UPDATE.pdf.

298 *Smoke Alarms in Private Rented Properties* Impact Assessment No: RPC14-CLG-2266, 2015.

299 SI No 1693.

300 The regulations were made under powers given by Energy Act 2013 s150.

301 MHCLG press release 19 March 2015.

failure to comply with these requirements (or by a local housing authority's failure to enforce them).

2.294 In *Flanagan and Suarez-Alvarez v Farid Malty*[302] the defendant was a private landlord. The local council (Kensington & Chelsea) had required him to undertake fire safety work including the construction of a partition to create a lobby and installation of fire-closing doors. The work was not carried out. In a later fire, the two claimant tenants were killed. In a claim brought by their personal representatives, judgment was obtained in default of defence. On the assessment of damages, the judge found that the landlord had been warned of the need for fire safety work by council officers and that, if the warnings had been heeded, neither claimant would have died. In addition to damages for bereavement, dependency etc, he awarded £5,000 aggravated damages in each case.

Resources (chronological order)

2.295
- *Fire Safety in Buildings*, British Safety Institute, BS 9999, 2008
- *Housing – fire safety: Guidance on fire safety provisions for certain types of existing housing*, LACORS, 2008
- *Fire safety in purpose-built flats*, Local Government Group, 2011
- *Approved Document B – Fire safety: Volume 1 – Dwelling houses* (2006 edition incorporating 2010 and 2013 amendments) *Department for Communities and Local Government* (DCLG), 2013
- *How to . . . communicate with tenants about fire safety*, Chartered Institute of Housing, November 2013
- *English Housing Survey: Fire and Fire Safety 2016 to 2017*, Ministry of Housing, Communities and Local Government (MHCLG), July 2018
- *The Smoke and Carbon Monoxide Alarm (England) Regulations 2015 Explanatory Booklet for local authorities*, DCLG, September 2015
- *The Smoke and Carbon Monoxide Alarm (England) Regulations 2015 Q&A Booklet for the Private Rented Sector – landlords and tenants*, DCLG, October 2015

Carbon monoxide

2.296 Carbon monoxide (CO) is a poisonous gas produced by incomplete burning of carbon-based fuels (primarily natural gas). It is colourless, odourless, and tasteless. When CO enters the human body, it

302 [1993] 30 April, West London County Court, HHJ Compston, unreported.

prevents the blood from taking oxygen to cells, tissues, and organs. It can cause serious injury or even death.

2.297 A gas appliance which is not burning fuel properly – with the result that CO is produced – will be in disrepair or at least will not in in 'proper working order'. This will also be a breach of LTA 1985 s9A where that applies to the tenancy because it amounts to a failure to keep the dwelling fit for habitation.

2.298 The appliance will need immediate decommissioning or repair to prevent injury to health from the emission of CO. For an example of the application of LTA s11 and DPA 1972 in a CO poisoning case arising from a faulty gas appliance, see *Sykes v Harry*.[303]

2.299 It is precisely in order to prevent such situations arising that the law imposes gas safety obligations on landlords and others (see 'Gas safety' at para 2.272 above). As indicated below, these obligations may not all be directly enforceable.

2.300 An alarm can provide some warning of CO emission. Any such alarm should comply with British Standard EN 50291 and carry a British or EU approval marking, such as a Kitemark. CO alarms should be installed and maintained in line with the manufacturer's instructions

2.301 The Smoke and Carbon Monoxide Alarm (England) Regulations 2015[304] came into force on 1 October 2015.[305] They require private landlords to ensure that during any period when premises are occupied under a tenancy: (1) a carbon monoxide alarm is equipped in any room of the premises which is used wholly or partly as living accommodation and contains a solid fuel burning combustion appliance; and (2) checks are made by or on behalf of the landlord to ensure that each prescribed alarm is in proper working order on the day any new tenancy begins.

2.302 Part 3 of the Regulations places enforcement duties on local housing authorities. If a local housing authority has reasonable grounds to believe that a landlord is in breach of a duty under the regulations, it must serve a remedial notice on the landlord. That triggers a landlord's duty to comply with a remedial notice. If the landlord fails to do so, the local authority must arrange for remedial action to be taken and may impose a penalty charge of up to £5,000. The regulations provide a landlord with rights of appeal and review.

303 [2001] EWCA Civ 167, [2001] QB 1014.

304 SI No 1693.

305 The regulations were made under powers given by Energy Act 2013 s150.

2.303 In March 2015, the UK Government announced £3 million funding to provide around 40,000 carbon monoxide alarms to be made available free from fire and rescue authorities to private sector landlords whose properties did not have alarms.[306]

2.304 It remains to be seen whether a tenant can establish any legal remedy if injured or likely to be injured as a result of a landlord's failure to comply with these new requirements (or by a local housing authority's failure to enforce them).

Resources

2.305
- *Carbon Monoxide: From Awareness to Action*, A report by the All-Party Parliamentary Carbon Monoxide Group, 2015
- *The Smoke and Carbon Monoxide Alarm (England) Regulations 2015 Q&A Booklet for the Private Rented Sector – landlords and tenants*, MHCLG, October 2015
- *The Smoke and Carbon Monoxide Alarm (England) Regulations 2015 Explanatory Booklet for local authorities*, MHCLG, September 2015
- *Carbon Monoxide Alarms: Tenants safe and secure in their homes*, A report by the All-Party Parliamentary Carbon Monoxide Group, 2017

Right to use common parts safely

2.306 Where LTA 1985 s9A applies to a tenancy, it is strongly arguable that a safe means of entrance, egress and escape from a dwelling, and safe use of the common parts, is necessary for the dwelling to be fit for habitation. See *Rendlesham Estates plc and others v Barr Ltd*.[307] See also paras 2.46 and 2.47.

2.307 DPA 1972 1972 s1 would equally apply where the lack of safety arises from build defects. However, DPA 1972 s4 liability is restricted to the dwelling.

2.308 LTA 1985 s11(1A) extends the implied repairing obligation to common parts of a building of which the dwelling forms part, so will be engaged if the lack of safety arises from a failure to repair (although this does not extend to an exterior path or garden). See *Edwards v Kumarasamy*[308] and see paras 2.78 and 2.79 above.

306 MHCLG press release 19 March 2015.

307 [2014] EWHC 3968 (TCC), [2015] 1 WLR 3663 at paras 70 and 71.

308 *Edwards v Kumarasamy* [2016] UKSC 40, [2016] AC 1334.

2.309 The Occupiers' Liability Act 1957 applies to common parts for tenants, occupiers and other visitors. See paras 2.95–2.99 above.

2.310 The HA 2004 powers of a local authority, and the HHSRS hazard assessment regime extend to common parts of a building. See chapter 5.

Related rights – notice, access and tenant-like conduct

The notice requirement

2.311 It is an implied term of all tenancy agreements which impose an obligation on the landlord to repair property rented out to a tenant that the landlord is not liable to carry out any repair *within* the demised premises unless and until he or she: (1) has been put on notice, or in any other way has knowledge, of the need for repair; *and* (2) has failed to carry out the repair within a reasonable period of time thereafter.[309] Although a common law rule, it has been consistently held to apply also where the repairing obligations are imposed by statute, eg, by LTA 1985 ss8 and 11, and the same rule extends to LTA 1985 s9A. The burden of proving both the essential matters is on the tenant.[310]

2.312 The landlord's knowledge of the defect must be proved even if the disrepair or unfitness is latent. A tenant injured by the collapse of a ceiling which no one could have expected to be liable to fall cannot recover damages from his or her landlord for breach of repairing obligations.[311]

2.313 It is the 'knowledge' of the landlord which is important. Usually this knowledge will arise from notice of disrepair or unfitness given by the tenant. However, a landlord may be imputed with knowledge if the disrepair or unfitness is brought to the attention of his or her workmen,[312] rent-collector or any other person (eg, a resident caretaker) employed by the landlord and having express or implied authority to receive complaints about property conditions on behalf of the landlord.

2.314 The route by which the landlord receives knowledge of the disrepair or unfitness is not significant, except that it has been

309 *Makin v Watkinson* (1870) LR 6 Ex 25; *O'Brien v Robinson* [1973] AC 912, [1973] 2 WLR 393, HL; *Morris v Liverpool CC* (1988) 20 HLR 498, [1988] 14 EG 59, CA.

310 *Morris v Liverpool CC* (1988) 20 HLR 498, [1988] 14 EG 59, CA.

311 *O'Brien v Robinson* [1973] AC 912, [1973] 2 WLR 393, HL.

312 *Sheldon v West Bromwich Corporation* (1984) 13 HLR 23, CA.

suggested that the informant must be a 'responsible source'.[313] In *Dinefwr BC v Jones,*[314] the council was held to have actual notice of the disrepair seen at the property by the council's EHO even though the EHO was not from the housing department and was inspecting the property after complaints relating to cleanliness rather than disrepair. The EHO, however, was not treated as having implied knowledge on behalf of the council about defects other than those obviously visible (that is not those which would have been discovered only on a thorough inspection). A tenant cannot necessarily rely on the proposition that, because the premises were inspected by the landlord or landlord's unqualified agent, it follows that the landlord knew of the defects in the premises. It is for the tenant to show that the landlord or unqualified agent saw the defect.

2.315 The *Jones*[315] case also indicates that knowledge will be established where the landlord receives information about the defects in a property from an independent valuer (in that case from the valuation officer following a right-to-buy application). This was confirmed in *Hall v Howard,*[316] where the landlord received an offer to purchase from a private tenant, accompanied by a surveyor's valuation report listing (and costing) repairs needed. Receipt of the report was sufficient to fix the landlord with knowledge of the defects. Similarly, service by a local authority of some form of statutory repair notice is sufficient to establish knowledge on the part of the landlord and thus, liability.[317]

2.316 The information received by the landlord must be sufficient to put a reasonable person on enquiry about whether works of repair or remedy are needed.[318] It will therefore be usual for the tenant to make the landlord aware of the disrepair or unfitness needing to be tackled, but the notice given need not particularise the degree or extent of the disrepair or unfitness nor the remedial works required.[319] Where the tenant informs the landlord that he or she will be preparing a detailed list of items of disrepair and estimates for the works required, the landlord is not treated as having knowledge of the

313 *Dinefwr BC v Jones* (1987) 19 HLR 445, CA.

314 (1987) 19 HLR 445, CA.

315 *Dinefwr BC v Jones* (1987) 19 HLR 445, CA.

316 (1988) 20 HLR 566, (1989) 57 P&CR 226, CA.

317 *McGreal v Wake* (1984) 13 HLR 107, CA.

318 *O'Brien v Robinson* [1973] AC 912, (1973) 2 WLR 393, HL; *Sheldon v West Bromwich Corporation* (1984) 13 HLR 23, CA; *British Telecommunications plc v Sun Life Assurance Society plc* [1996] Ch 69, [1995] 3 WLR 622, CA.

319 *Griffin v Pillet* [1926] 1 KB 17, KBD.

defects until the list and estimates are served.[320] Where no notice or knowledge can be established, the Defective Premises Act 1972 s4 may be helpful (see paras 2.108–2.128).

2.317 Even after a landlord has knowledge of disrepair, there is no breach of the repairing obligation until 'a reasonable time has elapsed in which the repair could have been carried out'.[321] There is no prescribed 'reasonable time', so the length of the period for completion of repairs will vary according to the circumstances in each case. A useful guide to what the government considers a reasonable period for ordinary minor repairs is given in Secure Tenants of Local Housing Authorities (Right to Repair) Regulations 1994 Sch 1.[322]

2.318 If the landlord has given some advance indication to the tenant of the times within which particular repairs will usually be completed (perhaps by showing 'target periods' in a tenants' handbook), these will be strongly indicative of what a 'reasonable time' would be for repairs falling within those categories. Some landlords may even have placed such time limits within the tenancy agreement (in which case they can be directly enforced). In other cases, the courts (and initially those advising tenants) will determine the reasonable period, taking into account a variety of factors. Obviously, the scale and severity of the disrepair or unfitness will be critical factors but also relevant will be: whether the tenant is actually living in the property: the availability of replacement parts; and (in the case of social landlords) the overall workload.[323] The burden of proving that a reasonable time has been exceeded lies on the tenant. This will require firm evidence rather than inference. For example, even where the repair required is the replacement of a missing or damaged front door and door frame, it does not necessarily follow that a landlord allowing a week to pass before effecting final repairs is in breach of LTA 1985 s11, where a temporary repair has been made.[324]

No need for notice of defects *outside* the demised premises

2.319 The implied term about 'knowledge' applies only to parts of a building which have been rented to the tenant. It does not apply to parts

320 *Al Hassani v Merrigan* (1988) 20 HLR 238, CA.
321 *Calabar Properties Ltd v Stitcher* [1984] 1 WLR 287, [1983] 3 All ER 759, CA at 298.
322 SI No 133.
323 *Morris v Liverpool CC* (1988) 20 HLR 498, CA.
324 *Morris v Liverpool CC* (1988) 20 HLR 498, CA.

which have been retained in the control of the landlord. When there is disrepair to part of a building which: (a) the landlord is contractually obliged to repair; and (b) the landlord continues to control, then the landlord is liable immediately disrepair occurs whether or not he or she knows or could have known of the need for repairs.[325]

2.320 This will be particularly important where a tenant is unable to prove that the landlord had 'knowledge'. But failure by the tenant to draw the defect to the landlord's attention in this type of case can, in some circumstances, be taken into account as a failure to mitigate.[326] The lack of any requirement for notice in relation to parts outside the property let to the tenant is also important in those disrepair or unfitness cases where the majority of the damage occurs immediately a defect arises and before any reasonable time to carry out a repair has elapsed, eg, in flooding cases.[327] In any event, reliance on the fact that there is no need for notice will increase the period of breach, because time will start to run immediately a defect occurs rather than after a reasonable time has elapsed, and may thereby increase any damages which may be recovered.[328]

2.321 It was suggested in *Charalambous v Earle (addendum to judgment)*[329] that this rule may need modification to take account of the practicalities of the modern relationship of residential landlords and tenants but this was said in the context of a long lease where there is a reciprocal obligation on lessees to contribute to the costs of the remedial works. In *Edwards v Kumarasamy*,[330] the Supreme Court upheld the general rule that no notice is required where the landlord retains the common parts and/or structure of the building, or in relation to parts that are not within the tenant's demise, but have been demised to other tenants by the same landlord. However, in addressing the situation where a landlord had let a flat to the tenant, but disrepair arose to the common parts which were not owned by the

325 *Melles & Co v Holme* [1918] 2 KB 100, KBD; *Bishop v Consolidated London Properties Ltd* (1933) 102 LJKB 257; *Loria v Hammer* [1989] 2 EGLR 249, ChD; *British Telecommunications plc v Sun Life Assurance Society plc* [1996] Ch 69, [1995] 3 WLR 622, CA; *Passley v Wandsworth LBC* (1998) 30 HLR 165, CA; *Charalambous v Earle (Addendum to judgment)* [2006] EWCA Civ 1338, [2007] HLR 8; *Edwards v Kumarasamy* [2016] UKSC 40, [2016] AC 1334.

326 *Minchburn v Peck* (1988) 20 HLR 392, CA.

327 See, eg *Passley v Wandsworth LBC* (1998) 30 HLR 165, CA.

328 *Charalambous v Earle (Addendum to judgment)* [2006] EWCA Civ 1338, [2007] HLR 8, CA.

329 [2006] EWCA Civ 1338, [2007] HLR 8.

330 [2016] UKSC 40, [2016] AC 1334.

landlord, and over which the landlord had at best an easement, the Supreme Court held that notice to the landlord was required.

> The potential harshness on a headlessee of a single flat of imposing a covenant to repair the common parts, which he has effectively transferred to the tenant his right to use, is mitigated by the need for notice of any disrepair before the covenant becomes activated.[331]

Rights of access by the landlord

2.322 For the purposes of carrying out repairs or inspecting for repairs, landlords may have rights of access under the terms of the tenancy agreement, at common law or under statute. In *Beaufort Park Resident's Management Ltd v Sabahipour*,[332] a tenant refused access to a director of the landlord company (with whom he had a difficult relationship) on the basis that he did not accept that the director had any authority or was suitably qualified to enter and inspect a leak he had reported. The Upper Tribunal found that the tenant was in breach of his lease because the director was the company's agent and the tenant was obliged to give him access for the purpose of examining the condition of the flat as stated in the lease.

2.323 In the absence of an express term, or some relevant statutory provision, a landlord has no power to enter tenanted property in order to carry out improvements.[333]

Access at common law

2.324 The landlord who is subject to an express or implied duty to keep premises 'in repair' will have the right at common law to enter to carry out those works (but no others):

> I have construed that covenant to mean that he shall put them into good condition if necessary and it is my judgment that the covenant carries with it an implied licence to the lessor to enter upon premises of the lessee and to occupy them for a reasonable time to do what he has covenanted to do.[334]

2.325 The right to enter to do repairs is subject to an obligation to give the tenant reasonable notice and must be exercised reasonably, although

331 *Edwards v Kumarasamy* [2016] UKSC 40, [2016] AC 1334 at 54.

332 [2011] UKUT 436 (LC).

333 *McDougall v Easington DC* (1989) 21 HLR 310, (1989) 58 P&CR 201, CA; *Yeoman's Row Management Ltd v Bodentien-Meyrick* [2002] EWCA Civ 860, [2003] L&TR 10.

334 *Saner v Bilton* (1878) 7 Ch D 815, Ch D at 824.

the tenant is not usually entitled to a copy of the specification of works.[335]

2.326 The landlord has the right to temporary vacant possession in order to carry out repairs only when vacant possession is essential.[336] In such cases, if the tenant refuses to move, the landlord can seek an injunction to obtain access to, and control of, the premises.[337] The grant of any such injunction is a matter for the discretion of the court and one is only likely to be granted if alternative accommodation is available while the works are carried out and the tenant's moving expenses are paid.

2.327 In the case of periodic tenancies of dwelling-houses, the landlord has an implied right to enter to repair defects which might cause personal injury.[338]

Access by statute

2.328 Most statutory repairing obligations carry within them express rights of entry for the landlord. LTA 1985 s9A(7) and (8) imply a tenant's covenant that the landlord, or any person authorised in writing by the landlord, may enter the dwelling for the purpose of viewing its condition and state of repair, subject to access being requested only at reasonable times of day and with at least 24 hours' notice in writing. The same provision is made at LTA 1985 s11(6).

2.329 In addition, Rent Act 1977 s148 gives landlords an express right to enter for the purpose of carrying out repairs in the case of protected or statutory tenancies. HA 1988 s16 gives the same right of access to the landlord of an assured tenant.

Use in a tenant-like manner

2.330 Under LTA 1985 s11(2), a landlord is not obliged to do repairs which the tenant is liable to do by virtue of his or her duty to use the premises in a tenant-like manner. In *Warren v Keen*,[339] Denning LJ described this duty as an obligation 'to do the little jobs around the place which a reasonable tenant would do' and included in his defin-

335 *Granada Theatres v Freehold Investments (Leytonstone) Ltd* [1959] Ch 592, [1959] 1 WLR 570, CA.

336 *McGreal v Wake* (1984) 13 HLR 107, CA.

337 See eg, *English Churches Housing Group v Shine* [2004] EWCA Civ 434, [2004] HLR 42.

338 *McAuley v Bristol CC* [1992] QB 134, [1991] 3 WLR 968, CA.

339 [1954] 1 QB 15, [1953] 3 WLR 702, CA.

ition turning the water off when the tenant went away, cleaning chimneys and windows, mending fuses and unblocking the sink. A local authority's view that changing a tap washer might be added to that list was rejected in *Islington LBC v Keane*,[340] where it was held that changing a tap washer was part of repairing a tap and its component parts and something most people would call a plumber to do. It therefore fell within LTA 1985 s11(1)(b). The express term suggesting that the tenant was liable for this defect was accordingly void.

2.331 Earlier, in *Churchill v Nottingham CC*,[341] it was held that, while cleaning a chimney might still be part of a tenant's duty to act in a tenant-like manner in respect of a small cottage on the moors, where wood or coal was still burned and the chimney used in the old fashioned way, in modern housing a tenant was not obliged to disconnect a fixed gas fire, remove the back plate and clean the flue behind it; this obligation fell on the landlord under LTA 1985 s11.

2.332 Under LTA 1985 s9A(2), a landlord is not liable to carry out works for which the tenant is responsible under:

i) the duty of the lessee to use the premises in a tenant-like manner, or
ii) an express covenant of the lessee of substantially the same effect as that duty;

2.333 In addition, under section 9A(3), the landlord is not liable for any unfitness to the dwelling wholly or mainly attributable to the tenant's breach of covenant. While there is no significant case law on fitness and the tenant's duty to use in a tenant-like manner, it seems clear that one of the main areas of dispute will be over the tenant's use giving rise to condensation and mould growth. Issues are likely to involve the extent to which the tenant use can be considered ordinary use, and the extent to which instructions such as keeping the windows open and the heating constantly on can be considered reasonable requirements for tenant-like conduct.

Attempts to take away rights

2.334 Statutory rights, whether by way of implied tenancy terms such as those in the LTA 1985 or outside the tenancy agreement – such as

340 December 2005 *Legal Action* 28, *Housing Law Casebook* 7th edn, paras R1.6 and R19.2, Clerkenwell County Court.

341 January 2001 *Legal Action* 25, *Housing Law Casebook* 7th edn, para R4.15, Nottingham County Court.

OLA 1957, or DPA 1972 – cannot be contractually excluded by the terms of the tenancy agreement.

2.335 The LTA 1985 makes express provision at section 9B(3) that the implied term in section 9A cannot be excluded or limited by agreement, nor can any penalty be imposed on the tenant for relying on the obligation. Similarly, LTA 1985 ss12(1)(a) and 11(4) make any attempt to exclude the section 11 implied repairing obligation, or to transfer liability for it to the tenant, void.

2.336 While common law rights such as those in negligence could, in principle, by excluded by an express contractual term, it is likely that such a term would be 'unfair' under the CRA 2015 and, as such, not binding.

Rights of non-tenants

2.337 The majority of rights are held by the tenant. For example, while under LTA 1985 s9A, a dwelling may be unfit if it presents a risk to the health and safety of any of the occupiers, but it is the tenant who can take action under the implied term. The same is true of the LTA 1985 s11 implied repair obligation. These contractual provisions can only be enforced by other occupants if they can bring themselves within the provisions of the Contracts (Rights of Third Parties) Act 1999 (see paras 3.47–3.51).

2.338 Similarly, common law nuisance claims can only be brought by the person with an interest in the land affected, which is the tenant.

2.339 However, both the OLA 1957 and DPA 1972 s4 liabilities are owed to most occupiers. The OLA 1957 liability extends to any person, whether tenant, member of household or visitor, with regard to the common parts. DPA 1972 s4 extends to 'all persons who might reasonably be expected to be affected by defects in the state of the premises'. That includes the tenant, their household and visitors.

2.340 Under the EPA 1990, 'any person aggrieved' by a statutory nuisance may bring a prosecution. This would include the tenant and any member of their household, or other occupiers of the dwelling. A complainant may not lose standing if they were subsequently evicted or they had become a trespasser.[342] See para 6.53.

2.341 There is no restriction on who can raise a complaint about conditions with the local authority and request an inspection under HA 2004. See para 5.21.

342 *Watkins v Aged Merchant Seamen's Homes* [2018] EWHC 2410 (Admin).

CHAPTER 3

Enforcing rights

continued

Introduction to the options

3.1 This chapter assumes that:

- the landlord is legally liable to undertake the repair or other works;
- where notice is necessary, the tenant has given notice of the disrepair or unfitness and the need for remedial works; and
- the landlord has failed to carry out the necessary works within a reasonable period (where such a period is applicable).[1]

3.2 In these circumstances, the landlord is in breach of a legal obligation and the tenant has a right to both financial compensation and an order requiring the landlord to carry out the necessary works (where any remain outstanding).

3.3 The tenant's adviser should first consider whether remedies other than issuing a claim are appropriate. These include:

- the tenant withholds rent;
- the tenant does the work;
- the tenant applies to a rent officer;
- the tenant applies to appoint a receiver or manager;
- the tenant pursues a complaints procedure (see para 3.229).

The tenant withholds rent

3.4 A tenant has no right in law simply to withhold rent in protest at a landlord's failure to carry out repairs or maintain the property in a state that is fit for human habitation.

3.5 In addition to provoking possession proceedings, tenants encouraging others to withhold rent could be taken to court for unlawful interference with the contracts (ie, the tenancy agreements) of other tenants.[2]

3.6 An adviser should not encourage a tenant to withhold rent. To do so invites possession proceedings, in which the tenant will be a defendant and therefore at a disadvantage, particularly an assured shorthold tenant where the accelerated possession procedure is available.

3.7 Even where the tenant has a greater level of security of tenure, all too often a tenant withholding rent is unable to resist spending any money set aside on other outgoings and, if the damages awarded do not exceed the amount withheld, there is a real risk of a possession

1 See paras 2.311–2.318.

2 See *Camden Nominees v Forcey* [1940] Ch 352, [1940] 2 All ER 1, ChD.

order. The dangers are well illustrated by the case of *Al Hassani v Merrigan*,[3] where the counterclaim for damages was dismissed; the money set aside could not meet the arrears, and the judge found it reasonable, in the circumstances, to grant a possession order for arrears of rent.

The tenant does the work

3.8 Where it is clear that the landlord is in breach of contractual repairing obligations, the tenant has a right at common law to carry out the necessary repairs (either personally or by engaging a contractor) and to recover the costs and expenses incurred by deducting them from future rent. The availability of this right to tenants was reaffirmed in the case of *Lee-Parker v Izzet (No 1)*.[4]

3.9 In order to rely on this right, tenants need show that they have behaved reasonably. Therefore, certain preliminary steps should be followed in order to exercise it:

- inform the landlord of the intention to take this form of action if works are not carried out;
- allow a further reasonable period for the landlord to comply with the obligations;
- obtain three estimates from properly qualified contractors for the cost of carrying out the remedial works and send copies of these to the landlord with a 'final warning' that the tenant will engage the contractor with the lowest tender unless the landlord carries out the work;
- engage the contractor at the lowest reasonable tender to have the work carried out;
- submit a copy of the contractor's invoice to the landlord and request reimbursement;
- if no money is forthcoming, settle the invoice and recoup the cost by deducting it from future rent.

3.10 This right, which is wholly separate from the right to 'set off against rent' (see paras 3.210–3.215) will provide a tenant who is sued for unpaid rent with a complete defence to the landlord's action.

3.11 This remedy can be invaluable where relatively low-cost works are needed (eg, replacing a part to a central heating boiler, fixing an extractor fan or mending a leaking toilet). However, it has the disadvantage that

3 (1988) 20 HLR 238, CA.

4 [1971] 1 WLR 1688, [1971] 3 All ER 1099, ChD.

the tenant is then responsible for any shortcomings in the standard of works done and only a court would be able to decide at what point a landlord would resume responsibility for any further defect that arose with the item that the tenant has worked on. It will be rare for a tenant to be able to afford to carry out a more expensive repair without first saving up rent with a view to eventually paying a contractor, as was the case in *Asco Developments & Newman v Lowes, Lewis and Gordon*.[5]

3.12 Where the problem relates to unfitness which isn't also a simple repair issue, it is inadvisable for the tenant to do the work. Tenants will not have the right to tackle design problems or structural defects or to make alterations without the landlord's consent.

3.13 Some tenancy agreements attempt to exclude the right to withhold rent. However, clear words are needed if the right is to be excluded[6]. For tenancies commencing on or after 1 October 2015 such a term is likely to offend the unfair contract terms provisions in the Consumer Rights Act 2015.[7] Indeed, a similar term prohibiting 'set-off' (see para 3.218) was held to be unenforceable in the county court case of *Cody v Philps*.[8]

3.14 Since 1 January 1986, secure tenants and, from 12 February 1997, introductory tenants of local authorities, have been able to use a statutory scheme allowing them to arrange minor repairs and recover the cost. In most respects it is more limited than the common law right. The scheme is found in the Housing Act (HA) 1985 s96[9] and HA 1996 s135, but it is hardly ever used in practice. Its scope is limited to repair work costing less than £250 and it requires the service of notices and counter-notices.[10]

The tenant applies to a rent officer

3.15 A tenant protected by the Rent Act (RA) 1977 can apply to the rent officer for a reduction in the registered rent if there has been a

5 (1978) 248 EG 683, ChD.

6 *Connaught Restaurants v Indoor Leisure Ltd* [1994] 1 WLR 501, [1974] 4 All ER 834, CA.

7 Parts 1 and 2 of the 2015 Act consolidate and replace the Unfair Terms in Consumer Contracts Regulations 1999 SI No 2083. These regulations still apply to terms in tenancy agreements which predate 1 October 2015.

8 December 2005 *Legal Action* 28, *Housing Law Casebook* 7th edn, para R19.11, West London County Court.

9 As amended by Leasehold Reform, Housing and Urban Development Act 1993 s121.

10 Further details can be found in the Secure Tenants of Local Housing Authorities (Right to Repair) Regulations 1994 SI No 133 as amended by 1994 SI No 844 and 1997 SI No 73. Note that demoted tenants do not have this right.

'change in the condition of the dwelling' since the last assessment.[11] However, this rarely arises nowadays, given the dwindling numbers of Rent Act tenants.

The tenant applies to appoint a receiver or manager

3.16 In the private rented sector, situations can arise where the identity of the landlord is not known, or the landlord cannot be traced and urgent works are required. In such cases, the remedy is to apply for the appointment of a receiver. The court has power to do this in any case where it appears just and convenient: see Part 69 of the Civil Procedure Rules (CPR) 1998. This remedy is not available to tenants of local authorities.[12] On the remuneration of the receiver, see *Evans v Clayhope Properties*.[13]

3.17 For situations where there are two or more flats in a single block, the procedure for appointment of a manager is now codified in the Landlord and Tenant Act (LTA) 1987 Part 2. This requires, in the usual case, that a preliminary 'warning notice' be served on the landlord or agent (section 22). If this does not produce the required effect, a tribunal[14] may, on application, appoint a manager to take over and run the block for the purpose of making good the disrepair (section 24). The appointment can be registered against the title of the property as a notice at the Land Registry to prevent the landlord avoiding the consequences of the order by selling on. Local authority and registered social landlords are exempt from this provision (section 58).

The tenant brings a claim in the county court

3.18 Claims brought by tenants will normally start as civil actions in the county court. In recent years, because of the limited availability of legal aid, many tenants have not been able to initiate claims but instead have raised counterclaims to possession proceedings for rent arrears (for discussion of defences and counterclaims see paras 3.210–3.228). Legal aid is more generally available for such counterclaims.

3.19 Although court proceedings take longer than some of the other remedies mentioned above, they can be a powerful way of securing a remedy for a tenant who has suffered at the hands of a recalcitrant

11 Rent Act 1977 s67(3)(a).

12 *Parker v Camden* LBC [1986] Ch 162, (1985) 17 HLR 380, CA.

13 [1988] 1 WLR 358, (1988) 20 HLR 176, CA.

14 The First-tier Tribunal (Property Chamber).

landlord. The court can order a landlord to carry out works on a property, can award damages and can make declarations. All of these remedies will be considered below.

3.20 It may often be the case that the defects of which the tenant complains constitute both disrepair and unfitness, while some may fall into one or the other category. However new rights under LTA 1985 s9A initially only apply to tenancies which were granted on or after 20 March 2019. They will apply to the majority of tenancies from 20 March 2020 (see para 2.29 for details of implementation).

3.21 Given the complexity of the court process, particularly where an order for works is being sought, a tenant would be well advised to seek legal representation if funding for the legal costs is available. The remainder of this part assumes that a tenant has consulted an adviser who is able to advise or represent him or her in court proceedings.

3.22 Advisers have differing approaches to managing cases. The tactics set out in this chapter have worked well in practice in disrepair cases but are by no means the only way of conducting a successful claim or counterclaim. They may need to be adapted to suit different advisers or the approaches of different local courts. Of course, the procedural rules cannot be approached with the same flexibility.

Before the claim

Taking initial instructions

3.23 Some advisers send the tenant a questionnaire to complete and bring to the first meeting. This works well with some tenants, but could be off-putting for a person disadvantaged by language or literacy difficulties. There is a schedule attached to the Pre-Action Protocol[15] in the CPR, and if a tenant can complete this, it saves time in the initial interview. Alternatively, a sample questionnaire is contained in appendix C to this book.

3.24 At an early stage, the adviser will have to consider how to fund the case – see chapter 4 for information about when funding might be available in the form of legal aid. Most claims will not be within the scope of legal aid so the funding arrangement will have to be based either upon a conditional fee agreement (CFA) or on an agreement that the tenant is responsible for the legal costs. Without an enforceable

15 www.justice.gov.uk/courts/procedure-rules/civil/protocol/prot_hou.

arrangement about costs with the client, there is no possibility of obtaining payment of those costs from the opponent.

3.25 It is important that the adviser establishes the tenant's requirements before or at the first interview. Sometimes the tenant will not want works carried out, but would prefer a move to other accommodation. Unfortunately, there is no private law remedy to obtain such a result and the possibility of a judicial review of a refusal by a social landlord to grant a transfer only arises in the most extreme circumstances. Judicial review proceedings are outside the ambit of this book.[16]

3.26 It is important to establish the landlord's identity as early as possible and the tenant should be asked to bring the original tenancy agreement, together with any other tenancy documents, to the first interview with the adviser. If there is any uncertainty about the identity of the landlord, the adviser can use LTA 1985 s1 to force the person receiving the rent to supply the tenant with the landlord's name and address. Copies of the register of title can be obtained online from the Land Registry to establish the ownership of the property, but the adviser should remember that the landlord may not be the registered title holder. It is quite possible that the landlord is the tenant of someone with superior title but is authorised to sublet the property.

3.27 The tenant should be advised to keep a diary of all future contact with the landlord, of the continuing effects of the disrepair or unfitness and of any unnecessary inconvenience and distress caused by works when they are eventually carried out.

3.28 The adviser may want to give the tenant a list to complete of any expenses and losses arising from the disrepair or unfitness, see appendix C. The tenant should be warned against the temptation of exaggerating such losses. In practice, the general damages, that is, the amount the court awards for inconvenience and distress, are often much larger than the financial losses, and any dishonesty at this stage will affect the credibility of the whole case. In addition, it will be necessary for the tenant to describe the damage to each piece of property for which a claim is made and how the unfitness or disrepair caused such damage.

3.29 Often the tenant will not have retained receipts and will have thrown goods away before giving the landlord the opportunity to inspect them. This can cause difficulties. For example, in *Heffernan*

16 See, for example, A Arden QC, J Bates and T Vanhegan, *Homelessness and Allocations*, Legal Action Group, 2018.

v Hackney LBC,[17] a claim for losses failed because of a lack of evidence. Sedley LJ said it was:

> . . . not permissible to come to court with bald assertions . . . unsupported by a single document showing payment or loss, and to leave [the judge] . . . like a blind man searching for a black hat in a dark room . . .

3.30 Even so, a tenant can successfully make a non-inflated claim for itemised goods destroyed, without receipts, because most judges accept the reality that tenants rarely keep them. When completing the list, the tenant might want to use the internet to obtain estimates for the replacement value of goods rather than spending hours going round the various shops where the goods were originally bought. For further consideration of 'special damages' see para 7.51.

Retaliatory action by landlords

3.31 Care will have to be taken when advising tenants of private landlords. Such tenants are likely to have assured shorthold tenancies (ASTs) with limited security of tenure. Landlords have in the past taken revenge on tenants who try to assert rights of repair by serving a notice under HA 1988 s21.[18] A valid section 21 notice obliges a court to end the tenancy. Deregulation Act (DA) 2015 s33(1) applies to all assured shorthold tenancies from 1 October 2018 in England (with some limited exemptions)[19] and is intended, among other things, to prevent retaliatory evictions. It provides some limited protection to a tenant suffering poor housing conditions including disrepair. It prevents a landlord from serving a valid section 21 notice within six months of being served with a 'relevant notice' (an improvement notice or an emergency remedial notice) by the local housing authority.[20] It also invalidates notices served following legitimate complaints made by a tenant.[21] Certain steps need to have been taken in order to benefit from this protection:

17 [2009] EWCA Civ 665, [2010] HLR 17.

18 Research indicates that private tenants in England who make formal complaints either to their local authority or an independent redress scheme are more likely to be issued with a section 21 notice than those who have not (*Touch and go: How to protect private renters from retaliatory eviction in England*, Citizens Advice, 2018).

19 DA 2015 s34.

20 DA 2015 s33(1) ie a notice served under HA 2004 ss11, 12 or 40(7).

21 DA 2015 s33(2).

- before the section 21 notice was given, the tenant must have complained to the landlord in writing, about the defects in the dwelling;
- the landlord must have failed to respond within 14 days of when the complaint was given with adequate proposals to remedy the defect within a reasonable timescale, or the landlord served a section 21 notice following the compliant;
- the tenant must then complain to the local authority about the same, or broadly the same defect;
- the authority must serve a relevant notice in response to the complaint;
- if the section 21 notice was not given before the tenant's complaint, it must have been given before the service of the relevant notice; and
- the relevant notice must have been served before any possession order is made by a court.[22]

3.32 The adviser should also bear in mind that, if the tenancy began or was renewed after 6 April 2007 and the landlord has not protected any deposit paid in an authorised scheme and served the prescribed information, as required by HA 2004 s213, then the landlord will be unable to rely on a notice served under HA 1988 s21.[23]

3.33 Where the tenancy began on or after 1 October 2015, the landlord must have provided the tenant with the booklet 'How to Rent: the checklist for renting in England', before being able to rely on a section 21 notice.[24]

3.34 For all tenancies, from 1 October 2018, the section 21 notice must be in a prescribed form.[25] For tenancies starting or after 1 October 2015, an Energy Performance Certificate[26] and an up to date Gas Safety Certificate[27] must have been served on the tenant.[28] A landlord who fails to give a new tenant a Gas Safety Certificate before they

22 DA 2015 s33(6).

23 HA 2004 s215(1A).

24 Assured Shorthold Tenancy Notices and Prescribed Requirements (England) Regulations 2015 SI No 1646 reg 3.

25 Assured Shorthold Tenancy Notices and Prescribed Requirements (England) (Amendment) Regulations 2015 SI No 1725.

26 Energy Performance of Buildings (England and Wales) Regulations 2012 SI No 3118 reg 6(5).

27 Gas Safety (Installation and Use) Regulations 1998 SI No 2451 reg 36(6).

28 HA 1988 s21A(1). DA 2015 s41(3) provides that the requirements should apply to all tenancies from 1 October 201, however at the date of publication the necessary amendment to the regulations have not been made.

occupy the property may not have complied adequately with the regulatory requirements.[29]

3.35 Similarly, where residential premises are required to be licensed, for example, certain houses in multiple occupation (HMOs), no valid section 21 notice can be served by a landlord of an unlicensed property, unless the landlord is in the process of applying for a licence.[30] Until the landlord regularises the position, the tenant will be more secure.

3.36 Even where the above provisions do not assist, the tenant may be willing to risk losing the tenancy rather than endure extremely poor conditions and the adviser should consider an interim injunction (see para 3.120). Where a tenant is in priority need as defined by HA 1996 Part 7 s189 and the property is in very bad condition, the local authority may have a duty to secure that suitable accommodation is made available and this may be a better alternative for the tenant.[31]

3.37 On 15 April 2019, the Government announced it intended to legislate to end 'no fault' evictions by way of section 21 and a consultation would follow.[32] For the remainder of this chapter it will be assumed that the tenant wants to take county court action.

Matters to consider after the first interview

Recoverability and proportionality of costs

3.38 The adviser needs to consider whether legal costs are likely to be awarded against the opponent and if so whether they will be sufficient to fund the case. If there is going to be a shortfall, the likelihood is that either the tenant will have to cover it or the adviser will not be paid. When deciding costs on a standard basis the court will only allow costs which are proportionate to the matters in issue.[33]

3.39 Costs incurred are proportionate if they bear a reasonable relationship to:

- The sums in issue in proceedings;
- The value of any non-monetary relief in issue in the proceedings;
- The complexity of the litigation;

29 See *Assured Property Services Ltd v Ooo* September 2017 *Legal Action* 31, Edmonton County Court, and *Caridon Property Ltd v Monty Shooltz* April 2018 *Legal Action* 37, [2018] EW Misc B9, Central London County Court.

30 HA 2004 s98.

31 HA 1996 ss175(3) and 193(2).

32 'Government announces end to unfair evictions', MHCLG press release, 15 April 2019.

33 CPR 44.3(2)(a).

- Any additional work generated by the conduct of any paying party; and
- Any wider factors involved in the proceedings, such as reputation or public importance.[34]

3.40 Other factors to which the court will also have regard when determining legal costs are:

a) the conduct of all the parties and the efforts made, if any, to resolve the dispute;
b) the amount or value of any money or property involved;
c) the importance of the matter to all the parties;
d) the particular complexity of the matter or the difficulty or novelty of the questions raised;
e) the skill, effort, specialised knowledge and responsibility involved;
f) the time spent on the case;
g) the place where and the circumstances in which work or any part of it was done; and
h) the receiving party's last approved or agreed budget.[35]

3.41 Costs which are disproportionate in amount may be disallowed or reduced even if they were reasonably or necessarily incurred.[36] Lord Justice Jackson states that the reason for this is:

> If parties wish to pursue claims or defences at disproportionate cost, they must do so, at least in part, at their own expense.[37]

3.42 Practitioners continue to test the limitations of this approach. Anecdotally, in disrepair cases it seems that costs judges award amounts that are sometimes much larger than the compensation recovered. They seem to appreciate that in such cases factors (a), (c) to (f) set out above will play a significant part in their decisions.

Limitation periods

3.43 The adviser needs to bear in mind that the landlord will have a potential defence to any claim for disrepair or unfitness that the tenant suffered before the limitation date. The time limits are set by the Limitation Act (LA) 1980 and start running from the date when the cause of action accrues and end with the date on which the claim is issued. The key date, therefore, is that on which the cause of

34 CPR 44.3(5).
35 CPR 44.4(3).
36 CPR 44.3(2)(a).
37 Lord Justice Jackson's *Review of Civil Litigation Costs – Final Report*, 2009, para 5.17 on p38.

action accrues, and this may vary. The basic limitation periods are three years in personal injury claims, six years for contract claims but 12 years for breach of long leases signed under seal which are therefore 'specialties' under LA 1980 s8.

3.44 The cause of action under a tenancy agreement or lease accrues at the date of breach of the obligation. Where premises are in disrepair or unfit, breach usually occurs when the landlord has knowledge of the disrepair or unfitness and has failed to remedy it within a reasonable period.[38] If works are not carried out, the cause of action is a continuing one but proceedings should be started within six years of the initial breach in order to ensure recovery of compensation for the whole period. If there has been a continuing breach of obligation for more than six years,[39] the damages will be limited to the circumstances over the six years preceding the launch of proceedings, if the landlord states they are relying on a limitation defence.

3.45 Where the claim is founded in tort, the same principles apply whether the duty of care which has been breached arises in common law or by statute. Actions based on a breach of the duty imposed by Defective Premises Act (DPA) 1972 s1 are subject to the usual rules on limitation, so the cause of action in most cases arises at the date of completion of the works (section 1(5)). Where the claim is for damage to property, eg under DPA 1972 s4, the initial six-year limitation period runs from the date of damage.[40]

3.46 Where a claim arises from a personal injury, the three-year limitation period runs from the date of injury, even though the landlord's tortious act may have occurred many years earlier.[41] Disrepair and unfitness claims may involve both personal injury and other heads of damages. If all of these claims are brought in one action, LA 1980 s11 will apply a three-year limitation period to all causes of action, including a claim for inconvenience and distress.[42] One solution is to ask the opponent to agree not to raise the limitation point. Alternatively, the claimant can make an application under LA 1980 s33 to extend the three-year limitation period.[43] Some advisers start

38 See para 2.317.

39 12 years in the case of a lease.

40 *Pirelli General Cable Works v Faber (Oscar) & Partners* [1983] 2 AC 1, [1983] 1 All ER 65, HL; *Ketteman v Hansel Properties* [1984] 1 WLR 1274, [1985] 1 All ER 352, HL; and see para 2.312 of this book regarding hidden defects.

41 *Rimmer v Liverpool CC* [1985] QB 1, (1984) 12 HLR 23, CA.

42 See *DR v Southwark LBC* December 2015 *Legal Action* 41, *Housing Law Casebook* 7th edn, para R18.42, Central London County Court.

43 See, eg, *Millington v Islington LBC* August 1999 *Legal Action* 25, *Housing Law Casebook* 7th edn, para R1.7, Clerkenwell County Court.

two separate legal actions – one for personal injury and the second for any other claims – and then ask the court to consolidate the two actions and hear them together. To avoid any claim that disproportionate costs have been incurred, this should only be done if the opponent has refused to agree to separate limitation periods in respect of the different claims in one action.

Who will be the claimant?

3.47 A remedy in contract is usually only available to the parties to the contract. So the tenant will be the claimant or, in the case of a joint tenancy, all of the tenants must be claimants unless the court orders otherwise.[44] Third parties such as children, other family members or lodgers may enforce contractual provisions only if they can bring themselves within the terms of the Contracts (Rights of Third Parties) Act (C(RTP)A) 1999 which applies to tenancies entered into on or after 11 May 2000.[45] They may particularly be able to do this if they are named as authorised occupiers in the tenancy agreement.

3.48 The cases of *Jarvis v Swan Tours Ltd* and *Jackson v Horizon Holidays*[46] have been applied to housing disrepair cases to allow tenants to claim damages for inconvenience and distress not only for themselves, but also for their families.

3.49 In cases where a non-tenant has suffered injury or damage to property (as opposed to inconvenience and distress or economic loss), that person may have a right to bring a claim in his or her own name using the DPA 1972 s4 or the Occupiers' Liability Act 1957 s2 (the latter statue will only apply where the issue relates to the common parts retained in the landlord's control).

3.50 In *Chin v Hackney LBC*,[47] a tenant brought an action for damages for disrepair and the claim was settled on terms that the landlord would carry out agreed works and pay damages. The tenant's disabled daughter then issued new proceedings for damages for personal injury caused to her by the housing conditions. The Court of Appeal allowed the daughter to bring her claim, stating that the new case was not '*res judicata*' (ie, already decided) because it was not between the same parties as the earlier case. However, the court made it clear

44 CPR 19.3.

45 C(RTP)A 1999 s10(2).

46 *Jarvis v Swan Tours Ltd* [1973] QB 233, [1973] 1 All ER 71, CA; *Jackson v Horizon Holidays* [1975] 1 WLR 1468, [1975] 3 All ER 92, CA. The application of the principles developed in these cases, involving holidays, to the law of landlord and tenant was noted in *McCall v Abelesz* [1976] QB 585, [1976] 2 WLR 151, CA.

47 [1996] 1 WLR 789, [1996] 1 All ER 973, CA.

that, where more than one member of a household has a claim arising from the same facts, these should all be brought in a single action and a wasted costs order should be considered where separate actions are issued. Even so, where separate actions are brought to preserve the six-year limitation period for the disrepair or unfitness claim, it is unlikely that a court would consider such a sanction.

3.51 *Murphy and Peers v Stockport MBC*[48] contains a useful analysis of the obstacles facing non-tenants who wish to be parties in housing disrepair actions. Mrs Murphy was the tenant and brought an action for damages for disrepair against her council landlord. Her children, who endured the disrepair along with their mother, were named as the second and third claimants. It was held that, in the absence of any claim for personal injury or damage to their personal property, the children could not rely on the duty of care in DPA 1972 s4. They could not sue in nuisance because they had no proprietary interest in their home. They could not rely on any express term as they were not parties to the tenancy agreement with the council and C(RTP)A 1999 did not apply because the children were not identified by name, class or description in the agreement. They could not rely on the implied term in LTA 1985 s11 and, applying *Lee v Leeds CC*,[49] that statute was not to be read as in any way extended by the Human Rights Act 1998. The best that the children could expect would be to have 'some element of a remedy on the coat-tails' of Mrs Murphy, by application of the rule in *Jackson v Horizon Holidays* (see para 3.48).

Pre-action Protocol

3.52 In county court cases, except in real emergencies,[50] the judge will expect the tenant to have followed a procedure set out in the Pre-action Protocol for Housing Disrepair Cases before starting court proceedings. The Protocol can be found on the Ministry of Justice website and reproduced in appendix B to this book.[51] It applies to all civil disrepair claims, but not to counterclaims nor to proceedings in the magistrates' court brought under the Environmental Protection Act 1990.[52] It aims to encourage the early exchange of information and settlement of

48 August 2002 *Legal Action* 27 *Housing Law Casebook* 7th edn, para R1.8, Stockport County Court;.

49 [2002] EWCA Civ 6, [2002] HLR 17.

50 In which case see interim injunctions at para 3.120.

51 www.justice.gov.uk/courts/procedure-rules/civil/protocol/prot_hou#1.1.

52 Protocol para 3.2.

claims without the need for court action. It is expected that the protocol will be revised to explicitly encompass claims under the new implied term in relation to fitness for habitation. In the meantime it is advisable to follow its scheme in any event, and it will often be the case that claims involve an element of both disrepair and unfitness.

3.53 The Protocol requires a letter to be sent to the landlord at the earliest opportunity, warning of a possible claim. If the tenant has all the information needed to start proceedings this can be a letter of claim (LOC).

3.54 The Protocol does not extend the statutory limitation period, so, if that is about to expire, the tenant should issue proceedings immediately rather than following the Protocol, unless the landlord quickly confirms that he or she will not rely on limitation as a defence (see paragraph 10 of the Protocol). The claim can then be stayed while the parties follow the Protocol.[53]

3.55 Similarly, the Protocol expects timings to be shortened in urgent cases. So where the conditions are a serious risk to health, the Protocol does not prevent the issue of proceedings and an early injunction application. Even so, the adviser would be well advised to have written some sort of warning letter to the landlord before launching into court action.

3.56 Paragraph 11 of the Protocol makes it clear that if, as a result of following the Protocol, the tenant's claim settles without litigation on terms that would have justified issuing proceedings, the landlord will pay the tenant's reasonable costs and expenses. In *Birmingham CC v Lee*,[54] the landlord carried out repairs during the Protocol period and then declined to pay the tenant's legal costs, given that the value of her claim was less than £5,000[55] and the claim therefore would be decided on the small claims track where costs would not usually be payable (see para 3.149). The Court of Appeal held that costs were properly payable up until the point that the repairs were carried out, even though the damages part of the claim was technically a small claims track claim.

3.57 Given that legal aid will only fund counterclaims to prevent the loss of the home or action to remove a serious risk of harm, the Protocol has little place in publicly funded legal work on housing conditions. Para 3.99 below deals with how to start a publicly funded case.

3.58 The Protocol will be dealt with below alongside other matters that the adviser will have to consider as the case progresses.

53 For guidance on limitation periods see para 3.43.

54 [2008] EWCA Civ 891, [2009] HLR 15.

55 £5,000 was the limit at the time; it is now £10,000.

First contact with the landlord

3.59 The Protocol requires the tenant to give the landlord 20 working days to respond to the LOC. A specimen LOC is set out in the Protocol and is reproduced in a slightly adapted form in appendix C. It should contain the following information:[56]

- the tenant's name, address of property, tenant's address if different, tenant's telephone number and when access is available;
- details of the defects, including any defects outstanding (the Protocol has a schedule that can be used for this purpose in its Annex C);
- a history of the defects;
- details of any notification previously given to the landlord;
- the effect of the defects on the tenant (including any injury claim);
- identities of all other person who plan to make a personal injury claim;
- details of any special damages;
- the name of a proposed expert;
- the proposed letter of instruction to expert (the standard letter in Annex B of the Protocol can be used for this purpose); and
- the tenant's disclosure of any relevant documents that are readily available.

3.60 It makes sense to send this letter as soon as possible after the first interview even if the adviser cannot include all of the information set out above. The adviser can then allow the 20-working-day period to run while gathering further information about the general and special damages claim.

3.61 The LOC should also request disclosure from the landlord of all relevant records or documents; paragraph 5.3 of the Protocol sets out a list. The LOC should also include the tenant's authorisation for release of the information to the adviser.

Landlord's response

3.62 The landlord should usually reply to the LOC within 20 working days of receiving it, disclosing all relevant records or documents and responding to the tenant's proposal for instructing an expert. If there is no response, the adviser can continue to gather evidence and then issue proceedings as soon as there is enough information to enable

56 Protocol para 5.

the adviser to do so. If such a letter is not received, the tenant's adviser should issue proceedings as soon as possible.

Instruction of expert(s)

3.63 Once the 20-working-day period allowed in the LOC has passed, the next step will usually be to obtain an expert's report. If the adviser's usual expert has a long waiting list, it can be a useful tactic to make a provisional appointment at the same time as sending off the LOC. The Protocol suggests that expert evidence will not always be necessary, and photographs or video footage of any defects may be enough. However, most tenants do not have the technical knowledge needed to prove causation – that is, that the poor housing conditions in photographs are caused by actionable disrepair. Evidence from an expert carries weight, and it is not usually possible for the adviser to be certain of the merit of the case without it. Only in the simplest of matters should the adviser dispense with the need to instruct an expert.

3.64 Where unfitness is the issue, conditions such as lack of heating, serious damp and mould growth, or inadequate sanitary conveniences might be proved without the need for an expert, if appropriately dealt with in a witness statement and with photographs. However, an expert report will be usually be necessary.

Choice of an expert

3.65 There is no advantage to a tenant in instructing a 'tame' expert who is tenant-biased. This is only likely to lead to an unsuccessful outcome at trial. CPR 35.3 states:

> (1) It is the duty of experts to help the court on the matters within their expertise.
> (2) This duty overrides any obligation to the person from whom experts have received instructions or by whom they are paid.

3.66 The adviser should instruct an expert who is aware of these duties and who will present the facts impartially. The expert must identify the causes of the disrepair and it can be fatal to the case if he or she does not appreciate this.

3.67 For example, in *Ball and Another v Plymouth CC*,[57] Mr and Mrs Ball complained of cold and damp. Their surveyor's report stated 'sweepingly' that the flat was suffering from condensation caused by damp penetration through external walls which in his professional

57 [2004] EWHC 134 (QB).

opinion was LTA 1985 s11 'disrepair'. No further details of the damp penetration were given. The landlord's expert reported that he could find no evidence of disrepair. It was a fast track trial, so neither surveyor gave evidence at court. The judge held that the burden of proof had not been satisfied and the tenants' claim failed.

3.68 If the adviser has not used an expert before, it is wise to seek recommendations from other practitioners specialising in housing disrepair. Usually, the appropriate expert in a disrepair case will be a qualified chartered surveyor with experience of (or training in) how to give evidence in court. However, some environmental health officers (EHOs) also have the necessary experience and knowledge to perform this function, although there is always a danger that if the landlord instructs a chartered surveyor, the judge might consider the landlord's expert to be more qualified. In cases involving fitness for habitation in addition to disrepair or alone, the advantage of obtaining an EHO's report may outweigh the risk, because EHOs are trained in public health matters and the report can also be used in evidence in a magistrates' court prosecution under the EPA 1990.

Example

The tenant complains of water dripping from the ceiling in wet weather and of damp and mould throughout the property. The adviser suspects penetrating damp, but cannot rule out the possibility that the property is suffering from condensation due to bad design. It could be that the drips are in fact water condensing on the cold ceiling as a result of the increased humidity in cold and wet conditions.

The adviser instructs an EHO with experience of giving evidence in the county court. If the report shows that the dampness is caused by a combination of disrepair and condensation due to lack of ventilation, or a design or construction defect, then the adviser can use the report in the county court for both disrepair and unfitness claims. In addition, as long as the EHO states that the property is prejudicial to health, the tenant could use the report to bring a prosecution in the magistrates' court (see chapter 6). However, the availability of a range of remedies in the county court, along with the possibility of public funding in appropriate cases, means that the magistrates' court may not be a preferred route. Additionally, the adviser can send a copy of the report to the local housing authority and ask that action be taken under the Housing Acts (see chapter 5).

3.69 Paragraph 7 of the Protocol sets out detailed steps to take if the parties are communicating with each other. They are supposed to try to agree the identity of a single expert who will be jointly instructed by both of them, with each party bearing half of the cost. The parties should give reasons for any objection to a proposed expert. If agreement is not possible, each party should instruct their own expert, but a joint inspection should be agreed. The Protocol states that the inspection should take place within 20 working days of the landlord's response to the LOC.[58]

3.70 The specimen letters in the Protocol require a landlord to give reasons for any objection to the expert proposed by the tenant. Tenants' advisers should not allow the landlord to reject an expert without giving an explanation, because it is an advantage to the tenant for the adviser to choose an expert known to be unbiased and reliable.

3.71 There are advantages and disadvantages to agreeing a single joint expert with the opponent. An advantage is that it minimises costs, and makes it difficult for the opponent to object to the cost, because the expert's fee is shared equally between the parties. It also makes it harder for the landlord to challenge the findings of the expert. The disadvantage is that the adviser cannot discuss the case with the expert, in confidence, for example, by telephoning to obtain a 'feel' of just how serious the disrepair or unfitness is. The joint expert is under a duty to record in writing any discussions and to send them to the other party.

3.72 CPR Practice Direction (PD) 35 para 3 sets out the form and content of an expert's report, which must contain a statement of truth and details of the expert's qualifications.

Further information from the landlord

3.73 Paragraph 6 of the Protocol requires the landlord to admit or deny liability and to give the reasons why it is denied, if that is the case. The landlord should make any allegation about lack of knowledge of the problem or difficulties in gaining access. A full schedule of intended works including anticipated start and completion dates and a timetable for the works should be included, as should any offer of compensation and costs. This information can be provided in the landlord's initial response, but at the latest must be given within 20 working days of receipt of the single joint expert's report, or the experts' agreed schedule following a joint inspection.

58 See Protocol para 7.4(a).

Personal injury claims

3.74 Bad housing often causes ill health such as coughs, colds and even asthma. There are advantages and disadvantages in making such injury claims along with the claim for inconvenience, distress and loss.

3.75 A potential advantage is that, where the claim includes a personal injury element, CPR 44.13 could give a claimant qualified cost protection from the whole of the defendant's costs known as Qualified One-way Costs Shifting (QOCS). In *Wagenaar v Weekend Travel Ltd*[59] Vos LJ said:

> Thus, in my judgment, CPR r 44.13 is applying QOCS to a single [personal injury] claim against a Defendant . . . [that] may also have other claims brought by the same Claimant within that single claim.

3.76 The *Wagenaar* case gave an example of a road traffic claim for personal injury which included related property damage. The definition in CPR 44 would also include a housing disrepair or unfitness claim which had a personal injury element.[60]

3.77 However, where a personal injury claim is brought alongside other claims, such as a claim for damages for distress and inconvenience and special damages, CPR 44.16(2)(b) also applies and cost protection is not automatic.[61] In *The Commissioner of Police of the Metropolis v Brown*[62] the court explained that mechanism of CPR 44.16(2) is to leave it to the court at the end of the case to decide whether, and if so to what extent, it is just to permit enforcement of a defendant's costs order. The following example was given of how the discretion may be exercised:

> In an ordinary claim arising out of an RTA, it might be thought unlikely that a court would consider it just to remove QOCS protection, simply because the injured claimant also sought compensation for damage to their car. But the discretion is there, and in an unusual RTA, for example where the personal injury claim is modest but the main issue in the case relates to damage to the car, the court might consider it just to remove QOCS protection.

3.78 The result, therefore, is that the court may allow the enforcement of costs orders at least against the damages for the non-personal injury

59 [2014] EWCA Civ 1105, [2015] 1 WLR 1968, at para 40.

60 See the example given in *Jeffreys v Commissioner of Police of the Metropolis* [2017] EWHC 1505 (QB), [2018] 1 WLR 3633 at para 52.

61 *Jeffreys v Commissioner of Police of the Metropolis* [2017] EWHC 1505 (QB), [2018] 1 WLR 3633.

62 [2018] EWHC 2046 (Admin).

parts of the claim where the personal injury element is not the main element of the claim.

3.79 The disadvantage of bringing an injury claim along with a disrepair or unfitness claim is that causation is often hard to prove. If the injury claim fails, it is quite likely that the costs of that part of the claim will be disallowed and will either have to be borne by the tenant out of the damages for the disrepair or unfitness or borne by the adviser who will not be paid for the work involved in pursuing that part of the claim.

3.80 Paragraph 3.5 of the Protocol states that if the injury can be proved with a GP report, then the claim for injury can be made using the Pre-action Protocol. However, if a consultant's report is going to be needed, the adviser must follow both the disrepair Protocol and the more protracted personal injury protocol, the Pre-Action Protocol for Personal Injury Claims.[63]

3.81 Most GPs are unfamiliar with civil court proceedings and are not very good at establishing a causal link between ill health and disrepair or unfitness. This is perhaps not surprising, given that there are often several inter-related causes to health conditions such as asthma. Where the ill health seems to give rise to a large financial claim, the adviser will need to give serious consideration to instructing a consultant with experience of medico-legal claims, albeit with the resulting delay. Where the ill health is minor, it may be sensible not to try to make a causal link; instead, the claim can allege that the inconvenience of living in bad housing was greater, given that the tenant was suffering ill health at the time. This will not gain the benefit of costs protection but will avoid the difficulty of proving a relatively small part of the claim – however, care must be taken to ensure that a personal injury claim is not pleaded by accident or inference.

Chronology and file statement

3.82 If the landlord complies with pre-action disclosure as set out in the Protocol, then the adviser will receive a large amount of documentary information, sometimes going back many years. An increasing number of tenants now correspond by email, and this can add to the weight of written evidence. All of these documents have to be collated and considered, because they may help or weaken the tenant's case. The best way to deal with such documentation is to

63 This can be found on justice.gov.uk with the Civil Procedure Rules.

prepare a chronology setting out the dates and most important events, and cross-referencing them to the documents. A sample chronology is set out in appendix C of this book.

3.83 Whether or not a chronology is used, a file statement (sometimes referred to as a 'proof of evidence') should be prepared. This should set out the full history of the disrepair or unfitness, and the inconvenience and distress suffered by the tenant. The dates and some of the facts can be based on the tenant's questionnaire and the chronology, but an interview will usually be necessary to bring out the ways in which the disrepair or unfitness has affected this particular tenant.

3.84 The adviser should consider whether a home visit can be justified to assist with the preparation of the statement. The facts will be much clearer, and the inconvenience and distress will be much better articulated, if the adviser has seen the condition and the layout of the premises. Landlords' representatives invariably object to the cost of such a home visit when the costs are assessed, but costs officers are usually prepared to allow the cost of one home visit by the adviser (although travel costs are often disallowed).

3.85 The file statement will eventually form the basis of a witness statement to be shown to the opponent, and it should therefore be in the tenant's own words as far as possible. If the tenant is unable to recall exact dates, then this should be made clear in the file statement. At this stage the document should disclose the weaknesses as well as the strengths of the case. Advisers might want to put in italics items that they know should eventually be excluded from the witness statement.[64]

3.86 The file statement should refer to any items that have been damaged by the disrepair or unfitness, such as electrical devices destroyed by water or clothing destroyed by damp. If this is a long list, it might be easier to refer to a separate schedule.

3.87 Both the chronology and the file statement will need to be updated when the expert's report is available so that the tenant can comment on it and confirm its accuracy.

3.88 The adviser should also consider obtaining statements from other members of the tenant's family, friends and possibly even health visitors and social workers about the effect of the disrepair or unfitness on the tenant. The cost of this exercise has to be balanced against the value of the claim because the CPR requires the costs to be

64 As to the adviser's duties in relation to the contents of a witness statement, see para 3.162 below.

proportionate to the amount of money involved and the complexity of the issues.[65]

Obtaining evidence

3.89 If the landlord does not respond or refuses to provide disclosure under the Protocol, there may not be enough evidence to issue proceedings. If so, the adviser should consider an application for pre-action disclosure under CPR 31.16. This will not be necessary if the expert's evidence clearly indicates disrepair or unfitness and if the tenant is likely to make a convincing witness. Pre-action disclosure orders are the exception rather than the rule but a tightly drawn list of what is needed makes such an application more likely to succeed. CPR 46.1(2) states that the starting point is that the applicant for disclosure will pay the costs of the person against whom the order is sought. However, it is possible to persuade the court to make a different order.[66] Failure by the landlord to comply with a Protocol is a relevant factor that should overturn this presumption.

Negotiations

3.90 Where the landlord is co-operating with the Protocol, the adviser will be well aware of the need to keep negotiating, while at the same time preparing the case for the prompt issue of proceedings. However, negotiations may not be enough to satisfy the court that the Protocol has been followed. Paragraph 2 of the Protocol makes it clear that litigation should be a last resort, and the parties should consider whether some form of alternative dispute resolution (ADR) procedure would be more suitable than litigation. ADR options mentioned in the Protocol include mediation, or for council or housing association tenants, internal complaints procedures or the Housing Ombudsman.

3.91 There can be costs sanctions for failing to consider ADR at the pre-action stage[67] so it might be wise for the adviser to propose it or to make a note on file if it seems inappropriate in a particular case. At this stage, the use of ADR should also be discussed with the client because the adviser will have to confirm to the court that this has

65 CPR 1.1(2) (c) and CPR 44.4(3).
66 CPR 46.1(3).
67 See Protocol para 4.1.

been done once the proceedings are underway. ADR is discussed in more detail in para 3.152.

Use of counsel

3.92 An inexperienced adviser should consult a barrister specialising in housing disrepair well before proceedings are issued. The barrister should be instructed to advise in writing on the merits and value of the claim (which is still archaically referred to as 'quantum' by most lawyers). If there is no approved list of housing counsel within the adviser's organisation, and the adviser cannot obtain a personal recommendation, then the annual 'Housing repairs: update' published in *Legal Action* has a list in its footnotes of barristers who have been active in recent cases and this is a good place to start.

3.93 Even an experienced housing adviser will often instruct counsel before issuing proceedings, either because of a restriction on a legal aid certificate or because it can be hard to find a barrister willing to act under a CFA if they have not been involved from an early stage and been able to have a say in the direction of the case.

Contact with the client

3.94 While the adviser is gathering the information necessary to issue proceedings, it is important to keep in contact with the tenant. Often the landlord will be carrying out repairs, sometimes to a poor standard, and the adviser will have to take details, since these may increase the claim further.

3.95 The adviser may have to deal with allegations that the tenant has refused admission to workmen and to persuade the tenant to continue to give access. The landlord's right to access is dealt with at paras 2.322–2.329. Any failure by the tenant to provide access which is unreasonable can lead to a reduction in damages and in some cases the claim could fail (see para 7.60). Failure to give access may lead to landlord to seek an injunction.[68]

3.96 Advisers should be careful not to allow the Protocol to delay the issue of proceedings unreasonably. It is important that the tenant sees that progress is being made, because if the momentum is lost through ineffective exchanges of correspondence, the tenant may lose confidence in the adviser and even give up a legitimate claim altogether.

68 *Liverpool Mutual Homes v Mensah* [2017] 8 WLUK 325, May 2019 *Legal Action* 29.

Letter before action

3.97 Once the investigations are complete, although not a Protocol requirement, the adviser should send a letter giving any details that were omitted from the LOC. This will often include a fuller history of notice given and more details of the inconvenience, distress, financial loss and ill health suffered by the tenant as a result of the disrepair or unfitness. The letter should ask for proposals for compensation and should ask for a full schedule of works, together with the anticipated date for completion of the works proposed.

3.98 The letter should make it clear that if satisfactory proposals are not received from the landlord within a relatively short period, perhaps 21 days, court proceedings will be started without further notice. If the landlord has not engaged with the Protocol by this stage, or if everything was included in the LOC, there is no need to send such a letter.

Legal aid cases

3.99 Since April 2013, legal aid has only been available to fund cases where:

- there are possession proceedings and the tenant has a defence to the claim, or a counterclaim based on adverse housing conditions; or
- the housing conditions present a serious risk of harm to the tenant or other occupiers of the tenant's dwelling.

3.100 In either situation, it would be normal for an adviser with a legal aid contract to grant emergency funding under delegated functions so that legal action can be taken without delay. In possession cases where a defence and counterclaim is raised, the legal aid may well pay for the tenant to defend the case through to trial (see paras 4.1–4.89). In 'serious harm' cases, the funding is likely to be limited to obtaining an interim injunction (see para 3.120). The adviser will need to draft particulars of claim, a witness statement and the application for the injunction. The adviser will need an expert to confirm the serious risk. It follows that much of the work set out in this chapter will have to be done. Once an injunction order has been implemented, the adviser will have to decide whether it is possible to continue the proceedings.

3.101 Few tenants will feel capable of acting in person in a county court claim. In some cases, the adviser will assist the tenant pro bono or put a conditional fee or a privately paying arrangement in place. If damages are eventually recovered, the cost of the work carried out under legal aid will attract the statutory charge and will have to be refunded to the Legal Aid Agency (LAA). If it is not possible or practical to continue the claim without public funding the adviser will need to end the proceedings by serving a notice of discharge of certificate along with a notice of discontinuance. The tenant will be protected from the costs claim that would usually follow by virtue of Legal Aid, Sentencing and Punishment of Offenders Act (LASPO) 2012 s21.[69]

3.102 For further consideration of the availability of legal aid funding, see paras 4.1–4.89.

Bringing a claim

Issuing proceedings

3.103 If the adviser is using counsel, this is the point at which instructions to settle court papers should be sent to the barrister, so that the adviser is ready to start proceedings as soon as any deadline in the final letter before claim has expired. Similarly, if there is a limitation on the legal aid funding certificate, this is the point at which the adviser should apply for the restriction to be lifted, unless the adviser's organisation has delegated powers to do this itself.

3.104 The adviser should check the scope and costs limitation on any legal aid funding certificate or any restriction on any legal expenses insurance policy before issuing the claim. If on legal aid, the adviser should also ensure that a notice of issue of the legal aid funding certificate has been served on the landlord, and if not, one should be prepared and served with the court papers.

3.105 Once the court timetable starts running, the adviser will have to meet tight deadlines and the effects of delay, especially where the rules have in built sanctions, can be draconian.[70] It is therefore wise to ensure at this stage that the tenant and any witnesses have confirmed the accuracy of, and signed, file statements, see para 3.82. If the opponent has complied with the Protocol it should be possible to include most of what will be needed to prove the case and taking

69 And see Civil Legal Aid (Costs) Regulations 2013 SI No 611 regs 5–8.

70 See *Mitchell v News Group Newspapers* [2013] EWCA Civ 1537, [2014] 1 WLR 795 as modified by *Denton and others v TH White Ltd and others, Decadent Vapours Ltd v Bevan and Others, Utilise TDS Limited v Davies and others* [2014] EWCA Civ 906, [2014] 1 WLR 3926.

such a step will enable the adviser to put in some sort of evidence if witnesses fail to co-operate later.

3.106 The adviser should remember that any proceedings brought on behalf of a child need to be brought by a person acting as the child's litigation friend and a Certificate of Suitability[71] needs to be filed.[72]

Which court?

3.107 The county court has jurisdiction to hear claims of any value and it is the obvious forum for disrepair and unfitness claims. If the claim is for compensation only, up to a value of £100,000, it can be started electronically using the Money Claims Online (MCOL) system.[73] In April 2018 the government introduced a new online service for small claims which are for compensation only, up to a value of £10,000, called Money Claims.[74] The intention is to expand this system to include higher value claims and for it to eventually replace the MCOL system. Currently, a claim for up to £10,000 can be made on either system. The online systems are not, however, available to tenants who need help with court fees.

3.108 If the claim is started on paper, it should be sent to the county court money claims centre.[75] If specific performance or an injunction is being sought, then the papers need to be sent to the county court hearing centre for the district in which the tenant's home is situated.[76]

3.109 Where there are complex construction issues, the claim can be started at a county court hearing centre specialising in construction matters. It will proceed as a county court case but in the Technology and Construction Court (TCC). CPR PD 60 para 3.4 lists the courts where a TCC judge is usually available.

The claim form

3.110 The claim form to use is form N1 and the template can be found on the Courts Service website.[77] It can be completed online and then printed. It must:

71 Court form N235.

72 CPR 21.5(3).

73 This can be accessed at: www.moneyclaim.gov.uk.

74 This can be accessed at: www.gov.uk/make-money-claim.

75 Currently at PO Box 527, Salford M5 0BY.

76 CPR 56.2(1)(c).

77 The easiest way to locate this form is to type 'Form N1' into an internet search engine and ensure that you are on the justice.gov.uk site.

- set out on the top right hand side that the case is being issued in the county court (assuming that this so) (if the case is being issued in the TCC, then this must be set out under the name of the hearing centre);[78]
- contain a concise statement of the nature of the claim;
- specify the remedy which the claimant seeks;
- refer to the fact that the particulars of claim are set out in a separate document;
- where the claimant is making a claim for money, contain a statement of value in accordance with CPR 16.3;
- name the claimant's preferred hearing centre;
- include an address at which the claimant resides; and
- where the landlord is an individual, include an address (with postcode) at which the landlord resides or carries on business (if this is known) – this applies even if the landlord's solicitors agree to accept service on the landlord's behalf.

3.111 Under CPR 16.3(4), where the tenant is seeking an order requiring the landlord to carry out work to the premises, the claimant must also state in the claim form –

(a) whether the estimated costs of those repairs or other work is –
  (i) not more than £1,000; or
  (ii) more than £1,000; and
(b) whether the value of any other claim for damages is –
  (i) not more than £1,000; or
  (ii) more than £1,000.

3.112 A court fee will be payable to 'HM Courts and Tribunal Service'. If the tenant needs an order for works, two fees are payable – one for the money claim and one for the claim for specific performance which is treated as an additional (non-money) claim.[79]

3.113 The claim form can be served by the court if so requested or returned to the claimant's adviser for service. It must be served within four months of the date it was issued.[80] Extensions are rarely granted and there is a very high burden to be satisfied if the application is made after the four-month period has expired.[81]

78 CPR 60 PD para 3.2.

79 For the amount of the fee, see leaflet EX50 on the Courts Service website. The easiest way to check the fee is to type 'court form EX50' into an internet search engine.

80 CPR 7.5(1).

81 CPR 7.6(3).

Particulars of claim

3.114 In 'disrepair', cases it is not practical to include full details of the case in the claim form and it is advisable to prepare a separate document setting out the particulars of the claim. This will be the same in 'unfitness' cases also, and claims may well be made for both disrepair and unfitness. The particulars of claim must be served within 14 days of service of the claim form or within the four-month limit for service of the claim form, whichever is the earliest.[82]

3.115 The particulars of claim should include a concise statement of the facts upon which the claimant relies and:

- all causes of action which are relevant, including express obligations, LTA 1985 s9A and s11, DPA 1972 s4, breach of covenants for quiet enjoyment, nuisance and where applicable, DPA 1972 s1;
- a description of the property, the occupiers and the current rent level;
- details of disrepair, unfitness, notice and damage; and
- that the claimant is seeking interest pursuant to County Courts Act 1984 s69;[83] if interest is not specifically pleaded, the claimant may lose the right to it.

3.116 The following documents should be annexed to and served with the particulars of claim:

- any written tenancy agreement (although contrary to the rule, many advisers save paper and the court's time by only appending the repairing clause and other relevant clauses of the agreement);[84]
- if a personal injury claim is included, a CPR-compliant medical report;[85] and
- a detailed schedule of any losses and expenses.[86]

It is also good practice to file the expert's report as an annex to the particulars of claim.

3.117 If exemplary or aggravated damages are claimed, which should be done rarely (see para 7.56), then these must be specifically pleaded.

3.118 A statement of value is only required on the claim form so that the court officers can calculate the correct court fee, but it is often also

82 CPR 7.4(1)(b) and (2).

83 It is not enough to state 'interest pursuant to statute', see CPR 16.4(2)(a)(ii).

84 CPR PD 16 para 7.3.

85 CPR PD 16 para 4.3.

86 CPR PD 16 para 4.2.

included in the particulars of claim. A specimen particulars of claim is set out in appendix C below.

3.119 It is important that the claim is precise and, if at all possible, advisers should avoid the need to amend the particulars subsequently, because this can have adverse costs consequences. Even so, it is often impossible to provide full details of some of the facts, for example of telephone calls made by the tenant to report the disrepair or unfitness. Defendants' barristers often attack particulars of claim, on the basis that they are too vague. The courts in general and Lord Woolf in particular[87] have disapproved of an overly strict approach to pleadings on the basis that as long as the parties know the case they have to meet, more can be provided in the witness statement[88] or in further information requested under CPR 18.

Interim injunctions

3.120 In cases of severe disrepair or unfitness, causing serious and continuing interference with the tenant's enjoyment of the property, or a fault or deficiency that presents a serious risk to health, the court can make an order forcing the landlord to carry out repairs before the full merits of the case have been tested at trial. This remedy is known as an interim injunction. An application for such an injunction will ensure that the matter is brought before a judge in a matter of days rather than months.

3.121 Despite the attractions of this method for securing immediate remedial works, the tenant needs to be aware that the interim injunction is an exceptional remedy granted purely to avoid the risk of further danger or damage and that, for these purposes, the landlord may successfully convince the court that basic 'patch' repairs or temporary works which reduce or eliminate the risk of harm until trial will be enough.

3.122 The case of *American Cyanamid Co v Ethicon Ltd*[89] sets out the matters that the tenant will be required to satisfy in order to obtain a mandatory interim injunction – namely that:

- there is a serious question to be tried (ie, a more than frivolous assertion that the landlord is in breach of a repairing or fitness obligation);

87 See *McPhilemy v Times Newspapers Ltd* [1999] EWCA Civ 1464, [1999] 3 All ER 775.

88 *Uddin and Another v Islington LBC* [2015] EWCA Civ 369, [2015] HLR 28.

89 [1975] AC 396, [1975] 2 WLR 316, HL.

- damages alone would not be adequate compensation (eg, because of a serious risk to health) or that the landlord would not be in a financial position to meet the damages to which the tenant would be entitled; and
- the tenant will be in a position to meet the costs incurred by the landlord in performing works required by the injunction, if it is later found that the order should not have been made.

If there is doubt about these last two factors, the balance of convenience (ie, comparative hardship) favours the tenant.

3.123 The leading authority on injunctions in disrepair cases is *Parker v Camden LBC*[90] and this, together with *Redland Bricks v Morris*,[91] requires that:

- the repair work required must be agreed by the parties or it must be clear what needs to be done (so there must be no substantial dispute between experts);
- the court will not order substantial works, eg the replacement of an entire heating system;
- the circumstances must be exceptional, eg an immediate risk to health;
- the terms of order sought must be sufficiently clear for the landlord to know exactly what remedial work has to be done and by what date; and
- the cost of carrying out the works must be taken into account.

It is expected that the same principles will apply in cases of unfitness.

3.124 Historically, judges have not followed such a strict approach in cases relating to housing conditions and, for example in London, interim injunctions have been routinely made by some courts against social landlords. Furthermore, where it is not possible to specify exactly what repair work is needed, the tenant can apply for an injunction requiring the landlord to investigate the cause of disrepair or the deficiency and/or the risk of harm and then by a specified date provide the court with a report setting out the work needed to remedy it with proposals for doing so.[92] This often proves just as effective as making an application for specified work to be ordered.

90 [1986] Ch 162, (1985) 17 HLR 380, CA.

91 [1970] AC 652, [1969] 2 WLR 1437, HL.

92 See appendix C for an example of an injunction.

3.125 In *Parker*, the court stated that an injunction may be granted where there is:

> . . . an undoubted breach of covenant giving rise to actual and immediate major discomfort and inconvenience and to a real risk of damage to health flowing from the admitted breach . . .[93]

3.126 An example of the procedure being usefully employed can be found in the county court case of *Sheridan v Broadbridge*.[94] There the landlord accepted that a range of remedial work was needed but did not accept that the works should be subject to an injunction. The judge was satisfied that at least one item (a rear staircase in danger of collapse) was sufficiently serious to pass the *Parker* test and made a mandatory order in respect of that and all the other outstanding works. He expressly held that, provided at least one item justified the making of the order, the injunction should cover all the work agreed to be required.

3.127 In practice, interim injunctions will usually be limited to works which would be relatively straightforward and effective in eliminating the risk of harm. In cases of fitness for habitation, for example where condensation dampness is the problem, improving or repairing ventilation, or installing a larger radiator.

3.128 If the application fails, the evidence put before the court suggesting risk to health or safety should at least justify a direction for an early trial. Any costs awarded against the tenant may be set off against a final award of costs or damages and in a legal aid case will not be assessed until the end of the case. However, the adviser should not hesitate to make an application for an injunction where there is a real risk to health or safety.

Interim injunction procedure

3.129 In an extremely urgent case, it is possible to go before the court without any paperwork, although the judge is likely to make the adviser undertake to file papers on the same or the next working day.[95]

3.130 In slightly less urgent cases, the adviser will need to complete a form N16A. The court will also expect to see a draft order and a witness statement from the tenant, explaining the reason for the urgency, confirming the injury or damage that will result if the work

93 [1986] Ch 162, (1985) 17 HLR 380, CA at 389.

94 September 1995 *Legal Action* 16, *Housing Law Casebook* 7th edn, para R21.1, Clerkenwell County Court.

95 CPR PD 25A para 4.3.

is not ordered and explaining why the tenant cannot carry out the work and then bring a damages claim. The expert's report should be exhibited to the tenant's witness statement or a separate witness statement should be prepared and signed by the expert. Once again, the expert's statement should make it clear why there is immediate danger to the tenant. Where it has not been possible to obtain a report, in the most obvious cases it may be sufficient to rely on photographs and a statement from the tenant.

3.131 In interim applications such as this, the tenant is under a duty to include all relevant information in the statement, including unhelpful matters. This is because the opponent will not have the opportunity to cross-examine the tenant, so the court expects the tenant to put all the facts before the judge.

3.132 In legal aid cases, the adviser must ensure that the scope of the legal aid as set out on the representation certificate includes applying for an injunction. If it does not, an application for an amendment must be granted by the LAA before the injunction application is made, otherwise the adviser will not be paid.

3.133 As a result of *American Cyanamid Co v Ethicon Ltd*,[96] it has become the practice for an injunction order to include an undertaking by the applicant to reimburse the respondent for any expense incurred as a result of obeying the injunction, should it later be decided that the order should not have been made. This is not an appropriate undertaking for a tenant of limited means to make and, if this is pointed out, most judges accept that it should not be required.[97] However, the tenant should be warned that, as already mentioned, if the application is unsuccessful or the judge makes no order on costs, then the costs of the injunction application could be payable by the tenant, which, at best will reduce the damages and at worst, leave the tenant with a bill to pay.

3.134 If the injunction application is successful, the adviser must ensure that the order makes provision for costs. If the injunction order is silent on the question of costs, then none will be payable, even if the tenant goes on to win the final claim. Judges often make an order for 'costs reserved', which means that, at the end of the case, the settlement order or the final court order will need to provide that those costs are payable by the landlord. This ('costs reserved') should be avoided if at all possible; particularly if the legal aid restrictions mean that the case is unlikely to go any further. If such an order is

96 [1975] AC 396, [1975] 2 WLR 316, HL.

97 See *Allen v Jambo Holdings Ltd* [1980] 1 WLR 1252, [1980] 2 All ER 502, CA.

made, and the case continues, the adviser should make a note on the file so that these costs are not forgotten.

3.135 If the court proceedings are already under way when the injunction application is made, a further court fee will be payable. If the application is made at the same time as the claim is lodged, then a fee additional to the usual one will be payable. Leaflet EX50,[98] sets out the level of fees, but it is surprisingly unclear about the fee for an injunction. Most practitioners assume that it is an 'application on notice where no other fee is specified'.

3.136 The adviser will have to decide whether to make the application for an injunction 'on notice', in which case the court is likely to set a date some weeks ahead or 'without notice' (also known as '*ex parte*'), in which case the court will fix the first available date to put the case before the judge. Often, the only way of securing a realistically early hearing date is to apply without notice, even though the adviser should still notify the landlord both of the intention to seek the injunction and of the hearing. The court will want to know what has been done to get the landlord to carry out the works being requested and what warnings have been given about seeking an injunction, even in an urgent case.

3.137 The adviser must ensure that the landlord is served with a copy of the notice of application for the injunction, including notice of the hearing date and with all the supporting papers. A certificate of service[99] should be filed at court before the hearing.

3.138 Although it is not usual for oral evidence to be given at an interim injunction hearing, the adviser should arrange for both the tenant and the expert to be at court. The tenant needs to be there to give instructions to the adviser and because it helps the judge to see how much the case matters to the tenant. The expert needs to be there, or at least be available at the end of a telephone, because it is usual for the landlord to come to court and try to negotiate some form of order or undertaking and the expert's assistance will be needed when wording an injunction/undertaking which identifies particular work.

3.139 The adviser should be wary of accepting an undertaking from a corporate body unless someone with executive responsibility, such as a director of a company or the head of housing of a local authority, is present at court to give the undertaking. Otherwise, it may well not be enforceable at a later date.

98 The easiest way to locate this is to type 'court form EX50' into an internet search engine.

99 See form N215.

3.140 If the landlord will not submit to an injunction, and if an undertaking is not acceptable to the tenant, then it is unlikely that an order will be made at the first hearing and the application will probably be adjourned to a later date with more time available. Usually, by the time the matter is scheduled to return to court, the works will have been done, because landlords take injunction applications extremely seriously.

3.141 Where the injunction has been obtained using the 'without notice' procedure and the landlord was not present at the hearing, then the court will order that the matter comes back to court shortly afterwards so that the landlord can attend.

Interim applications

3.142 Once the period for filing an acknowledgment of service of the claim has passed, the adviser should consider making an application for an interim payment under CPR 25.6 and 25.7. The court can award an interim payment only if the landlord has admitted liability, judgment has been obtained for damages to be assessed or for a sum of money or the court is satisfied that, if the matter went to trial, the tenant would be likely to obtain judgment for a substantial amount. This is often the case in disrepair claims and the psychological advantage of obtaining an interim payment at this stage is tremendous. Usually, any damages recovered in this way will be held by the solicitor until the costs have also been paid.

3.143 If the tenant's claim is purely for money and the landlord fails to file a defence, the tenant's adviser should enter judgment in default; see CPR 12.4(1). If there is outstanding disrepair or unfitness and the tenant is making a claim for specific performance, the adviser will have to apply on notice for the defendant to be debarred from defending, see CPR 12.4(2) (a) and CPR 23. In either case, the court will still have to consider the claim at a disposal hearing[100] and may direct that certain steps be taken to enable it to do this, such as that a witness statement is filed.

3.144 If a defence is filed but the adviser thinks that it is very weak, an application for summary judgment can be made at this stage. CPR 24.2 allows a court to give summary judgment if it considers that the defendant has no real prospect of successfully defending the claim and there is no other compelling reason why there should be a trial. There is, therefore, a high burden on the tenant but an application can be a useful tactic where the adviser knows from

100 CPR 12.7 and PD 24 para 7.

experience that the landlord is simply buying time and ultimately will not fight a trial.

3.145 The adviser should ensure that the tenant is aware that costs could be awarded in favour of the landlord if the application for an interim remedy is unsuccessful and this will reduce any damages eventually obtained.

3.146 The court rules require that, 24 hours before the hearing of an application, a schedule of costs in form N260 must be served on the opponent and a copy filed at court.[101]

Allocation and alternative dispute resolution

3.147 Once the court has seen the landlord's defence, a directions questionnaire (DQ) will be sent to each party. The purpose is for the court to obtain enough information to manage the case actively from this point. It is very important that the completed form is returned to court within the time specified because the court can strike out the tenant's claim if the adviser fails to do this.[102]

3.148 The notice accompanying the DQ indicates which of the court's three procedural tracks its court officer has considered is the most appropriate for the case and asks the parties to apply if they disagree. If there are works outstanding, then as long as the cost of the works exceeds £1,000, the claim will be allocated to the fast track or to the multi-track.

3.149 If the cost of works is likely to be less than £1,000, then the case will be allocated to the court's small claims track, unless the value of the damages claim exceeds £1,000. If there are no works outstanding, then the case will be allocated to the small claims track *unless* the value of the claim exceeds £10,000.[103] Costs are not payable on the small claims track, so most advisers cannot afford to assist with cases that are allocated to that track.

3.150 CPR 26.6(4) states that the fast track is the normal track for cases with a value of less than £25,000 if they can be tried in less than a day and there is no need for extensive oral evidence from experts. Judges seem to allocate disrepair cases to the fast track as a matter of course, even though most of them have a complex history and are unlikely to be disposed of in one day. Given the limited advocacy costs payable for fast track trials, advisers should argue in the DQ that any case with a

101 CPR PD 24 para 9.2 and PD 44 para 9.5.

102 CPR 26.3.

103 CPR 26.6(1)(a) and (b).

long history and multiple documents is too complex to be allocated to the fast track. Claims purely for specific performance, where there are complex issues of building construction may not be suitable for the fast track, unless a joint expert has been appointed, in which case it should just about be possible to complete the trial within a day.

3.151 All cases being dealt with by the TCC are treated as being allocated to the multi track.[104]

3.152 The DQ asks whether the parties want a one-month stay to attempt to settle the case and whether the court should arrange a mediation appointment. ADR is regarded with some suspicion by tenants' advisers, on the basis that requests for stays are often delaying tactics on the part of landlords. Where works are still outstanding by this stage, many months after the adviser's first contact with the landlord, nothing short of a mandatory order is likely to resolve the matter. It is doubtful that a landlord will agree through mediation to an order that could ultimately result in imprisonment for default. The tenant's adviser will therefore want to press on towards trial without risking further delay through mediation. However, any offer by the landlord to mediate should be seriously considered as the court can take an unreasonable refusal by the tenant into account when it is exercising its discretion in awarding costs.

3.153 Where the remedial work has been done and the claim is purely financial, mediation can bring a settlement about in much less time and at much less cost than through litigation and is to be encouraged. The procedure at a mediation is non-adversarial and the adviser's role will be very different from the role of representing the tenant at a trial. Even so, the adviser will need to prepare the case for the mediation, warning the tenant of both the strengths and weaknesses and helping the tenant to decide how far to compromise in order to reach a settlement. The usual rule for mediation is that each party bears their own legal costs but it is sometimes possible to persuade the landlord to agree in advance to pay them, regardless of the outcome. In any event, advisers must ensure that the costs of the mediation are to be treated as part of the costs of the proceedings, so that they can be recovered if the mediation is not successful. Further information about mediation can be found on the Ministry of Justice website and on the website of the Civil Mediation Council.[105]

3.154 Both parties should try, if possible, to agree the timetable for carrying out the steps necessary to prepare the case for trial (these

104 CPR 60.6(1).

105 www.civilmediation.justice.gov.uk and www.civilmediation.org.

steps are known as 'directions'). There are standard wordings on the Ministry of Justice website[106] and courts like these to be kept to.

3.155 If the parties have not selected a joint expert, the directions should provide either that one is now appointed or that the parties have permission to rely on their own expert evidence. CPR PD 35.8 requires that the directions order is served on the expert.

3.156 The DQ asks for an estimate of the likely trial costs for cases likely to be allocated to the multi track. In such cases the court requires a costs budget on a prescribed form.[107] The adviser should send this to the opponent and attempt to agree the budget if possible. Failure to file the costs budget with the DQ (or before, if there has been an earlier hearing) carries the draconian sanction that no costs other than court fees are likely to be recoverable.[108]

3.157 The adviser should serve a copy of the proposed DQ and any costs budget on the landlord's representative as soon as possible and in any event a few days before it is due to be filed at court.

3.158 Once the DQ and fee have been filed at court, there is likely to be a delay of a few weeks while the papers are put before a district judge and a directions order is made. Of course, the adviser can start carrying out the proposed directions while waiting for the sealed order, but if the landlord delays there is unlikely to be a sanction.

3.159 A district judge will: (a) consider the DQ; (b) confirm or change the track allocation; and (c) order directions. If the claim is allocated to the multi track, a costs and case management conference will be listed to approve the budgets. Once the sealed directions order is received, the adviser should diarise the directions and ensure compliance with them. In order to maintain progress, the adviser should consider applying to the court if the landlord is failing to comply with the time limits. Maintaining the pressure on the opponent is likely to bring the landlord to the negotiating table and, if repairs are outstanding, the sooner that a mandatory order is obtained, the better for the tenant's welfare.

Disclosure

3.160 The court's directions will provide for each party to disclose any documents that have not already been revealed in the Protocol

106 Search 'standard directions order'.

107 Precedent H, see CPR PD 3E.

108 CPR 3.14 as illustrated in *Mitchell v News Group Newspapers* [2013] EWCA Civ 1537, [2014] 1 WLR 795.

process – see CPR 31.6. Corporate landlords often fail to divulge all relevant documents that they have in their possession. For example, the tenant may have made a formal complaint, in which case the landlord's complaints department will have a file relating to the disrepair or unfitness. Similarly, any expert employed by a corporate landlord is likely to have a separate file, and unless the papers were prepared in contemplation of court proceedings, the documents will be disclosable. The adviser has to consider carefully at this stage whether the cost of forcing the landlord to produce such documents is justified by the improvement in the tenant's prospects of success. There may be enough evidence almost to guarantee a successful outcome without the need for specific disclosure. In heavily contested cases, however, this possibility should not be overlooked, see CPR 31.12.

3.161 Advisers should remember that tenants are obliged to disclose all relevant documents that either help or hinder their case, unless the documents are privileged.[109] The tenant must sign the disclosure form personally[110] and must resist any temptation to omit unhelpful documents from the list. The duty of disclosure is ongoing and any documents that come into existence after the list has been served must be disclosed, unless they are privileged.

Witness statements

3.162 The statements that have already been prepared now need to be put in a form that is suitable for witness statements.[111] The tenant's evidence will need to be updated so that the tenant includes factual information that refutes allegations made in the defence and gives context to any documents disclosed by the landlord. The tenant will also need to update the position on the works of repair, mention any distress caused by repair works that have been carried out in an inconsiderate manner and, if necessary, give further details of the claim for special damages.

3.163 At this stage, refer back to the particulars of claim to make sure you have included all the disrepair or unfitness which you originally relied on and still want to pursue. Make sure you have dealt with the issue of notice for each element, and access if this has been raised in

109 Legal privilege includes communications between the tenant and adviser and papers prepared in contemplation of litigation. Further detail is beyond the scope of this book.

110 CPR 31.10(6).

111 CPR PD 32 paras 17–22.

the defence. In unfitness cases, the landlord may also have alleged that the problem has arisen due to the tenant's 'un-tenant like' behaviour or other breach of the tenant's covenants (see para 2.330). This should be fully addressed in the statement.

3.164 Don't forget to deal in detail with how the disrepair or unfitness caused the loss or damage that you are claiming for (see special damages at para 7.51), including distress and inconvenience.

3.165 CPR 32.4 states that only material that would be admissible if the witness was giving oral evidence should be included in a witness statement. It is not its function to make submissions or arguments about why the tenant has a strong case; to do so is to confuse the role of a witness with the role of an advocate.[112]

3.166 Witness statements stand in place of initial oral evidence given under oath. The evidence must be 'the truth the whole truth and nothing but the truth'.[113] Unless the statement is being adduced at an interim hearing, the statement need not reveal unhelpful facts.[114] Such matters are for the opponent's advocate to draw out through cross examination. However care should be taken that excluding material does not render untrue or misleading anything which remains in the statement.

3.167 The witness statement will contain a statement of truth declaring that the witness believes the statement to be true. The witness must sign this statement. It is a contempt of court punishable by imprisonment for a person to deliberately to make false statements in a witness statement and the adviser is under a duty to explain this to a witness.[115]

3.168 It is hoped that the adviser will not be in a position where a witness is no longer co-operating. However, CPR 32.9 provides for service of a witness summary setting out what the adviser expects the witness to say, if a signed witness statement cannot be obtained.

3.169 If the witness statement or witness summary is not served within the time specified in the directions, then the witness may not be called to give evidence unless the court gives permission.[116] An application for permission will have to be made relying on the principles relevant to applications for relief from sanctions.

112 *JD Wetherspoon Plc v Harris and Others* [2013] EWHC 1088 (Ch), [2013] 1 WLR 3296.

113 See, for example, the Chancery Guide, chapter 19.

114 See Bar Standards Board 'The Preparation of Witness Statements': www.barstandardsboard.org.uk.

115 CPR 32.14.

116 CPR 32.10.

Preparations for trial

3.170 Once witness evidence has been exchanged, the adviser should consider instructing a barrister to advise on the strength of the case in the light of all the papers. The adviser might want to arrange a site visit by the barrister. Some barristers are reluctant to spend the time in doing this, but others say that it is invaluable.

3.171 The court will send out a Listing Questionnaire, also known as the pre-trial checklist,[117] which must be completed and returned within a tight time-scale. It ensures that the case is ready to be tried. Advisers must be in no doubt that the court will regard postponement of a trial as a last resort and will very likely impose costs sanctions for any such delay. The adviser should consider whether any further directions are required, for example, that the tenant should have permission to call oral evidence from the expert. A detailed costs estimate must be filed with the checklist and in multi-track cases this should be accompanied by a trial timetable. The trial advocate is the most appropriate person to draft this timetable. A hearing fee for the trial is payable when the checklist is filed.

3.172 The adviser should never be tempted to delay progress towards a trial while negotiating with the landlord or landlord's representatives. The best settlements are achieved while the landlord is under the pressure of an approaching trial.

Settling a case

3.173 Early settlement through ADR is discussed at para 3.147. Part 36 of the CPR encourages early settlements of litigation by placing costs and interest penalties on a party who refuses to accept a reasonable offer. There are good reasons for a tenant to take advantage of this provision: the interest penalty can benefit the tenant by increasing the damages, and the costs penalty can mean that costs which might otherwise be borne by the tenant are paid by the landlord on the 'indemnity basis'.[118]

3.174 There are formalities that should be observed when wording a Part 36 offer (see CPR 36.5 and a form[119] which if used, avoids mistakes). A time limited offer can now be a valid Part 36 offer[120] – as

117 Form N170.

118 For an explanation of the difference between 'standard' and 'indemnity' costs see CPR 44.3.

119 Form N242A.

120 CPR 36.9 (4)(b) as amended in April 2015.

long as an offer stays open for 21 days it can now state that it is withdrawn thereafter.[121]

3.175 A Part 36 offer can be made before the proceedings are issued but, in any event, serious consideration should be given to making such an offer when the particulars of claim are served. Usually there is a bracket within which the damages are likely to fall. One strategy is to pitch the financial part of the offer at the low end of this bracket, to increase the chances of beating it in court if the matter proceeds to trial and to tempt the landlord into a settlement. On the other hand, it may be better to propose a settlement offer at the very top of the bracket because, if the adviser makes an offer at the bottom of the scale and it is not accepted, this is likely to lower the landlord's expectations of what might be awarded and consequently lower the likely eventual settlement. If this approach is adopted the client should be advised that the offer is made with a view to negotiation, so that expectations are not created.

3.176 The correct approach in any particular case will depend on the tenant's temperament and attitude to the court case. Many tenants would rather have less money at an earlier stage than endure the anxiety and uncertainty of litigation, especially once the repairs have been carried out. The adviser must take instructions, explain the pros and cons of both strategies and then let the tenant decide, carefully recording and getting the tenant to sign confirmation of that decision.

3.177 Any offer in respect of damages should be put on the understanding that, if the repairs have not been carried out by the stipulated date, further damages will be claimable.

3.178 The offer may invite the landlord to submit to a court order requiring outstanding repair work to be completed within a specified time period. The landlord is likely to want such terms to be included in a Tomlin order[122] as opposed to an order for specific performance, which is effectively a mandatory injunction.

3.179 A Tomlin order recites that a settlement has been achieved, but all the details of the settlement are included in a schedule to the order, which is not a public document. It can include provisions that go beyond the power of the court; for example, it can provide that the work has to be done to the satisfaction of the tenant's expert or that the landlord has to re-house the tenant. It can therefore be a useful

121 Of course, once an offer is withdrawn it no longer has the costs consequences that it would have carried if it had stayed open until trial, see CPR 36.17(7).

122 Named after Mr Justice Tomlin, from his judgment in *Dashwood v Dashwood* [1927] WN 276, ChD.

form of settlement. However, given the delay that can arise if the landlord then fails to carry out the works agreed, Tomlin orders should be resisted in cases of serious disrepair. If a Tomlin order is used, the adviser must ensure that it gives permission to restore the case for enforcement purposes. Permission may be required to restore in other circumstances. See appendix C below for a precedent.

3.180 A well-advised landlord will take the initiative by making a Part 36 offer. A tenant who fails to accept a reasonable offer which is not then bettered at trial will be ordered to pay the landlord's costs incurred from 21 days after the date of the offer. A tenant will have to pay such costs out of any damages awarded. This could significantly reduce or even extinguish the amount recovered. Where the case is funded by a conditional fee agreement (CFA), the adviser may well require the tenant to accept an offer at the lower end of the damages bracket and it will be a breach of the terms of the CFA to reject this advice. All of this must be fully explained to the tenant.

3.181 It is possible for the landlord to make a Part 36 offer to settle the financial part of the claim while still defending the claim for specific performance. The fact that works are still outstanding and the case must continue to trial should not be an excuse for failing to accept a reasonable Part 36 offer for damages.

3.182 If the adviser recommends a settlement to the tenant, he or she should be sure to warn that it will be some months before the tenant receives the money and that there will be a deduction from the damages to pay any success fee or Legal Aid Statutory Charge. The adviser should tell the tenant at the outset and it should be repeated that any shortfall between the costs obtained from the landlord and the true costs of the case will have to come out of the damages. If the tenant is not advised of these matters before agreeing to the settlement, the tenant is likely to feel ambushed and this may cause unnecessary and unfortunate friction between the tenant and the adviser.

Trial

3.183 As soon as the hearing date is notified by the court, the adviser must inform the tenant, all witnesses, the expert and counsel. The adviser should discuss with the barrister the latest date by which the barrister will want to receive the brief for trial.

3.184 If the tenant is the claimant, the adviser must prepare four identical bundles of all documents that either party might want to refer to a trial; these are known as trial bundles. CPR 39.5 and PD32 paras 27.3–27.15 set out what should be included in a bundle and how it should be organised. The adviser should supply counsel with the draft index to the bundle for comment. Bundles should be agreed with the opponent where possible and must be filed at court not more than seven and not less than three working days before trial[123] and that the copy that is provided to the landlord's representative must be identical to the two that will go to the court for the use of the judge and the witnesses.

3.185 The court rules require that two days before a fast track trial a schedule of costs in form N260 must be served on the opponent and filed at court.[124]

3.186 The trial takes place before a district or circuit judge, who considers the evidence, both in the form of written statements and under cross-examination, listens to the arguments on both sides and then delivers judgment.

Final orders

Mandatory orders for works

3.187 If any works remain outstanding, the tenant's representative will seek an order at trial that the landlord comply with the applicable repairing or fitness obligation. The order will be for specific performance of the express or implied terms of the tenancy agreement. For non-contractual repairing obligations, the equivalent remedy is a mandatory injunction. The duty imposed by the DPA 1972 s4 (see paras 2.108–2.128) can also be enforced by injunction.[125] Specific performance is a remedy available at common law[126] and by statute.

3.188 LTA 1985 s17(1) provides:

> In proceedings in which a tenant of a dwelling alleges a breach on the part of his landlord of a repairing covenant relating to any part of the premises in which the dwelling is comprised, the court may order specific performance of the covenant, whether or not the breach relates to a part of the premises let to the tenant and notwithstanding any equitable rule restricting the scope of the remedy, whether on the basis of a lack of mutuality or otherwise.

123 CPR 39.5(2).

124 CPR PD 44 para 9.5.

125 *Barrett v Lounova (1982) Ltd* [1990] 1 QB 348, [1989] 1 All ER 351, CA.

126 *Jeune v Queens Cross Properties Ltd* [1974] Ch 97, [1973] 3 All ER 97, CA.

3.189 LTA 1985 s9A(5) provides:

> Where in any proceedings before a court it is alleged that a lessor is in breach of an obligation under the implied covenant, the court may order specific performance of the obligation (regardless of any equitable rule restricting the scope of that remedy).

3.190 Several points arise:

- For the purposes of the LTA 1985, 'lease' and 'tenancy' have the same meaning and both expressions includes a sub-lease or sub-tenant.[127] For the purposes of LTA 1985 s17(1) 'tenant' includes a statutory tenant.[128]
- Specific performance of obligations to maintain common parts can be ordered on the application of a tenant of one flat in a property containing several dwellings.
- The old equitable rules that 'the applicant must have clean hands' (ie, must not also be in breach of obligations, eg, for payment of rent) and that 'an order must be capable of supervision by the court' may be disregarded, but the grant of specific performance remains entirely at the discretion of the court.

3.191 It will not be a defence for the landlord to raise the prospect of severe financial hardship as a result of the terms of the order. Indeed, in *Francis v Cowliffe Ltd*,[129] an order for the provision and maintenance of lifts was made notwithstanding the very real prospect of bankruptcy of the landlord as a result of compliance. However in unfitness cases works may be limited by what can be done at 'reasonable expense' (See para 2.44).

Service of orders

3.192 Any mandatory order must be served personally on the landlord[130] and, in cases of corporate landlords such as local authorities, housing associations or companies, on a person with executive power to ensure that the work is done. A certificate of service should always be obtained. Under CPR 81.9 an order to do or not do an act may not be enforced unless it displays on the front a warning known as a penal notice. The penal notice should be in the terms stated in CPR PD 81 para 1 and the adviser should ask for it to be attached. Inserting a penal notice has been confirmed to be an executive act which should

127 LTA 1985 s36(2)(a).

128 LTA 1985 s17(2).

129 (1976) 239 EG 977, DC.

130 CPR 81.5(1) and 81.6.

be carried out by a court official on request.[131] However, a penal notice is not always a pre-requisite to committal proceedings and such a defect may be waived if no injustice has been caused,[132] for example where the landlord was aware that they could be committed to prison for breach of the order.[133]

3.193 The adviser should also ensure that any time limits set out in an injunction should run from the date that the order is served rather than from the date it is made.

> **Example**
>
> On 2 April the tenant obtains an order compelling the landlord to overhaul a roof by 26 April. The sealed order with penal notice is not received by the adviser until 15 April. The landlord then proves elusive, and the adviser is unable to effect service until 27 April. By that time the order has expired and if the landlord does not comply with it, it will be unenforceable unless the adviser applies to court for new time limits. This can be avoided if the order said that the roof had to be overhauled within 28 days of service of the order upon the landlord.

Declarations

3.194 The county court has power to make a binding declaration, even if it is the only relief sought.[134] Where a mandatory order is unlikely to be effective (because it either cannot be served or will not be complied with) and the tenant would prefer to carry out the works and recoup the costs from future rent, or simply where an injunction is refused, the grant of a declaration may be a useful alternative remedy. In a disrepair or unfitness case, the court could be invited to make a declaration providing that:

1) the landlord is in breach of a specified repairing or fitness obligation;
2) the tenant is entitled to do the necessary works in default;
3) the works may be financed by deduction from future rent; and

131 *R v Wandsworth County Council ex p Munn* (1994) 26 HLR 697, QBD.

132 CPR PD 81 para 16.2.

133 See also *R (MA) v Croydon LBC* [2009] EWHC 2474 (Admin), [2010] 1 WLR 1658 regarding orders made against a public body.

134 CPR 40.20.

4) the tenant's compliance with stages 2) and 3) will not constitute breach by the tenant of any express terms of the tenancy agreement which prima facie prohibit such action.

3.195 The court also has power to make an interim declaration.[135]

Compensation and costs

3.196 The court can, of course, award damages and costs. Compensation is discussed in chapter 7. The adviser should ensure that any settlement or judgment order provides for the landlord to pay costs as agreed or assessed by the court, and may at this stage include in the settlement, or ask the court to make, an order that the landlord pay a reasonable sum on account of costs.[136] The costs will include the costs of implementing a court order, which may involve liaising with the tenant while work is being carried out.

3.197 Costs are usually awarded on the standard basis and the criteria for assessment is discussed at paras 3.38–3.42 above.

3.198 Where costs are recovered but not paid within 14 days the receiving party is usually entitled to interest on the costs at eight per cent.[137]

3.199 If the tenant loses and is legally aided then they will be protected from the costs claim that would usually follow by virtue of LASPO s26(1).[138]

Enforcing an order

Remedies for breach of mandatory orders

3.200 Failure to perform works directed in an order of specific performance or by injunction is punishable by committal for contempt. It is unlikely that a landlord will be put in prison on a first non-compliance and a court may impose a fine as an alternative. Even so, proceedings to commit the landlord for contempt of court are a very effective way to ensure that the work is done. The procedure is set out in CPR 81. All requirements should be carefully followed:

- The order to be enforced must contain a penal notice. If it does not, you will generally have to return to court to get one included.

135 CPR 25.1(b).

136 CPR 44.2(8).

137 CPR 40.8(1); Judgments Act 1838 s17; County Court Act 1984 s74; County Courts (Interest on Judgment Debts) Order 1991 No 1184 art 5.

138 And see the Civil Legal Aid (Costs) Regulations 2013 SI No 611 regs 5–8.

- Check that the order was personally served on the landlord before the end of the time limit for doing the act.
- Check that the time limits have been breached. Often extensions of time will have been agreed for the specified work to be done. However these should be carefully limited and no longer than is absolutely necessary. When such an agreement has been made, you should either apply for the original order to be varied, or put the agreement in writing and personally serve the varied order or the new agreement on the landlord.[139]
- Identify in detail each breach of the court order.

3.201 A committal application is made using the procedure under Part 23 and it must:

- set out the full grounds for the application numbering each breach separately;
- be supported by one or more affidavits containing all the evidence you will be relying on;
- contain a prominent notice stating the possible consequences of the court making a committal order and of the landlord not attending the hearing; and
- be personally served on the landlord along with the notice of the hearing date.[140]

3.202 As an alternative to the use of committal, the court may order that necessary action may be done either by the tenant or by some person appointed by the court with the costs borne by the landlord.[141]

3.203 In addition, CPR 69 also allows a court faced with a breach of a mandatory order to direct that the necessary action be taken by a receiver on behalf of the tenant at the expense of the landlord. The court may select and direct the individual who is to carry out the action required. The availability of this remedy for repairs cases against private landlords was confirmed in *Parker v Camden LBC*.[142] The court may enforce the financial element of the procedure, either by directing a payment into court (as in *Barrett v Lounova (1982) Ltd*[143]) or by an order of sequestration on the landlord's assets.

139 CPR 81.5.

140 CPR 81.10 and PD 81 para 13.

141 CPR 70.2A.

142 [1986] Ch 162, [1985] 2 All ER 141, CA.

143 [1990] 1 QB 348, CA.

3.204 If there is a real risk that the landlord will sell a property to avoid the effect of judgment, or will dispose of assets to avoid an award of damages, the tenant can apply for a freezing injunction.[144]

3.205 If damages or costs are not paid by the landlord, the adviser can use a variety of remedies to secure payment:

- a warrant of control to seize goods held by the landlord;[145]
- a third party debt order, which is often very effective against local authorities;[146]
- a charging order, which can be very effective against private landlords who own the premises;[147]
- an attachment of earnings order;[148]
- the appointment of a receiver;[149]
- a statutory demand[150] threatening to petition for bankruptcy, but only if the intention is to follow it through with such an application.

3.206 The costs of *enforcing*, as opposed to *implementing*, the final order will not be included in the original judgment so the adviser must apply separately for them. Similarly, the adviser will need to check that the wording of the retainer, for example in the CFA, before any enforcement action is taken.

Enforcing a Tomlin order

3.207 Where a Tomlin order has been agreed (see para 3.179), the timescales for works to be done will be contained in the schedule to the order. The terms in the schedule do not form part of the order itself and cannot be directly enforced through a committal application.

3.208 Where the landlord fails to carry out the works in accordance with the schedule, the adviser will have to bring the matter back to court in order to obtain an order for performance of the relevant terms, with a penal notice attached. This can be done by applying for an injunction on a form N16A. This will inevitably involve allowing the landlord some further time. However this should be as limited as possible.

144 CPR 25.1(1)(f).
145 CPR 83.15.
146 CPR 72.
147 CPR 73.
148 CPR 89.
149 CPR 69.
150 Insolvency Act 1986 s268(1)(a).

3.209 The court may allow a tenant to claim damages for breach of the Tomlin order by an application in the same action without the need for a new claim to be issued.[151] Alternatively, an agreement that this is the case can be included in a recital to the Tomlin order.

The tenant raises their rights when taken to court by the landlord

Defences and counterclaims

3.210 In many cases, the tenant seeks advice only when possession proceedings have been started as a result of rent arrears. If there is disrepair or unfitness, it will be possible to reduce or even extinguish the arrears by counterclaiming for a sum equal to the damages to which the tenant is entitled as a result of the landlord's default. This is the case even though the damages are unliquidated, in that they have not yet been assessed by the court.[152] Where the amount of damages matches or exceeds the rent arrears, the tenant is entitled to an equitable set-off amounting to a complete defence to the landlord's possession action,[153] and to payment of the damages which exceed the arrears.

3.211 Equitable set-off has the advantage over the common law right to recoup from rent discussed in para 3.4 above, in that it goes beyond costs of remedial works and can include ordinary (general) damages for inconvenience and distress to which the tenant is entitled as a result of the landlord's default. The set-off should be formally stated in the defence to the landlord's claim and will usually be accompanied by a counterclaim setting out the breach complained of and the damage suffered.[154]

3.212 It must be shown that the right to set-off emerges from a landlord's breach of obligations and that it would be unfair (inequitable) to allow the landlord to recover the amount claimed in the face of the landlord's breach and the tenant's counterclaim. Such conditions will usually be automatically satisfied in the case of damages resulting from the landlord's breach of a contractual obligation.

151 *Bargain Pages v Midland Independent Newspapers* [2003] EWHC 1887 (Ch), approved in *Starlight Shipping Co v Allianz Marine & Aviation Versicherungs AG* [2013] UKSC 70, [2014] 1 All ER 590 at para 79.

152 *British Allianz v International Marine* [1980] QB 137, [1979] 2 All ER 1063, QBD.

153 *Televantos v McCulloch* (1991) 23 HLR 412, [1991] 1 EGLR 123, CA.

154 See the example of a defence and counterclaim in appendix C.

3.213 Note that, where the tenancy has been assigned to a new landlord, the tenant is not entitled to set off damages arising before the assignment in a claim for rent arrears which have arisen after the assignment.[155] However, if rent arrears are assigned to the new landlord, then the tenant can set off damages for disrepair that arose when those arrears accrued.[156] It is expected that the same principle will apply in unfitness cases, with the proviso that no damages can accrue prior to the implied term taking effect for that tenancy (see para 2.57).

3.214 The remedy of counterclaim and set-off is invaluable where the landlord is relying on the 'potentially draconian'[157] power in HA 1988 Sch 2 Ground 8 to seek possession against an assured tenant (where the judge usually has no choice but to grant a possession order if at least eight weeks' rent is owed if the rent if paid weekly or fortnightly or two months' rent is owed if the rent is paid monthly) and where the set-off could extinguish the arrears or reduce them to less than eight weeks' or two months' rent. This should be raised with the judge at the first opportunity at the first hearing of the possession claim, along with some evidence of the nature and extent of the defects if there has been no opportunity to prepare a defence and counterclaim.

3.215 Where the tenant is asking for rent arrears to be set-off against a disrepair or unfitness counterclaim, there is no time limit on that part of the defence.[158] This means that the tenant may benefit from a counterclaim for in excess of six years' worth of loss.[159]

3.216 Legal aid is available for defences and counterclaims as the tenant's home is at risk, even where prospects of success are at least marginal.[160] A specimen defence and counterclaim is set out in appendix C of this book.

3.217 A court fee based on the value of the counterclaim is payable and CPR 20.4(2) states that the defendant will need permission to make a counterclaim unless it is filed with the defence.

155 *Edlington Properties Ltd v JH Fenner & Co Ltd* [2006] EWCA Civ 403, [2004] 1 WLR 2853.

156 See *Muscat v Smith* [2003] EWCA Civ 962, [2004] HLR 6.

157 *North British Housing Association Ltd v Matthews* [2004] EWCA Civ 1736, [2005] HLR 17, CA, per Dyson LJ at para 33.

158 Limitation Act 1980 s36(2); and see *Filross Securities Ltd v Midgeley* (1999) 31 HLR 465.

159 See eg *Islington LBC v Keane* December 2005 *Legal Action* 28, *Housing Law Casebook* 7th edn, para R.16.

160 Civil Legal Aid (Merits Criteria) Regulations 2013 SI No 104 as amended by Civil Legal Aid (Merits Criteria) (Amendment) Regulations 2016 SI No 782. See also paras 4.46–4.47.

3.218 The defence should include a paragraph asking the court to set off the tenant's damages against any rent arrears. If the adviser omits to do this, the rent arrears cannot be extinguished by the counterclaim and the tenant remains at risk of a possession order. A term in the tenancy agreement prohibiting set-off may be unfair.[161] As mentioned at para 3.213, a tenant is not entitled to set off damages for disrepair incurred when the property was owned by a previous landlord in a claim brought by a new landlord, unless the old arrears have been assigned to the new landlord, and that landlord is suing for them.[162]

3.219 The defence and counterclaim may well have to be drafted without the benefit of an expert's report, because even if a court has given 28 days for the defence and counterclaim to be filed, it is unlikely that the adviser will be able to obtain and consider a report within that period.

3.220 The value of the counterclaim is not considered by the court when ascertaining 'value' for the purposes of allocating the case to a procedural track.

3.221 The adviser should check the wording of any legal aid funding certificate carefully to see whether it authorises the making of a counterclaim. It is not sufficient for it to state that the funding is to defend a possession claim. If necessary, the adviser should apply for an amendment of the scope of the certificate before starting work.

3.222 Filing a counterclaim will buy the tenant precious time in a rent arrears possession claim, because any decision about possession will usually be delayed until after the trial of the counterclaim. *Al Hassani v Merrigan*,[163] mentioned in para 3.7, illustrates how important it is that such time is used wisely by the tenant. In particular, the adviser should ensure that the tenant now pays the rent as and when it falls due and that any problems with budgeting or housing benefit are addressed. Even if the adviser believes that the counterclaim is likely to exceed the amount of the rent arrears, the tenant should be advised to reduce the arrears by making regular payments. Judges can be inconsistent in the amount of damages awarded and if the adviser's prediction about damages proves to be over-optimistic, the tenant may end up relying on reasonableness as a defence to the possession

161 *Cody v Philps* December 2005 *Legal Action* 28, *Housing Law Casebook* 7th edn, para R19.11 and see Unfair Terms in Consumer Contract Regulations 1999 for tenancies which began before 1 October 2015 and Consumer Rights Act 2015 Sch 2 Part 1 para 2 for those which began after 1 October 2015.

162 *Edlington Properties Ltd v Fenner and Co Ltd* [2006] EWCA Civ 403, [2006] 1 WLR 1583.

163 (1988) 20 HLR 238, CA.

claim, rather than on the counterclaim. In such circumstances, unless the tenant can demonstrate that finances are now under control and that paying both rent and arrears has been established as a regular habit, the tenant's tenancy will be in jeopardy.

3.223 For similar reasons, the adviser should not be tempted to treat a counterclaim as a reason for allowing the trial to be delayed any longer than is absolutely necessary. If a case drifts, the danger is that the tenant will fall behind with the rent again and may even be in the position of owing more rent by the time the case comes to trial than was owed when the possession proceedings were started.

3.224 If, at trial, the damages awarded under the counterclaim exceed the arrears, any possession claim based solely on arrears of rent should be dismissed. If the court gives judgment for specified amounts on both the claim and the counterclaim, then the judge can make a separate order on costs against each party – see CPR 40.13. This could mean that the tenant's costs are reduced or even extinguished by the costs awarded to the landlord. Separate orders should therefore be avoided.

3.225 Advisers should note that there is no obligation to raise a counterclaim as part of possession proceedings. It is not an abuse of process for a tenant to start fresh proceedings, claiming damages for disrepair or unfitness, after the possession proceedings have finished.[164]

Counterclaims after a warrant has been issued

3.226 It is possible to counterclaim in order to set off damages for disrepair or unfitness against arrears even after a possession order has been made, but not executed. In practice this usually happens when a notice of eviction has been received by the tenant and they turn to an adviser for help in suspending the warrant. Legal aid is available in these circumstances because the tenant's home is at risk. While the counterclaim is not a defence at this stage, if the arrears are extinguished by the set off then discharge of the possession order can be sought. This should also be included in any settlement or court order.

3.227 In contrast to the position when a counterclaim is served with a defence, where a possession order has already been made the adviser must apply on form N244 for permission to bring the counterclaim.[165]

164 *Henley v Bloom* [2010] EWCA Civ 202, [2010] 1 WLR 1770.
165 CPR 20.7(3)(b).

3.228 With respect to time limits, a counterclaim may be treated as being brought at the date of the claim itself.[166] This can enable the tenant to claim for periods that would otherwise be time barred, and may be the case where an order has previously been suspended and warrants stayed on a number of occasions, although a court might refuse to allow a very stale counterclaim where the alleged disrepair predated the arrears.[167]

The tenant makes a complaint

Complaints procedures

3.229 In the private rented sector, if a tenant gives notice of a defect or problem with their home and the landlord does not take any action, there is, at the moment, no more formal complaints procedure to which they can turn unless the landlord is a member of a voluntary scheme. However, in January 2019 the government announced plans to require private landlords to join a new housing redress scheme which will deal with complaints from private tenants,[168] and has proposed a new Housing Complaints Resolution Service.

3.230 Tenants of social landlords, that is tenants of local authorities and private registered providers such as housing associations, have access to both their landlord's internal complaints procedure and, if that fails to resolve the problem, to the Housing Ombudsman.

3.231 Local authorities and other social housing providers will have internal complaints procedures which may also incorporate internal appeals. Bringing a formal complaint this way may seem like a daunting process to tenants but, in relatively minor cases, it will be a more proportionate remedy than court proceedings. The tenant or adviser must familiarise themselves with the internal complaints process of the landlord, which can usually be found on its website.

3.232 If, despite the complaint, the landlord has failed to put things right, a social tenant will have access to the Housing Ombudsman. There is a filter system for referrals of complaints by 'designated

166 Limitation Act 1980 s35(1)(b).

167 *Midland Heart Ltd v Idawah* [2014] EW Misc B48 (11 July 2014), December 2014 *Legal Action* 25, *Housing Law Casebook* 7th edn, para R19.13.

168 'James Brokenshire announces overhaul of broken housing complaints system', MHCLG press release 24 January 2019.

persons',[169] however some direct access to the ombudsman is available:[170]

3.233 The tenant should contact a 'designated person', which is an MP, a local councillor or a member of the landlord's tenant panel. If the designated person cannot resolve the problem with the tenant's landlord, then they can refer the complaint to the Housing Ombudsman.

3.234 Alternatively, the tenant can complain directly to the Housing Ombudsman:

- where the tenant has exhausted the internal complaints procedure of the landlord and eight weeks have elapsed since those procedures were exhausted; or
- the Housing Ombudsman is satisfied that a designated person has refused to refer the complaint; or
- a designated person has agreed that the tenant can complain to the Housing Ombudsman direct.

The Housing Ombudsman

3.235 Whether the complaint is referred by a designated person or comes directly from the tenant, any complaint to the Housing Ombudsman must normally be made within 12 months of the end of the internal complaints procedure.

3.236 The Housing Ombudsman will first consider whether the complaint can be resolved quickly under its early resolution procedure. If this is not possible, the Housing Ombudsman will investigate the matter under its formal investigation process and may appoint an independent surveyor to help in the investigation of a complaint.

3.237 Even though the full investigation of a complaint can take over a year, the formal process of instituting a complaint is often sufficient to propel a landlord into action. The Housing Ombudsman does not expect tenants to take court action in order to have repairs done. Accordingly, the Housing Ombudsman will investigate complaints even in cases where the tenant could clearly bring legal proceedings. Perhaps most usefully, it will investigate complaints of maladministration where there is no redress by way of civil action, eg complaints in relation to improvement works.

3.238 The Housing Ombudsman will not usually recommend that the landlord pay the tenant's legal costs, so funding legal representation may be a problem.

169 HA 1996 Sch 2 para 7A(3).
170 HA 1996 Sch 2 para 7B.

3.239 Past investigations of complaints have led to recommendations for public apologies and compensation, but in recent years the compensation awarded has often been much less than that which might have been obtained by seeking redress in the courts. The Housing Ombudsman does not publish the findings it makes on complaints, but a selection of case studies is available on its website.[171]

171 www.housing-ombudsman.org.uk.

CHAPTER 4

Funding a claim about housing conditions

continued

Legal aid

Introduction

4.1 Legal aid is a taxpayer-funded national scheme which can, in some circumstances, pay a tenant's lawyers to take a legal claim (or bring a counterclaim) for poor housing conditions. It can also provide a tenant with protection against being held responsible for a successful landlord's costs.

4.2 The Legal Aid, Sentencing and Punishment of Offenders Act (LASPO) 2012 came into force on 1 April 2013 and severely restricted legal aid for housing advice and legal representation work.[1] Schedule 1 to LASPO 2012 sets out an exhaustive list of the situations in which legal aid is still available.

4.3 Legal aid is administered by the Legal Aid Agency (LAA) which is an executive agency of the Ministry of Justice. The LAA will only fund work carried out by advisers ('providers') who have signed a contract with them. The civil contract between the LAA and provider organisations is known as the Standard Civil Contract.

4.4 A number of regulations have been made under LASPO 2012. The Lord Chancellor's Guidance (LCG) issued under LASPO 2012 s4[2] is also an important source of reference for providers of civil legal aid; housing conditions cases receive special attention in Part 12 of that guidance.

4.5 LASPO 2012, the regulations and guidance can be accessed online on the government's LAA website,[3] and advisers will also find the updates on the LAG Legal Aid Handbook website[4] invaluable.

4.6 For the purposes of cases relating to poor housing conditions, legal aid comes in two main types: *Legal Help*, also known as controlled work, which enables the adviser to provide a limited amount of legal advice and assistance to a tenant or licensee (referred to for the remainder of this chapter as 'tenant'), but not to take, issue or conduct court proceedings; and *Legal Representation*, also known as licensed or certificated work, which enables a tenant to bring or defend court proceedings.

1 See 'Sorting myths from facts over housing cases', November 2014 *Legal Action* 7: www.lag.org.uk/article/202414/sorting-myths-from-facts-over-housing-cases.

2 www.gov.uk/government/uploads/system/uploads/attachment_data/file/404988/legal-aid-lord-chancellors-guidance.pdf (updated January 2018).

3 www.gov.uk/guidance/funding-and-costs-assessment-for-civil-and-crime-matters.

4 www.legalaidhandbook.com.

4.7 To obtain legal aid, the tenant has to satisfy tests of scope, merits and financial eligibility. The tests for scope and eligibility are the same for all levels of service but the merits test varies depending upon whether the adviser is providing Legal Help or Legal Representation, see paras 4.27 and 4.43 below.

Scope

4.8 Civil legal aid for housing conditions cases is limited to three situations:

1) bringing a counterclaim to defend possession proceedings;
2) bringing a claim to reduce or remove a serious risk of harm to occupants of a dwelling; or
3) judicial reviews of a public body

Each of these is considered in turn below.

Counterclaims in possession proceedings

4.9 LASPO 2012 Sch 1 para 33 allows the use of legal aid to defend claims for possession or eviction in relation to a person's home. A 'home' can be a house, caravan, houseboat or other vehicle or structure if it is the person's only or main residence, as long as they have the right to be in occupation.[5] The defence can include a counterclaim for damages based on breach of tenancy or the commission of various specified torts, not including negligence.[6] Disrepair and unfitness counterclaims are only in scope insofar as the counterclaim constitutes a defence to possession proceedings. They are therefore only in scope to defend possession claims based on rent arrears, the defence being that the alleged arrears are not owed due to an equitable set-off (see para 3.210 on right to set-off). A disrepair or unfitness counterclaim will not be in scope for a non-arrears-based possession claim.

4.10 Part 7.4 of the LCG states that legal aid should not be granted where the tenant has withheld rent in order to provoke possession proceedings so that their disrepair claim can be brought as a counterclaim.[7] Most tenants who withhold rent do so not to provoke proceedings but in order to push a landlord into carrying out repairs (see para 3.4 on withholding rent); it should be rare that this exclusion will apply.

5 LASPO 2012 Sch 1 Pt 1 para 33(9).
6 See LASPO 2012 Sch 1 Pt 1 para 33(6) and Pt 2 paras 3–6 and 8.
7 See para 3.210.

4.11 Disrepair or unfitness counterclaims can be raised after a possession claim has been adjourned, or even after a possession order has been made if the eviction has not yet been carried out.[8] It is therefore worth asking tenants who approach with disrepair or unfitness problems but no apparent ongoing possession proceedings about their history. There must be outstanding arrears in order for the counterclaim to potentially prevent eviction and so fall within the provisions of LASPO 2012. If the counterclaim is filed after the defence, then the court's permission is required.[9]

Serious risk of harm

4.12 LASPO 2012 Sch 1 para 35 allows the use of legal aid to bring a claim designed to remove or reduce a 'serious risk of harm' to a tenant or a 'relevant member' of the tenant's family where:

- the risk arises from a deficiency in the tenant's home;
- the home is rented or leased from another person; and
- the legal services are provided with a view to securing that the other person makes arrangements to remove or reduce the risk.

4.13 'Deficiency' is defined in LASPO 2012 Sch 1 para 35(4) as 'any deficiency, whether arising as a result of the construction of a building, an absence of maintenance or repair, or otherwise'. This is a wide and useful definition. It covers deficiencies in the home arising from lack of maintenance and lack of repair but also includes problems caused by poor design such as condensation dampness. Not only Landlord and Tenant Act (LTA) 1985 ss9A and 11 unfitness and disrepair claims, but also Environmental Protection Act (EPA) 1990 and claims in tort are also in scope.

4.14 Relevant members of the tenant's family are defined in LASPO 2012 Sch 1 para 35(3) in two categories: children and adult relatives. Children are defined as persons under 18.[10] Children must be the tenant's children or children for whom the tenant has parental responsibility. Adult relatives are persons connected with the tenant through 'full blood, half-blood, marriage or civil partnership or cohabitants'. Cohabitants are 'two persons who are neither married to each other nor civil partners of each other but are living together

8 *Rahman v Sterling Credit Ltd* [2001] 1 WLR 496, (2001) 33 HLR 63, CA; and *Midland Heart Ltd v Idawah* [2014] EW Misc B48.

9 Civil Procedure Rules (CPR) 20.4.

10 See LASPO 2012 Sch 1 Part 1 para 35(4).

as husband and wife or as if they were civil partners'.[11] The deficient premises must be the home of the adult relative if they are to be counted as a relevant family member.

4.15 The LCG identifies a number of factors that it says may be taken into account when determining whether the 'serious risk' test is met, namely whether:

- the deficiency has already resulted in harm to the tenant or a relevant family member;
- as a result of the deficiency, an existing health condition is worsened (for example, where an applicant who has asthma is living in a damp home, or where an applicant who has rheumatism is living in a home with no heating);
- the applicant or relevant family members affected by the deficiency are in a high-risk age group – such as the elderly and very young children – and therefore more susceptible to any deficiency;
- the applicant is vulnerable due to a disability (for example, a leaking roof which causes flooring to be damp may be viewed as significantly more serious if the applicant has particular mobility problems, or where important medical equipment was placed in jeopardy as a result of the deficiency);
- there are relevant environmental conditions (for example, broken heating may be a much more serious deficiency during the winter);
- there are multiple deficiencies which could, taken cumulatively, be of greater seriousness than individually (for example, damp conditions combined with a broken window could exacerbate the health risks associated with excess cold);
- a single deficiency poses multiple risks (for example, a roof in a state of disrepair could lead to hazards of excess cold, structural collapse, damp and mould);
- a deficiency affects rooms or areas that are shared (this may be a relevant factor if, for example, risks of infection could be increased in shared areas where disrepair is not dealt with);
- the expert instructed under the Pre-action Protocol reports that the deficiency is likely to deteriorate further in the near future; and
- the local authority has already identified hazards which arise from deficiencies in the home, for example under the Housing Health and Safety Rating System (HHSRS).[12]

11 See LASPO 2012 Sch 1 Pt 1 para 35(4); and Family Law Act 1996 s62(1).

12 Lord Chancellor's Guidance (LCG) para 12.10.

4.16 If any of the factors set out above are present, the adviser should be sure to point them out in any legal aid application. However, this is not an exhaustive list, and some of the items are an unnecessarily restrictive interpretation of LASPO 2012. For example, there is much research to show that significant amounts of mould in a home pose a serious risk to the health of its occupants[13] – there should therefore be no need to show that the tenant is in a high-risk group or already has a health condition that may be made worse by the mould.

4.17 It is notable that only work to remedy those defects which cause or contribute to a serious risk of harm is in scope (except for in a counterclaim). For this reason, and because work to recover damages is not in scope, the 'serious risk of harm' cases under legal aid are problematic. They are appropriate where there is an immediate risk which has been ongoing for a relatively short time, such as a broken boiler.

Example

An elderly tenant has a broken boiler in winter. He also has a damaged front door, a leaking pipe within his bathroom wall causing a damp patch and some dislodged roof slates causing occasional slight water ingress. Only the broken boiler is likely to be a deficiency causing a serious risk of harm. It is arguable that the two sources of water ingress contribute to the risk of harm by making the property colder. However, work to compel the landlord to fix the front door is never in scope. Once the boiler is fixed, the serious risk to harm is removed and funding will not continue to allow the provider to do work to compel the landlord to remedy the water ingress. If the boiler is fixed after issue of proceedings but the claim is not settled, the tenant may be stuck with unresolved proceedings at an early stage and no order for costs. He must find an alternative method of funding representation or proceed alone.

13 In 2011, Mendell and others published a review of scientific studies and concluded that evident dampness or mould was consistently associated with asthma, allergies and respiratory infections ('Respiratory and Allergic Health Effects of Dampness, Mold, and Dampness-Related Agents: A Review of the Epidemiologic Evidence', Environmental Health Perspectives, 2011 June 119(6): 748–756).

Judicial reviews

4.18 If a legal services provider has a public law legal aid contract with the LAA, they may provide civil legal services in relation to a judicial review of an enactment, decision, act or omission so long as the judicial review is of benefit to an individual and does not relate to immigration or other excluded categories irrelevant to housing conditions.[14] Providers with public law contracts therefore have a wide scope to take action. For example, they can request a judicial review of a local authority's failures to prosecute private landlords or housing associations for breaches of the Housing Act (HA) 2004 (see chapter 5).

Financial eligibility

4.19 The main provisions governing the determination of financial eligibility for Legal Help and Legal Representation are the Civil Legal Aid (Financial Resources and Payment for Services) Regulations ('FR Regs') 2013[15] as amended. There is also useful guidance to LAA caseworkers on the LAA website.[16]

4.20 In *Legal Help* cases, the means test is conducted by the legal services provider and a sample of cases is audited subsequently by the LAA to ensure that the client was properly assessed and that adequate proof of means was obtained. LAA caseworkers carry out the means test for *Legal Representation*. Where urgent legal representation is needed and it is in the interest of justice to do so, providers may 'delegate functions' to assess whether an applicant is eligible for legal aid and grant them an emergency certificate lasting eight weeks and covering only the most urgent steps to be taken[17]. LAA caseworkers will then assess eligibility in line with their normal time limits. If the applicant is found to be eligible then a full legal aid certificate will be granted. If the LAA assess that the applicant was not eligible on financial grounds then their certificate will be revoked and the LAA will charge them for all costs billed to the LAA. The adviser therefore has to ascertain that the client is likely to qualify and must obtain the necessary evidence before delegating functions.

14 LASPO 2012 Sch 1 para 19.

15 SI No 480.

16 *Guide to Determining Financial Eligibility for Controlled Work and Family Mediation*, April 2018 (updated September 2018); and *Civil representation guide to determining financial eligibility for certificated work*, April 2014, v1.

17 Civil Legal Aid (Merits Criteria) Regulations 2013 reg 46.

4.21 Tenants receiving certain types of state benefits are eligible for legal aid without the need for a detailed means test, as long as their capital is within a specified limit.[18] This is known as 'passporting'.

4.22 The means of spouses or partners, including partners of the same sex, are aggregated for the purposes of assessment.

4.23 Standard allowances are made for dependants and for certain outgoings, such as employment costs. Net rent can be deducted up to a maximum allowance, currently £545 per month, unless the tenant has children who live with them. In possession proceedings for rent arrears, the net rent due (after housing benefit), as opposed to what the tenant is actually paying can be taken into account.[19]

4.24 Advisers can make use of an online civil legal aid eligibility calculator (a link entitled 'work out who qualifies for legal aid' is on the LAA webpage). The calculator can provide an indication of financial eligibility and possible contributions and should import the financial information into Legal Help forms. However, it is not a replacement for the detailed guidance set out in the FR Regs. Identical information entered into the eligibility calculator and the LAA's Client and Cost Management System (CCMS)[20] can yield different conclusions as to the level of contribution due. The eligibility calculator can be a useful initial indicator but clients should be warned of the potential for inconsistencies at an early stage.

Legal Help

4.25 Legal Help (also known as controlled work) can only be provided for housing condition cases that fall within LASPO 2012 Sch 1.[21] The Schedule excludes the provision of general information about the law and the legal system, the issuing or conducting of court proceedings, advocacy or instructing an advocate in proceedings.

18 Currently £8,000: see FR Regs 2013 SI No 480 reg 6. If the applicant is over 60 the 'Pensioner's Disregard' may apply: FR Regs 2013 reg 41.

19 *R (Southwark Law Centre) v Legal Services Commission* [2007] EWHC 1715 (Admin), [2008] HLR 12 and now reflected in FR Regs 2013 reg 28(5).

20 CCMS is the LAA's online system used by civil and family legal aid providers and others assigned to work on their cases. It covers the whole process for certificated civil and family legal aid work, from submitting legal aid applications to paying bills.

21 That is, counterclaims or claims of serious risk of harm, see LASPO 2012 Sch 1 Pts 33 and 35 and the Lord Chancellor's Guidance. See paras 4.8–4.17.

4.26 In order to receive Legal Help, the tenant must attend the adviser's office in person, unless there is a good reason why this is not possible.[22]

The merits test for Legal Help

4.27 At the stage where a Legal Help form is signed, it is too early for an adviser to properly assess the merits of the case. Even so, the circumstances must satisfy the 'sufficient benefit test', ie that:

- it is reasonable for the tenant to be provided with Legal Help, having regard to any potential sources of funding for the tenant other than under legal aid; and
- there is likely to be sufficient benefit to the tenant, having regard to all the circumstances of the case, including those of the tenant, to justify the cost of providing Legal Help.[23]

4.28 It follows that the adviser will only be paid for assisting a tenant with poor housing conditions using Legal Help where possession proceedings are threatened or underway or where there is a 'credible allegation' that the conditions pose a serious risk to the health and safety of occupants of a dwelling.[24]

The extent of Legal Help

4.29 Where the merits criteria are satisfied (see above), Legal Help will cover the preliminary investigation of a 'serious risk to health' claim, including:

- establishing the strength of the tenant's case;
- reasonable endeavours to determine the identity of the landlord, the ownership of the property in question, and whether the landlord is likely to be able to meet any money judgment or is insured (if these can be ascertained);
- whether liability is likely to be contested and, if so, on what basis and with what merit;
- initial correspondence with the landlord (see para 3.59);
- the completion of an application for legal aid on CCMS;
- advice on bringing claims under the EPA 1990 and service of a notice on the owner/responsible person (see chapter 6);

22 Civil Legal Aid (Procedure) Regulations 2012 SI No 3098 reg 22(1)(b)(ii).
23 Civil Legal Aid (Merits Criteria) Regulations 2013 SI No 104 reg 32.
24 LCG para 12.6.

- advice on bringing a claim under LTA 1985 s9A (see chapter 3); or
- advice to resolve the existence of hazards under the HHSRS (under the HA 2004) (see chapter 5).

This does not mean engaging in extensive correspondence or waiting indefinitely for a response from the other party.

4.30 The LCG envisages that an expert's report to establish the nature of the alleged deficiencies and the risk to the tenant's health will normally be obtained under Legal Help.[25] This may mean that in 'serious harm' cases the early stages of the Housing Disrepair Pre-action Protocol may have to be followed while still on Legal Help; although given the urgency, the timescales may well need to be shortened. Where the tenant wants to defend possession proceedings it will probably not be appropriate to obtain an expert's report until proceedings have been started, at which time Legal Help should be replaced with a representation certificate.

4.31 The 2018 Standard Civil Contract's Category Specific Rules for Housing and Debt say at para 10.10 that an expert must not be instructed to prepare a report outside of the Pre-action Protocol except in two situations.

4.32 The first is when the report is required urgently to seek an injunction. In this scenario the report would be within the Protocol in any event so long as a Letter of Claim had been sent first – the Protocol time limits could be considerably shortened.

4.33 The second is when:

> . . . it appears the condition of the property may constitute a statutory nuisance, the landlord has been given notice of the condition and a request for remedial works within a reasonable period of time and that time period has elapsed and the landlord has not made arrangements to take appropriate action.

This means in practice that notice under EPA 1990 s82 must have expired without remedy of the statutory nuisance being abated before an expert can be instructed. It is wise to arrange for the expert to inspect as soon as possible after the notice expires, but to not actually instruct them to do so until the day after the notice has expired, to avoid giving the landlord an extended period to abate the nuisance.

4.34 Investigation of any claim, or combination of claims, should be carried out under one Legal Help matter start. The focus of the

25 LCG paras 12.6 and 12.7.

matter in a 'serious risk to health' claim is on the state of the property rather than a specific set of proceedings. Where the potential claim is a counterclaim in possession proceedings, however, Legal Help can only be used for issues specific to the potential counterclaim.

Payment for Legal Help work

4.35 Payment to advisers is set at standard fixed fees per case, which are based on past national averages for housing work.[26] Extra payment can be made as an 'escape fee' if the costs on hourly rates reach above a threshold,[27] in which case providers can apply to be paid separately at hourly rates.

Help at Court

4.36 Help at Court authorises assistance and advocacy for a client in relation to a particular hearing, without the adviser formally acting as legal representative in the proceedings. In housing conditions cases the use of Help at Court is likely to be limited to cases with sufficient merit but where, because of low value, a tenant needs to argue at a hearing that their claim should not be allocated to the small claims track (see para 4.44).

The boundary between Legal Help and Legal Representation

4.37 The LCG guidance acknowledges that there is considerable overlap between these two levels of legal aid. Legal Help will allow initial investigative work to be carried out to the point where sufficient information is available to assess whether the merits criteria set out in LASPO 2012 and the LCG are satisfied. At that point, the adviser should apply for Legal Representation to continue to investigate and to prepare court proceedings.

4.38 The adviser can follow the Pre-action Protocol, so far as it applies, either under Legal Help or under Legal Representation.[28]

4.39 The adviser is not expected to carry out extensive investigations under Legal Help. In cases where at least six hours of investigation are needed before the adviser can assess the merit of the case, Investigative

26 Currently £157 per case. See Civil Legal Aid (Remuneration) Regulations 2013 SI No 422 Sch 1 Pt 1 Table 1.

27 The threshold is set out in the Remuneration Regs Sch 1 Pt 1 Table 1 and is currently £471. The hourly rate is currently £52.65 inside London and £48.24 elsewhere.

28 LCG para 6.9(d).

Representation – which is a form of Legal Representation – should be used (see para 4.41). In practice, most cases requiring a certificate will proceed straight from Legal Help to Legal Representation and most will start with Legal Representation granted on an emergency basis.

Legal Representation

4.40 Legal Representation (also sometimes called licensed work or certificated work) is a level of civil legal aid service under LASPO 2012, the grant of which authorises legal representation for a party to civil proceedings or for a person who is contemplating taking proceedings. EPA 1990 claims are not covered by Legal Representation as they are not civil claims. The pre-issue work on these EPA 1990 cases may be done under Legal Help, but an alternative funding method must be secured in order to proceed to issue.

4.41 Legal Representation takes two forms: Full Representation and Investigative Representation. Investigative Representation is limited to investigation of the strength of a proposed claim, which might include an application for pre-action disclosure.[29]

4.42 Applications for Full Representation must be made online using CCMS.

The merits test for Legal Representation

4.43 Civil Legal Aid (Merits Criteria) Regulations ('Merits Regs') 2013[30] regs 7 and 8 apply to all housing conditions cases where Legal Representation is sought. The LAA must be satisfied that the likely benefits of the proceedings to the individual justify the likely costs, having regard to the prospects of success and all the other circumstances of the case. The 'reasonable private paying individual test' must also be met, ie 'a reasonable private paying individual would be prepared to start or continue the proceedings having regard to the prospects of success and all the other circumstances of the case'.

4.44 Merits Regs 2013 reg 39 also applies; it requires that:

- the tenant does not have access to other potential sources of funding (other than a conditional fee agreement (CFA)) from which it would be reasonable to fund the case;

29 Civil Legal Aid (Procedure) Regulations 2012 SI No 3098 reg 9.
30 SI No 104.

- the case is unsuitable for a conditional fee agreement;
- there is no person other than the tenant, including a person who might benefit from the proceedings, who can reasonably be expected to bring the proceedings;
- the tenant has exhausted all reasonable alternatives to bringing proceedings including any complaints system, ombudsman scheme or other form of alternative dispute resolution;
- there is a need for representation in all the circumstances of the case including:
  i) the nature and complexity of the issues;
  ii) the existence of other proceedings; and
  iii) the interests of other parties to the proceedings; and
- the proceedings are not likely to be allocated to the small claims track.

4.45 The LCG at para 7.14 suggests that other sources of funding could include legal expenses insurance or collective funding by a group of individuals who stand to benefit and who could potentially gather a fighting fund for the litigation.

4.46 In addition, the tenant has to show that the case has a sufficient prospect of success to justify the funding. Merits Regs 2013 reg 5 as amended classifies 'prospects' as:

- 'very good', which means an 80 per cent or more chance of obtaining a successful outcome;
- 'good', which means a 60 per cent to 79 per cent chance of obtaining a successful outcome;
- 'moderate', which means a 50 per cent to 59 per cent chance of obtaining a successful outcome;
- 'borderline', which means that the case is not 'unclear' but that it is not possible, by reason of disputed law, fact or expert evidence, to:
  i) decide that the chance of obtaining a successful outcome is 50 per cent or more; or
  ii) classify the prospects as marginal or poor;
- 'marginal', which means a 45 per cent to 49 per cent chance of obtaining a successful outcome;
- 'poor', which means less than a 45 per cent chance of obtaining a successful outcome; or
- 'unclear', which means there are identifiable investigations which could be carried out, after which it should be possible to estimate of the prospects of success. An application for Investigative Representation may well be justified for this category.

4.47 To bring a counterclaim in possession proceedings, where the counterclaim forms a defence, and a possession order has not already been made, the tenant must usually have a defence to the claim with at least a 'marginal' prospect of success, and to bring a claim for specific performance in cases of serious risk of harm, the tenant should have at least a 'moderate' prospect of success.[31] The 'moderate' prospect also applies to a counterclaim brought after a possession order has been made. In addition, in specific performance cases the landlord must have been notified of the disrepair or unfitness and have had a reasonable opportunity to resolve the problem.[32]

4.48 Merits Regs 2013 reg 39(b) requires that the case must be unsuitable for a CFA. The LCG suggests that most disrepair claims for specific performance will be suitable for a CFA as long as the tenant can obtain legal expenses insurance. The LCG states that a tenant should try to find insurance with a deferred premium that can be paid out of damages recovered at the end of the case and provides that evidence may be required of attempts to obtain such a policy.[33] If the claim includes damages sufficient to pay for an insurance premium then the prospects of success considered appropriate for a CFA are 60 per cent or more. Where the claim does not include damages then the suggested appropriate prospects of success are 80 per cent or more, and the claim must not involve significant expenditure on disbursements. The same should apply to unfitness claims.

4.49 Although not specifically mentioned in the LCG, the vulnerability of the tenant could affect suitability for a CFA. If the tenant has poor mental health, meaning that they are likely to fail to give instructions to the solicitor or access to the landlord for long periods then the risk to the tenant and instructing solicitor will be too great for a CFA to be appropriate. Without legal aid, the tenant will have no protection from paying the landlord's legal costs if they lose the proceedings. The prospects of success will be reduced. See 'Assessing the risk' at para 4.112 below for other factors affecting the prospects of success of a CFA.

4.50 Where there is disrepair or unfitness that has not been remedied then, subject to the client's financial eligibility and merits, a full Legal Representation certificate will be granted so long as:

31 Merits Regs 2013 regs 43, 61 and 62 as amended.

32 Merits Regs 2013 reg 62.

33 LCG part 7.1.

- there is a serious risk of harm; and
- the case is unlikely to be allocated to the small claims track[34] (ie, the cost of repairs or damages are likely to exceed £1,000[35]).

4.51 In 'serious harm' cases, once the defect causing a serious risk of harm has been remedied, a certificate will be discharged and the LAA will pay for no further work other than the costs claim. This is problematic, as the serious risk of harm can be removed, or the tenant decanted, leaving other defects outstanding and ongoing court proceedings which the tenant is left fighting without representation. If such a scenario arises, the LAA should be notified and a request made for representation to continue to obtain an order for costs. In counterclaims to possession proceedings there is no such issue and the proceedings and counterclaim will be funded to their conclusion so long as the prospects of success and other tests continue to be met.

4.52 Even where the repairs have already been carried out, the tenant is likely to be allowed to pursue a small disrepair or unfitness counterclaim if it will significantly reduce the outstanding rent arrears by way of set-off. This will be the case especially where it is the only way of defeating a possession claim founded on Ground 8 of HA 1988 Sch 2, the mandatory ground for possession based on two months' or eight weeks' rent arrears.

Example

A tenant is faced with possession proceedings. The landlord is a housing association relying on Ground 8 of HA 2988 Sch 2 on the basis of £1,500 rent arrears where the monthly rent is £600, ie the arrears are more than two months' rent. The tenant does not have the means to reduce the arrears to below the two months' rent threshold. The adviser asks whether there have been any disrepair problems and the tenant confirms that, despite complaints, a year ago there was no hot water and heating at the property for three months, but the problem has now been fixed. This would not justify a free-standing application for legal aid to bring a claim, because there is no current threat to health. It *will* justify applying for legal aid to *defend* and counterclaim in the proceedings, because the damages awarded on the counterclaim will reduce the arrears to below two months' rent and will therefore enable a court to refuse an order for possession.

34 Merits Regs 2013 reg 39(f).

35 CPR 26.6(1)(b).

Emergency Legal Representation

4.53 Emergency Legal Representation (ELR) is dealt with in Civil Legal Aid (Procedure) Regulations ('Procedure Regs') 2012[36] Part 5, Merits Regs 2013 reg 46 and in LCG Part 7.27. ELR may be justified if the merits criteria are met and 'it is in the interests of justice to provide representation'.[37] The 'interests of justice' test is satisfied if legal intervention is required before there would be time for the LAA to process a normal application for representation, and that without legal intervention there is a serious risk of:

- loss of life, liberty or physical safety;
- the loss of the client's home;
- a miscarriage of justice;
- unreasonable hardship to the applicant; or
- irretrievable problems in handling the case,

and there are no other appropriate options available to deal with the risk. The time for the LAA to process an application can be found on the LAA current website, but is often 20 working days.[38]

4.54 Delay by the tenant in dealing with the proceedings could be a ground for refusing an emergency certificate, but only if the further delay necessary to process a full application would not cause the sort of risks referred to above.[39]

4.55 The LAA gives most legal aid providers the power to carry out certain functions on its behalf; this is known as having 'delegated functions' (formerly 'devolved powers'). Where an organisation has this authority, it can use its delegated functions to grant ELR in an appropriate case. The exercise of the function must be reported on CCMS. The report must be submitted within five working days of the grant of ELR. Where the organisation does not have this power, or they are unsure about the tenant's means and would prefer the LAA to assess them, an emergency application must be submitted on CCMS.

4.56 The scope of an emergency certificate, setting out the steps that can be taken, can be amended by a provider with delegated functions within the first eight weeks after granting ELR provided that the

36 SI No 3098.

37 Merits Regs 2013 reg 46(b).

38 To find the current process time put 'legal aid guidance – civil processing dates' into a search engine.

39 Merits Regs 2013 reg 11(6); and LCG para 7.29.

certificate has not been issued by the LAA during that period.[40] Similarly the financial limit on an emergency certificate can be extended under delegated functions up to £10,000 but only before the full certificate has been issued or refused by the LAA and only to do urgent work. Any amendment made with delegated functions must be reported to the LAA on CCMS.

4.57 The duration of the certificate (eight weeks) cannot be extended except by the LAA. The adviser must take care to diarise the date that the certificate will expire and, if a full certificate has not been received to replace it, ensure that an application for an extension is lodged well before that date. If the emergency certificate expires without the date being extended, it ceases to be in force and no further work may be carried out under it until the substantive certificate is granted.[41] If work is carried out in this period, the adviser will not be paid for it, even if a substantive certificate is subsequently granted. The adviser needs to be aware of this trap.

Applying for a Representation Certificate

4.58 Applications for a Representation Certificate must be made on CCMS. There are a number of 'Quick Guides' on the LAA system to instruct providers how to use the system. The CCMS system is not at all user-friendly. It is repetitive, subject to frequent crashes (meaning it cannot be accessed whatsoever at many times), and is extremely time-consuming to use. The tenant must sign a declaration stating that all the information input to the system is correct before submitting the application. The majority of applications for a Representation Certificate will be for an emergency certificate, because there is a fast-approaching step in possession proceedings needed or because there is a serious risk of harm warranting an application for an interim injunction. In many cases, the CCMS application will have to be prepared in the first meeting with the tenant so that they can sign the application then and there without the need to return. It is therefore vital that the tenant brings the necessary evidence about their financial means and, where relevant, documents relating to the possession claim, with them to the first meeting.

4.59 The information and documents which are necessary for a CCMS application are discussed below. However this is not an exhaustive list, and what is required will depend on the tenant's circumstances.

40 *Guidance on completing Form CIVAPP8*, April 2013, v1.1 para 6.

41 LAA's Costs Assessment Guidance 2013 para 10.15.

Means documents

4.60 The FR Regs 2013 do not prescribe which supporting documents are acceptable as proof of means, and so alternatives can be provided if the documents suggested by the LAA are not available. However, the application will be processed more quickly if the tenant can find the documents suggested by the LAA.

4.61 If the tenant receives a passported benefit, CCMS should check on the DWP database and instantly confirm whether the benefit is being received. This works effectively. It should therefore not be necessary for the tenant to provide any other proof of benefit or other income. If the database does not find that the benefit is being received, a call to the Department for Work and Pensions (DWP) to ascertain the situation with the tenant in attendance to give consent is the best next step rather than sending the tenant away to find documents. If the tenant is in receipt of universal credit, they will not have confirmation letters. It may be that the tenant is in receipt of a contribution-based rather than income-based benefit and therefore is not passported.

4.62 In all cases, the last three months' bank accounts for every bank account that the tenant and (if relevant) the tenant's partner has are needed. The date requirements are strict. If the application is made on 3 January 2019, then bank statements are needed from 3 November 2018 to 3 January 2019 inclusive. If the tenant has online banking, then these statements can be printed in the adviser's office. If the tenant does not, the tenant should go to the bank to get an up-to-date print-out before the meeting.

4.63 If the tenant does not receive a passported benefit, he or she will need to provide appropriate evidence as set out in part 15 of the Means Assessment Guidance.

Merits documents/information

4.64 The court case number, name of the court and date that proceedings were started are needed if proceedings have already been started – for example, when defending a possession claim.

4.65 If the tenant has building, contents or motor insurance, a copy of the policy schedule is needed to confirm that legal expenses insurance is not included.

Completing the application

4.66 When making an application for legal aid to defend possession proceedings and counterclaim for disrepair on CCMS, an adviser has to answer the same questions twice – first in relation to defending proceedings, and then in relation to the counterclaim. It is almost impossible to estimate which proportion of the costs are applicable to defending possession proceedings and which to the disrepair counterclaim as there is a considerable overlap. The LAA accepts putting the same figures in twice, covering the proceedings as a whole. This can affect the cost benefit analysis calculation that CCMS automatically does with the figures, however this is irrelevant. The proceedings are of overwhelming importance to the tenant as they concern the roof over the tenant's head, so the certificate should be granted whatever the cost benefit ratio is.

Amending certificates

4.67 Only the LAA can amend a substantive certificate. The provider can use delegated functions to amend an emergency certificate while it is live. To obtain an amendment of the certificate, the adviser applies on CCMS. It is not necessary for the tenant to re-sign the declarations unless a means re-assessment is done. The provider can tick the box saying that the tenant has signed the necessary declarations so long as they have the original signed declarations on file.

Notice of issue of certificate

4.68 Procedure Regs 2012 reg 38 requires a legally-aided party to give notice to the opponent of the fact that the case is being funded by the LAA. The 'notice of issue of certificate' is on LAA form NOTICE 1[42] and must tell the opponent that only the client's solicitor or the LAA can give a valid receipt for any damages or costs paid. Failure to serve such a form before the issue of proceedings can affect the tenant's right to recover the legal costs from the landlord. All amendments to the scope of a certificate and the issue of a substantive certificate after an emergency certificate must be similarly notified to the opponent, but the adviser should not show the representation certificate to the opponent or reveal the limitations because these are privileged and would give the opponent a tactical advantage.

Responsibilities of the tenant

4.69 Some certificates require tenants to make monthly financial contributions towards the cost of legal representation. It is important to

42 www.gov.uk/government/publications/notices-certificate-extensionamendment-and-withdrawalrevocation.

stress to tenants the need to keep up regular payments. If they are not paid, the certificate is likely to be suspended, so that no further work may be done by the adviser, and ultimately it may be discharged.

4.70 Tenants must also be reminded that they have an ongoing duty to notify any changes in circumstances to the LAA (via their adviser) for the duration of their case. Some changes may result in a review of the tenant's financial eligibility, for example, if the tenant starts to live with another adult, so that their joint incomes should be aggregated for the purpose of assessing eligibility, or if the tenant takes a new job at a different rate of pay.

The statutory charge

4.71 Where the tenant's case is funded by the LAA, that agency has first call on any property recovered or preserved for the tenant (usually damages in housing disrepair or unfitness cases). This is known as the 'statutory charge'.[43]

4.72 The statutory charge does not apply to any property recovered or preserved under Legal Help alone, ie, where no other level of service is granted before that recovery or preservation.[44]

4.73 However, any property recovered or preserved on behalf of the tenant as a result of work carried out under a Legal Representation certificate will be subject to the statutory charge. The charge will also cover work done under Legal Help, if the work was in connection with the same dispute or proceedings for which the Legal Representation certificate was subsequently issued.[45]

4.74 It is usual for winning tenants to recover costs from their landlords. However, these 'party' costs will exclude costs relating purely to funding issues and, for example, costs of hearings where no orders for costs against the opponent were made, or disbursements for reports that were unhelpful and could not be used in the litigation. It may also exclude unnecessary contact with the tenant such as excessive telephone calls.

4.75 It is, therefore, important to advise tenants in writing at the outset of their case, and at regular intervals throughout, that the statutory charge will bite on their damages. The LAA leaflet 'paying for your legal aid' should be provided to the tenant in the first meeting. Any costs not recovered from the opponent will reduce the tenant's

43 See LASPO 2012 s25; and Civil Legal Aid (Statutory Charge) Regulations 2013 SI No 503 (in both cases as amended and replaced from time to time).

44 Civil Legal Aid (Statutory Charge) Regulations 2013 reg 4(1).

45 Civil Legal Aid (Statutory Charge) Regulations 2013 reg 4(2).

compensation. It follows that it is vital for the adviser to seek appropriate costs orders against opponents, whether at interim hearings, at trial or as part of any settlement and to try and avoid any unnecessary work.

4.76 Damages recovered should be paid to the LAA, where they will be utilised to pay any costs and disbursements which the LAA is liable to pay to the adviser and any counsel. In practice, where costs are going to be recovered from an opponent, solicitors send only enough of the damages to the LAA to cover the costs they intend to claim from the LAA (usually the legal aid only costs which are not recoverable from the opponent). They then give an undertaking on CCMS that the claim for legal aid costs will not exceed what they have sent.

4.77 Once such an undertaking has been given to the LAA, the balance of any damages may be released to the tenant. However, advisers should be wary of releasing damages in this way before costs are actually recovered from an opponent. If, for any reason, the opponent does not pay (eg, because of insolvency), the adviser will be held to the undertaking to the LAA, which will act as a limit on the costs payable by the LAA to the adviser.

Payments to the adviser

4.78 As the case progresses the adviser can ask the LAA to reimburse any expenses such as court fees and expert's fees that have been paid. The adviser can also ask for periodic payments on account of costs. The claim is made electronically through the LAA case management system

4.79 If the case has been successful, damages and costs should be paid by the landlord. In these circumstances, provided there has been an order for costs or an agreement to pay them, the adviser can claim party and party costs from the opponent.[46] This claim will be at whatever hourly rate the local court or the Senior Courts Cost Office (SCCO) normally award; this will be many times higher than the legal aid rate.[47] Once the costs have been recovered, the adviser informs the LAA of the outcome on CCMS. The LAA will then recoup any payments it has made on account and the legal aid certificate is discharged.

46 Full details of the process can be found in the Senior Courts Costs Office Guide at: www.gov.uk/government/uploads/system/uploads/attachment_data/file/430874/senior-courts-costs-office-guide.pdf.

47 Legal aid rate is currently £63.00 per hour (London rate) and £59.40 per hour (non-London rate).

4.80 If the case has failed, then the adviser can have the legal aid certificate discharged. If there have been court proceedings, the costs will be checked by the court on behalf of the LAA. If proceedings were not started, then the assessment process will be carried out by the LAA unless the assessable costs are over £2,500, in which case they will be assessed by the court. More detailed guidance as to who should assess costs is set out in the Costs Assessment Guidance 2018 at para 14. When considering the £2,500 limit, the total amount of costs is calculated as the profit costs and disbursements of all providers, plus all counsel's fees.[48] VAT is not included. An uplift on costs is included. Claims must be submitted within three months of the final assessment of costs by the court or within three months of discharge of the legal aid certificate, as appropriate, and there can be reductions in payments if claims are made late.[49]

4.81 Claims to the LAA are made via creation of a bill on CCMS.

Exceptional Case Funding

4.82 Where a potential claim for poor housing conditions falls wholly or partly outside of scope under the LASPO 2012, it may be possible to apply for Exceptional Case Funding (ECF), at least against social landlords, however in practice few such applications are granted. Any application would have to meet the criteria for ECF funding. The tenant's rights under the European Convention on Human Rights (ECHR) must be engaged. For a housing conditions claim against a social landlord, it will generally be arguable that Article 8 (right to respect for private and family life) and, possibly, Article 1 of Protocol 1 (right to peaceful enjoyment of possessions), if the tenant's belongings are at risk, are engaged. Article 6 (the right to a fair trial), may also be relevant.

4.83 Once that hurdle is surmounted, the adviser will need to address the following three issues:

- the importance of what is at stake;
- the complexity of the tenant's case;
- the tenant's ability to represent him or herself effectively.

4.84 With respect to the importance of what is at stake, proceedings that are purely about damages are less likely to be considered important than proceedings that bear directly on the nature and quality of the tenant's home life. However, the tenant's family life is significantly affected, or

48 Costs Assessment Guidance 2018 v1 para 14.14.

49 CPR 47.18(2) and 47.8.

the tenant's losses or expenses impact on the tenant's ability to meet his or her family's basic needs, this is clearly of importance.

4.85 The legal, factual and procedural complexity of the tenant's case are all relevant. Obtaining and analysing expert evidence, conducting cross-examination at trial, presenting complex legal submissions, understanding evidential requirements and testing of evidence can all be complex procedures that a tenant will not be able to understand or carry out themselves.

4.86 The tenant's mental and physical health, level of education, or ability in English may all be relevant to the tenant's ability to present his or her case effectively. What is important overall is the tenant's ability, or lack of it, to understand and carry out the necessary steps in his or her case. If the landlord is represented, the inequality of arms will be heightened. In housing condition cases that rely heavily on evidence, no assistance that the court may give to the tenant who is conducting his or her own case will be able to compensate for a lack of understanding and preparation of the evidence required.

4.87 In relation to damages claims for housing conditions, the LGC to LAA decision-makers on ECF applications states:[50]

- Where the applicant is seeking to claim damages, what is the level of damages sought? Do they include damages to compensate for items of particular importance to the applicant, such as damage to important medical equipment?
- To what extent is expert evidence necessary to resolve disputes concerning the allegations of disrepair, the medical effects of disrepair or the nature of remedial work required?

4.88 All exceptional funding applications are also subject to the legal aid means and merits criteria.

4.89 Further guidance on an application for ECF is beyond the scope of this book. Advisers are referred to guides and support by the Public Law Project.[51]

Legal expenses insurance

4.90 Some tenants who seek advice will already have legal expenses insurance, perhaps as part of a home contents or motor insurance policy.

50 *Lord Chancellor's Exceptional Funding Guidance (Non-Inquests)*, 2018, para 58.

51 Eg *How to get legal aid Exceptional Case Funding (ECF) in housing law*, Public Law Project, July 2018.

In an appropriate case, a claim might be made on this insurance in the hope that the insurer will be prepared to meet the tenant's own legal costs of bringing a claim about housing conditions. A solicitor has an obligation to consider this possibility in every case.[52]

4.91 Legal expenses insurance might take the form of a stand-alone legal expenses insurance policy, or it may be an addition to some other insurance – for example, home contents insurance. Occasionally, legal expenses insurance is provided as an incidental benefit of having a credit card or bank account, but cover might be limited, eg to telephone legal advice from a solicitor on the insurance company's panel.

4.92 Some policies exclude landlord and tenant disputes, in which case the policyholder cannot use the insurance to fund a claim related to housing conditions. Most policies require notification of a possible claim within 90 days of the date that the policyholder first becomes aware of it. Since tenants usually endure disrepair for many months before consulting an adviser, most tenants find that the insurer declines cover on the basis that it has suffered prejudice as a result of delay. However, it is always advisable to check the exact position.

4.93 The Insurance Companies (Legal Expenses Insurance) Regulations 1990[53] require an insurer to give a policyholder freedom of choice of a solicitor, but most insurance companies insist that the policyholder consults a solicitor on an approved panel, and they will only allow freedom of choice at the point where litigation is about to commence (although the chosen solicitor must agree to the insurer's standard terms of appointment).

4.94 Once legal expenses insurance funding is in place, there will be no need for the adviser and tenant to apply for legal aid or sign a CFA. However, if a claim is pursued with the benefit of legal expenses insurance, the adviser must become acquainted with the sometimes onerous reporting conditions that may apply to such insurance, and keep to those conditions. It is important that both tenant and adviser are clear about any restrictions that the policy may place on their freedom to conduct the litigation, especially where opponents' offers to settle are concerned. Policies sometimes give insurers the right to withdraw insurance cover unless an offer is accepted, even if the adviser considers it too low.

52 *SRA Handbook*, Version 21, December 2018, outcome 1.6 and indicative behaviour 1.16.

53 SI No 1159.

Conditional fee agreements

Introduction to conditional fee agreements

4.95 Conditional fee agreements, known as CFAs (and more popularly as 'no win, no fee' agreements) were introduced by the Courts and Legal Services Act 1990. They allow a solicitor to agree not to charge for the solicitor's legal fees unless the tenant wins the case. To that extent, the Act modifies the indemnity principle under which a solicitor cannot submit a bill to an opponent for more than the tenant would be liable to pay.

4.96 Few tenants are able to afford to pay a solicitor privately so, where a tenant is ineligible for legal aid and has no legal expenses insurance, a CFA may be the only way of funding a case.[54] However, before signing a CFA, solicitors are under a professional duty to discuss with the tenant how the tenant will pay the solicitor's fees, in particular whether the tenant should apply for legal aid (and whether the tenant's own costs are covered by insurance or may be paid by someone else, such as an employer or trade union).[55]

4.97 Counterclaims are rarely suitable for CFAs because the prospects of full cost recovery are not sufficient. That is because the landlord may cover some or all of the costs of their own claim against the tenant.

4.98 Under a CFA, the solicitor is entitled to charge the tenant a 'success fee' if the case is won in civil proceedings. This is to compensate for the risk of not being paid at all and the fact that the solicitor is not remunerated until the end of the case. The success fee is a percentage of the profit costs, namely, the costs that the solicitor is charging, excluding expenses such as court fees and VAT. Some solicitors do not charge a success fee. Others restrict the amount by placing a cap upon it, for example that they will not take more than a quarter of the tenant's damages even if the fee comes to more than that. A cap limiting the deduction from damages is compulsory in any case which has an element of personal injury.[56]

54 *Flatman v Germany; Weddall v Barchester Health Care Ltd* [2013] EWCA Civ 278, [2013] 1 WLR 2676, CA confirms that a solicitor is not liable for a third party costs order if they use a CFA to fund a case on behalf of an impecunious client nor if they fund disbursements.

55 *SRA Handbook*, Version 21, December 2018, outcome 1.6 and indicative behaviour 1.16.

56 Courts and Legal Services Act 1990 s58(4B)(c), Conditional Fee Agreements Order 2013 SI No 680 art 5. Currently 25 per cent of total damages including VAT.

4.99 Prosecutions under the EPA 1990 are specifically permitted to be funded under a CFA, although no success fee can be charged.[57]

Requirements of a conditional fee agreement

4.100 Some of the rules that made CFAs unenforceable were relaxed in 2005 but it is still easy for a relatively small technical breach to prevent solicitors from being paid for their work. The pre-2005 'costs war'[58] has continued to an extent,[59] so solicitors using this model of funding need to be very familiar with the relevant legislation.

4.101 Section 58 of the Courts and Legal Services Act 1990 (as amended by Access to Justice Act 1999 s27 and LASPO 2012 s44) requires that CFA agreements:

- are in writing;
- do not relate to criminal or family proceedings (except for prosecutions under the EPA 1990); and
- specify the success fee, which must be calculated with reference to the legal costs and must not exceed that specified by the Lord Chancellor (currently 100 per cent).

In certain proceedings, the fee is capped at a specified percentage of the damages.[60] At present, the only proceedings that are regulated in this way are those that include a claim for personal injury.[61]

4.102 If the section 58 requirements are not met, then the agreement is unenforceable and, by virtue of the indemnity principle, the losing party is not liable for the winning party's costs. In *Birmingham City Council v Forde*,[62] a disrepair case, it was held that it is possible to rectify a defect in a CFA by asking a tenant to sign a replacement agreement. The rectification must occur before judgment or settlement.[63]

57 Courts and Legal Services Act 1990 s58A(1)(a), Conditional Fee Agreements Order art 2.

58 For examples of this costs war in disrepair cases see *Bowen v Bridgend CBC* [2004] EWHC 9010 (Costs); *Birmingham CC v Crook* [2007] EWHC 1415 (QB) and *Birmingham CC v Forde* [2009] EWHC 12 (QB), [2009] 1 WLR 2732.

59 *Sibthorpe and Another v Southwark LBC* [2011] EWCA Civ 25, [2011] HLR 19.

60 Courts and Legal Services Act 1999 s58(4A).

61 Conditional Fee Agreements Order 2013 SI No 689 art 4.

62 [2009] EWHC 12 (QB), [2009] 1 WLR 2732. Permission to appeal was refused, see [2009] EWCA Civ 865.

63 *Brierley v Prescott* [2006] EWHC 90062 (Costs) and *Oyston v Royal Bank of Scotland* [2006] EWHC 90053 (Costs).

4.103 The CFA does not have to be signed to have effect[64] but any prudent solicitor will obtain the tenant's signature in order to show that the tenant agreed to its terms. Nor do the terms of the CFA have to be contained in one document.[65]

4.104 *Engeham v London & Quadrant Housing Trust Ltd and Academy Plumbing Ltd*[66] is an example of the dangers of a clerical error in a CFA. The claim was brought against two defendants, but only the claim against the first defendant was covered by the wording on the CFA. The second defendant agreed to pay costs and damages. The costs were disallowed. It is not clear from the case report whether the claimant raised the possibility of rectification of the CFA.

Right to information and right to cancel

4.105 The Consumer Contracts (Information, Cancellation and Additional Charges) Regulations ('CCICA Regs') 2013[67] apply to CFAs. CCICA Regs 2013 Sch 1 sets out information that must be included in contracts that are made at the solicitor's premises. The requirements set out in Schedule 1 relate to transparency and, if the solicitor's terms and conditions satisfy the Solicitors Regulation Authority's (SRA's) requirements, then it is very likely that they also comply with Schedule 1.

4.106 If a CFA is signed 'off premises' (that is, during or following a home visit) or 'at a distance' (without a face-to-face meeting with the tenant) then Schedule 2 of the CCICA Regs applies. The solicitor must give the tenant a written notice of the right to cancel together with a prescribed cancellation form. Where a tenant has not been given the notice, the right to cancel the CFA extends for up to 54 weeks.[68] This means that the solicitor has no right to claim for work done either from the tenant or the opponent until after that period has elapsed. Even more worryingly, CCICA Regs 2013 reg 19 makes it a criminal offence to fail to inform the tenant of the right to cancel. Solicitors should consider the regulations carefully.

64 *Utting v McBain* [2007] EWHC 3293 (QB), [2008] 3 Costs LR 442.

65 *Jones v Wrexham Borough Council* [2007] EWCA Civ 1356, [2008] 1 WLR 1590 paras 27 and 86.

66 Reported in December 2013/January 2014 *Legal Action* 17.

67 SI No 3134.

68 CCICA Regs 2013 reg 31.

Professional duties

4.107 There are further professional requirements relating to CFAs which apply to all solicitors. These are set out the Solicitors' Code of Conduct 2011.[69] As a minimum, the solicitor should explain the following to the tenant, both at the outset and, when appropriate, as the matter progresses:

- whether there are other methods of funding that might be more suitable than a CFA;
- the circumstances in which the tenant may be liable for the costs and whether the solicitor will seek payment of these from the tenant, if entitled to do so;
- if the solicitor intends to seek payment for any or all of the costs from the tenant, the tenant's right to an assessment of those costs; and
- an estimate of those costs.

4.108 The solicitor should also provide the usual 'client care' information about how the service is going to be delivered to the tenant and how they might complain if dissatisfied. The Law Society has issued a Practice Note to guide practitioners about the use of client care letters.[70]

Model CFA

4.109 The Law Society has produced a new 'model' CFA for use in personal injury cases which is available on its website and can be adapted by solicitors to make it suitable for housing condition claims.

4.110 The model CFA is a 12-page agreement containing the statutory and basic requirements. Solicitors will also need to draft a 'client care letter' to provide the further information that is required by the SRA code of conduct (see para 4.107). Some solicitors prefer to incorporate all the necessary information into one letter, which becomes the CFA.

4.111 The adapted CFA should contain terms stating that the tenant will give access for works to be carried out and will ensure that no rent arrears accrue or, if there are modest arrears, that these are cleared by the tenant, if necessary by regular instalments. The solicitor would be well advised to withdraw from the arrangement if the

69 See *SRA Handbook*, Version 21, December 2018, at O(1.6) and O(1.13) and IB (1.5), IB(1.16) and IB(1.17).

70 To access this, go to the Law Society's home page (www.lawsociety.org.uk), click on 'Advice and practice notes' and then 'client care information'. Users need a Law Society account to gain access.

tenant breaches these terms, because the likelihood is that the claim will fail and neither damages nor costs will be recovered.

Assessing the risk

4.112 Before the solicitor enters into a CFA with a tenant, it is prudent to carry out a thorough risk assessment. This can be a pro forma document, kept on the file, assessing all the facts of the case on which the solicitor is about to embark.

4.113 In particular, the solicitor should consider at the outset:

- any issues of limitation;
- the identity and solvency of the proposed defendant;
- how the facts can be proved, whether the tenant will make a good witness and whether expert evidence will be necessary;
- whether the tenant seems to have the fortitude to see the case through to a conclusion;
- how liability will be proved;
- any issues of causation;
- the likely value of the claim and the likely track to which proceedings will be allocated;
- the likelihood of the case settling or going to trial;
- general litigation risk; and
- any other special factor that might affect the prospects of success.

4.114 This risk assessment will inform the solicitor about the advisability of undertaking the case on the speculative basis which a CFA represents. A copy should be discussed with and approved by a senior colleague before a CFA is offered to the tenant; and it is good practice to give a copy to the tenant before he or she signs the CFA.

4.115 Not only will the risk assessment help the solicitor to avoid taking on a weak or, worse, a hopeless case, it will also prove invaluable in the task of setting the appropriate success fee for the CFA and justifying that success fee if the costs are challenged by the tenant at the end of the case.

Setting the success fee

4.116 Since the success fee is irrecoverable from the opponent in relation to any CFA entered into after 1 April 2013, it must be paid by the tenant. This is only realistic if the tenant has a claim for damages as well as for specific performance. The tenant has a right to challenge the success fee and must be told of this and reminded of the right when the fee is taken. There is no obligation to charge a success fee and some practitioners avoid problems by not charging one. If a success fee is to be charged, as stated above, it is calculated with reference to the costs net of VAT and disbursements.

4.117 The level should reflect the risk of pursuing the case. The more likely the case is to succeed, the lower the fee should be. There is a 'ready reckoner' that was first explained in *Conditional Fees – a survival guide.*[71] This produces the following figures:

Prospects of success %	Success fee %
100	0
90	11
80	25
75	33.3
70	43
65	54
60	67
50	100

4.118 A success fee of more than 100 per cent of the legal fees makes the whole CFA unenforceable[72] so, even if the solicitor is foolhardy enough to take on a case with a less than 50 per cent chance of success, the uplift will remain at 100 per cent.

4.119 The factors that a court will take into account when assessing the success fee will include:

- the risk that the costs, fees or expenses might not be recovered from the opponent;
- the legal representative's arrangement with the tenant for payment of disbursements such as court fees (if the tenant is paying these then the success fee should be lower than if they are being paid by the solicitor); and
- what other methods of funding were available to the tenant.

4.120 In *Bowen v Bridgend County Borough Council,*[73] a straightforward housing disrepair claim, Master Hurst found that a 25 per cent uplift was appropriate.

71 Michael Napier, Fiona Bawdon and Gordon Wignall, Law Society Publishing (2nd edn, 2001).

72 Courts and Legal Services Act 1998 s58(4)(c); and the Conditional Fee Agreements Order 2013 SI No 689 art 3.

73 [2004] EWHC 9010 (Costs).

4.121 Staged success fees are now common and are popular with judges.[74] In *Designer Guild Ltd v Russell Williams (Textiles) Ltd (trading as Washington DC) (No 2)*,[75] the House of Lords noted that:

> . . . there is an argument for saying that in any case which reached trial a success fee of 100 per cent is easily justified because both sides presumably believe that they have an arguable and winnable case.

It is therefore generally accepted that any case that goes to trial justifies a 100 per cent success fee.

4.122 In *Birmingham CC v Forde*,[76] the CFA in a housing disrepair claim provided for a success fee of 100 per cent of basic charges if the claim concluded at trial, or 75 per cent if the claim concluded before a trial had commenced but after proceedings had been issued, or 50 per cent if the claim concluded before proceedings were issued. Many practitioners adopt a similar formula but with a 25 per cent fee for pre-issue work.

Capping the deduction from damages

4.123 Unsurprisingly, before most tenants sign a CFA they want to know how much they are likely to pay at the end of the case, even if this is going to be deducted from their compensation rather than paid from their own resources. Unless the case includes an injury claim, there is no obligation to limit how much of the tenant's damages the solicitor will take. Even so, many practitioners give a guarantee that as long as the tenant keeps to the terms of the CFA, they will not lose more than 25 per cent from any damages awarded. Usually this cap includes all of the possible deductions that a solicitor might make – that is, deductions for the success fee, unrecovered disbursements and solicitor's costs that are not recoverable from the opponent. Note that these agreements use the word 'awarded' rather than 'recovered'. This is because if a tenant accrues rent arrears as the case progresses, it is only fair that those arrears should come out of the tenant's share of the damages. A cap may not be appropriate where it is unlikely that almost all of the costs are going to be recovered from the opponent, for example where certain parts of the claim have less prospect of success than others but both solicitor and tenant agree that they should be pursued.

74 *Callery v Gray (No 1)* [2001] EWCA Civ 1117, [2001] 1 WLR 2112; *Peacock v MGN Ltd* [2010] EWHC 90174 (Costs).

75 [2003] EWHC 9024 (Costs), 20 February 2003, SCCO. For the full report, see [2003] 2 Costs LR 204.

76 [2009] EWHC 12 (QB), [2009] 1 WLR 2732.

After-the-event insurance

4.124 When acting for a tenant under a CFA, it is desirable to have after-the-event (ATE) legal expenses insurance in place to protect the tenant against the risk of having to pay the opponent's costs should the tenant lose the case.

4.125 A list of ATE insurance providers is printed from time to time in the Law Society's publication *Litigation Funding* but, rather than approach insurers directly, the usual course is to submit an application to a specialist broker, such as 'The Judge'. Their website[77] contains a downloadable proposal form, which must be signed by both solicitor and tenant. A case summary and counsel's advice on merits are often needed to support an application.

4.126 As with all insurance products, the solicitor and tenant should pay very close attention to the often detailed small print of each policy in order to understand the terms and conditions on which insurance is offered.

4.127 The premiums have traditionally been high and are no longer recoverable from the opponent.[78] The reality is that ATE legal expenses insurance is hard to find for most cases of modest value. If insurance cannot be obtained, then the risk of having to pay the opponent's costs, if unsuccessful, should be fully explained to the tenant. Some tenants are willing to take the risk of pursuing a claim without insurance.

4.128 Because the insurance premium is no longer recoverable from the opponent, there is no need to inform the opponent whether insurance is in place.

Paying for disbursements and counsel

4.129 The solicitor may ask the tenant to meet disbursements as they occur, but this arrangement needs to be agreed in advance. If the tenant cannot afford to pay for disbursements, the solicitor will have to do so on the tenant's behalf. The tenant might be asked to make small monthly instalment payments towards the disbursements by standing order. In a case where the disbursements are likely to be very high, the solicitor may apply for specialist 'disbursement funding', which is offered by several banks and brokers. It may not be appropriate to agree to cap the success fee in such a case.

77 www.thejudgeglobal.com/.
78 LASPO 2012 s46.

4.130 As mentioned above, an element of the success fee can reflect the fact that the solicitor is carrying the cost of disbursements until the end of the case (when it is hoped that they will be recovered from the opponent).

4.131 Many barristers are willing to undertake work under a CFA. They will want to consider the papers and carry out their own risk assessment before agreeing to take the case on. There will have to be negotiation with counsel's clerk as to whether the solicitor can afford to pay them a success fee and, if so, whether this will be capped. The solicitor should bear in mind that, if the tenant has been given a guarantee that only a percentage of damages will be taken, any success fee paid to counsel will reduce the amount that the solicitor will receive.

4.132 If the tenant wins the case, the solicitor will be liable to pay the barrister under the CFA, regardless of whether the barrister's fees are recovered from the opponent. The solicitor may wish to retain sufficient damages from the tenant, until those costs are recovered. Paying parties are as likely to challenge the level of the barrister's success fee as they are to challenge the level of the solicitor's success fee. Some barristers are willing to agree to limit their fees to those recovered on their behalf from the opponent.

The final bills

4.133 The tenant must be sent final bills for both the success fee and for the final costs figure (by settlement or assessment).

4.134 In *Allen v Brethertons LLP*,[79] Master Leonard held that neither a success fee nor base costs could be taken by the solicitors until bills had been sent to the client. The final bill also starts the time limits for the tenant to apply for detailed assessment of the solicitor's bill.[80] This is not common in housing conditions matters, but has been in personal injury, where the client seeks to challenge base costs as a way of challenging the amount of the success fee.

79 [2018] EWHC B15 (Costs).

80 If the tenant applies within one month, the bill will be assessed. Between one month and 12 months the tenant can apply to the court to exercise a discretion to order assessment. After 12 months, there is no assessment unless there are special circumstances.

Challenges to CFAs

4.135 The paying party may seek to challenge the validity of a CFA on technical grounds. If a CFA is declared to be unenforceable by the court, then the solicitor will not be entitled to payment of costs (at all), though disbursements incurred on behalf of tenants are still usually recoverable on the basis of quantum meruit.[81]

4.136 In *Hollins v Russell*,[82] it was recommended that a copy of the agreement should be produced to the paying party as part of the costs assessment procedure at the end of the case. Some solicitors have refused to produce the agreement to the opponent on the ground of privilege. However, para 18.2 of the Senior Courts Costs Office Guide 2018 states that it should be usual for a CFA (redacted where appropriate) to be disclosed if a success fee is claimed.

4.137 If faced with a serious challenge to the validity of the CFA, the solicitor may wish to consult specialist costs counsel.

Other sources of funding and support

4.138 Other limited sources of funding and support may be available to tenants who wish to bring a claim related to their housing conditions but do not qualify for legal aid and do not have legal expenses insurance.

4.139 If a tenant is a member of a trade union, the tenant's subscription might give him or her access free legal help with problems relating to housing conditions.

4.140 A Citizens Advice Bureau[83], Law Centre[84] or legal advice clinic[85] may be able to offer a tenant free legal advice. And in appropriate cases, they may also be able to refer a tenant to Advocate, a service through which counsel may provide free advice and legal representation in court.[86]

81 The principle of payment of a reasonable sum in the absence of a contractual obligation. For an example of quantum meruit being employed in a housing CFA case see: *Bowen v Bridgend County Borough Council* [2004] EWHC 9010 (Costs).

82 [2003] EWCA Civ 718, [2003] 1 WLR 2487.

83 www.citizensadvice.org.uk/.

84 www.lawcentres.org.uk/i-am-looking-for-advice.

85 www.lawworks.org.uk.

86 www.weareadvocate.org.uk/.

CHAPTER 5

Private and housing association tenants: involving the local council

> It is simply unacceptable that people are living in cramped, unsafe accommodation provided by landlords who are more interested in a quick profit than the safety or welfare of their tenants.[1]
>
> . . . a small number of rogue or criminal landlords knowingly rent out unsafe and substandard accommodation. We are determined to crack down on these landlords so that they either improve the service they provide or leave the sector.[2]

Introduction

5.1 Poor housing standards are not only of concern to those who occupy unsatisfactory housing – the wider community rightly takes an interest in the quality and safety of the housing stock. It is in everyone's interests that housing should be safe, sound, healthy to live in and not become an eyesore or otherwise adversely impact on the local environment.

5.2 To ensure that these objectives are attained, numerous Housing Acts and other legislative measures – designed to achieve basic minimum conditions in the housing stock – have been on the statute book for over a century. They cast responsibilities on local councils to see that housing in their districts meets basic standards. The standards prescribed and the methods of achieving them have changed over time and it is not necessary to trace the history.[3] The modern approach is largely contained in the Housing Act (HA) 2004.

5.3 In this chapter, those aspects of the housing legislation that are of most assistance to the individual tenant or other occupier will be considered. The text seeks to show how the provisions can be used to help tenants who want to enjoy improved standards of safety, comfort and security in their homes where remedial action is not forthcoming from their landlords.

5.4 Particular advantages and attractions of use of the HA 2004 provisions are that they:

- are not limited to those conditions which amount to 'disrepair' (although the Homes (Fitness for Human Habitation) Act 2018 enables tenant action on conditions other than disrepair);

1 Housing Minister Brandon Lewis MP, 6 November 2015, MHCLG Press Release, *New measures to tackle rogue landlords and overcrowded housing.*

2 From the Introduction to *Tackling rogue landlords and improving the private rental sector: Government's Response*, MHCLG, November 2015.

3 For a synopsis of the relevant history see See D Ormandy, 'Assessing housing conditions: the HHSRS past, present and future', [2014] 17 *Journal of Housing Law* 84.

- carry no obligation of prior notification to the landlord;
- cover latent or inherent defects (although the Homes (Fitness for Human Habitation) Act 2018 may enable tenant action on such defects);
- operate irrespective of the security of tenure of the occupiers;
- deal with problems of design, layout and inadequate facilities (although the Homes (Fitness for Human Habitation) Act 2018 may enable tenant action in this regard);
- operate at no financial cost or financial risk to the tenant;
- in some cases, provide a degree of protection against the retaliatory eviction of a tenant who has triggered action under this legislation;[4] and
- may entitle the tenant to apply for a rent repayment order, if the landlord fails to comply with a notice given under the HA 2004 by a local housing authority.[5] (There is no form of funding available for applications to the First-tier Tribunal for a Rent Repayment Order.)

5.5 As might be expected, the housing legislation does not focus exclusively on the condition of an individual room, flat or house. While the conditions faced by a particular tenant or occupier in his or her home are the focus of this book, this chapter sets out a brief review of the wider powers available to a local council to tackle both:

- individual properties which contain more than one person's home or one household's home ('houses in multiple occupation' or HMOs); and
- groups of properties which form a block, street or area and need to be addressed on a wider basis ('area action').

5.6 Before turning to the detail, it is essential to emphasise that very little of this housing legislation imposes legal obligations on landlords which are directly enforceable by tenants and other occupiers themselves. Instead, the legislation works by casting powers and duties on local housing authorities[6] (primarily, district and borough councils). These powers and duties range from undertaking the initial inspection of residential premises to applying the ultimate sanctions of

4 DA 2015 ss33–34.

5 Since 6 April 2017 tenants can apply to the First-tier Tribunal (Property Chamber) for a Rent Repayment Order even in situations where the Local Authority has not taken steps to prosecute a breach, although the breach will have to be proved to the criminal standard and must have taken place after 6 April 2017. HPA 2016 Chapter 4.

6 Defined in Housing Act (HA) 2004 s261(2).

emptying or demolishing housing stock which does not meet minimum standards.

5.7 It is therefore imperative that tenants and their advisers understand how to trigger action by the relevant local housing authority. It is much more important to know how to get the local housing authority to take up issues and pursue them than to be familiar with the minutiae of the technical assessments that local housing authority officers undertake. It is results that count, much more than the method by which they are achieved.

5.8 For that reason, this chapter first outlines how the powers of local housing authorities can best be invoked, before turning to describe the applicable duties and the available powers they hold.

5.9 There is no lack of enthusiasm on the part of the courts for upholding or enforcing the legislation relating to housing conditions. The judiciary has sanctioned policies of bold use of the housing legislation in attempts to eradicate bad housing. Lord Denning MR said some 40 years ago:

> It seems to me that the policy of Parliament was to make the owners of houses keep them in proper repair. Not only so as to keep up the stock of houses, but also to see that protected tenants should be able to have their houses properly kept up. It would be deplorable if there were no means of compelling owners of old houses to keep them in proper repair; or if the owners could let them fall into disrepair as a means of evicting tenants. Of course, if the state of the house is so bad that it should be condemned whoever was occupying it then let it be demolished or closed or purchased. But if it is worth repairing, then it should be repaired, no matter whether it is occupied by a protected tenant or an unprotected tenant.[7]

5.10 Despite the willingness of the judiciary to back effective use of the legislation by local housing authorities to tackle poor conditions, particularly in the private rented sector, there is a significant number of properties in England in a very unsatisfactory state:[8]

- One in six privately rented homes (16 per cent) present a severe threat to health or safety, falling short of the statutory minimum standard for safe housing.

7 *Hillbank Properties v Hackney LBC* [1978] QB 998 at 1009, (1982) 3 HLR 73 at 82, CA.

8 *A nation of renters: how England moved from secure family homes towards rundown rentals*, CAB & NPI, May 2015, p10: www.npi.org.uk/publications/housing-and-homelessness/nation-renters-how-england-moved-secure-family-homes-towards/. The English Housing Survey data for subsequent years suggests the position has not changed significantly since 2015.

- Nearly one in ten privately rented homes (eight per cent) have serious damp, while 10 per cent pose a risk of a dangerous fall, and six per cent are excessively cold.
- In total, 740,000 households live in a privately rented home that is physically unsafe.
- Half a million (510,000) children live in privately rented homes that are unsafe.

5.11 One obvious limitation of the fact that enforcement of minimum housing standards has been placed in the hands of local housing authorities is that the occupiers of housing stock owned by that same authority cannot trigger the enforcement process. The special position of council tenants in relation to the housing legislation is therefore addressed separately, later in this chapter (at para 5.93). The entry into force of the Homes (Fitness for Human Habitation) Act 2018 has provided options for council tenants to take steps to enforce adequate housing conditions. As social tenancies come to fall under the new requirements of Landlord and Tenant Act (LTA) 1985 s9A, the tenants will be able to bring civil claims against their landlords in respect of housing conditions.

5.12 Another feature of this housing legislation is that much of it is concerned with bad housing conditions that can give rise to risks to health or cause nuisance. Those conditions are also the target of the new LTA 1985 s9A, and also of the environmental health legislation reviewed in chapter 6 of this book. The latter legislation may also be enforced by the same local housing authorities. Tenants and their advisers therefore need to encourage local housing authority officers to review their full portfolio of powers and responsibilities and to deploy the remedial action most likely to be effective in addressing the deficiencies at a particular property.

Getting prepared to take action

5.13 Before taking even the first steps to invoke the exercise of local housing authority powers, tenants and their advisers need to understand what might be achievable and what consequences might follow from involving the local housing authority.

5.14 Tenants and their advisers will find that a broad outline of local housing authority powers and duties under the HA 2004 is given in the remainder of this chapter. However, that is no substitute for the need to have access to the primary materials. In discussion and in correspondence with local housing authorities, advisers will certainly need to make reference to extracts from the HA 2004 itself, to the regulations and the orders made under it,[9] and to the key statutory guidance issued on its implementation.[10] Although much of the primary material is available on the internet, those seeking a detailed treatment will find it in a good textbook or handbook such as *Using the Housing Act 2004*.[11]

5.15 Before invoking action by a local housing authority, any adviser will also need some appreciation of how the particular local housing authority has organised itself to utilise its HA 2004 powers and to enforce the statutory requirements. Most local housing authorities have delegated their Housing Act responsibilities to their local environmental health officers (EHOs). Advisers will need to know where the local EHOs are based, how they are deployed (whether by geographical patch or by regulatory subject area), when and how they may best be contacted, and what local procedures have been adopted for the exercise of enforcement powers.

5.16 Most crucially, the focus must be on what the tenant wishes to achieve and whether involving the local housing authority will help or hinder that objective. If the tenant wants to secure re-housing (most often from the private rented sector into social rented housing), invoking the Housing Act powers of the local housing authority may prove counter-productive. If the measures taken do actually improve the condition of the tenant's home, that may result in a lowering of priority on any waiting list where priority has been given on account of unsatisfactory housing conditions.[12] Likewise, if it might be possible to have the tenant accepted by the local housing authority as being 'homeless' – because conditions are so poor that it is not reasonable to remain in occupation[13] – the prospects of success with that approach will reduce if conditions are improved. On the other hand, some enforcement activity may result in permanent displacement of the tenant, triggering an obligation on the local housing authority to

9 Particularly, the Housing, Health and Safety Rating System (England) Regulations 2005 (HHSRS Regs 2005) SI No 3208.

10 Communities and Local Government (CLG), *Housing Health and Safety Rating System Enforcement Guidance, Housing Act 2004 Part 1: Housing Conditions* (the 'Enforcement Guidance'), August 2006, issued under HA 2004 s9; and CLG, *HHSRS Operating Guidance – Housing Act 2004: Guidance about inspections and assessment of hazards given under Section 9* (the 'Operating Guidance'), February 2006.

11 Carr, Cottle and Ormandy, *Using the Housing Act 2004*, Jordans, 2008.

12 HA 1996 s166A(3)(c) (England).

13 HA 1996 s175(3) (England).

secure re-housing and possibly pay compensation (see para 5.91 below).

5.17 Even more important, if the tenant is a private sector tenant with only the limited security of an assured shorthold tenancy (or even an unprotected tenancy) the tenant and any adviser will need to consider the real risk that, if the local housing authority is called-in to take action, the landlord may retaliate by seeking recovery of possession[14] (or perhaps by seeking an increased rent at the next opportunity). In some cases, this possibility of repossession can be precisely what the tenant in fact wants. If the tenant is in a priority need category for the purposes of homelessness legislation, he or she may be pleased to have the prospect of an unanswerable possession claim generated as the landlord's response to the local housing authority's enforcement of Housing Act powers.

5.18 If the landlord does 'retaliate', by serving a notice of possession under HA 1988 s21 and the tenant does not want to leave, an adviser should check the relevant legal provisions governing the validity of a section 21 notice and in particular whether:

- for tenancies granted or renewed[15] after 1 October 2015, the tenant is protected by the provisions designed to tackle retaliatory eviction (see para 3.31);
- for the same group of tenants, the notice is in the prescribed form;
- the premises are in an unlicensed building for which the landlord should have a licence under the applicable housing legislation but does not;
- the landlord has failed to protect, under an approved deposit protection scheme, any deposit that the tenant has paid or has failed to give the tenant prescribed information about the protection of the deposit;
- the landlord has failed to provide a gas safety certificate;
- the landlord has failed to provide an energy performance certificate; and/or

14 This concept of 'retaliatory eviction' is described in D Crewe, *The tenant's dilemma – Warning: your home is at risk if you dare complain*, Citizens Advice, June 2007. In some countries it provides a defence to possession proceedings: see, eg Civil Code of California, section 1942.5. In England, it can now provide a defence to some private sector tenants: DA 2015 s33.

15 'Renewal' for this purpose does not include the triggering after 1 October 2015 of a statutory periodic tenancy which follows automatically on the expiry of a fixed tenancy granted before that date.

- the landlord has failed to provide certain prescribed material (currently the official leaflet *How to rent: the checklist for renting in England*).[16]

5.19 In any of those circumstances, the landlord may be unable to rely on the HA 1988 s21 notice to recover possession.[17]

Mobilising the local housing authority

5.20 All local housing authorities are under a statutory duty to keep housing conditions in their area under review, with a view to identifying any action that may be needed under the HA 2004 and related legislation.[18] Sadly, very few local housing authorities interpret this as requiring a systematic inspection of all housing in their districts, whether by a rolling programme of inspections or otherwise. It is often said that they lack the financial and other resources to undertake such exercises or deal with the consequences they may throw up. Local housing authorities are not even required by the HA 2004 to inspect properties that they themselves make available for homeless households as suitable accommodation.[19] The Secretary of State has reserved powers to give directions to local housing authorities about undertaking their review duties but has not yet exercised them.[20]

5.21 More commonly, individual properties are brought to the attention of local housing authorities by complaints from tenants and their advisers or by referral from others (such as fire authorities and other agencies).[21]

16 www.gov.uk/government/publications/how-to-rent.

17 HA 2004 ss75, 98 and s215; DA 2015 ss33 and 34; and the Assured Shorthold Tenancy Notices and Prescribed Requirements (England) Regulations 2015 SI No 1646 as amended.

18 HA 2004 s3(1).

19 *Firoozmand v Lambeth LBC* [2015] EWCA Civ 952, [2015] HLR 45.

20 HA 2004 s3(3)(a).

21 One report found that most local housing authorities take action in response to 'complaint or service requests, rather than as the result of . . . any coherent strategic approach': Dr Stephen Battersby, *Are private sector tenants being adequately protected – a study of the Housing Act 2004, Housing Health & Safety Rating System and local authority interventions in England*, June 2011 (see too, by the same author, an earlier paper *Housing enforcement activity by local authorities in England & Wales*). A follow up survey by the Chartered Institute of Environmental Health found that 'the vast majority of local authorities take a reactive approach to inspections': Bob Mayho, *Housing (enforcement survey): results and commentary*, CIEH, November 2011.

5.22 If a local housing authority considers, whether by reason of a complaint or as part of its own review of its district, that it would be appropriate for any residential premises to be inspected under the HA 2004 Part 1 (Housing Conditions), then the local housing authority *must* arrange for an inspection to be carried out.[22]

5.23 The statutory Enforcement Guidance[23] rather curiously describes the duty to inspect in these terms:

> While there is not an express duty on local authorities to inspect properties where they think there might be hazards, sections 3 and 4 of the Act, when taken together, imply that an authority should have good reason not to investigate further.[24]

5.24 The better view is that where the information that it has received causes the local housing authority to consider that an inspection would be appropriate, then it is under a mandatory statutory duty to inspect.

5.25 The Enforcement Guidance recognises that requests for inspections may be received at a rate too great for a local housing authority to carry out an immediate inspection on receipt of each request. It suggests that:

> Authorities will need to prioritise inspections and in doing so may have regard to their wider housing strategies and the individual circumstances of the case before them. Local authorities may feel that priority should be given to complaints or referrals from sources such as social services child protection teams, the police, the fire and rescue authority and Warm Front managers, and also from other occupiers, directly or indirectly through local councillors.[25]

5.26 Research has suggested that tenants will benefit from the request for inspection (and any pressure for subsequent action) being channelled through and pursued by an adviser. One report found that:

> . . . a majority of the authorities investigated maintained that it was the presence of a local voluntary housing advice centre or law centre which encouraged strictest compliance with statutory powers.[26]

5.27 Although local housing authorities have substantial powers to tackle unsatisfactory rented housing, a frequent difficulty for advisers is in mobilising an authority into taking any action, even an initial

22 HA 2004 s4(2).

23 See note 10 above.

24 Enforcement Guidance para [2.6].

25 Enforcement Guidance para [2.8].

26 Hawke and Taylor, 'Compulsory repair of individual physically substandard housing', [1984] *Journal of Social Welfare Law* 129 at 132.

inspection. The UK Government guidance recommends that local housing authorities each 'have a clearly publicised contact number and email address for reporting bad practice among landlords and letting agents',[27] however, this is often not the case. Advisers must be prepared to press the local housing authority forcefully on the need for action. Initially, this may take the form of letters, emails and telephone calls to the local housing authority's EHOs. If the officers fail to act, approaches to local councillors or the local Member of Parliament may be necessary.

5.28 If such pressure produces no response within a reasonable period, advisers should consider obtaining and presenting an 'official complaint'. This is *not* the same as a complaint under the local housing authority's ordinary complaints procedure.

5.29 Under HA 2004 s4, a justice of the peace (JP) for an area may make an 'official complaint' to the local housing authority that a Category 1 or Category 2 hazard (see para 5.4) is present on the premises.[28] On receipt of such an official complaint, the local housing authority is bound to:

- inspect the premises;[29] and
- consider a report from the inspecting officer if the officer is of the opinion that such a hazard does exist at the premises.[30]

A similar official complaint may be made by a parish or community council, with like effect.[31] See appendix C for a draft request for an official complaint and the text of a sample complaint.

5.30 It is not procedurally difficult to arrange for such an official complaint to be made. Advisers can draft all the necessary documents themselves and need only satisfy a JP, parish council or community council that particular premises have a Category 1 or Category 2 hazard. That can be done by inviting a visit to the premises or by providing a short report (perhaps with photographs).

5.31 As far as official complaints made by JPs are concerned, practice varies considerably in arrangements made at local magistrates' courts for dealing with these cases. Most justices' clerks will simply make an *ad hoc* arrangement for a magistrate to be available to consider a paper or personal request. However, the speediest method

27 *Improving the Private Rented Sector and Tackling Bad Practice: A Guide for Local Authorities*, DCLG, March 2015, para 29.

28 HA 2004 s4(3)(a).

29 HA 2004 s4(2).

30 HA 2004 s4(6).

31 HA 2004 s4(3)(b).

is to set up an official complaint on an informal basis with a JP known personally to the adviser or tenant or to arrange for a local parish or community councillor to raise the matter at a parish council or community council meeting.

5.32 Unfortunately, the HA 2004 contains no statutory timetable or deadline within which local housing authorities must respond to invitations to inspect or to official complaints. All the Act provides is that where, following an official complaint, the inspecting EHO concludes that there are hazards on the premises he or she must report to the local housing authority without delay and the local housing authority must consider this report as soon as possible.[32]

5.33 If a local housing authority is dilatory in arranging an inspection on request, or in responding to an official complaint (see para 5.29), or even in taking action following an inspection, the tenant will need to bring a claim for judicial review in the Administrative Court (after giving notice by way of a pre-action protocol letter[33]) seeking a mandatory order requiring the local housing authority to act. Experience would suggest that receipt by a local housing authority's legal department of notice of intention to take such proceedings is usually sufficient to galvanise the local housing authority into action.

5.34 In certain cases, particularly those exemplifying systemic delay or inaction, complaint through the local housing authority's own internal complaints procedure and ultimately to the Local Government Ombudsmen may be worthwhile. Failure by a local housing authority to act, when it is known that a property may require statutory action, is maladministration, notwithstanding the resource implications for local housing authorities of enforcing the legislation.

5.35 Four common explanations tendered by local housing authority officers for failure to take prompt and effective action are: 1) problems securing access to premises; 2) inability to identify the landlord or owner of the property; 3) the need to follow elaborate procedures set out in the local enforcement protocol; and 4) lack of financial resources. Advisers should be ready to meet all these points:

1) **Access** Obviously, the local housing authority should be furnished with all necessary contact details so that the tenant can give access to the tenanted areas. Beyond that, and for access in relation to common parts and other parts retained by the landlord or let to others, HA 2004 s239(3) gives local housing authority officials powers of entry to premises at any reasonable time. Although

32 HA 2004 s4(6) and (7).

33 Civil Procedure Rules, *Pre-action Protocol for Judicial Review.*

24 hours' notice should usually be given,[34] immediate access may be obtained without notice when it is necessary to ascertain whether certain offences are being committed[35] or where emergency remedial action is required.[36] Further detail about the procedure for undertaking the inspection, once access is secured, is given in the statutory Operating Guidance.[37]

2) **Information** The tenant ought to be in a position to readily identify the landlord from the tenancy agreement, rent book or notice given by the landlord under the provisions of Landlord and Tenant Act (LTA) 1987 s48. That information can be passed to the local housing authority. If the tenant does not have the landlord's details (eg because they usually deal with an agent) the details must be supplied if the tenant makes a written request for them to the person receiving the rent.[38] However, some local housing authorities prefer to make their own official requests for information about ownership and the identity of the landlord (not least because there can be criminal sanctions for a landlord or agents failure to comply) and will not take enforcement action until they have received a response.[39]
3) **Procedural delay** Each local housing authority will have adopted its own local 'policy and procedure' code regulating its enforcement activities (including HA 2004 enforcement). Advisers should secure a copy. Appropriate compliance with the published procedures should produce speedy rather than delayed action. Advisers will need to ensure that any time-scales published in the local code are complied with. The central government guidance to local housing authorities states that 'authorities should not delay too long or hesitate to use the legal powers at their disposal if a landlord fails to remedy an issue, or ignores repeated attempts of contact by officials'.[40]
4) **Lack of resources** Each local housing authority should have allocated resources to fund action to tackle bad housing in its area. In

34 HA 2004 s239(5).

35 HA 2004 s239(6).

36 HA 2004 s40(6).

37 Operating Guidance, chapter 4 and annex B.

38 Landlord and Tenant Act 1985 (LTA 1985) s1.

39 For examples of the difficulties that can arise as to the correct person to be served with a HA 2004 notice see *Hastings BC v Braear Developments Ltd* [2015] UKUT 145 (LC) and *Wood v Kingston Upon Hull CC* [2015] UKUT 0165 (LC).

40 *Improving the private rented sector and tackling bad practice: a guide for local authorities*, DCLG, March 2015, para 40.

November 2015, the UK Government announced distribution of a further £5 million among 65 local housing authorities in England specifically to enable them to:[41]

- increase inspections of property;
- carry out more raids;
- initiate more enforcement action and prosecutions; and
- demolish sheds and buildings that are prohibited.

That followed an announcement in March 2015 that the UK Government had already 'made available £6.7 million to a number of local authorities to help tackle the acute and complex problems they face in tackling rogue landlords'.[42]

5.36 In November 2018 the government announced Rogue Landlord Enforcement grants worth £2 million aimed at the development of best practice among local authorities in enforcement activities to raise standards in the private rented sector.[43]

5.37 Obviously, at the end of an inspection the tenant and adviser will want to know what has been noted and what action will be taken. Although it is good practice, rather than a legislative requirement, that copies of inspection records be provided, the Housing Health and Safety Rating System Regulations (HHSRS Regs) 2005[44] require that inspection records are prepared and retained[45] and the Operating Guidance advises that:

> . . . any inspection should ensure that sufficient clear information is recorded to substantiate the findings and provide the evidence to support the judgments and decisions. That information should be recorded in a form which is logical and readily understandable, in particular by occupiers and owners.[46]

Assessment of the property

5.38 Under the legislation which the HA 2004 replaced, local housing authority EHOs were looking to see whether premises were 'unfit for human habitation' or 'in substantial disrepair'. As described in chapter 6, those EHOs were using the Environmental Protection

41 *New funding to crack down on rogue landlords and tackle 'beds in sheds'*, DCLG press release, 11 November 2015.

42 Lord Ahmad of Wimbledon, Written statement to the House of Lords, 13 March 2015.

43 Rogue Landlord Enforcement Grant, MHCLG, November 2018.

44 SI No 3208.

45 HHSRS Regs 2005 reg 5.

46 Operating Guidance, annex B, para [B2].

Act (EPA) 1990 to identify whether premises are a 'statutory nuisance'. However, an inspection and assessment under HA 2004 Part 1 seeks to identify and address what the Act terms as 'hazards'.

5.39 For the purposes of the HA 2004, a 'hazard' means any risk of *harm* to the *health* or safety of an actual or potential occupier of a dwelling which arises from a *deficiency* in the dwelling or in any *building* or land in the vicinity.[47]

5.40 The Act provides supplementary interpretations for each of the words italicised. 'Harm' includes temporary harm.[48] 'Health' includes mental health.[49] 'Building' includes parts of a building.[50] 'Deficiency' may arise as a result of construction, absence of maintenance, want of repair or otherwise.[51]

5.41 The task of the local housing authority is to identify whether any hazards are present and then to classify them. The most serious hazards are Category 1 hazards. The next most serious hazards are classified as Category 2. In short, if a Category 1 hazard is identified, the local housing authority will be under a duty to take action. If a Category 2 hazard is found, the local housing authority is under no obligation to act, but has the statutory power to do so. In most circumstances, therefore, the tenant will want the assessment to produce a finding that there is a Category 1 hazard.

5.42 The process of assessment is highly technical (arguably, unnecessarily so). It is carried out by local housing authority officials in accordance with detailed provisions in the Act, the regulations made under it, the Operating Guidance, and the Enforcement Guidance, together running over many hundreds of pages. In 2013, the report of an inquiry into the private rented sector recommended that the government should consult on a 'simpler more straightforward set of quality standards for housing in the sector.'[52] Such a consultation exercise was then undertaken. In its report on the results, the government concluded that it was not necessary 'to update the methodology or produce a revised version of the operational guidance'.[53] Instead, it published a layperson's guide: *Renting a safe home: a guide for tenants*, which was

47 HA 2004 s2(1).
48 HA 2004 s2(4).
49 HA 2004 s2(5).
50 HA 2004 s2(4).
51 HA 2004 s2(1).
52 House of Commons Select Committee on Communities and Local Government, *First report of session 2013/14*, HLC 50, July 2013.
53 *Review of property conditions in the private rented sector: Government response*, DCLG, March 2015.

updated in 2018 and now published as *How to rent a safe home.*[54] Advisers seeking to help tenants invoke a local housing authority's inspection and assessment procedure should ensure that those tenants are provided with copies. In late 2018, the Government announced that there will be a further review of the HHSRS and its operation.[55]

5.43 In short summary, the process is as follows:

1) an assessment is made of the likelihood of a person suffering any harm as a result of the hazard (this includes potential occupiers and their vulnerabilities, not just the current occupiers);
2) an assessment is then made of the range of probable harmful consequences of that hazard;
3) the results of the two strands of assessment are combined to produce a numerical score (using a prescribed methodology);
4) the numerical score is considered against a range of scores grouped into prescribed bands;
5) if the banding is A, B or C, the hazard is a Category 1 hazard; and
6) any lower banding is a Category 2 hazard.

5.44 For the purposes of illustration only, take a property affected by dampness and mould growth. 'Damp and mould growth' is a hazard of a prescribed description if there is a risk of harm from exposure to house dust mites, damp, mould or fungal spores.[56] The classes of potentially relevant harmful consequences are listed in the regulations and range from 'death' and 'regular severe pneumonia' in Class 1 to regular serious coughs and colds in Class 4.[57] The task of assessment involves a calculation of the degree of risk of some harm from the dampness or mould growth and the likely severity of the harm it may cause. That assessment is then reduced to numbers and percentages.[58] The numbers then fall into numerical score ranges identifying the appropriate band for those numbers.[59] If the dampness and mould is assessed as falling in bands A, B or C it will be a Category 1 hazard.[60] If in any other band, it will be a Category 2 hazard. The hazards are discussed in more detail below.

5.45 This short description of the assessment process should suffice to demonstrate that assessment is something of an 'art' as well as a

54 Current edition at the time of writing MHCLG, 26 June 2018.
55 MHCLG press release 26 October 2018.
56 HHSRS Regs 2005 reg 3 and Sch 1.
57 HHSRS Regs 2005 reg 2 and Sch 2.
58 HHSRS Regs 2005 reg 6.
59 HHSRS Regs 2005 reg 7.
60 HHSRS Regs 2005 reg 8.

science. It is not a field into which the non-specialist should trespass unguided. Those seeking to delve a little further will greatly benefit from both the House of Commons Library Briefing Paper *Housing, Health and Safety Rating System (HHSRS) 01917*[61] and the *Housing Health and Safety Rating System – Guidance for Landlords and Property Related Professionals*.[62]

5.46 If the tenant or adviser is dissatisfied with an assessment, the best course of action is to ask for a re-assessment by a second officer of the local housing authority or, failing that, to commission an inspection and report from an independent environmental health expert. Advisers personally taking on the daunting task of seeking to influence the making of, or a revision of, an assessment will need to become very familiar with the extensive statutory guidance contained in the Operating Guidance,[63] which is the primary negotiating tool on the subject.

The HHSRS Hazards

5.47 The 29 prescribed descriptions of hazards in the HHSRS Regs 2005[64] are extensive, covering risks to health and safety arising from the design and condition of the building, and also its occupation:

Damp and mould growth

1. Exposure to house dust mites, damp, mould or fungal growths.

Excess cold

2. Exposure to low temperatures.

Excess heat

3. Exposure to high temperatures.

Asbestos and MMF

4. Exposure to asbestos fibres or manufactured mineral fibres.

Biocides

5. Exposure to chemicals used to treat timber and mould growth.

Carbon monoxide and fuel combustion products

6. Exposure to–

   (a) carbon monoxide;

61 19 May 2016.

62 DCLG, May 2006.

63 See note 10 above.

64 HHSRS Regs 2005 Sch 1.

(b) nitrogen dioxide;

(c) sulphur dioxide and smoke.

Lead

7. The ingestion of lead.

Radiation

8. Exposure to radiation.

Uncombusted fuel gas

9. Exposure to uncombusted fuel gas.

Volatile organic compounds

10. Exposure to volatile organic compounds.

Crowding and space

11. A lack of adequate space for living and sleeping.

Entry by intruders

12. Difficulties in keeping the dwelling or HMO secure against unauthorised entry.

Lighting

13. A lack of adequate lighting.

Noise

14. Exposure to noise.

Domestic hygiene, pests and refuse

15. (1) Poor design, layout or construction such that the dwelling or HMO cannot readily be kept clean.

(2) Exposure to pests.

(3) An inadequate provision for the hygienic storage and disposal of household waste.

Food safety

16. An inadequate provision of facilities for the storage, preparation and cooking of food.

Personal hygiene, sanitation and drainage

17. An inadequate provision of–

(a) facilities for maintaining good personal hygiene;

(b) sanitation and drainage.

Water supply

18. An inadequate supply of water free from contamination, for drinking and other domestic purposes.

Falls associated with baths etc

19. Falls associated with toilets, baths, showers or other washing facilities.

Falling on level surfaces etc

20. Falling on any level surface or falling between surfaces where the change in level is less than 300 millimetres.

Falling on stairs etc

21. Falling on stairs, steps or ramps where the change in level is 300 millimetres or more.

Falling between levels

22. Falling between levels where the difference in levels is 300 millimetres or more.

Electrical hazards

23. Exposure to electricity.

Fire

24. Exposure to uncontrolled fire and associated smoke.

Flames, hot surfaces etc

25. Contact with–

(a) controlled fire or flames;

(b) hot objects, liquid or vapours.

Collision and entrapment

26. Collision with, or entrapment of body parts in, doors, windows or other architectural features.

Explosions

27. An explosion at the dwelling or HMO.

Position and operability of amenities etc

28. The position, location and operability of amenities, fittings and equipment.

Structural collapse and falling elements

29. The collapse of the whole or part of the dwelling or HMO.

5.48 The approach to the hazards is not concerned with issues of repair, or, as will become clear, with the interests of the current tenant. The hazards are instead conceived of in terms of risks to health and safety of potential occupiers of the building. So, while some hazards address defects that might be considered to be repair problems (eg: adequate water supply; structural collapse; electrical safety; excess cold; deficient lighting; gas leaks and carbon monoxide), others are more concerned with the safety of the physical layout of the building (for example: falling on stairs or level surfaces; falls associated with baths; positioning of fittings and amenities; or difficulty in cleaning due to layout). Other hazards address the security of the property, and overcrowding.

5.49 While some hazards will arise from issues with the condition or design of the property that can be remedied for the benefit of the current tenant, others might have their remedy in ending the current tenancy. (For example, overcrowding, or falling hazards where the tenant is elderly or at a greater risk of falls.) The issues that this presents should be considered before seeking an inspection.

5.50 However, the HHSRS Regs hazards do address common issues faced by tenants, such as:

- mould growth;
- inadequate or defective electrical, heating, water and sanitary installations;
- inadequate fire safety to the dwelling, or building;
- excess cold, or excess heat;
- pest infestation;
- lack of physical security; and
- unsafe doors and windows.

5.51 On fire safety, the government issued an *Addendum for the profile for the hazard of fire and in relation to cladding systems on high rise residential buildings* to the HHSRS Operating Guidance on 1 December 2018.[65] This specifically addresses the issue of unsafe cladding on high rise buildings and the approach to be taken under HA 2004, in the wake of the Grenfell Tower tragedy and the large number of high-rise residential buildings in the private sector with similar cladding.

65 MHCLG December 2018. Available at https://assets.publishing.service.gov.uk/government/uploads/system/uploads/attachment_data/file/760150/Housing_Health_and_Safety_Rating_System_WEB.pdf.

Selecting the appropriate action

5.52 Once a local housing authority has made its assessment of the hazard, the results will dictate the necessity for action. If a Category 1 hazard has been identified, the local housing authority take what it considers to be the most appropriate enforcement action from the available statutory menu of options (considered below).[66] If the assessment has identified a Category 2 hazard, the local housing authority has a power (but is not under a duty) to take enforcement action.

5.53 The tenant or adviser faced with an assessment of only a Category 2 hazard should not assume that no action will be taken. The Enforcement Guidance expressly states that:

> Authorities have a general power under section 7 to take enforcement action in relation to Category 2 hazards. But aside from hazards which are at the upper range, in band D for example, residential property may contain a number of more modestly rated hazards which appear to create a more serious situation when looked at together. There may for example be a minor hazard to health from damp in the bathroom ceiling, plus a moderate fall hazard from a loose but not actually broken handrail on the stairs, plus a food hygiene hazard from old-fashioned preparation facilities in the kitchen. In this example, the hazards do not combine in any measurable way. However, the situation in the property may be considered unsatisfactory because the occupants encounter one hazard after another as they move around. Such a property may be perceived as less safe than one with a single high-scoring hazard.
>
> There may be pressure on authorities, particularly from tenants, to act against a number of moderate hazards on the grounds that they present a picture of a run-down property, even though no single hazard is evidence of a serious risk to health and safety. HHSRS is designed to deal with all hazards, no matter how serious, which arise from deficiencies in and around the home. Therefore, *even minor Category 2 hazards need not go un-addressed*, if the local housing authority considers that it is appropriate in all the circumstances to take action in relation to those hazards. Authorities can use their powers to deal with single or multiple Category 2 hazards. More generally, authorities may also decide that they will *always* act on certain bands of Category 2 hazards.[67] [Emphasis added]

5.54 If reference to that Guidance does not produce the desired result from the tenant's or the adviser's perspective, where an initial

66 The Enforcement Guidance does not match the HA 2004 in this regard. It suggests that informal resolution should be attempted. Unfortunately, this has led to a reluctance to serve any form of notice, even where it is mandatory to do so, as with a category 1 hazard.

67 Enforcement Guidance paras [4.16]–[4.17].

Category 2 assessment has been made, the local housing authority can be asked to exercise its discretion and take action given particular factual circumstances. A local housing authority that responded that it *never* took action in respect of Category 2 hazards notwithstanding the Enforcement Guidance – perhaps on the basis of a lack of resources – would be unlawfully fettering its discretion and should be made subject to judicial review proceedings. If a reasoned explanation is proffered for why no action is going to be taken on the Category 2 hazard in the particular case, the preferred course may be to invite a further inspection (perhaps following a tenant's representations) or to commission an independent inspection and report – with a view to reconsideration and the assessment moving into Category 1.

5.55 The range of enforcement actions available to the local housing authority includes:[68]

- service of a hazard awareness notice;
- issuing an improvement notice;
- making a prohibition order;
- making a demolition order;
- declaring a clearance area;

and (where a Category 1 hazard is present and posing an immediate risk):

- emergency remedial action; or
- making an emergency prohibition order.

5.56 The different alternatives are described more fully below. Advisers pressing for one course of action to be pursued in preference to others should become familiar with the extensive statutory guidance contained in the Enforcement Guidance,[69] which is the primary negotiating tool on the selection of options to be pursued.[70] Where the tenant is likely to need protection from a 'retaliatory eviction' by the landlord (see para 5.18), it will be essential that the local housing authority serves an improvement notice under HA 2004 ss11–12 or an emergency remedial action notice, as those are the only forms of notice capable of triggering the protection offered by Deregulation Act (DA) 2015.[71]

68 HA 2004 s5(2).

69 See note 10.

70 Appeals by landlords against the selection of particular enforcement measures are also building up a significant body of case-law on the correct choice of enforcement tool. See, for examples, *Bolton MBC v Patel* [2010] UKUT 334 (LC); *Bristol CC v Aldford Two* LLP [2011] UKUT 130 (LC); and *Liverpool CC v Kassim* [2012] UKUT 169 (LC).

71 DA 2015 s33(13) defining 'relevant notice'.

5.57 If only one option is possible, the local housing authority must take that action.[72] In all other circumstances, the local housing authority has a choice to make as to which is the most appropriate course of action and it must take the form of action it selects.[73] Although no two options can be pursued at the same time in respect of the same hazard, the choice is not once-and-for-all. If the preferred measure does not secure the desired result, the local housing authority may then try again with the same action or select a different one.[74] In determining which route to pursue, the local housing authority is required to have regard to guidance issued by the Secretary of State. The current guidance is given in the Enforcement Guidance.

5.58 The process of 'option selection' is intended to be both participatory and transparent. On participation, the Enforcement Guidance says:

> Enforcement policies should take account of the circumstances and views of *tenants*, landlords and owners. Policies should also provide for consultation [with] social services, tenancy support, housing needs and housing management officers, *where there are vulnerable occupants*, for the purposes of *agreeing* a suitable approach to hazards.[75] [Emphasis added]

5.59 In respect of transparency, the local housing authority must draw up a statement explaining why a particular option was selected rather than the others.[76] That statement then accompanies any notice served in pursuit of the preferred option.[77]

5.60 Obviously, either the tenant or landlord may be disappointed by the selection made by the local housing authority. If the selection results in service of an improvement notice, a prohibition order, an emergency prohibition order or the taking of emergency remedial action, 'the person served' (which may include the tenant) has, in each case, a right of appeal to the First-tier Tribunal (Property Chamber). That tribunal can confirm, vary or quash the notice. But the tenant is unlikely to wish to appeal against a notice that has actually been served. More likely, the tenant will wish to have achieved a more compelling form of action than that adopted by the local housing authority or a more immediate one.

72 HA 2004 s5(3).
73 HA 2004 s5(4).
74 HA 2004 s5(5).
75 Enforcement Guidance, para [2.16].
76 HA 2004 ss8(2) and 8(3).
77 HA 2004 s8(4).

5.61 The tenant would certainly have sufficient interest in a decision about which course of action to adopt to seek to challenge it by way of judicial review on the usual administrative law principles (eg failure to take into account some relevant consideration). However, in *R v Southwark LBC ex p Cordwell*,[78] a case under the pre-HA 2004 regime, the Court of Appeal indicated that relief sought by way of judicial review would only be granted in exceptional cases. It was for the local housing authority to decide on the most satisfactory course of action for the purposes of the Housing Acts. The court would not conduct a fine analysis of what was, of necessity, an inherently imprecise process of evaluation of relevant material, in order to form a different view from the local housing authority about the reasonableness of one course of action over another.

5.62 If judicial review is not an option, perhaps because the concern is with the manner in which the local housing authority went about reaching its decision rather than with the decision itself, a complaint under the local housing authority's complaints procedure – and ultimately to the ombudsman[79] – may provide satisfaction.

Forms of action and their enforcement

Hazard awareness notice

5.63 This is simply a notice advising the recipient of the presence at the premises of a Category 1 or 2 hazard.[80] It identifies the hazard and suggests action that may be taken. Not least because it requires no action, it carries no right of appeal. Its only usefulness to a tenant may be that:

- it serves as formal notice of disrepair[81] if it identifies 'disrepair' (or its effect) as the hazard;
- it serves as formal notice of unfitness[82] if it identifies hazards that amount to a risk to the health and safety of the actual occupiers;
- it may be presented to the local housing authority as evidence of the presence of adverse conditions justifying greater priority for

78 (1995) 27 HLR 594, CA.

79 In England, the Local Government and Social Care Ombudsman.

80 HA 2004 s28 (Category 1) or s29 (Category 2).

81 Where there is requirement that the landlord has knowledge of the need for repair in order to trigger to a landlord's obligations: see paras 2.311–2.318.

82 Where there is a requirement that the landlord has knowledge of unfitness affecting the dwelling: see paras 2.311–2.318.

the tenant on the local housing authority's waiting list for social housing;[83] or

- it may be used as evidence to satisfy the local housing authority that the tenant is homeless because the premises are no longer reasonable to continue to occupy.[84]

5.64 Most tenants and their advisers will have been expecting a firmer response than service of a hazard awareness notice if the problem at the premises is serious or urgent. For challenges to the decision to serve a hazards awareness notice rather than take stronger action, see para 5.60.

Improvement notice

5.65 This form of notice requires the person on whom it is served to take the form of remedial action specified in the notice that will address the identified hazard or hazards.[85] The notice will spell out the work required, when it must start (not earlier than 28 days after service[86]), when it must finish and what result must be achieved. It must contain statutorily prescribed information, including the rights of appeal.[87]

5.66 For most tenants, this will be the form of action they *most* seek: a clear statutory notice telling the landlord what must be done – whether by way of repair *or* improvement *or* both – to address the present state of the property and containing a timetable for action. Service of an improvement notice will also trigger some protection from retaliatory eviction by the landlord: DA 2015 s33. Just as importantly, non-compliance with an improvement notice constitutes a criminal offence. The prospect of a criminal record, significant initial fine and a daily fine thereafter until compliance, is frequently such as to galvanise even initially recalcitrant landlords. Since 6 April 2017, a local authority can impose a civil penalty of up to £30,000 for non-compliance, in place of a prosecution.[88]

83 See para 5.91.

84 See para 5.91.

85 HA 2004 ss11 (Category 1 hazards) and 12 (Category 2 hazards).

86 *Odeniran v Southend-on-Sea BC* [2013] EWHC 3888 (Admin), [2014] HLR 11.

87 HA 2004 s13.

88 HPA 2016 s126. Guidance on *Civil Penalties under the Housing and Planning Act 2016* MHCLG 6 April 2017. Can be found at https://www.gov.uk/government/publications/civil-penalties-under-the-housing-and-planning-act-2016.

Prohibition order

5.67 Such an order prohibits the use of the premises for such categories of use as it describes.[89] Most relevantly, it may prohibit use of the premises as a dwelling. But it is more flexible in scope than that. It may simply operate until some particular facility is installed or it may prohibit occupation only by a specified group (eg young children). The order will describe the hazard and the action that would need to be taken before the order would be revoked. If the hazard is eliminated (whether by repair, improvement or otherwise) the order must be revoked.

5.68 Depending on the tenant's objective in invoking the local housing authority's HA 2004 assessment procedure, this may be either a preferred or less desirable outcome. In particular, the effect of the order is to enable the landlord to seek and obtain possession without the tenant being able to rely on the Rent Acts or the HA 1988.[90] On the other hand, for those in 'priority need', a prohibition order may serve as a passport to homelessness assistance from the local housing authority. Indeed, for any tenant, the service of a prohibition order may hold out the prospect of rehousing and compensation: see para 5.91.

Demolition order

5.69 As is evident from its title, this is perhaps the most draconian form of enforcement method available to the local housing authority. The procedures for making, service and enforcement of demolition orders are set out in HA 1985 Part 9. But a complete replacement definition of 'demolition order' was inserted into section 265 of that Act by HA 2004 s46 and other extensive amendments to Part 9 have been made by other provisions of HA 2004. A demolition order cannot be made in respect of a 'listed' building, however serious the hazard.

5.70 A demolition order requires the owner to demolish the premises after they have been vacated and clear the site. It gives rise to powers to demolish in default and recover expenses. A common (and obvious) response on the part of a recipient of a demolition order is to suggest that the building will cease to be used for human habitation and that a prohibition order would suffice. If not satisfied by that

89 HA 2004 ss20 (Category 1 hazards) and 21 (Category 2 hazards).

90 HA 2004 s33.

response, the local housing authority must take further steps, including service of any necessary notices, leading to the demolition of the property.[91]

5.71 Again, depending on the tenant's objective in invoking the local housing authority's HA 2004 assessment procedure, this may be a preferred or less desirable outcome. In particular, the effect of the order is to enable the landlord to seek and obtain possession without the tenant being able to rely on the Rent Acts or the HA 1988.[92] For those in 'priority need', a demolition order may serve as a passport to homelessness assistance from the local housing authority. Indeed, for any tenant the service of a demolition order may not be the disaster its name suggests given the rights to compensation and rehousing of occupiers that it carries: see para 5.91.

Declaring a clearance area

5.72 This form of action is available where the local housing authority is satisfied that each residential building in an area (however small) contains a Category 1 hazard and that any non-residential buildings in that area are dangerous.[93] Again, this carries implications for displacement, rehousing and compensation of tenants: see para 5.91.

5.73 Provisions for area clearance require separate treatment and are explored more fully in the discussion of area action (below) at para 5.103.

Emergency action

5.74 Where the situation discovered by the local housing authority is particularly serious, it may decide to take emergency action where there is 'imminent risk of serious harm'. That action may take the form of actually entering the premises and setting about emergency remedial works[94] (for which the costs will be recovered from the landlord) or it may involve the local housing authority serving an emergency prohibition order immediately preventing further occupation of the premises.[95]

91 *R v Epsom and Ewell Corporation ex p RB Property Investments (Eastern)* [1964] 1 WLR 1060, [1964] 2 All ER 832, DC.

92 HA 1985 s270.

93 HA 1985 s289 as substituted by HA 2004 s47.

94 HA 2004 ss40–42.

95 HA 2004 s43. For example, on 30 July 2009, Calderdale Metropolitan Borough Council served an emergency prohibition order, prohibiting use of a privately owned residential tower block on the grounds of fire safety.

5.75 Advisers with clients presenting accounts of what are essentially 'life or limb' defects may immediately want to contact the local housing authority and press for emergency remedial action. As well as having access to the statutory provisions, the adviser may need to refer the local housing authority's officers to the appropriate passages in the statutory Enforcement Guidance.

5.76 The service of notice of emergency remedial action under HA 2004 s40(7) will trigger the provisions of the DA 2015 s33 giving the tenant some protection from retaliatory eviction. However, in a dangerous situation the adviser should never rely on action by the local housing authority alone and should consider helping the tenant make an interim injunction application in civil proceedings, if the defect arises from breach of the landlord's contractual or other obligations to the tenant or other occupier: see paras 3.120–3.14.

Suspending action

5.77 Having resolved to serve an improvement notice or prohibition order (as described above) the local housing authority may decide to exercise its powers to suspend the operation of the notice[96] or order.[97] In such a case, the notice or order will be endorsed to identify a specified time after which the suspension will lapse or an event which would cause the suspension to lapse.

5.78 While these provisions may sensibly allow time for events to unfold (eg for particular tenants to move in or out), suspension may prejudice the interests of the occupiers. For example, one appeal by a tenant to a residential property tribunal (now First-tier Tribunal) was concerned with the period for which (if at all) a notice should be suspended.[98] In that case, the tenant wanted the suspension lifted or limited so that she would be rendered homeless. Given the seriousness of the hazard, the tribunal agreed to limit the period of suspension. More importantly, the suspension of a notice will have the effect of depriving the tenant of the protection from retaliatory eviction given by DA 2015 s33.[99]

96 HA 2004 s14.

97 HA 2004 s23.

98 *Khadija Ali v Bristol CC* [2007] 15 May, Bristol RPT (ref: CH1/00HB/HPO/2007/0005) helpfully noted with summaries of other prohibition order appeals in Carr, Cottle and Ormandy, *Using the Housing Act 2004*, Jordans, 2008, p194.

99 DA 2015 s33(9).

Purchase of the property

5.79 If the local housing authority considers that it could use the premises, containing a Category 1 hazard, for temporary accommodation it may buy the property instead of making a demolition order or prohibition order.[100] Notwithstanding that the premises are, obviously, a serious hazard and that the local housing authority has decided that they are best dealt with by being emptied or demolished, the local housing authority is entitled to carry out patch repairs to the purchased property and let it to tenants.[101] Given the state that such a property may be in, even after patch repairs, the statutorily implied covenant of fitness at LTA 1985 s9A[102] is excluded from any temporary letting of such a property by the local housing authority.

5.80 Premises retained by local housing authorities are notoriously used as 'short life' accommodation or as 'temporary housing' for homeless families. Advisers should ensure that they are not so used unless the premises are 'suitable' accommodation for the purposes of discharging any housing functions relating to the homeless.[103] Any attempt by the local housing authority to retain such purchased property as a permanent part of the housing stock will be struck down by the courts.[104]

Enforcement

5.81 Tenants and their advisers will not be interested merely in the speed with which the local housing authority acts and the form of notice it serves – they will want to secure positive enforcement of the obligations which any notices or orders impose on landlords.

5.82 For example, non-compliance with either an improvement notice[105] or a prohibition order[106] is a criminal offence punishable by an unlimited fine. Where a prohibition order is breached, a daily

100 HA 1985 s300(1).
101 HA 1985 s302 (as amended).
102 HA 1985 s302 (as amended by Homes (Fitness for Human Habitation) Act 2018 s1(6)).
103 HA 1996 Part 7 (Homelessness) ss206(1) and 210 (England).
104 *Victoria Square Property Co v Southwark LBC* [1978] I WLR 463, [1978] 2 All ER 281, CA; and see *R v Birmingham CC ex p Sale* (1983) 9 HLR 33, (1983) 82 LGR 69, QBD.
105 HA 2004 s30.
106 HA 2004 s32.

fine of £20 can be imposed for each *day* after conviction that the premises are occupied. Since 6 April 2017, local authorities have been able to levy a civil penalty of up to £30,000 for non-compliance, in place of a criminal prosecution.[107] As the local authority is able to retain the entire penalty, rather than a proportion of any fine on conviction, and does not face the costs of bringing a prosecution, this development may encourage local authorities to a more active approach to enforcement. Since 6 April 2018, failure to comply with an improvement notice or prohibition order is also a 'banning order offence'[108] which enables a local authority to seek an order from the First-tier Tribunal banning a landlord from letting housing in England.[109] Non-statutory guidance on banning orders has been published.[110]

5.83 Central government has advised local housing authorities that, when prosecuting:

> It is the responsibility of council officers to ensure magistrates have a full and tangible understanding of the harm suffered by the tenant and how the harm had been caused by the landlord. Schedule 16, Part 6 of the Crime and Courts Act 2013, allows the court to take account of assets as well as income when setting a financial penalty.[111]

5.84 However, prosecution is at the option of the local housing authority and some are not adept at handling such prosecutions. Others would prefer to pursue informal 'encouragement' of bad landlords. A review of 24 local authority prosecutions found that:[112]

> Prosecution is a final resort: except in one case presenting serious risk to life, the councils tried to encourage and persuade the landlord to secure improvements to bring the property to the standard required by law.

107 HPA 2016 s126. Statutory Guidance *Civil penalties under the Housing and Planning Act 2016* MHCLG last updated 6 April 2018 is at www.gov.uk/government/publications/civil-penalties-under-the-housing-and-planning-act-2016.

108 Housing and Planning Act 2016 (Banning Order Offences) Regulations 2018 SI No 216.

109 HPA 2016 Part 2 Chapter 2.

110 *Banning Order Offences under the Housing and Planning Act 2016*, MHCLG April 2018, at https://assets.publishing.service.gov.uk/government/uploads/system/uploads/attachment_data/file/697643/Banning_order_guidance.pdf.

111 *Improving the Private Rented Sector and Tackling Bad Practice: A Guide for Local Authorities*, DCLG, March 2015, para 89.

112 *Prosecuting landlords for poor property conditions*, Local Government Association, June 2014.

5.85 However, there is a limit to the extent to which local housing authorities should pursue informal alternatives to prosecution. The UK Government's advice is that:[113]

> A number of cynical landlords are experienced enough to take advantage of a local authority offering advice and use delaying tactics to avoid undertaking the necessary work. It is important to avoid wasteful informal engagement. Landlords should respond to advice and informal engagement promptly, failure to do so should be met with prompt robust enforcement action and the beginning of prosecution proceedings.

5.86 In recent years, enforcement action has remained extremely patchy. Formal enforcement activity in many councils is still low, with many preferring to take an informal approach instead.[114] FOI research in 2015 found that formal enforcement activity (hazard awareness notices, improvement and prohibition notices, as defined under the Housing Act 2004) had fallen by 40 per cent since the previous Parliament. Freedom of Information Act requests in 2018 showed all local authorities in England combined took enforcement action on category 1 hazards on a total of 10,069 occasions in 2017.[115]

5.87 What the tenant and his or her adviser need in any particular case is tough enforcement action by the local housing authority in the face of landlord non-compliance. HA 2004 Sch 3, read with the terms of the Enforcement Guidance, provides ample scope for local housing authorities to assist tenants in such circumstances – not least by undertaking the necessary works themselves and recovering the costs of doing so directly from the landlord. That approach should be followed, whether or not the landlord is also prosecuted.

Rehousing and compensation for displaced tenants

5.88 To address particularly serious defects in rented premises, the temporary or permanent departure of the tenant(s) may be necessary.

113 *Improving the Private Rented Sector and Tackling Bad Practice: A Guide for Local Authorities*, DCLG, March 2015, para 90.

114 *Rogue Landlords in London: A survey of local authority enforcement in the private rented sector* Pidgeon C (2016); and *The challenge of tackling unsafe and unhealthy housing: report of a survey of local authorities for Karen Buck MP*, Battersby S (2015).

115 *The Independent* 20 January 2018, at: www.independent.co.uk/news/uk/politics/councils-rented-homes-99-per-cent-unsafe-generation-rent-properties-karen-buck-property-a8168896.html.

5.89 Where the tenants need to leave temporarily while work is being carried out, the local housing authority should assist with the provision (or facilitation) of alternative temporary accommodation[116] and perhaps suspend the commencement date for works under an improvement notice until the tenants are temporarily relocated.

5.90 Prohibition orders will (unless suspended) raise a spectre of potentially long-term displacement.[117] No doubt for that reason, the Enforcement Guidance advises that, when considering whether to serve a prohibition order, the local housing authority should also:

> . . . have regard to the risk of exclusion of vulnerable people from the accommodation;
>
> consider the availability of local accommodation for rehousing any displaced occupants. Rehousing in such cases is for the local housing authority to consider, particularly where they may have a duty to provide accommodation. It is unrealistic to expect a landlord owning a small number of properties to re-house the tenant. Landlords have no legal responsibility to re-house their tenants as a result of action by the local housing authority, although the tenant may be able to seek redress; and
>
> consider whether it is appropriate to offer financial advice or assistance.[118]

5.91 Where a person is permanently displaced from residential accommodation as a result of a prohibition order, demolition notice or area clearance and suitable alternative accommodation is not available, the local housing authority is under a duty to secure that he or she will be provided with other accommodation.[119] However, the duty is that the local housing authority 'do its best',[120] and it can offer temporary accommodation until permanent accommodation is available.[121] Any permanent accommodation need not be offered on the same terms as those on which the previous accommodation was held. But, the displaced tenant will not need to queue up on the waiting list or bid for properties through the housing allocation scheme adopted by the local housing authority under HA 1996 Part 6. That is because rehousing of such displaced tenants does not count as an allocation

116 Enforcement Guidance, para [5.21].

117 For an example of rehousing and compensation issues in respect of the tenancy of a rented property subject to a suspended prohibition order see *Complaint against Islington LBC* (14 013 91), 30 June 2015, Local Government and Social Care Ombudsman.

118 Enforcement Guidance, para 5.23.

119 Land Compensation Act 1973 s39.

120 *R v Bristol Corporation ex p Hendy* [1974] 1 WLR 498, [1974] 1 All ER 1047, CA.

121 *R v East Hertfordshire DC ex p Smith* (1991) 23 HLR 26, CA.

at all,[122] enabling displaced tenants to be dealt with by direct offers outside the usual procedures.

5.92 Such displaced occupiers will also usually be entitled to a home loss payment (currently a minimum of £6,100[123]) and compensation for moving and redecoration costs (in the form of a disturbance payment).[124]

Council tenants

5.93 The position of private sector and housing association tenants in relation to the HA 2004 is as described above. However, where a council tenant's landlord is the local housing authority itself, that tenant does not enjoy the full benefits of HA 2004 Part 1. Because a local housing authority cannot properly serve Housing Act notices upon itself, it cannot fully apply the Housing Acts in respect of its own properties.[125] The High Court has rejected the contention that this 'discrimination' against council tenants infringes the Human Rights Act 1998.[126]

5.94 A part of the stated rationale for the Homes (Fitness for Human Habitation) Act 2018 in its passage through Parliament was to address this issue, so that a council tenant can enforce against their landlord for poor housing conditions, (including issues that would amount to a Category 1 and possibly Category 2 hazard), via LTA 1985 s9A. See paras 2.32–2.59.

5.95 Government guidance, issued over 30 years ago, encouraged local housing authorities to make extra-statutory local arrangements to deal with unsatisfactory council housing.[127] It urged them to introduce and publish arrangements so that:

- if a council tenant sought the help of an EHO about the condition of a property; and

122 HA 1996 s160(4) and the Allocation of Housing (England) Regulations 2002 SI No 3264 reg 3(2).

123 Home Loss Payments (Prescribed Amounts) (England) Regulations 2017 SI No 769.

124 Land Compensation Act 1973 Part III (as amended).

125 *R v Cardiff CC ex p Cross* (1983) 6 HLR 1, CA.

126 *R (Erskine) v Lambeth LBC* [2003] EWHC 2479 (Admin); December 2003 *Legal Action* 9.

127 Department of the Environment Circular 21/84 para 117, Welsh Office Circular 42/84.

- in the EHO's opinion the condition was such that, if it were a private property, action under the Housing Acts would be necessary; then
- the EHO would give notice to the Director of Housing, who would ensure that necessary works were carried out within a reasonable period.

5.96 It is worth exploring whether any particular local housing authority drew up and retained such quasi-statutory local arrangements. If not, the council tenant may need to abandon the possibility of any benefit from reliance on HA 2004 and concentrate on pursuing other remedies explored in this book, in particular via LTA 1985 s9A when that applies to the tenancy.

5.97 Where council property is *transferred* to a housing association, the local housing authority may invoke its HA 2004 powers and duties almost immediately post-transfer. Indeed, if it has disposed of particularly unsatisfactory housing, the local housing authority may wish to take action while its information about poor conditions is still up to date.

Houses in multiple occupation

5.98 Some of the worst instances of landlord neglect and disrepair, and of poor housing conditions generally, are to be found in properties subject to more than one tenancy or occupancy – for example, in houses poorly converted into bedsits or flats, in hostels, in so-called 'hotels' or in 'lodging houses'. Any house or flat is defined as being in 'multiple occupation' (an 'HMO') if it contains two or more households.[128] There are estimated to be over 450,000 HMOs in England.

5.99 Local housing authorities have long had extensive powers to control the standards, the provision of facilities, the number of occupants, and the means of escape from fire in such multi-occupied properties.[129] In addition, the local housing authority has powers to intervene where there are problems of disrepair, lack of maintenance and other unsatisfactory aspects in the state of the property. In each case, a local housing authority can do the work necessary to bring the

128 For the very detailed definition of different types of HMO see HA 2004 ss254–260 and the Licensing of Houses in Multiple Occupation (Prescribed Descriptions) (England) Order 2006 SI No 371.

129 See D Ormandy and R Burridge, 'Houses in Multiple Occupation' in *Environmental Health Standards in Housing*, 1988, Sweet & Maxwell, chapter 6 for an historic account.

property up to standard if the manager of the HMO will not do so. Failure to comply may result in prosecution or civil penalty and the authority may do the necessary works in default and recoup its costs. Ultimately, the authority may compulsorily purchase the property.[130]

5.100 The majority of the powers to tackle poor housing standards in HMOs are now contained in Part 1 of the 2004 Act (see above) and in specific management regulations for HMOs made under HA 2004 s234.[131]

5.101 Because of the particular need to maintain standards in HMOs, a requirement for mandatory licensing of most HMOs is now set out in HA 2004 Part 2. On 1 October 2018, new regulations came into force extending the definition of HMOs that require mandatory licensing and setting minimum room sizes for occupation.[132] That mandatory licensing scheme can be extended to additional types of HMOs by individual local housing authorities. The detail of the main licensing scheme and its local extensions are outside the scope of this book.[133]

5.102 Tenants experiencing problems in HMOs should first ask the local housing authority whether their HMO has a licence (because if it should do but does not, rent paid may be recoverable by an application for a rent repayment order and possession cannot be obtained from an assured shorthold tenant relying on notice given under HA 1988 s21). They should at the same time invite an inspection by an EHO with a view to use of the HA 2004 powers and the enforcement of the HMO regulations.

Area action

5.103 Local housing authorities have long had extensive powers to address areas of unsatisfactory housing in their districts.[134] Although the mass

130 The relevant legislation is helpfully gathered on the website of the National HMO Network at www.nationalhmonetwork.com.

131 Management of Houses in Multiple Occupation (England) Regulations 2006 SI No 372.

132 The Licensing of Houses in Multiple Occupation (Prescribed Description) (England) Order 2018 SI No 221.

133 An outline of the provisions is given in *Houses in multiple occupation and residential property licensing reform: guidance for local housing authorities* MHCLG, June 2018 and updated December 2018, and see Squier and Cullen, 'Tackling rogue landlords: Housing Act 2004, Parts 2 and 3' [2014] 17 *Journal of Housing Law* 78.

134 R Burridge and D Ormandy (eds), *Unhealthy housing: research, remedies and reform*, Routledge & Chapman, 1993, chapters 14–16.

clearance and demolition programmes directed at 'slums' in the 20th century are no longer being adopted, local housing authorities have retained powers to address areas of unsatisfactory housing. In the 21st century these are still being used to tackle small residual pockets of the worst housing and to underpin strategies for 'renewal' of particular districts. A tenant's home may be included in one of them.

5.104 The powers to tackle such areas of unsatisfactory housing are in addition to those statutory provisions enabling local authorities to deal with individual unsatisfactory houses and flats through the HA 2004 (as described above) and/or the EPA 1990 (see chapter 6).

5.105 Where the most appropriate action is the clearance of the unsatisfactory housing, the authority may declare a *clearance* area under HA 1985 s289, as amended by HA 2004. On the other hand, if housing can be renovated and rehabilitated, the appropriate action is declaration of a *renewal* area under the Local Government and Housing Act (LGHA) 1989.

5.106 Tenants caught up in such area action may be relieved to see the local housing authority taking steps which may result in them being suitably rehoused and compensated (see para 5.91) for the loss of their homes. But, of necessity, there is often a long lead-time between the local housing authority deciding to use its powers and the actual work starting. Meanwhile, the landlord will remain under any contractual obligations to repair and keep fit for habitation, subject to any modification of the extent of those obligations having regard to the reduced 'life expectancy' of the premises: see para 2.88. The local housing authority might use its other powers under the HA 2004 or EPA 1990 to achieve at least patch repairs before rehousing and demolition or renewal are put in hand.

5.107 Those tenants who would rather that a different form of action was undertaken to tackle the poor condition of their home may wish to challenge the local housing authority's decisions in the manner described in para 5.60. They will also want to check carefully that the authority is operating within the strict parameters of the tight statutory conditions about how, for example, clearance areas are to be set up, organized and seen through to completion.

Clearance areas

5.108 A clearance area is an area which is to be cleared of all buildings. A clearance area may be declared if the local housing authority is satisfied that:[135]

135 Housing Act 1985 s289 as heavily modified by HA 2004 s47.

- each of the residential buildings in the area contains a Category 1 hazard, and the other buildings (if any) in the area are dangerous or harmful to the health or safety of the inhabitants of the area; or
- the residential buildings in the area are dangerous or harmful to the health or safety of the inhabitants of the area as a result of their bad arrangement or the narrowness or bad arrangement of the streets and the other buildings (if any) in the area are dangerous or harmful to the health or safety of the inhabitants of the area; or
- each of the residential buildings in the area contains a Category 2 hazard, the other buildings (if any) in the area are dangerous or harmful to the health or safety of the inhabitants of the area, and the circumstances of the case are circumstances specified or described in an order made by the Secretary of State.

5.109 Declaration of a clearance area leads to a process of acquisition by compulsory purchase of the properties in that area and their subsequent demolition. The cleared site is then available to the local housing authority for its own purposes – usually the provision of new housing.

5.110 The local housing authority must:[136]

- ensure that owners and occupiers are informed at an early stage and consulted;
- ensure that it has sufficient resources to carry the scheme through and to accommodate any displaced persons who are unable to secure their own accommodation; and
- pay compensation to displaced owners and some occupiers.

Renewal areas

5.111 Since April 1990, local authorities have had powers to take area action in respect of unsatisfactory housing through the declaration of renewal areas. The statutory arrangements are in the LGHA 1989 Part 7 as since substantially modified and amended.

5.112 A renewal area may be declared where a local housing authority is satisfied that the living conditions in an area within their district, consisting primarily of housing accommodation, are unsatisfactory, and that those conditions can most effectively be dealt with by declaring the area to be a renewal area.

136 See Enforcement Guidance, para 5.48.

5.113 Before making such a declaration, the local housing authority must consider a report which has reviewed:

- the living conditions in the area concerned;
- the ways in which those conditions may be improved (whether by the declaration of a renewal area or otherwise);
- the powers available to the authority (including powers available apart from the LGHA 1989) if the area is declared to be a renewal area;
- the authority's detailed proposals for the exercise of those powers during the period that the area will be a renewal area (if so declared);
- the cost of those proposals;
- the financial resources available, or likely to be available, to the authority (from whatever source) for implementing those proposals; and
- the representations (if any) made to the authority in relation to those proposals.

5.114 A programme of public consultation is also required before declaration. Declaration vests the local housing authority with considerable additional powers over housing in the area (including the right compulsorily to acquire and repair property) and may attract additional central government and privately funded financial help to the area. The powers are to be exercised with the objects of:

- securing the improvement or repair of the premises, either by the authority or by a person to whom they propose to dispose of the premises;
- the proper and effective management and use of the housing accommodation, either by the authority or by a person to whom they propose to dispose of the premises comprising the accommodation; and
- the well-being of the persons for the time being residing in the area.

Conclusion

5.115 The procedures for dealing with statutorily unsatisfactory properties outlined in this chapter may sometimes constitute a double-edged sword. They may just as easily leave a landlord with vacant possession or a cleared site, as provide the tenant with a repaired home. Even those tenants who would qualify for rehousing by the local housing authority may languish in defective property for substantial periods awaiting an offer of accommodation, notwithstanding their statutory priorities.

5.116 It is for these reasons that advisers should be pressing local housing authorities to use their available HA 2004 powers early and creatively, to tackle bad housing long before it sinks into a condition warranting the prohibition of occupation or even demolition. It is to be hoped that the provisions of DA 2015, offering some measure of protection from retaliatory eviction, will trigger more frequent calls for the use of these provisions by, and for, tenants, although the evidence on the number of notices served by councils suggests that the impact is at best, very limited.

5.117 The Housing and Planning Act (HPA) 2016, and subsequent regulations, have added to enforcement powers of local authorities and enhanced tenants' ability to seek rent repayment orders. Measures include:

- the introduction of a database of landlords and letting agents who have been convicted of certain criminal offences, including non-compliance with HA 2004 notices (in force from April 2018);[137]
- banning landlords and letting agents from letting property where they have been convicted of serious offences; including non-compliance with HA 2004 notices (in force from April 2018);[138]
- enabling local housing authorities to issue civil penalty notices as an alternative to prosecution for certain breaches of housing legislation, with revenue from penalties to be retained by the council (in force from April 2017); and
- extending rent repayment orders to cover situations where the landlord has failed to rectify a serious health and safety hazard in the property and enabling tenants to seek a rent repayment order regardless of any prosecution or lack of it by the local authority.[139] Local authorities would be permitted to retain that money for housing purposes where the rent was paid through housing benefit or universal credit (in force April 2017).

5.118 Whether these additional powers encourage local authorities to a more active investigation and enforcement regime remains to be seen. However, for tenancies to which the new LTA 1985 s9A applies, tenants will now have the ability to take action on poor housing conditions themselves, without reliance on the local authority.

137 HPA 2016 Chapter 3.
138 HPA 2016 Chapter 2.
139 HPA 2016 Chapter 4.

CHAPTER 6

Using the Environmental Protection Act 1990 to tackle poor housing conditions

continued

Introduction

6.1 This chapter explains how the provisions of the Environmental Protection Act (EPA) 1990 can be used by tenants and their advisers to tackle poor housing conditions. It explains the powers available to local councils to take action under the Act and then the arrangements for individual tenants to take proceedings to obtain remedies and compensation.

6.2 Although the Act is less than 30 years old, statutes like it have been aimed at poor housing conditions for generations. Since the mid-19th century, the UK Parliament has sought to protect the general public from the worst effects of poor housing conditions by passing public health legislation. These laws, which were largely consolidated into the Public Health Act (PHA) 1936, have been amended subsequently and are now recast in the EPA 1990 Part 3.[1] See appendix A for the text of the key provisions in EPA 1990 ss79–82.

6.3 Much of this legislation can be used by tenants, occupiers and their neighbours to force landlords of bad housing to carry out necessary works, and to improve the condition of property which they own. EPA 1990 Part 3 is concerned with tackling the effects of bad housing, that is, the poor conditions which occupiers and others face as a result of poor design, disrepair and other housing defects.

6.4 The EPA 1990 can be a particularly useful weapon in those circumstances where premises are unhealthy or otherwise in poor condition but there is no civil remedy, such as described in chapters 2 and 3, because there is no breach of contract or any other civil 'wrong' or tort.

6.5 In particular, the EPA 1990 has proved invaluable in assisting tenants living in damp housing where the cause of the dampness is condensation due to bad design or poor construction. The black mould produced by such conditions has been shown to cause ill health such as asthma (see paras 2.192–2.225). Fortunately, the incidence of condensation-ridden housing has declined over the last 20 years. This, coupled with the limits that decided cases[2] have placed on using the Act, meant that EPA 1990 prosecutions had been becoming

1 As amended by the Environment Act 1995 and the Clean Neighbourhoods and Environment Act 2005.

2 For example, *Birmingham CC v Oakley* [2000] UKHL 59, [2001] 33 HLR 283.

less common. However, in the last decade there has been something of a revival[3] in prosecutions.[4]

The Environmental Protection Act 1990

6.6 The key to the use of the EPA 1990 by tenants against landlords responsible for bad housing conditions, is the concept of the 'statutory nuisance'.

6.7 Statutory nuisances are defined as arising in the specific circumstances set out in the EPA 1990 and related legislation. The following, contained in the EPA 1990 and PHA 1936, are the 'statutory nuisances' most immediately relevant to housing conditions (references are to the EPA 1990 unless otherwise stated):

- 'any premises in such a state as to be prejudicial to health or a nuisance' (EPA 1990 s79(1)(a));
- 'any accumulation or deposit which is prejudicial to health or a nuisance' (EPA 1990 s79(1)(e));
- 'any insects emanating from relevant industrial, trade or business premises and being prejudicial to health or a nuisance' (EPA 1990 s79(1)(fa));[5]
- any other matter declared by any enactment to be a statutory nuisance' (EPA 1990 s79(1)(h));
- 'any tent, van, shed or similar structure used for human habitation which is in such a state or so overcrowded as to be prejudicial to health; or the use of which, by reason of the absence of proper sanitary accommodation or otherwise, gives rise, whether on the site or on other land, to a nuisance or to conditions prejudicial to health' (PHA 1936 s268, as amended by EPA 1990 Sch 15 para 4);
- 'any well, tank, cistern or water-butt used for the supply of water for domestic purposes which is so placed, constructed or kept as to render the water therein liable to contamination prejudicial to health' (PHA 1936 s141, as amended by EPA 1990 Sch 15 para 4);

3 See, for example, Timothy Waitt, 'The dangers of damp', *Inside Housing* 30 August 2013.

4 See, for more recent examples, the cases of *Dingwall v Lambeth LBC*, December 2014 *Legal Action* 29, Camberwell Green Magistrates' Court; *Duke v Uthayakanthan*, December 2015 *Legal Action* 42, Camberwell Green Magistrates' Court and *Dor v Woodhouse Estates Ltd* March 2018 *Legal Action* 36, North London Magistrates' Court.

5 Added by Clean Neighbourhoods and Environment Act 2005 s101.

- 'any pond, pool, ditch, gutter or watercourse which is so foul or in such a state as to be prejudicial to health or a nuisance' (PHA 1936 s259, as amended by EPA 1990 Sch 15 para 4);
- 'noise emitted from premises so as to be prejudicial to health or a nuisance' (EPA 1990 s79(1)(g)).

6.8 Most species of statutory nuisance contain two distinct limbs, which are to be read as alternatives and treated quite separately, ie 'prejudicial to health' or a 'nuisance'.

6.9 Several of the listed statutory nuisances deal with matters likely to be common in dwellings out of repair (blocked gutters, polluted water tanks, defective cisterns etc) but the one of most relevance to unhealthy housing conditions is contained in section 79(1)(a). Each element of section 79(1)(a) requires close attention, especially as some of its elements are replicated in the other forms of statutory nuisance.

The elements of EPA 1990 s79(1)(a)

'Any premises'

6.10 'Premises' are defined by the EPA 1990 to include all land and vessels.[6] Both the private rented sector and social housing are covered. The courts have held that the Act directs attention to the condition of the premises, rather than to the way in which they are used.[7] Indeed, the premises need not even be occupied.[8]

6.11 In the case of a block of flats, the 'premises' for the purposes of section 79 may be an individual flat or flats. It is possible to allege a statutory nuisance in relation to an entire block only if the issue relates to the condition of the common parts or if there is a problem 'not confined to any one constituent unit in the block and which can only be related to the entire block'.[9]

6.12 An open site without any permanent buildings (eg, a travellers' site) may also be 'premises' for the purpose of section 79. The EPA 1990 powers can be used to eliminate statutory nuisances on caravan sites and other areas of land used for residential purposes.[10]

6 EPA 1990 s79(7).

7 *Birmingham CC v Oakley* [2000] UKHL 59, [2001] 33 HLR 283.

8 *Coventry CC v Doyle* [1981] 1 WLR 1325, [1981] 2 All ER 184, DC.

9 *Birmingham DC v McMahon and Others* (1987) 19 HLR 452, QBD at 457.

10 *R v Secretary of State for the Environment ex p Ward* [1984] 1 WLR 834, [1984] 2 All ER 556, QBD at 560.

'in such a state'

6.13 A statutory nuisance arises if the state of the premises as a whole is such as to be prejudicial to health or a nuisance. This may arise either from a single major item (eg a putrid water tank) or from the accumulation of a number of minor items. It is the effect of the defects which gives rise to the statutory nuisance rather than the fault itself.

6.14 In *Birmingham CC v Oakley*,[11] it was said that the object of section 79(1)(a) is to provide a means for the summary removal of noxious matters and the Act must be restricted to public health matters. So, a poor arrangement of rooms, where a toilet without a wash hand basin was situated next to a kitchen, could not render premises in such a 'state' as to be prejudicial to health. Similarly, in *R v Bristol CC ex p Everett*,[12] a steep staircase, where there was a likelihood of accident, could not be considered a statutory nuisance. However, the circumstances in both these situations can be addressed using the other provisions discussed in chapter 5 of this book.

'prejudicial to health'

6.15 A statutory nuisance will arise where premises are in such a state, through disrepair or otherwise, as to be 'prejudicial to health'. That is defined by the EPA 1990 s79(7) to mean 'injurious or likely to cause injury, to health'. Both actual and potential ill health are covered.

6.16 The courts have held that the requirement 'prejudicial to health' will be satisfied simply where the state of the premises is such as would cause a well person to become ill or the health of a sick person to deteriorate further.[13] Accordingly, a statutory nuisance exists where *any* premises are in such poor condition as to cause potential or actual detriment to the health of the tenant or other occupiers. The test is, however, objective in the sense that no account is taken of any occupier's particular vulnerability.[14]

6.17 'Health', although not defined by the EPA 1990, should be interpreted broadly to include physical and mental health, particularly to incorporate the medically recognised stress associated with living in bad housing. Mere interference with comfort will not bring a case within the 'health' limb[15] nor will defects which are merely

11 [2000] UKHL 59, [2001] 33 HLR 283.
12 [1999] 1 WLR 92, [1999] 31 HLR 1102, CA.
13 *Malton Borough Health Board v Malton Farmers Manure Co* (1879) 4 Ex D 302.
14 *Cunningham v Birmingham CC* (1988) 30 HLR 158, [1998] Env LR 1, DC.
15 *Salford CC v McNally* [1976] AC 379, HL, per Lord Wilberforce.

decorative (such as stained wallpaper[16]) or which simply constitute an 'eyesore'.[17]

6.18 Examples of premises which are 'prejudicial to health' include those suffering from dampness, condensation, mould growth, or infestations[18] but not those which simply lack sound insulation.[19]

'or a nuisance'

6.19 The EPA 1990 does not define 'nuisance'. In *National Coal Board v Neath BC*,[20] the Divisional Court held that to fall within section 79(1)(a), the 'nuisance' must be either:

- a public nuisance at common law; or
- a private nuisance at common law.

6.20 At common law, a *public* nuisance arises where an act or omission affects adversely the comfort or quality of life of the public generally, or a class of citizens.

6.21 At common law, a *private* nuisance is a substantial interference by the owner or occupier of property with the use and enjoyment of neighbouring property.

6.22 Given this restrictive interpretation of 'nuisance' in section 79, it follows that a statutory nuisance based on this limb 'cannot arise if what has taken place affects only the person or persons occupying the premises.'[21] If the conditions arise within the premises and are a nuisance only to the tenant or other occupier, a 'statutory nuisance' will not arise unless the prejudice to health 'limb' of section 79 can be satisfied.

6.23 Moreover, only certain types of nuisance may be within the section. The courts have required that the nuisance must be of such a nature as to relate to matters of public health.[22] Conditions short of

16 *Springett v Harold* [1954] 1 WLR 521, [1954] 1 All ER 568, QBD.

17 *Coventry CC v Cartwright* [1975] 1 WLR 845, [1975] 2 All ER 99, DC.

18 See, eg, *Dent v Haringey LBC* December 1999 *Legal Action* 18, *Housing Law Casebook* 7th edn, para R25.37, Wood Green Crown Court; *Ogunlowo v Southwark LBC* December 2005 *Legal Action* 29, *Housing Law Casebook* 7th edn, para R25.44, Camberwell Magistrates' Court.

19 *R (Vella) v Lambeth LBC and London and Quadrant Housing Trust* [2005] EWHC 2473 (Admin), [2006] HLR 12, which overruled *Southwark LBC v Ince* (1989) 21 HLR 504.

20 [1976] 2 All ER 478, DC.

21 *National Coal Board v Thorne* [1976] 1 WLR 543, 74 LGR 429, DC, per Watkins J at 546.

22 *Great Western Railway Co v Bishop* (1872) LR 7 QB 550; *Bishop Auckland Local Board v British Auckland Iron and Steel Co Ltd* (1883) 10 QBD 138, considered in *Coventry CC v Cartwright* [1975] 1 WLR 845, [1975] 2 All ER 99, DC.

prejudice to health, such as offensive smells, noise and dirt, may be within the term 'nuisance'. Traffic noise is not.[23]

6.24 Using the 'nuisance' limb of section 79(1)(a), action can be taken against 'statutory nuisance' arising from poor housing conditions in immediately adjacent property (including common parts retained by the landlord). Examples include: leaking lavatory overflows, unhygienic rubbish chutes, back-surges of sewage, blocked pipes and gutters, and noisy central heating boilers.

6.25 Where premises *are* in such a state as to cause potential or actual injury to health, or constitute a nuisance, the consequent statutory nuisance may be tackled either by action by the local authority or through direct action by the occupier.

Action by local authorities

6.26 The existence of statutory nuisances may be brought to the attention of local authorities either by their own systematic inspections of their districts or, more commonly, by complaints from tenants and others. The investigation of statutory nuisances and enforcement of environmental protection legislation are usually delegated to individual environmental health officers (EHOs). For these purposes, EHOs have a right to enter and inspect premises which may be in such a state as to be a statutory nuisance.[24]

6.27 Once satisfied of the existence of a statutory nuisance (or the likelihood of a statutory nuisance arising or recurring), a local authority is legally bound to take action,[25] using the powers available to it under the EPA 1990 or the Housing Act (HA) 2004 (see chapter 5). Although obliged to follow the statutory procedures to tackle statutory nuisances, some authorities will first give the landlord an 'informal notice' that EPA 1990 sanctions are being considered.[26] But, if a local authority is aware of a statutory nuisance it cannot simply do nothing. As the Court of Appeal has recently said:

23 *Haringey LBC v Jowett* [1999] EHLR 410, (2000) 32 HLR 308, DC.

24 EPA 1990 Sch 3 para 2.

25 *Cocker v Cardwell* (1869) LR 5 QB 15.

26 Some local authorities publish 'enforcement protocols' on their websites setting out when they will take action and when they will try to resolve the matter by other means.

> An unreasonable failure to act to prevent a continuing statutory nuisance may be the subject of challenge in judicial review proceedings.[27]

However, in the same case, the court noted that:

> Public bodies are often under staffed and under resourced and do not have the same direct concerns to uphold environmental standards as do members of the public.[28]

6.28 Advice about what a tenant may do if a local authority fails to take action under its statutory powers, or is slow in doing so, is given in chapter 5 at para 5.20.

Abatement notices

6.29 The first formality is service by the local authority of an abatement notice under EPA 1990 s80(1) on the person responsible for the nuisance. The notice requires the person served (in practice, usually the landlord) to abate the nuisance (or prevent it arising or recurring) and to execute 'such works, and the taking of such other steps as may be necessary' for that purpose. The notice also gives a time limit for completion of remedial works.[29]

6.30 The abatement notice must be sufficiently clear to enable the landlord to understand what is required, bearing in mind the risk of exposure to penal sanctions for non-compliance. In straightforward cases, the notice need not spell out precisely what works are required, but can simply require that a certain result be achieved.[30] However, in more complex cases, the abatement notice must specify the works required and these works must be capable of remedying the nuisance.[31]

6.31 The local authority is required to serve the abatement notice on 'the person responsible for the nuisance': EPA 1990 s80(2)(a). He or

27 *Austin v Miller Argent (South Wales) Ltd* [2014] EWCA Civ 1012, [2015] 1 WLR 62 at [16].

28 *Austin v Miller Argent (South Wales) Ltd* [2014] EWCA Civ 1012, [2015] 1 WLR 62 at [18].

29 This preliminary step is not part of the court proceedings, see *R (Ethos Recycling Ltd) v Barking & Dagenham Magistrates' Court and another* [2009] EWHC 2885 (Admin), [2010] Env LR 25.

30 *Budd v Colchester BC* [1999] BLGR 601, (1999) *Times* 14 April, CA.

31 *Network Housing Association Ltd v Westminster CC* (1994) 27 HLR 189, DC. See also *Millard v Wastall* [1898] 1 QB 342; *Whatling v Rees* (1914) 84 LJKB 1122; *R v Wheatley* (1885) 16 QBD 34; *R v Secretary of State for the Environment ex p Watney Mann (Midlands)* [1976] JPL 368; and *Elvington Park Ltd and Another v City of York Council* [2009] EWHC 1805 (Admin), [2010] Env LR 10.

she is defined by EPA 1990 s79(7) as being 'the person to whose act, default or sufferance the nuisance is attributable'.

6.32 In cases of structural defects (eg, statutory nuisances arising from disrepair), the abatement notice must be served on the 'owner',[32] ie, the person who does (or would) receive the rent.[33]

6.33 If the person causing the nuisance cannot be found (as is frequently the case with the very worst housing conditions) the local authority can serve notice on the owner *or* occupier.[34]

6.34 Where more than one person is responsible for a statutory nuisance, notice may be served on each person whether or not their conduct or default alone would amount to a nuisance.[35]

6.35 The person served with an abatement notice has a right of appeal to a magistrates' court (to be exercised within 21 days of the date notice is served[36]) by way of complaint.[37] The grounds of appeal are set out in the Statutory Nuisance (Appeals) Regulations 1995.[38] The grounds include defects or errors in the abatement notice or that the notice might lawfully have been served on a third party as well as the appellant. The court has power to quash or vary the abatement notice or dismiss the appeal.

6.36 If the abatement notice is neither appealed nor complied with, the person served is guilty of an offence if the failure to comply is without reasonable excuse.[39] The EPA 1990 imposes no statutory duty to prosecute for non-compliance with abatement notices and is silent about whether private prosecutions may be brought by occupiers directly in place of local authorities unwilling to take further action.

6.37 If the offence of failure to comply is proven, the landlord or other person served is liable to a fine up to level 5 on the standard scale[40] and a further fine of one-tenth the level 5 scale for each further day of

32 EPA 1990 s80(2)(b).

33 *Camden LBC v Gunby* [2000] 1 WLR 465, (2000) 32 HLR 572, QBD.

34 EPA 1990 s80(2)(c).

35 EPA 1990 s81(1).

36 EPA 1990 s80(3).

37 EPA 1990 Sch 3 para 1(2).

38 1995 SI No 2644 as amended by 2006 SI No 771.

39 EPA 1990 s80(4). The excuse must be 'reasonable' eg it is no justification for generating loud noise that constitutes a statutory nuisance to say that it was being done to drown-out other local noise: *Waltham Forest LBC v Mitoo* [2016] EWHC 2159 (Admin).

40 In *Darlington BC v Munnelly*, December 2015 *Legal Action* 42, the landlord was fined £1,000 even after a guilty plea; £500 in costs was also awarded.

non-compliance following conviction.[41] The original abatement notice continues to bind the person served and the incentive for compliance with it is the prospect of incurring daily fines. There is, accordingly, no need for a nuisance order (see below).

6.38 Whether or not it prosecutes for non-compliance, the local authority can itself abate the nuisance 'and do whatever may be necessary' for execution of the original abatement notice.[42] It can then recover its costs from the person served or from the present owner of the property.[43]

High Court actions

6.39 If the local authority is satisfied that it would be inappropriate to deal with a statutory nuisance by using the magistrates' court procedure outlined above, it may take any necessary legal proceedings against the owner in the High Court.[44] Such proceedings have the advantage of giving access to broader remedies, eg injunctions, and wide-ranging means of enforcement. They are useful where the owner persistently defaults or repeatedly delays the process. For the procedure in a High Court action under the EPA 1990, see *Warwick RDC v Miller-Mead*.[45]

Emergency procedures

6.40 Frequently, the delays inherent in the enforcement procedures described above render them inappropriate for tackling situations of 'prejudice to health'. A streamlined procedure for these urgent cases is to be found in section 76 of the Building Act 1984, set out in appendix A.

6.41 Where an authority is satisfied (usually as a result of an urgent tenant complaint) that a statutory nuisance exists and that unreasonable delay would be caused by following the normal EPA 1990 procedure, it may serve the landlord with a notice stating its intention to do the remedial works and specifying the defects it intends to remedy.

41 EPA 1990 s80(5). Level 5 is now an unlimited fine. See Legal Aid, Sentencing and Punishment of Offenders Act (LASPO) 2012 s85. The imposition of a daily fine is discretionary: *Canterbury CC v Ferris* [1997] Env LR D14.

42 EPA 1990 s81(3).

43 EPA 1990 s81(4).

44 EPA 1990 s81(4).

45 [1962] Ch 441, [1962] 2 WLR 284, CA.

6.42 Nine days after service, the local authority can carry out all the necessary work identified in the notice and can recover its costs and expenses from the person on whom the notice is served. Landlords can prevent this procedure taking effect only if, within seven days of service of the notice, they serve a counter-notice on the local authority indicating that they intend to remedy the defects. The local authority cannot act thereafter unless:

- the landlord fails to start remedial works within a reasonable time; or
- having been started, remedial works proceed unreasonably slowly or make no progress at all.

In either of these circumstances, the local authority can then act, carry out the works and recover the full cost from the landlord.

6.43 Advisers assisting tenants in situations where housing conditions are sufficiently serious to constitute a statutory nuisance by reason of prejudice to health, should always consider pressing the EHO to use this 'nine-day notice' procedure.

Recurring nuisances

6.44 Under the EPA 1990 a local authority can serve an abatement notice requiring works, not only when it is satisfied that a nuisance exists, but also where it is satisfied that:

- a nuisance is likely to occur; or
- a nuisance is likely to recur.

6.45 The notice can either prohibit or restrict the nuisance from arising or recurring and require the necessary works for those purposes.[46]

Action by tenants and other occupiers

Private sector tenants and occupiers

6.46 Private sector or housing association tenants will usually look to the EHOs employed by local authorities to take the necessary administrative and legal proceedings to eradicate statutory nuisances arising at their homes, using the powers described above.

6.47 Advisers consulted by private tenants suffering prejudice to health or nuisance should consider involving the local authority's EHO by

46 EPA 1990 s80(1).

requesting a visit and inspection of the tenant's property.[47] The tenant must be warned that taking such action could lead to the ending of the tenancy, for example if the premises are in such poor condition as to lead to an order that they should no longer be occupied. Nowadays, there is protection from retaliatory evictions for assured shorthold tenants as long as they follow the procedures set out in the Deregulation Act 2015[48] and if the local housing authority serves an improvement notice or an emergency remedial action notice under the Housing Acts.[49] Local housing authorities should therefore be pressed to serve such notices in conjunction with any other action taken. If a complaint about housing conditions is made to a local authority, the tenant should liaise closely with the EHO and ensure that the abatement procedures are fully used, including the nine-day notice procedure for urgent cases (see para 6.40). In any subsequent prosecution of the landlord, the tenant may well be a witness for the local authority.

6.48 There are five situations, however, which may give rise to difficulty:

1) *The EHO fails to carry out an inspection, or there is an unreasonable delay before a visit is made* A local authority is required to investigate individual complaints (EPA 1990 s79(1)). In the event of a clear default, a complaint may be made to the Secretary of State,[50] who may direct the authority to inspect. Alternatively, a complaint may be made to the Local Government and Social Care Ombudsman. In the interim, consideration can be given to bringing a private prosecution (see para 6.50 onwards).
2) *The EHO carries out an inspection but does not agree that a statutory nuisance has arisen* In such circumstances, advisers should ask for the matter to be reconsidered, ensuring that the EHO is supplied with all the available medical information about the prejudice to the health of the tenant, or complaints from other tenants about the nuisance. An EHO may be persuaded to revisit and reconsider if presented with a convincing report from an independent expert engaged by the tenant.
3) *The EHO is not prepared to find that premises constitute a statutory nuisance, even after reconsideration* In this eventuality, the EHO

47 See para 5.20.

48 See para 5.17–5.18.

49 See chapter 5.

50 Currently, the Secretary of State for the Department of Environment Food and Rural Affairs.

should be asked whether there are any Category 1 or Category 2 hazards for the purposes of Housing Act 2004 and, if so, what action will be taken: see chapter 5. Alternatively, the tenant will need to establish the existence of the nuisance by instructing an independent EHO and, if satisfied that a statutory nuisance can be proved, take proceedings directly against the landlord using the section 82 procedure (see paragraph 6.50 onwards).

4) *The EHO agrees that there is a statutory nuisance, but fails to take remedial action within a reasonable time using the EPA 1990 procedures* The duty of the local authority to serve an abatement notice is a mandatory statutory duty.[51] The tenant can challenge the failure to take action, if aggrieved by the breach of statutory duty, and apply in judicial review proceedings[52] in the Administrative Court for an order directing the local authority to use the powers available to it.[53] Alternatively, complaint may be made to the Local Government and Social Care Ombudsman.[54] However, this may be secondary to the urgent need to remedy the statutory nuisance, in which case the tenant should initiate proceedings directly against the landlord in the magistrates' court, using the section 82 procedure, and secure the attendance of the EHO as a witness (see para 6.50 onwards).
5) *The EHO behaves improperly or unprofessionally* If the difficulty for the tenant arises from the improper or unprofessional behaviour of the EHO (eg, where the tenant is subject to racist remarks or has some evidence of corruption), complaint should be made to the chief EHO of the local authority concerned. If this produces no satisfaction, the matter should be raised with the professional association of EHOs, the Chartered Institution of Environmental Health.

Council tenants and occupiers

6.49 Council tenants are largely outside the usual provisions for the enforcement of the public health legislation simply because EHOs, as local government officers, cannot serve statutory notices on their own

51 *Cocker v Cardwell* (1869) LR 5 QB 15; *McPhail v Islington LBC* [1970] 2 QB 197, [1970] 2 WLR 583, CA at 586.

52 *Austin v Miller Argent (South Wales) Ltd* [2014] EWCA Civ 1012, [2015] 1 WLR 62 at [16].

53 EPA 1990 s80(1).

54 If the property is owned by the council itself, or another social landlord, complaint could be made to the Housing Ombudsman Service.

local authorities.[55] The council tenant must therefore use the enforcement procedure contained in EPA 1990 s82: see para 6.50 onwards.

EPA 1990 section 82 proceedings

6.50 The procedure for direct action by a tenant against their landlord is contained in EPA 1990 section 82 which is set out in full in appendix A.

6.51 Under this section, action may be taken against a local authority by a *council* tenant for the abatement of a statutory nuisance. This is the case even if the council is only providing the accommodation in exercise of its powers as a local housing authority.[56]

6.52 Similarly, section 82 can be used by a *private* sector or housing association tenant where the local authority is not itself taking proceedings to compel the landlord to deal with a statutory nuisance at the property.

6.53 Proceedings may be initiated by any 'person aggrieved' by the statutory nuisance. Although this will usually be the tenant or licensee, the provision extends to all other occupiers of the premises, such as the tenant's family or lodgers. The courts take a very broad approach. In *Watkins v Aged Merchant Seamen's Homes*[57] the EPA 1990 was used by a former licensee of alms-house accommodation and she was treated as a 'person aggrieved' even after a possession order had been made against her. The judge said:

> Whether a complainant is a 'person aggrieved' for the purposes of section 82(1) of the 1990 Act is always a question of fact and degree. It is normally, although not necessarily in every case, sufficient for a complainant to be a 'person aggrieved' if the complainant is in actual occupation, whether or not lawful occupation. If the legality of the occupation is a matter of bona fide dispute at the time the complaint is made, then it is likely, though not axiomatic, that the complainant will be found to be a person aggrieved.[58]

6.54 Under section 82, proceedings brought by individual tenants are criminal proceedings from the outset[59] even though the Act itself

55 See *Cardiff CC v Cross* (1982) 6 HLR 1, CA.

56 *R v Epping (Waltham Abbey) JJ ex p Burlinson* [1948] 1 KB 79, [1947] 2 All ER 537, KBD.

57 [2018] EWHC 2410 (Admin), [2019] Env LR 2, May 2019 *Legal Action* 29.

58 [2018] EWHC 2410 (Admin), [2019] Env LR 2 at [48]. See also *Pemberton v Southwark LBC* [2000] 1 WLR 1672, (2000) 32 HLR 784 in which a trespasser was permitted to bring a 'nuisance' claim.

59 *Botross v Hammersmith and Fulham LBC* (1994) 27 HLR 179, DC.

refers to an action started by way of complaint.[60] The document starting a magistrates' court prosecution is usually described as an '*information*' but since both the terms 'complaint' and 'information' are referred to in the legislation and case-law, they will also be used interchangeably in this chapter.

Funding

6.55 If a tenant has the resources, they could privately fund action taken under the EPA 1990. For those without such means, the form of legal aid funding known as Legal Representation[61] is *not available* for the private prosecution of criminal cases, nor for the enforcement of orders made under section 82. However, preparatory work can be undertaken by using the other form of legal aid, known as Legal Help.[62]

6.56 A conditional fee agreement (CFA) might be available if the nuisance has not been remedied by the time that the tenant is in a position to start a prosecution (see para 6.127). It is unlikely that a CFA will be available at an early stage of the case because it is difficult to assess the prospects of success without an expert's report. Also, there is a high risk that the landlord will abate the nuisance before there is any prospect of recovering legal costs, see para 6.81 below.

Overview of procedure

6.57 In summary, the process for using EPA 1990 s82 works in the following way:

- The tenant sends a letter to the landlord giving notice that a statutory notice exists and giving the landlord 21 days to abate it.
- When the 21 days has expired and the nuisance has not been remedied, the tenant asks the magistrates' court to issue a summons by providing the court officer with an information form and supporting documents.
- The court allocates a date for both the parties to attend and returns the summons to the tenant for service upon the landlord.

60 *R v Newham East JJ ex p Hunt* [1976] 1 WLR 420, [1976] 1 All ER 839, DC and Magistrates' Courts Act 1980 s50.

61 See chapter 4.

62 See chapter 4 at para 4.25.

- At the first hearing, if the landlord pleads guilty, a nuisance order is made. If there is a dispute over compensation or costs, that part of the case is usually adjourned to a later date.
- If the landlord pleads not guilty, the court gives directions and adjourns the case to a date when there is sufficient time for the case to be tried.
- If successful, the proceedings produce a nuisance order under section 82(2), breach of which constitutes a further criminal offence: EPA 1990 s82(8).

See appendix C for precedent documents for use of these procedures.

Preparatory work

6.58 Preparation for action under EPA 1990 s82 will usually include:

- The engagement of an independent EHO to inspect the premises, take photographs and samples, and prepare a report.[63]
- Preparation of letters, statements of the tenant and other members of the household relating to conditions at the premises, including statements which may be submitted under the Criminal Justice Act (CJA) 1967 s9.
- Preparation of a schedule of items destroyed or damaged by the statutory nuisance, including other financial loss, to be submitted for consideration of a compensation order.
- Assisting the tenant to disclose information to which the landlord is entitled.

Procedure

6.59 The procedure in the magistrates' court is regulated by the Criminal Procedure Rules (Crim PR) and Practice Directions (PDs) which are revised annually and can be found on the Ministry of Justice website.[64] The overriding objective is set out at Crim PR r1.1 and is to deal with a case 'justly'. This is stated to include:

(a) acquitting the innocent and convicting the guilty;
(b) dealing with the prosecution and the defence fairly;
(c) recognising the rights of a defendant, particularly those under Article 6 of the European Convention on Human Rights;

63 Advisers may find such EHOs via the Health and Housing Group, Star Street, Ware, Hertfordshire, SG12 7AA, tel: 01920 465384.

64 www.justice.gov.uk/courts/procedure-rules/criminal/.

(d) respecting the interests of witnesses, and victims and keeping them informed of the progress of the case;
(e) dealing with the case efficiently and expeditiously;
(f) ensuring that appropriate information is available to the court when sentence is considered; and
(g) dealing with the case in ways that take into account–
  (i) the gravity of the offence alleged,
  (ii) the complexity of what is in issue,
  (iii) the severity of the consequences for the defendant and others affected, and
  (iv) the needs of other cases.

6.60 Crim PR r1.2 puts both prosecution and defence under a duty to prepare and conduct the case in accordance with the overriding objective, to comply with the rules and with any directions made by the court and to inform the court and the other participants in the case of any failure to take a procedural step required by the rules. Crim PR r3.3 requires both parties to communicate throughout the case in order to assist the court to achieve the overriding objective. For the landlord, this includes a duty to:

- indicate whether the landlord is likely to plead guilty; and
- clarify what is agreed and what is disputed.

6.61 Both landlord and tenant must establish and then communicate to the court:

- what information, or other material, is required by one party of another, and why; and
- what is to be done, by whom, and when (without or, if necessary, with a direction).

6.62 The court is supposed to actively manage all cases[65] and it can impose costs sanctions for non-compliance with the procedural rules.[66]

The expert

6.63 The success of a section 82 case will turn mainly on factual and expert evidence about 'prejudice to health' or 'nuisance' and the tenant's adviser will want to obtain and rely on a written expert's

65 Crim PR rr3.2 and 3.4.
66 Crim PR r3.5(6)(b).

report on the condition of the premises. It was held in *O'Toole v Knowsley MBC*[67] that an EHO is qualified to assess whether premises are prejudicial to health and no additional medical evidence, for example from a general practitioner (GP), is necessary. In *Southwark LBC v Simpson*,[68] it was stated that a chartered surveyor without expertise in public health matters will not have the knowledge required to give admissible opinion in an EPA 1990 case.

6.64 The tenant's adviser must serve the expert's report on the court and on the landlord as soon as practicable[69] and must then inform the EHO that the report has been so served.[70] In EPA 1990 proceedings, the report will usually have been served before the prosecution starts but any additional expert evidence must be dealt with according to this rule and breach of it may lead to the tenant not being allowed to introduce the evidence.[71]

6.65 The EHO's duties to the court are set out in Crim PR r19.2 and are much the same as in civil proceedings (see para 3.65).

6.66 Where both parties want to rely on different experts the court may direct that the experts discuss the issues and then prepare a statement setting out the matters upon which they agree and disagree.[72]

6.67 Lay magistrates and District Judges of a magistrates' court are not entitled to reject the evidence of an EHO called on behalf of the tenant unless that evidence is challenged or contradicted by an EHO for the landlord:

> ... when it comes to deciding whether the condition of premises is or is not liable or likely to be injurious to health one is moving outside the field where a tribunal is entitled to draw on its own experience. That is a matter upon which the tribunal needs informed expert evidence.[73]

Even so, it is the bench and not the expert who will decide, based on the whole of the evidence, factual and expert, whether the offence is made out.[74]

67 (2000) 32 HLR 420, [1999] EHLR 420, QBD.
68 (1999) 31 HLR 725, DC.
69 Crim PR r19.3(3)(b).
70 Crim PR r19.5.
71 Crim PR r19.3(4).
72 Crim PR r19.6(2)(b).
73 *Patel v Mehtab* (1982) 5 HLR 78, QBD, per Donaldson LJ at 82.
74 *R (Hackney LBC) v Rottenberg* [2007] EWHC 166 (Admin), [2007] Env LR 24.

Notice of the intended proceedings

6.68 Before the tenant starts court proceedings, the landlord must be given at least 21 days' notice specifying the matter complained of: EPA 1990 s82(6) and (7). The notice must provide reasonable details of the alleged statutory nuisance but need not be comprehensive or set out what remedial works are required.[75]

6.69 The notice must be served on the person responsible for the nuisance. Part 4 of Crim PR states that documents can be served by hand, by first class post, or where the landlord has given a document exchange (DX) or electronic (email) address, at that address unless they have refused to accept service by that method. The dates of deemed service are a little more generous to landlords than those in the civil courts so advisers need to consider Crim PR r4.11.

6.70 EPA 1990 s160 provides that where the landlord is a local authority, the notice must be served on a clerk to that authority. Since most town clerks have been replaced by chief executives, this can pose a problem. There are two conflicting cases on this point.[76] The notice should be sent to the principal office of the authority unless the landlord has specified another address as envisaged by EPA 1990 s160.[77] Advisers should therefore take the precaution of sending one copy of the notice to the chief executive's office but addressed to 'the clerk' and a second copy to the council's solicitor.

The information

6.71 The person aggrieved by the existence of a statutory nuisance sends a formal written statement, described as an 'information' to the magistrates' court. That then triggers the issue of a summons to the landlord from the court.

6.72 This is a straightforward process involving completion of a prescribed information form which is delivered to the court officer at

75 *R v Liverpool Crown Court ex p Cooke* [1996] 4 All ER 589, [1997] 1 WLR 700, DC; *East Staffordshire v Fairless* [1998] EWHC 954 (Admin), (1999) 31 HLR 677, *R (Fullers Farming Limited) v Milton Keynes Council* [[2011] EWHC 3784 (Admin), [2012] Env LR 17.

76 *R v Birmingham CC ex p Ireland* [1999] 2 All ER 609, QBD; and *Leeds v Islington LBC* [1998] Env LR 655, (1999) 31 HLR 545, QBD.

77 In *Leeds v Islington LBC* [1998] Env LR 655, (1999) 31 HLR 545, QBD, an address on the rent book for service of notices under Landlord and Tenant Act 1987 s47 was held to be unacceptable for service of a notice under EPA 1990 s82(6).

the tenant's local magistrates' court.[78] The information must contain a statement of the offence, setting out:

- An indication of the capacity in which the landlord is to be served (ie, as the person responsible for the nuisance or the 'owner' if either the nuisance arises from a structural defect, or the person responsible for the nuisance cannot be found).[79] If the tenant cannot contact or trace the landlord, the information may even be laid against the 'managing agents' who receive the tenant's rent.[80] An information can also be laid against a social housing provider which is utilising privately-owned housing.[81]
- The nature of the alleged nuisance in ordinary language[82] and enough detail for the landlord to understand what is being complained of, and what is needed to abate it.[83] (The EHO report, if attached to the information, will usually be more than adequate.)
- That the statutory nuisance arises under section 79(1)(a) and/or section 82 (prejudice to health or a nuisance) rather than one of the other variants of statutory nuisance (smoke, effluvia, noise etc), if that is the case.[84]

6.73 It would be usual for the tenant to be in occupation of the premises at the date the information is delivered to the Court (see para 6.53), but the absence of the tenant (perhaps driven to live elsewhere temporarily by the poor conditions) is not fatal to an application.[85] Nor is the departure of the tenant after the summons is issued.[86]

6.74 It is permissible to send an information immediately after expiry of the 21-day notice period under section 82(6).[87]

78 Crim PR r7.2(1).

79 EPA 1990 s82(4) and (5). Small defects in the information can and should be remedied by section 124 of the Magistrates' Courts Act 1980, see *Wandsworth LBC v Rashid* [2009] EWHC 1844 (Admin), [2010] Env LR 22.

80 *Dhorre v Woodhouse Estates Ltd*, North London Magistrates' Court, DJ (MC) Rimmer, noted as *Dore v Woodhouse Estates Ltd* March 2018 *Legal Action* 36, applying *Camden LBC v Gunby* [2000] 7 WLR 465, (2000) 32 HLR 572.

81 *Ozmus v West Hampstead Housing Association*, *Housing Law Casebook* 7th edn, para R25.29, Wood Green Crown Court.

82 Crim PR r7.3(1)(a)(i).

83 Crim PR r7.3(1)(b).

84 Crim PR r7.3(1)(a)(ii).

85 *Jones v Public Trustee* September 1988 *Legal Action* 21, Hastings Magistrates' Court.

86 *Watkins v Aged Merchant Seamen's Homes* [2018] EWHC 2410 (Admin), [2019] Env LR 2.

87 *R v Dudley Magistrates' Court ex p Hollis* [1998] 1 All ER 759, (1998) 30 HLR 902, DC.

6.75 Although many of the busiest magistrates' courts are familiar with applications made under EPA 1990 s82, advisers should be careful not to take the issue of a summons for granted in other areas. It is good practice to ensure that the information is accompanied by a statement from the tenant,[88] the expert's report, a copy of EPA 1990 s82 and a request for an early hearing date. It is sensible to give the tenant's postal address as c/o the adviser to ensure that all documents reach the adviser in good time.

6.76 No fee is payable.[89]

6.77 On receipt of the information, the court will issue a summons to require the landlord to attend a hearing on a specified date.[90] The function of the court, when issuing a summons is judicial, ie, there is a discretion to issue, or to refuse to issue the summons, which must be exercised judicially. It would, however, be wrong to refuse to issue a summons merely because the landlord also faced civil proceedings, at least when the scope of the civil proceedings is not co-extensive with the scope of the EPA 1990 proceedings.[91] Minor and obvious errors in drawing up the summons will not invalidate the proceedings.[92]

6.78 In order to have jurisdiction, the court must be satisfied that *at the date of the information*:

- the notice under section 82(6) (see para 6.68) has been served and 21 days have elapsed since service; and
- there is a statutory nuisance (rather than the prospect of a nuisance arising or recurring);[93] and
- the tenant was 'aggrieved' (see para 6.53) by the statutory nuisance *at that date*.[94] If any work is carried out by the landlord after

88 It is recommended that this complies with Criminal Justice Act 1967 s9.

89 Magistrates' Courts Fees Order 2008 SI No 1052 reg 3 (1)(a) – these are criminal proceedings: *Botross v Hammersmith and Fulham LBC* (1994) 27 HLR 179, DC.

90 Crim PR r7.4(3)(a).

91 *R v Highbury Corner Magistrates' Court ex p Edwards* (1994) 26 HLR 682, DC.

92 *Fernandez v Broad* [1996] CLY 2759, Div Crt. In that case, the information was laid under EPA 1990 s82 against a private landlord but both it and the subsequent summons described the owner of the property as 'the said council'. The court would not allow the proceedings to be frustrated 'by the taking of technical points'. The decision was approved on its facts in *R (Essence Bars (London) Ltd (t/a Essence)) v Wimbledon Magistrates' Court* [2016] EWCA Civ 63, [2016] 1 WLR 3265 at [52].

93 EPA 1990 s82(1).

94 *Hilton v Hopwood* (1899) 44 SJ 96. See too *Watkins v Aged Merchant Seamen's Homes* [2018] EWHC 2410 (Admin), May 2019 *Legal Action* 29.

the date of the EHO's inspection report, it may be necessary to arrange a re-inspection by the EHO before the information is put before the court.

6.79 There is provision in the rules for the tenant's representative to serve the summons and then notify the court officer that this has been done.[95] Alternatively, the court can serve the summons.

The first hearing

6.80 The court will often inform the tenant directly of the hearing date, so the adviser should ensure that the tenant realises that they must pass this date on to the adviser as soon as possible.

6.81 Even if the remedial works are started after the laying of the information, the tenant and adviser should attend on the hearing date to secure an order for costs (see below). Note that the case could proceed to hearing even if the tenants have been re-housed, because removing the tenant does not remedy the statutory nuisance.[96]

6.82 Advisers may well find that, at the first hearing date, the case appears in a list of many others, on the basis that it will be effective only if there is a guilty plea and agreement on matters such as the works to be covered by an order.

6.83 The tenant may feel able to present the case at an uncontested hearing. If not, both solicitors and barristers have the right to address the court. Some barristers are willing to act in EPA 1990 prosecutions under a conditional fee agreement (CFA).[97] If a barrister is instructed without a CFA, the adviser will be liable for his or her fee.

6.84 The adviser should remind those representing the landlord that they must tell the tenant as soon as possible whether a guilty or not guilty plea is to be entered. If the landlord is pleading guilty, it may be possible to agree a works schedule and at the hearing the magistrates can be invited to make an order requiring the landlord to abate the nuisance within a specified time and to carry out the works necessary for that purpose.[98] If, by the hearing date, the nuisance has abated (whether naturally or as a result of remedial measures) but the court is satisfied that recurrence is likely, it can make an order

95 Crim PR r7.4(6)(a).

96 *Lambeth LBC v Stubbs* (1980) 255 EG 789, (1980) 78 LGR 650, DC, followed and applied in *Coventry CC v Doyle* [1981] 1 WLR 1325, [1981] 2 All ER 184, DC.

97 See chapter 4 on funding.

98 EPA 1990 s82(2).

prohibiting recurrence and requiring works to prevent recurrence.[99] The court's powers at this stage mirror those of the local authority itself to serve an abatement notice as described at para 6.29 (save that the magistrates have no jurisdiction to prevent first occurrence of a nuisance). In order to secure the most appropriate orders, tenants and their advisers should have drafts available for the court to consider.

6.85 If the landlord does not confirm that a guilty plea is to be entered, the adviser should complete the first section of a procedural form entitled *'Preparation for effective trial'*.[100] The form is intended to assist the court to make appropriate directions to prepare the case for trial. The adviser should send the form to the landlord in good time for the landlord to complete it and bring it to the first hearing. Much of the form contains questions that are irrelevant to an EPA 1990 prosecution so some advisers prepare a list of supplementary questions to elicit the nature of the defence and send this with the court form.

6.86 If the landlord does *not* plead guilty at the first hearing, they may well request an adjournment. Magistrates are not entitled to adjourn simply to allow for works to be done before trial and thus deprive the tenant of the right to a compensation order.[101] Even so, if the tenant opposes an adjournment then the landlord can be sure of obtaining one from the court by pleading not guilty, in which case the court is likely to give directions and then fix a one-day or two-day trial well into in the future. The tenant should be reminded not to lose sight of the primary object of the proceedings, namely to force the landlord to do work. One approach is to agree to one short adjournment of perhaps 14 or 21 days and, if the landlord is not prepared to plead guilty by the second hearing, to insist (at that second hearing) on an effective trial date being fixed. Only as an adviser becomes familiar with a regular opponent will the best tactics become apparent.

6.87 The tenant must have a list of dates when the EHO will be unable to attend court so that the trial date can be fixed for a date when the EHO and the tenant are available.

6.88 A misguided tenant might at this stage try to prevent the landlord from carrying out work before trial in order to secure a conviction.

99 EPA 1990 s82(2)(b).

100 www.justice.gov.uk/courts/procedure-rules/criminal/docs/2014/crimpr-part3-magistrates-courts-trial-preparation-form.pdf.

101 *R v Dudley Magistrates' Court ex p Hollis* [1998] 1 All ER 759, DC.

Such a strategy will backfire because it will be held that the landlord is not liable for the continuance of the nuisance and the summons will be dismissed.[102]

Negotiations

6.89 Advisers should be aware that the duties of a prosecutor, to ensure that the guilty are convicted, prevent the sort of settlement negotiations that are common in civil litigation. Out of court resolutions can take place but it is improper to use the prosecution as a means to extract compensation and costs from a landlord who does not admit guilt. Many of the duties of a private prosecutor are the same as for the Crown, so the adviser should refer to the Code for Crown Prosecutors.[103] In particular, the adviser should read the Full Code Test, the Threshold Test and the section of the Code relating to out of court disposals.

Preparing for the trial

6.90 Unless the tenant is going to present the case, an advocate should be booked as soon as the trial date is known. The adviser should also ensure that the EHO is informed of the trial date and asked to attend.

6.91 Crim PR Part 15 reflects the Criminal Procedure and Investigations Act (CPIA) 1996 which requires the prosecuting tenant '*as soon as is reasonably practicable after . . . the accused pleads not guilty*'[104] to disclose to the landlord any information or documents that may undermine the tenant's case.[105] This duty of disclosure continues until the end of the case.[106] If there is no such material the tenant must confirm this to the landlord in a written statement.[107] The tenant must inform the court office of any such disclosure.[108]

102 *Quigley v Liverpool Housing Trust* [1999] EWHC 593 (Admin), [2000] EHLR 130, [2000] Env LR D9; and *Jones v Walsall MBC* [2002] EWHC 1232 (Admin), [2003] Env LR 5.

103 www.cps.gov.uk/publications/code_for_crown_prosecutors/disposals.html/.

104 CPIA 1996 s13(1)(a).

105 CPIA 1996 s3 as amended by CJA 2003.

106 CPIA 1996 s7A.

107 CPIA 1996 3(1)(b).

108 Crim PR r15.2.

Examples

(1) An adviser learns from a witness that the tenant's flat became affected by damp only when the tenant overcrowded the flat by subletting rooms. The subtenants have now left and the landlord is unaware of the subletting. This evidence cannot be ignored; the adviser must tell the tenant to either abandon the prosecution or provide the landlord with details of the witness and the substance of the evidence.
(2) An adviser obtains a report from an EHO stating that the tenant's home is *not* prejudicial to health. The tenant offers to pay for a second report in the hope that the second EHO will have a more helpful opinion. The adviser must tell the tenant that even if a second report is obtained, the first one will have to be shown to the landlord.

6.92 Because this is a summary prosecution, the landlord is not obliged to give the tenant notice of what issues he or she is going to raise in the defence.[109] This means that the tenant has to prepare to prove every element of the offence, as set out in para 6.7. If the landlord wants further information from the tenant, the voluntary disclosure procedure set out in CPIA 1996 s6A can be used. The landlord will serve a statement setting out the general nature of the defence; a copy must be sent to the court. On receipt of the defence statement, the tenant must either:

- disclose any material which in the light of the defence statement might be reasonably expected to assist the defence; or
- confirm in writing that there is no such material.

6.93 CPIA 1996 s8 and Crim PR r15.5 provide a procedure to force the prosecuting tenant to produce documents or information if the landlord believes that the tenant is withholding material that would assist in defending the case.

6.94 If the landlord wants to rely on expert evidence the usual direction is that it must be served within 28 days of the first hearing.

6.95 Section 9 of the Criminal Justice Act 1967 allows written statements to be tendered in evidence at a magistrates' court trial. The

109 CPIA 1996 ss1(2) and 5(1)(a) although the *effective trial* form is helpful here, see para 6.85 above. If invited and reminded of the overriding objectives, many landlords will do so.

adviser may want to make use of this provision to rely on evidence from a witness who would prefer not to attend trial. The statement must be in a prescribed form with the criminal version of the statement of truth. It must be sent to the court as soon as possible. The court officer will then serve it on the landlord, who has seven days in which to object to the statement being tendered in evidence.[110] If an objection is made, the evidence will not be admissible unless the witness attends court.

6.96 In certain circumstances, the tenant can rely on hearsay evidence such as the landlord's repair records. In such a case, the adviser should refer to a specialist criminal procedure text for more detail.

6.97 About two weeks before the date set for the trial, the adviser should try to find out from the landlord's representative whether the intention is still to fight the case. If, in fact, the landlord is now going to plead guilty, then, as long as the landlord's representative confirms this in writing, the court can be informed and some of the time set aside can be allocated to another matter.

6.98 The adviser should be careful to comply with the court's directions and to apply promptly if a variation is needed. There are sanctions for failures such as costs orders or refusal to allow evidence to be adduced.

6.99 If the intention is still to plead not guilty, the advocate will want to see a full proof of evidence from the tenant and any other witnesses. Although a trial bundle[111] is not strictly required for a magistrates' court trial, many advocates expect to be given one to assist with the preparation of the case. Normally, the adviser should ensure that there is a well organised, comprehensive, indexed and paginated bundle of documents available for the use of the court and, where possible, with the content having been agreed in advance. Some advisers find that, whether or not required by the rules or an order, it can be helpful to submit a skeleton argument at or before the trial

6.100 In a contested case, it is worth checking that none of the sitting justices are in any obvious way associated with the interests of the landlord.[112] In particular, where the case is being brought against a local authority none of those sitting should be members of that authority.[113]

110 Crim PR r27 but it is possible to obtain permission to make a late objection.

111 See Civil Procedure Rules PD39A.

112 *R v Smethwick JJ ex p Hand* (1980) *Times* 4 December, DC.

113 Courts Act 2003 s41.

Trial

6.101 The procedure for a magistrates' court trial is set out in Crim PR r24.3.3 and the adviser should read it carefully.

6.102 At the close of the evidence, the justices are required to make certain findings, including:

- the actual condition of the premises: (i) at the date of the laying of the tenant's information and (ii) at the date of hearing;
- whether the condition at the date of the serving of the information constituted a statutory nuisance, and whether the statutory nuisance still exists or is likely to recur; and
- identifying the person responsible for the statutory nuisance, or the owner.

6.103 The existence of a statutory nuisance and the cause of that nuisance have to be proved to the criminal standard of proof, ie, beyond reasonable doubt. It follows that if any of the points above have not been proved with admissible evidence, there will be no conviction.

6.104 The landlord will not be the 'person responsible' if the court decides that the real cause of the nuisance is the tenant's own conduct, eg, failure to use the heating system supplied or otherwise to behave reasonably.[114]

6.105 The fact that the matter complained of does not arise from any breach of the landlord's obligations may be persuasive in showing that it was not caused by any act or default of the landlord, but is not conclusive.[115] However, where the nuisance arises from any defect of a structural nature (eg, dampness resulting from a hole in the roof), the landlord is liable in the capacity of 'owner', irrespective of repairing obligations, once a statutory nuisance is proved.[116] It is necessary to have evidence at the trial to prove ownership.

Nuisance orders

6.106 If the matters listed at para 6.102 are found in favour of the tenant, the court must make an order against the landlord requiring:

114 *Dover DC v Farrar* (1982) 2 HLR 32, DC; *GLC v Tower Hamlets LBC* (1984) 15 HLR 54, DC; *Warner v Lambeth LBC* (1984) 15 HLR 40, DC; *Carr v Hackney LBC* (1996) 28 HLR 747, DC.

115 *Birmingham DC v Kelly and Others* (1985) 17 HLR 572, QBD, at 579.

116 *Coventry CC v Doyle* [1981] 1 WLR 1325, [1981] 2 All ER 184, DC and EPA 1990 s82(4)(b).

- such work as the court considers necessary to abate the nuisance, within a stipulated time limit; and/or
- sufficient works to prevent a recurrence of the nuisance.

6.107 The work required must be specified by the court in the nuisance order,[117] and so advisers should ensure that the court is supplied with a full and detailed draft order. Where there has been agreement on the facts, advisers should arrange that the fullest possible order is agreed in advance with the landlord and put before the justices. Much may be achieved through hard bargaining on the terms of orders 'at the door of the court' and the tenant's expert can assist with negotiations on the wording of the order. Whether or not the order is agreed, evidence in support of it must be given, since the decision about the extent of the works necessary to abate the nuisance should be made by the court itself.[118] The order may properly require works to be done which go beyond the terms of any contractual repairing obligation on the landlord. The order can for instance, require improvement work or the installation of fixtures, fittings and facilities not present at the commencement of the tenancy.[119]

6.108 The court has a wide discretion about the form and content of the order and, in considering the remedial works to be specified, can properly have regard to the future life of the property. The justices must 'look at the whole circumstances of the case and try and make an order which is in its terms sensible and just, having regard to the entire prevailing situation'.[120] If the order is being made against a local authority, the court is also entitled to have regard to the general obligations that the council owes to its tenants and to the extent of its resources.[121]

6.109 Although, in many cases, the landlord will attempt to convince the court that simple 'patch' repairs will cure the statutory nuisance, advisers should be bold in pressing for substantial orders for work sufficient to prevent recurrence of the nuisance. With the assistance of expert witnesses, tenants in past cases have been able to persuade courts to make formidable orders for remedial works, including improvements which, because of the limits of landlord obligations in

117 *Network Housing Association v Westminster CC* (1995) 27 HLR 189, DC.

118 *Birmingham DC v Kelly and Others* (1985) 17 HLR 572, QBD.

119 *Birmingham DC v Kelly and Others* (1985) 17 HLR 572, QBD.

120 *Nottingham City DC v Newton* [1974] 1 WLR 923, [1974] 2 All ER 760, QBD, per Widgery LCJ at 766.

121 *Salford CC v McNally* [1976] AC 379, HL; *Birmingham DC v Kelly and Others* (1985) 17 HLR 572, QBD.

civil law, would not have been achieved in the county court. For example, in *Birmingham DC v Kelly and Others*,[122] the magistrates ordered installation of gas-fired central heating, secondary double glazing, roof insulation, filling of cavity walls and electrical re-wiring.

6.110 Where the only effective way to abate the statutory nuisance is to have the whole property demolished, a nuisance order requiring demolition may be made.[123] Where the property is unfit, the court can prohibit occupation.[124] It is therefore wise, when a property is in very poor condition, to ensure that the tenant realises that re-location may be the consequence of bringing proceedings.

Enforcement

6.111 The landlord will usually comply with the terms of the nuisance order before expiry of the time stated in the order. If he or she fails without reasonable excuse to comply with 'any requirement' of an order made in section 82 proceedings, the landlord commits a further criminal offence: EPA 1990 s82(8). The tenant may then bring a prosecution for that non-compliance in the same magistrates' court where the order was made. Indeed, if the order in the earlier part of section 82 proceedings was made against a private or housing association landlord, the local authority could bring the further prosecution even though it was the tenant who first obtained the order in default of the local authority acting. The prosecution is launched by serving further information. If the magistrate is satisfied that an offence has occurred, the magistrates' court (or its clerk) will issue a summons requiring the attendance of the landlord for trial. Tenants should press for early hearing dates as the daily fine, which is the real pressure on the landlord to comply with the order, bites only from the date of conviction, not from when the order is breached or the information laid.

6.112 Tenants should try to establish in advance whether the landlord will be pleading guilty or not guilty to the offence of non-compliance. In particular tenants should be alert to the prospect of the landlord relying on section 82(8), the 'reasonable excuse' defence. This is undefined and potentially very wide ranging.

6.113 If the magistrates are satisfied about non-compliance, or there is a guilty plea, a further conviction will be entered.

122 (1985) 17 HLR 572, QBD.

123 *Brown v Biggleswade Union* (1879) 43 JP 554.

124 EPA 1990 s82(3).

Penalties

6.114 Where the initial prosecution under EPA 1990 s82(1) results in a nuisance order, the court enters a conviction and may impose an unlimited fine: s82(2).[125] The penalty for failure to comply with a nuisance order is a second fine. The magistrates have a discretion whether to impose the daily fine and will be assisted by any information about the landlord's earlier convictions relating to other properties owned.

6.115 Some guidance as to setting the amount of the fine was provided in *R (Islington LBC) v Inner London Crown Court.*[126] In that case, the premises had been fitted with new windows that provided inadequate ventilation and, as a result, the tenant's flat was suffering from condensation and mould growth; conditions that Lord Justice Brooke described as 'deplorable'. He stated that a fine in the region of £500 would be 'clearly too low', but he quashed a fine of £4,000 as being too high, given that the premises were fit for human habitation, the council had pleaded guilty and at the time of sentencing had nearly completed the schedule of works. The case was remitted for sentencing to the Crown Court, where the fine was reduced to £1,500.

6.116 The tenant's advocate, when acting as prosecutor, represents the public interest. As such, that advocate should be ready to assist the court to reach its decision as to an appropriate sentence.[127] At the sentencing stage, the tenant's advocate should inform the court of:

- the impact of the statutory nuisance on the tenant and their family;[128]
- any relevant sentencing guidelines and guideline cases;[129]
- any known previous convictions (the adviser will find it helpful to keep a database of previous EPA prosecutions for this purpose); and
- the appropriate sentencing range in the light of the above factors.

125 Since 2014 there is no standard scale, only guidelines.

126 [2003] EWHC 2500 (Admin), [2004] HLR 31, December 2004 *Legal Action* 15.

127 *Attorney General's guidelines on the acceptance of pleas and the prosecutor's role in the sentencing exercise* (revised 2009).

128 See the CPS sentencing guidelines as to putting a 'victim personal statement' before the court. If this is done it should conform with section 9 of the CJA 1967.

129 The relevant guidance for EPA prosecutions is found in the Sentencing Council's *Definitive Guideline for Environmental Offences* and the recommended penalties are heavy, see: www.sentencingcouncil.org.uk/wp-content/uploads/Final_Environmental_Offences_Definitive_Guideline_web1.pdf/.

Compensation

6.117 In addition to any penalty, a compensation order[130] should be made in favour of the tenant for harm they have suffered and for damage to their property. Section 63 of the Legal Aid, Sentencing and Punishment of Offenders Act 2012 (LASPO) requires that a court must consider making a compensation order in any case where it has power to do so.[131] This requirement is in addition to the requirement that the court should give reasons if it does not make a compensation order.[132] In a 'prejudice to health' case, actual ill health will usually have been proved and recompense should follow. A compensation order provides a 'speedy, summary and cheap' method of obtaining financial compensation without the need to bring separate civil proceedings.[133] Full details of any personal injury should be provided,[134] although in the absence of such evidence an award for anxiety and distress can be made.[135] There is no limit on the amount of the award.[136] It is not necessary to show that the landlord would have been liable in civil proceedings to pay compensation,[137] but some evidence of the actual loss suffered must be available: mere representations are insufficient.[138]

6.118 The decision in *R v Liverpool Crown Court ex p Cooke*[139] has greatly limited the value of compensation awards and effectively means that the longest period of inconvenience and distress that can be claimed is six months. Often, it will be much shorter. In *Cooke*, the Divisional Court held that, when assessing compensation, magistrates were not entitled to take into account the whole period for which the nuisance

130 Powers of Criminal Courts (Sentencing) Act (PCC(S)A) 2000 s130; *Herbert v Lambeth LBC* (1992) 24 HLR 299, DC; and *Botross v Hammersmith and Fulham LBC* (1994) 27 HLR 179, DC.

131 PCC(S)A 2000 s130(2A).

132 PCC(S)A 2000 s130(3).

133 *R v Dorton* (1987) 9 Cr App R(S) 514, [1988] Crim LR 254, CA.

134 *R v Cooper* (1982) 4 Cr App R(S) 555, [1982] Crim LR 308, CA.

135 *Bond v Chief Constable of Kent* [1983] 1 WLR 40, [1983] 1 All ER 456, DC.

136 In *Duke v Uthayakanthan* December 2015 *Legal Action* 42, Camberwell Green Magistrates Court, the court awarded £1000 compensation for cockroach infestation. The same amount has been awarded for a flying beetle infestation: *Dent v Haringey LBC* December 1999 *Legal Action* 18, *Housing Law Casebook* 7th edn, para R25.37.

137 *R v Chappell* (1985) 80 Cr App R 31, [1984] Crim LR 574, CA.

138 *R v Horsham Justices ex p Richards* [1985] 2 All ER 1114, [1985] 1 WLR 986, DC; and *R v Amey* [1983] 1 WLR 345, [1983] 1 All ER 865, CA.

139 [1996] 4 All ER 589, (1997) 29 HLR 249, QBD.

existed. Since there is no 'offence' under section 82 unless a nuisance is proved to exist on the date of hearing, it follows that the earliest date that compensation can be awarded from will be the date that the 21-day statutory notice expires, see para 6.68. If the statutory notice has expired more than six months before the information was laid, then compensation will run from six months before the date that the information was laid. The Divisional Court reiterated earlier warnings from appeal courts that the power to make compensation orders should be exercised only in simple and clear cases. The Divisional Court indicated in *Cooke* that in the context of the relatively short period of liability 'many, if not most' claims ought to be simple and straightforward. *Cooke* preceded LASPO 2012 s63 and might be decided differently today.

6.119 Even so, the Divisional Court in *Davenport v Walsall MBC*[140] dismissed an appeal from magistrates who refused to make a compensation order on the ground that the case was too complicated; though it was a relevant factor that there was likely to be no civil remedy. It was a feature of the case that the landlord had pleaded guilty and so the magistrates did not have a substantial pool of information about the case. The Divisional Court indicated that it did not wish to encourage magistrates to be 'over-eager to resort to assertions of complexity' but that it would only interfere if the 'decision falls outside the scope of their legitimate discretion'.

6.120 Care should be taken in identifying the actual loss in respect of which compensation is sought because, in any subsequent civil action for damages, credit will have to be given for the amount of the compensation order where the award is for the same 'injury, loss or damage'.[141] If a civil claim is going to be brought, the magistrates should always be asked to award compensation for those items which will not attract civil damages. The adviser should avoid adversely affecting the civil damages claim when coming to a settlement of the section 82 prosecution. However, there is county court authority for the proposition that the clearest evidence would be needed to show that an agreement reached in the magistrates' court would be treated as a compromise in a prospective civil claim.[142]

140 (1996) 28 HLR 754, [1997] Env LR 24, DC.

141 PCC(S)A 2000 s134(2).

142 *Middlemast v Hammersmith and Fulham LBC* May 1997 *Legal Action* 20, *Housing Law Casebook* 7th edn, para, R25.48, West London County Court.

6.121 On the other hand, often the only chance for a tenant to be compensated is in the magistrates' court. In *Issa v Hackney LBC,*[143] the tenant's home was prejudicial to health owing to bad design, even though there was no breach of any civil obligation on the landlord. The council landlord was fined and ordered to carry out remedial works. The tenant's children had suffered asthma and they brought a county court claim against the council for damages. They relied as their cause of action on the council's failure to comply with the EPA 1990 and the conviction that their parent had obtained. The Court of Appeal held that the EPA 1990 does not give rise to a private law right of action. There is no civil liability on landlords unless there is actionable breach of contract or a tort: see chapter 2.

Appeals

6.122 An appeal against conviction may be made by the landlord to the Crown Court.[144] The appeal takes the form of a rehearing but the court concerns itself only with the matters as they stood at the date of the hearing before the justices.[145] Either party can appeal to the Divisional Court of the Queen's Bench Division by way of case stated. Alternatively, the procedure for judicial review by the Administrative Court is available to both parties. Judicial review may be necessary, for example, to compel the magistrates in EPA 1990 proceedings to award costs.[146] Any order made by the magistrates' court which is scheduled to take effect before an appeal can be heard must be complied with.[147]

Costs

6.123 The EPA 1990 makes specific provision for costs awards in section 82 proceedings: section 82(12). Where the court is satisfied that the statutory nuisance existed at the date that the information was laid then, irrespective of whether the nuisance still exists or is likely to

143 [1997] 1 All ER 999, (1997) 29 HLR 640, CA.

144 EPA 1990 s73.

145 *Northern Ireland Trailers v Preston Corporation* [1972] 1 WLR 203, [1972] 1 All ER 260.

146 See *R v Dudley Magistrates' Court ex p Hollis* [1998] 1 All ER 759, DC.

147 *Hammersmith LBC v Magnum Automated Forecourts Ltd* [1978] 1 WLR 50, [1977] 1 All ER 401, CA.

recur at the date of the hearing, the court must order the landlord to pay the costs. The sum ordered to be paid is 'such amount as the court considers reasonably sufficient to compensate the tenant for any expenses properly incurred by him in the proceedings'.[148] This is a more generous test than standard assessment in the county court.

6.124 The costs incurred 'in the proceedings' may, at least arguably, include the costs of bringing the proceedings ie costs incurred before issue of the summons.[149]

6.125 There being no fixed scales for the award of costs, and no special rules for assessment of costs, the court has to make a broad assessment as to what figure will be just and reasonable in all the circumstances. The award should be sufficient to cover experts' fees, legal costs, tenant's loss of earnings etc. Tenants have recovered costs in excess of £10,000 where the case has been defended to a late stage necessitating substantial preparation time. There is no formal procedure to assess the costs and the magistrates have a wide jurisdiction. Decisions on costs can be reached without the need for pleadings or formal bills[150] but in *Taylor v Walsall and District Property and Investment Co*[151] it was made clear that the informant is expected as 'a matter of routine' to give advance notice to the landlord of any claim for costs and the landlord should indicate in advance whether that claim is accepted or challenged. The same case encouraged the use of the equivalent of Civil Procedure Rules Part 36 offers. Perhaps the best way for the adviser to approach costs is to produce a schedule similar in form to that used for summary assessment of costs in the county court.[152]

6.126 Costs remain 'properly incurred' when the tenant pursues an application for a compensation order at an adjourned hearing, even though the magistrates decide not to make a compensation order, providing the application was proper, ie, was not 'doomed from the outset'.[153]

148 EPA 1990 s82(12).

149 *R (Hale) v North Sefton Justices* [2002] EWHC 257 (Admin), [2002] All ER (D) 10 (Jan), (2002) *Times* 29 January (Costs incurred for a solicitor's attendance – when the defendant was on bail but before being charged – are expenses incurred 'in the proceedings').

150 *R v Southend Stipendiary Magistrate ex p Rochford DC* [1994] Env LR 1, QBD.

151 (1998) 30 HLR 1062, DC.

152 See County Court form N260.

153 *Davenport v Walsall MBC* (1996) 28 HLR 754, [1997] Env LR 24, DC.

6.127 Costs will only be 'properly incurred' if the complainant has signed a valid conditional fee agreement[154] or is liable under a private retainer to pay those costs to the adviser. A success fee cannot be charged for an EPA 1990 prosecution.[155] Costs are not properly incurred if there is an unlawful contingency fee arrangement. In *Hughes v Kingston upon Hull CC*,[156] a magistrate made a finding that Mr Hughes, a pensioner on income support, was not aware of any liability for costs to his solicitor. The Court of Appeal held that Mr Hughes was unable to seek an order for costs against the council because the agreement with his solicitors was a contingency fee and therefore contrary to public policy.

6.128 The adviser can reserve the right to waive payment of fees, but there must be a letter of retainer setting out the tenant's liability to pay costs, win or lose, together with applicable rates. In *Carr v Leeds CC; Wells and Coles v Barnsley MBC*,[157] the court decided that a retainer was not a sham where the tenants did not have the means to pay their solicitors but clearly believed themselves to have a liability for costs.

6.129 Where the court has made an order for costs or compensation to be paid, the landlord must send any payments to the magistrates' court office. A court official might then send costs or compensation direct to the tenant, rather than to the adviser. This can leave the adviser out of pocket because the tenant may well think that the whole sum is compensation and spend it. Some courts will agree to send the costs to the adviser if the tenant signs a prior letter of authority to that effect and the clerk can be asked to make a note on the court file. Even with such a letter, some magistrates' courts will keep to their usual procedure. Where the case is compromised, the adviser can make it a condition that the landlord pays the costs to the adviser rather than the tenant. In these circumstances, the tenant's representative should tell the magistrates that there is no need for a costs order because they have been agreed privately between the parties. If the costs are not paid by the landlord, the tenant could instruct the adviser to bring a civil claim to sue on the compromise.

6.130 Costs for a failed prosecution can in certain circumstances be paid to a landlord out of Central Funds.[158] The magistrates have no

154 Courts and Legal Services Act 1990 s58A(1)(a).

155 Conditional Fee Agreements Order 2013 SI No 689 art 2.

156 [1999] QB 1193, [1999] 2 All ER 49, CA.

157 (2000) 32 HLR 753, [2000] COD 10, DC.

158 Prosecution of Offences Act 1985 s16; Crim PR r45.4 and *Bentley-Thomas v Winkfield Parish Council* [2013] EWHC 356 (Admin), [2013] Env LR D7, but the hourly rates are low and corporations cannot claim costs.

general discretion to award costs against an unsuccessful tenant. However, there is power to do so if, in the magistrates' opinion, the landlord's costs were incurred as a result of an unnecessary or improper act or omission on the part of the tenant.[159] If the magistrates believe that the fault lies on the part of the tenant's legal adviser or representative then they can make a 'wasted costs order' against that person.[160] Such orders are rare.

Environmental Protection Act 1990 and the Housing Acts

6.131 Local authorities have a statutory duty to take action where premises are in such a state as to be a statutory nuisance under the EPA 1990. However, if any premises are in such poor condition as to amount to a Category 1 hazard, the local authority has a statutory duty to take action under the HA 2004.[161] This alternative has an advantage to a private tenant in that it gives some protection from retaliatory eviction.[162] On the other hand, HA 2004 remedies do not enable a tenant to claim compensation for enduring unhealthy housing.

6.132 The courts have made it clear that local authorities should not use the statutory nuisance procedure to force full-scale repairs on landlords of unfit housing[163] but must instead use the Housing Act procedure.[164]

6.133 On the other hand, the fact that *council* property is unfit or hazardous (even to the extent of simply awaiting demolition) is no bar to the tenant taking proceedings under section 82, and gives the tenant the possibility of recovering compensation as well as improvements. It should be borne in mind that in such cases magistrates are invited, when drawing up orders, to take into account the prospective life of the property.[165]

159 *R v Enfield Justices ex p Whittle* June 1993 *Legal Action* 15, *Housing Law Casebook* 7th edn, para R25.29, DC.

160 Prosecution of Offences Act 1985 s19A; and Crim PR r45.8.

161 See chapter 5.

162 See Deregulation Act 2015 s33.

163 *Salisbury Corporation v Roles* [1948] WN 412, (1948) 92 SJ 618, DC.

164 *R v Kerrier DC ex p Guppys (Bridport)* (1976) 32 P & CR 411, CA.

165 *Salford CC v McNally* [1976] AC 379, HL.

Note of warning

6.134 EPA 1990 procedures provide a swift and straightforward remedy for bad housing conditions and impose salutary penalties on landlords, including council landlords. However, as this chapter has shown, some care must be taken by advisers when helping tenants considering such action.

6.135 EPA 1990 s82 proceedings are *criminal* proceedings and carry a higher burden of proof. Landlords have their reputation to consider and will fight these cases hard. Social landlords (local authorities or housing associations), in particular, almost inevitably indicate a Not Guilty plea at the first hearing. However, in practice, very few cases ended up being tried. Most are settled on terms, sometimes in conjunction with settlement of civil court proceedings, and usually when the nuisance is abated between the first hearing and trial.

6.136 In light of these matters, advisers should be certain of their evidence before starting prosecutions. If the case is contested, the trial could take several days and the tenant's expert could be required at court for the whole period. At trial, if any element of the offence is not proven by the tenant, for example that the landlord is the 'owner' of the property, then the magistrates will dismiss the case. If the proceedings result in an acquittal, the tenant's adviser will have incurred heavy costs and expenses, which the tenant will not have to pay if the adviser is acting under a CFA. The tenant will be unlikely to be able to afford to pay their legal costs if the adviser was acting under a private retainer.

6.137 Most advisers use the EPA 1990 when it is the only available remedy, for example because the statutory nuisance is caused by a design fault rather than by something falling within a contractual or other civil obligation of the landlord (eg because it has not rendered the dwelling unfit for human habitation).

CHAPTER 7

Compensation

continued

General principles of compensation awarded in the civil courts

7.1 A detailed analysis of the principles governing the award of compensation by the civil courts for breach of contract or for other civil wrongs is beyond the scope of this book but is given in *McGregor on Damages* (20th edn);[1] *Chitty on Contract* (33rd edn);[2] and *Clerk & Lindsell on Torts* (22nd edn).[3] A very brief analysis of the principles as they apply to housing conditions cases is set out below.

7.2 In a 'disrepair' case, a tenant will be able to recover financial compensation known as 'damages' for loss which is caused by the landlord's breach of contract or other civil wrong (tort) and which is not too remote.

7.3 There have been few reported cases in relation to compensation awarded for a breach of the term implied by previous statutory provisions that the landlord must keep a property 'fit for human habitation', and such cases are now very old. It remains to be seen how the law develops in this area in the light of the new implied covenant of fitness (Landlord and Tenant Act (LTA) 1985 s9A), but it may be expected that a tenant would have the same remedy in damages for breach of the term as they do for breach of the repairing obligation. In previous fitness cases, compensation has been awarded for personal injury,[4] and in *Horrex v Pidwell*,[5] applying the dicta in *Walker v Hobbs & Co*,[6] the county court held that the tenant could recover for damage to furniture, damage to decorations and for inconvenience and discomfort. In *Johnson v Sheffield CC* general damages were awarded for breach of an express term that the council would supply a house 'fit to live in'.[7]

7.4 The tenant will have to prove, on the balance of probabilities, that the breach of contract or the tort was the effective or dominant cause of the loss. In contract, the voluntary intervening act of a third party will generally break the chain of causation, except where it is part of a landlord's contractual duty to protect the tenant from such acts.[8]

1 Sweet & Maxwell.
2 Sweet & Maxwell.
3 Sweet & Maxwell.
4 *Summers v Salford Corporation* [1943] AC 283, HL.
5 1958 CLY 1461.
6 (1889) 23 QBD 458.
7 August 1994 *Legal Action* 16.
8 See *Stansbie v Troman* [1948] 2 KB 48, [1948] 1 All ER 599, CA.

7.5 In *Marshall v Rubypoint*,[9] a tenant of a flat claimed damages for loss caused by a burglary which occurred when the landlord had failed to repair the communal front entrance door. The Court of Appeal held that a door which is obviously broken, and which can easily be pushed open, is an invitation to would-be burglars and that the disrepair of the door, and hence the breach of contract, was causative of the burglary. Similarly, in *Vye v English Churches Housing Group*[10] the landlord was held liable to a tenant who was assaulted on the common staircase by an intruder when the front entrance door was in disrepair.

7.6 The position is slightly different in tort where a landlord will not usually be liable for the intervening act of a third party which is likely to be treated as a new independent cause. In these situations, a tenant is likely to be better off bringing the claim in contract.

7.7 Causation is most often an issue in cases where claims are made for damages for personal injury caused or exacerbated by housing conditions (see para 3.74). Medical evidence will usually be required to prove this is the case.

7.8 A tenant will not be able to recover loss which is too remote. In *contract*:

> . . . the damages . . . should be such as may fairly and reasonably be considered either arising naturally, ie according to the usual course of things, from such breach of contract itself, or such as may reasonably be supposed to have been in the contemplation of the parties at the time they made the contract as the probable result of it.[11]

In *tort*, the test is whether damage is of such a kind as the reasonable person should have foreseen, but so long as the kind of damage is foreseeable, and occurs, the extent of the damage need not have been foreseen nor the precise manner of its incidence.

7.9 In *Mira v Aylmer Square Investments Ltd*,[12] a leaseholder who lost profits from subletting, by reason of his landlord's breach of the lease, was awarded damages because the length of the lease, its provisions relating to subletting and the common practice of subletting in that part of London meant the loss was reasonably foreseeable. The landlord was also held liable for the tenant's losses in *Marshall v Rubypoint*.[13] The Court of Appeal rejected the landlord's contention

9 (1997) 29 HLR 850, CA.

10 November 2003 *Legal Action* 11, Lambeth County Court.

11 *Hadley v Baxendale* (1854) 9 Exch 341.

12 (1990) 22 HLR 182, CA.

13 (1997) 29 HLR 850, CA.

that the presence of a functioning internal door to the tenant's flat rendered the losses from the burglary too remote. By contrast, in *Berryman v Hounslow LBC*,[14] where a tenant claimed damages for a slipped disc sustained from walking up the stairs to her fifth floor flat because the lift did not work, it was held that the injury was not a foreseeable consequence of the breach of duty to keep the lift in working order. Similarly, in *Ryan v Islington LBC*,[15] it was held that the fact that disrepair might cause a council tenant to be unable to complete the statutory purchase of her home, and thus obtain a discount, would not have been in the contemplation of the parties when the secure tenancy was granted; the loss was too remote to be recoverable.

7.10 In *Eaton Square Properties Ltd v Shaw*,[16] a tenant who moved to new premises was unable to claim for lost income from a business which she said she was unable to pursue because she had spent so much time dealing with her landlord's alleged breach of an agreement to do works. It was held that the purpose of the move was to make the tenant's accommodation fit for occupation, not to further or assist her business. Any economic loss which the tenant might have been able to prove was unconnected to her relationship with her landlord and could not be said to have arisen from any breach of the landlord and tenant relationship.

Damages in housing conditions cases

7.11 Where a tenant has succeeded in establishing:

- breach of the landlord's repairing or fitness obligation;
- a nuisance;
- that the landlord's negligence or breach of statutory duty has caused personal injury or damage to property,

the appropriate remedy in most cases will be an award of damages, ie, financial compensation. If the case has not yet come to trial but the claim for damages is clear, an application may usefully be made for an award of interim damages under Civil Procedure Rule (CPR) 25.6 (see para 3.142).

14 (1997) 30 HLR 567, CA.
15 [2009] EWCA Civ 578.
16 [2011] EWHC 2115 (QB).

7.12 Obviously, the landlord remains liable to compensate the tenant for damage suffered as the result of a breach of the express or implied terms of the contract or in tort, even if the landlord has carried out works before judgment or before the issue of proceedings; the tenant has an accrued cause of action as soon as the landlord's default causes loss.

The purpose of damages

7.13 The fundamental principle in awarding damages in cases about housing conditions is that the amount allowed should as far as possible place the tenant in the position he or she would have been in if he or she 'had not suffered the wrong complained of, be that wrong a tort or breach of contract'.[17]

7.14 The purpose of awarding damages will go no further than that. The object is not 'to punish the landlord but, so far as money can, to restore the tenant to the position he would have been in had there been no breach'.[18]

The approach to assessment

7.15 Bearing in mind the principles to be applied, the courts have offered only broad guidance on the assessment of damages, although the usual rule, that both general and special damages will be available, has been applied in disrepair cases. An assessment cannot be achieved by applying one set of rules to all cases regardless of the circumstances of the particular case. The facts of each case must be looked at to see what damage the tenant has suffered and how he or she may be fairly compensated by a monetary award:

> So, the true measure of damages for persons ... occupying land, whether in tort or contract, depends on the position of the plaintiffs and all the circumstances in which they have suffered loss and damage.[19]

17 *Dodd Properties (Kent) Ltd v Canterbury CC* [1980] 1 WLR 433, [1980] 1 All ER 928, CA.

18 *Calabar Properties Ltd v Stitcher* [1984] 1 WLR 287, [1983] 3 All ER 759, CA.

19 *Dodd Properties (Kent) Ltd v Canterbury CC* [1980] 1 WLR 433, [1980] 1 All ER 928, CA.

General damages

Tenants who remain in occupation

7.16 If the tenant remains in residence during a period of disrepair or unfitness, general damages will be an award for loss of amenity[20] which includes all the inconvenience, disappointment, discomfort, mental distress and loss of enjoyment suffered by the tenant, as well as damages for any ill health caused by the disrepair.[21]

7.17 The period attracting compensation runs from 1) the date when the landlord has had a reasonable time to carry out the works up to 2) the date that the works are carried out. In cases where knowledge is not a precondition of liability (see para 2.319), the start date will be the date that the tenant starts to suffer inconvenience as a result of the disrepair or unfitness. In cases where the disrepair *or unfitness* is ongoing at the date of trial, the damages will be awarded up to the date of trial.

7.18 There are a number of different approaches to calculating general damages for the delay in carrying out remedial works. In *Wallace v Manchester CC*[22] the Court of Appeal confirmed that the tenant's claim for loss while living in a dwelling in poor condition is for the loss of comfort and convenience. The appropriate method to calculate the damages could be:

- a global award for discomfort and inconvenience; or
- a notional reduction in rent; or
- a combination of reduced rental value and an award for discomfort and inconvenience.

There is no requirement to assess damages separately under each of the first two methods as they are merely different ways of expressing the same concept.[23]

7.19 Historically, the courts have used all three methods for calculating damages, but are increasingly using a notional reduction in rent. Advisers will need to carefully consider which approach is likely to maximise damages in any particular case.

20 *Moorjani v Durban Estates Ltd* [2015] EWCA Civ 1252, [2016] HLR 6.
21 *Calabar Properties Ltd v Stitcher* [1984] 1 WLR 287, [1983] 3 All ER 759, CA.
22 (1998) 30 HLR 1111, [1998] L&TR 279, CA.
23 See Timothy Waitt 'Damages for disrepair claims: time for a rethink?' [2008] Vol 11 (4) *Journal of Housing Law* 67.

Reduction in rental value

7.20 The award of general damages can be assessed as the:

> . . . difference in value to the tenant . . . between the house in the condition in which it now is and the house in the condition in which it would be if the landlord on receipt of notice had fulfilled its obligation to repair.[24]

7.21 In *Moorjani v Durban Estates Ltd*, the Court of Appeal held that the purpose of an award of damages was to give compensation for the impairment to the rights of amenity afforded to the lessee by the lease:

> The lessee pays a premium for the assignable right to the enjoyment of occupation of a specific property for a period usually longer than his own lifetime, the quality of which is underpinned the lessor's repairing and reinstatement obligations. It is nothing to the point that the lessor incurs no cost in their performance (since that is met either from insurance or service charge). The quality of enjoyment is underpinned by the lessor's promise to carry out those obligations diligently and in due time, rather than to neglect or delay in their performance.[25]

7.22 The calculation of the value of this loss to the tenant will vary according to the circumstances of the case.

7.23 Courts can use the rent as an indicator of the 'value' of the tenancy to the tenant when calculating the level of general damages.[26] If this method is used, the court looks either at the rent due under the tenancy or at the notional market rental value for leaseholder claims and then awards a 'discount' representing the extent of loss of use and enjoyment suffered by the tenant. For example, if the rent were £120 per week and the poor conditions are significantly disruptive, a weekly figure of £40 might provide a starting point for damages.

7.24 This rather artificial approach can result in very high awards where high rents are charged, eg, to homeless families in temporary accommodation. However, it can also result in compensation being underestimated, particularly where the rent is relatively low compared with the hardship suffered. In such cases it will be preferable to seek damages on a global basis (see para 7.30 below).

7.25 It has been held that the fact that the rent had been registered as a fair rent, and therefore in a sense had been fixed with regard to the

24 *Hewitt v Rowlands* (1924) 93 LJKB 729.

25 [2015] EWCA Civ 1252, [2016] HLR 6.

26 *McCoy & Co v Clark* (1984) 13 HLR 82, CA.

state of repair, should not reduce the level of damages.[27] However, in exceptional circumstances, a very low rent, which already recognised the poor quality of the premises, can properly result in a lower award of damages.[28]

7.26 There are a number of cases (albeit now somewhat dated) in which, it was held to be wrong, on the facts of those cases, to limit damages to the amount of the rent.[29] In *Personal Representatives of Chiodi v De Marney*[30] the Court of Appeal would not interfere with the assessment of general damages of £30 per week where the contractual rent for the entire premises was only £8 per week. However, more recently, the Court of Appeal has indicated that it should be exceptional for damages for discomfort and inconvenience to exceed the rent payable:

> Whilst we accept that there will be cases in which the level of distress and/or inconvenience experienced by a tenant may require an award in excess of the level of rent payable . . . clear reasons need to be given by the court for taking that course, and the facts of the case – notably the conduct of the landlord – must warrant such an award.[31]

7.27 The Court of Appeal has also approved diminution in rental value as a correct measure of damages in cases where only a nominal rent is payable, for example, premises let on long leases with a ground rent. In *Earle v Charalambous*,[32] the court decided that, for a long leaseholder, the actual rent paid would be ignored but the damages would still be calculated by reference to diminution of market rental value: 'a notional judgment of the resulting reduction in [market] rental value is likely to be the most appropriate starting point for the assessment of damages'.[33] The Court of Appeal also rejected the view that expert valuation evidence was necessary. The judge was entitled to accept the tenant's own evidence about the rental values of equivalent properties.

27 *Sturolson & Co v Mauroux* (1988) 20 HLR 332, CA; see also *Pirachia v Mavadia* December 2007 *Legal Action* 30, *Housing Law Casebook* 7th edn, para R18.75 (referring to 4th edn, para P11.50A), Lambeth County Court.

28 *Newham LBC v Patel* [1978] 13 HLR 77, CA.

29 *Personal Representatives of Chiodi v De Marney* (1989) 21 HLR 6, CA; *Credit Suisse v Beegas Nominees Ltd* [1994] 4 All ER 803, [1994] 1 EGLR 76, ChD; *Hussein v Mehlman* [1992] 2 EGLR 287, Wood Green Trial Centre.

30 (1989) 21 HLR 6, CA.

31 *English Churches Housing Group v Shine* [2004] EWCA Civ 434, [2004] HLR 42.

32 [2006] EWCA Civ 1090, [2007] HLR 8.

33 [2006] EWCA Civ 1090, [2007] HLR 8 para 32.

7.28 Where general damages are awarded on the basis of a proportion of rental value, no reduction in the damages ought to be made where the rent is paid by way of housing benefit, even when the defendant landlord is also the local authority. In *Wallace v Manchester CC*[34] the Court of Appeal made it clear that the fact that a tenant is in receipt of housing benefit is irrelevant to any award of damages. The source of the money used to pay rent is irrelevant to the extent of the discomfort and inconvenience suffered by the tenant.

7.29 Given that an award of damages based on loss of rental value is simply a method of quantifying general damages, it does not attract the higher level of interest that special damages awards attract.

Global awards

7.30 Older cases show the courts making global awards for distress and inconvenience based on the judge's view of the severity of the conditions. In October 1988, the Court of Appeal held that £250 for 12 months' disrepair was 'little more than nominal or cosmetic'.[35] If this figure is uprated for inflation as at December 2018, it is authority for damages of least £652.05 per annum to be awarded even in the most minor of cases. In July 1998, the Court of Appeal 'assumed without deciding' that there was a tariff of £1,000 to £2,750 per annum for disrepair cases. This equates in December 2018 to a bracket of between £1,752.15 and £4,818.40.[36] More recent cases show that the worst cases of disrepair can attract global awards in excess of £6,500 per annum.[37]

7.31 The Court of Appeal has stated that where a judge makes a global award of damages he or she 'would be well advised to cross-check the prospective award by reference to the rent payable for the period equivalent to the duration of the landlord's breach of covenant'.[38] As a result, reduction in rental value has become the most common way of quantifying general damages. This is evident from the examples of awards given at the end of this chapter.

34 (1998) 30 HLR 1111, [1998] L&TR 279, CA.

35 *Davies v Peterson* (1989) 21 HLR 63, CA.

36 *Wallace v Manchester CC* (1998) 30 HLR 1111, CA at 1123.

37 See eg *Vergara v Lambeth LBC and Southbank Homes* August 2002 *Legal Action* 30, *Housing Law Casebook* 7th edn, para R18.93, where £4,500 per annum was awarded in September 2001 (worth £7,285.71 in January 2019).

38 *Wallace v Manchester CC* (1998) 30 HLR 1111, CA, per Morritt LJ, p1121.

Combination awards

7.32 In some cases, advisers have sought to assess a likely award of compensation using both the tenant's notional monetary loss (loss of rental value) and a sum for any discomfort, injury or inconvenience suffered, in order to achieve a higher award of general damages.

7.33 For example, in *Sturolson & Co v Mauroux*,[39] the Court of Appeal did not comment adversely on the approach of a county court judge who first applied the 'discounting' method to assess the degree of loss of value to the tenant of the tenancy itself and then went on to add to it a substantial award for inconvenience, discomfort and injury to health (although the correctness of the county court judge's approach was not, in that respect, challenged).

7.34 A county court judge followed the same approach in *Brent LBC v Carmel (Murphy)*.[40] The Court of Appeal refused to interfere with the level of damages awarded, either on the ground that it was excessive or on the ground that it was calculated on a wrong basis. However, such an approach is now unlikely to be followed, given the indication from the Court of Appeal in *Wallace v Manchester CC*[41] that diminution in value is merely one method of evaluating general damages for distress and inconvenience.

Damages for enduring the remedial works

7.35 Damages are not usually recoverable for the distress and inconvenience caused by the undertaking of remedial works themselves, unless the works would not have been necessary if the landlord had performed its repairing obligations when it should have done. Alternatively, the works may be so extensive that a failure to rehouse a tenant during the works may amount to a breach of the covenant of quiet enjoyment for which damages may be awarded.[42]

Damages for moving to temporary accommodation

7.36 If the tenant is required to move out (either temporarily while works are being undertaken or, if conditions are sufficiently serious, before remedial work even starts) any specific costs of removal or alternative accommodation can be recovered as special damages (provided they

39 (1988) 20 HLR 332, CA.

40 (1995) 28 HLR 203, CA.

41 (1998) 30 HLR 1111, [1998] L&TR 279, CA.

42 *Thornton & Jarrett v Birmingham* November 2004 *Legal Action* 27, *Housing Law Casebook* 7th edn, para R18.89.

arise from the breach of contract or tort).[43] In addition, a separate element of general damages will be awarded for the inconvenience of having to move and live for a time in temporary accommodation.[44] This award will be increased if promises about the length of stay in temporary housing are broken by the landlord.[45]

Damages for personal injury

7.37 If it can be shown that the landlord's breach of contract or duty of care caused personal injury (mental or physical) then damages for that injury can be recovered.[46] Damages for personal injury were awarded for breach of the obligation to keep a house 'reasonably fit for human habitation' in *Summers v Salford Corporation*.[47] Advisers will wish to refer to the Judicial College Guidelines[48] as well as to reported cases in *Kemp & Kemp: Quantum of Damages*[49] for guidance on the level of compensation for particular injuries.

Tenants not in occupation

7.38 If the tenant has rented the property for the purpose of subletting it (or is going away temporarily and wishes to sublet) and as a result of the adverse housing conditions can only sub-let for a reduced rent or cannot sublet it at all, the damages awarded will be measured by the loss of rental income from the subletting.[50]

7.39 If a long lessee is driven out of occupation by the adverse housing conditions and forced to sell the lease (or bought the lease intending to offer it for re-sale), then the damages awarded can be measured as the difference between the selling price and the price he or she would

43 *Earle v Charalmbous* [2006] EWCA Civ 1090, [2007] HLR 8.

44 *Vergara v Lambeth LBC and Hyde Southbank Homes*, August 2002 *Legal Action* 30; *Housing Law Casebook* 7th edn, para R18.93.

45 *Lubren v Lambeth LBC* (1988) 20 HLR 165, CA.

46 *McCoy v Clark* (1984) 13 HLR 87, CA; *Attica v British Gas Plc* [1988] QB 304, [1987] 3 WLR 1101, CA; *Sykes v Harry* [2001] EWCA Civ 167, [2001] QB 1014; *Lips v Older* [2004] EWHC 1686 (QB); *Ashgar v Barnet LBC and Minoan Investments Ltd* December 2013 *Legal Action* 15; *Housing Law Casebook* 7th edn, para R18.30.

47 [1943] AC 243.

48 *Judicial College Guidelines for the Assessment of general damages in personal injury cases*, 14th edn, OUP, 2017.

49 Sweet & Maxwell.

50 *Calabar Properties v Stitcher* [1984] 1 WLR 287, [1983] 3 All ER 759, CA; *Mira v Aylmer Square Investments Ltd* (1989) 21 HLR 284, CA; *Wallace v Manchester CC* (1998) 30 HLR 1111, [1998] L&TR 279, CA.

have obtained if the landlord had carried out the works.[51] Indeed, if it can be established that the landlord deliberately prepared the leasehold premises for sale to the present lessee in such a way as to disguise a serious problem, the lessee may recover damages in deceit as well as for breach of contractual obligation.[52]

7.40 Even if a tenant or long lessee is out of occupation for reasons unconnected to the adverse housing conditions, he or she can still claim damages for loss of amenity. In *Moorjani v Durban Estates Limited*[53] the Court of Appeal considered the issue of whether a long leaseholder of a residential flat could claim to have suffered loss arising from disrepair (which although serious, was not sufficient to render the flat uninhabitable) during a period when, for reasons unconnected with the disrepair, he had chosen to live elsewhere, leaving the flat vacant.

7.41 The underlying issue of principle was identified as whether the loss caused by such a breach lies in the impairment of the amenity value of the lessee's proprietary interest in the flat or in the experience of discomfort, inconvenience and distress which the lessee actually suffers. In most cases this difficulty does not arise, either because the lessee remains in the property so that the personal loss of amenity and inconvenience is equivalent (at least in value) to the impaired amenity of the flat. Or the lessee vacates because of the disrepair so that the non-use of the flat can properly be said to have been caused by the breach.

7.42 The Court of Appeal, having reviewed the law on damages for disrepair and the earlier case-law summarised above, found that the losses caused to the lessee by the lessor's breach consist of the impairment to the rights of amenity afforded to the lessee by the lease, of which discomfort, inconvenience and distress (even the deterioration of the health of a loved one) are only symptoms. It was not, therefore, a fatal obstacle to a claim for damages for that impairment in the lessee's rights that the lessee may have chosen not to make full use, or even any use, of the premises during part or even all of the relevant period, for reasons unconnected with the disrepair itself. However, it did not follow that the use or non-use of the lessee's property rights during the period of disrepair was irrelevant for all

51 *Calabar Properties v Stitcher* [1984] 1 WLR 287, [1983] 3 All ER 759, CA; *City and Metropolitan Properties v Greycroft Ltd* [1987] 1 WLR 1085, [1987] 3 All ER 839, ChD, at 842–3; *Credit Suisse v Beegas Nominees Ltd* [1994] 4 All ER 803, [1994] 1 EGLR 76, ChD; *Gorman and Lane v Lambeth LBC*, December 2009 *Legal Action* 23.

52 *Gordon v Selico* (1986) 18 HLR 219, CA.

53 [2015] EWCA Civ 1252, [2016] HLR 6.

purposes; it could be relevant as mitigation of loss. The court is entitled and obliged to temper the rigour of the rules which seek to implement the compensatory principle which lies at the heart of the law of damages, where particular circumstances make it just to do so. In particular circumstances, this may mean quantification of damages in excess of the current rental value. In other cases, the particular circumstances of the lessee may tend to reduce rather than aggravate the damages and not merely where the relevant conduct consists of what may conventionally be described as mitigation.

7.43 Accordingly, the Court of Appeal found that the trial judge had been wrong to treat the lessee's non-occupation of his flat during most of the period of disrepair as fatal to his claim for compensation for loss of amenity. The lessee had suffered precisely the same loss as would have been suffered by a lessee who, in comparable circumstances, had remained in flat throughout, namely a serious although temporary impairment of the rights in relation to the flat, for which he had paid a full premium. The starting point for the valuation of that impairment ought to be by reference to the rental value of the flat during the relevant period, with a very substantial percentage discount to reflect the judge's conclusion that the disrepair in the flat was cosmetic and did not render it uninhabitable.

7.44 The damages to be awarded where a lessee chose not to occupy the flat for the relevant period should be substantially reduced as the effect of the impairment of rights was very much less than it would have been upon a lessee who, as is usual in these cases, remains in occupation throughout. The trial judge's award of damages was therefore set aside and the Court of Appeal substituted its own award on the basis that it would have been a waste of time and money to remit it to the county court for redetermination.

Updating and uprating awards

7.45 Advisers must remember to update awards made in previous cases to take account of inflation because this can make a significant difference to the amount, especially for older cases. For example, the informal tariff referred to in *Wallace v Manchester CC* of £1,000 to £2,750 per annum in 1998 would have been worth approximately £1,752.15 and £4,818.40 per annum in December 2018. Updating is usually done by using the inflation tables in *Kemp & Kemp: Quantum of Damages*,[54] which updates from January of one year to January of

54 Sweet & Maxwell.

another year by using a multiplier. However, it is possible to update to the nearest month by using the Retail Price Index (RPI) itself.

7.46 As part of the reforms of legal aid, which were effected by the Legal Aid, Sentencing and Punishment of Offenders Act (LASPO) 2012, the recoverability of success fees from losing defendants in cases funded by conditional fee agreements (CFAs), was ended. To partially compensate claimants for the reduction in their damages as a result of the deduction of success fee in CFAs, it was proposed that general damages in personal injury cases should be increased by ten per cent. In *Simmons v Castle*[55] the Court of Appeal ordered that general damages awards should increase by ten per cent for any judgment delivered after 1 April 2013. In this personal injury case, the court noted that this increase should apply to all claims in nuisance or tort, if the tort causes suffering, distress or inconvenience to any individual. This appeared to exclude contractual claims including disrepair claims under the LTA 1985 s11. Following representations, the judgment was revised to clarify that the ten per cent uplift is to be given to general damages in all civil claims for 'four types of damage in relation to both tort and contract cases, namely 'pain and suffering and loss of amenity', 'physical inconvenience and discomfort', 'social discredit', and 'mental distress'.[56] This clearly covers general damages in disrepair and unfitness claims.

7.47 Advisers seeking or negotiating damages must now ensure that they seek an additional ten per cent in general damages, presumably by either uprating rental figures by ten per cent and then calculating damages or by calculating the likely award and then uprating this by ten per cent. It is likely that this will be a further incentive to calculate general damages by reference to diminution in rental value given that it will be clear how to uprate such an award, whereas global awards are inherently more arbitrary.

7.48 The ten per cent uplift does not apply to claims funded under CFAs signed before 1 April 2012.[57]

Conclusion

7.49 General damages represent compensation for loss of amenity, specifically the inconvenience and loss of enjoyment suffered by the tenant. Accordingly, the courts will expect the tenant to give notice in

55 [2012] EWCA Civ 1039, [2013] 1 WLR 1239.

56 At [48] and [50].

57 *Simmons v Castle* [2012] EWCA Civ 1288, [2013] 1 WLR 1239.

the particulars of claim or counterclaim about the nature of the loss suffered; it will not be sufficient just to claim 'damages'.[58] The claim may also embrace the effects of the adverse conditions on other members of the tenant's family,[59] although family members with claims in their own right, eg personal injury claims under the Defective Premises Act 1972 s4 usually have to be joined to the action as claimants.[60]

7.50 There are few recent appellate decisions in relation to quantum of general damages, given the relatively low levels of such awards and the disproportionate costs which would be involved in appealing any such decisions.[61] However, the annual 'Housing repairs update' in *Legal Action* summarises county court cases where damages have been awarded against residential landlords. As a guide to the current 'going rate' for the assessment of general damages for adverse housing conditions, see para 7.68 onwards.

Special damages

7.51 The tenant is entitled to recover damages representing the loss in value of items of furniture and other personal belongings destroyed or damaged as a result of the landlord's breach of obligation or tort. The most common examples are carpets, furniture, curtains and clothing corrupted by dampness. Additionally, special damages may be sought for other specific loss capable of calculation in monetary terms, for example:

- cleaning costs;
- loss of earnings, eg from time taken off work for missed appointments;
- extra heating costs or the costs of a dehumidifier (eg for 'drying-out' dampness);
- the costs of alternative accommodation;
- the cost of repairs, cleaning up and redecoration;
- travelling and medical costs (eg arising from personal injury); or

58 *Perestrello e Companhia Limitada v United Paint Co Ltd (No 1)* [1969] 1 WLR 570, [1969] 3 All ER 479, CA, at 485.

59 *Jackson v Horizon Holidays Ltd* [1975] 1 WLR 1468, [1975] 3 All ER 92, CA; *Jarvis v Swan Tours* [1973] 1 QB 233, [1972] 3 WLR 954, CA. The application of the principles developed in these cases involving holidays to the law of landlord and tenant was noted in *McCall v Abelesz* [1976] QB 585, [1976] 2 WLR 151, CA.

60 *C (a minor) v Hackney LBC* [1996] 1 WLR 89, [1996] 1 All ER 973, CA.

61 See *Vass v Pank* July 2001 *Legal Action* 25, CA.

- the cost of eating out (eg if food storage or cooking facilities have been damaged).

The above list is of examples only. Those acting for the tenant should ensure that consideration is given to pleading all losses which, as a matter of fact, are caused by the adverse conditions.

7.52 If tenants themselves carry out works of repair, clearing up or redecoration, damages will be awarded to compensate for any expenses reasonably incurred.[62] Even if the works actually improve the property, no reduction is made from the damages on account of this element of betterment, if the tenant was unable to make good the damage without betterment.[63] These specific costs may be pleaded as special damages.

7.53 Courts will often make a deduction to allow for betterment in respect of special damages claims for damaged belongings. However, on the basis of the rationale set out in *Harbutt's Plasticine Ltd v Wayne Tank and Pump Co Ltd*,[64] there should be no such deduction where it is not possible or reasonable to obtain secondhand replacements. This was accepted in *Clark v Affinity Sutton Homes Ltd*,[65] where the district judge awarded the full claim in respect of carpets with no deduction for depreciation on the basis it would be difficult if not impossible to purchase second hand carpets. The burden of proving that there should be a deduction for betterment will be on the landlord.[66]

7.54 If the disrepair or unfitness renders the premises uninhabitable, the tenant may recover as damages any expenses reasonably incurred in taking alternative accommodation from the date that the premises could no longer be occupied, up to the date of assessment of damages or completion of remedial works.[67] Such damages will include the costs of any removals, storage of furniture, etc. Such costs should be specifically pleaded as special damages.

7.55 Each specific item for which special damages are claimed must be identified in the pleadings, and at trial it will be necessary to prove the loss in respect of each item. It is therefore vital that the tenant collects and retains where possible all receipts, accounts and invoices relating to items replaced or repaired. Where there is likely

62 *Calabar Properties v Stitcher* [1984] 1 WLR 287, [1983] 3 All ER 759, CA.

63 *McGreal v Wake* (1984) 13 HLR 107, CA.

64 [1970] 1 QB 447, [1970] 2 WLR 198, CA.

65 December 2014 *Legal Action* 27, *Housing Law Casebook* 7th edn, para R18.38.

66 *Lagden v O'Connor* [2003] UKHL 64, [2004] 1 AC 1067 per Lord Hope at [34].

67 *Calabar Properties v Stitcher* [1984] 1 WLR 287, [1983] 3 All ER 759, CA.

to be a dispute over the damages claimed, the tenant would be well advised to retain (or at least photograph) any damaged item pending the trial.

Aggravated and exemplary damages

7.56 Aggravated and exemplary damages are not usually recovered in claims about housing conditions because of the limited circumstances in which they can be awarded. Aggravated and exemplary damages can be awarded only in tort, not in contract.

7.57 *Aggravated* damages are awarded to compensate a person for injury to his or her feelings of dignity and pride and for aggravation generally. *Exemplary* damages are punitive and are awarded to indicate the courts disapproval of the conduct in question. Exemplary damages can be awarded in a disrepair case only where there has been oppressive conduct by local government officers or where the landlord's conduct has been calculated to make a profit which may well exceed the compensation payable to the tenant.[68] Aggravated and exemplary damages are usually only awarded in unlawful eviction cases, but can be claimed in a disrepair case, where appropriate, eg where the landlord has deliberately neglected essential repairs as part of a plan to drive the tenant out.[69]

Tenants' failure to mitigate their loss

7.58 In an action for damages for breach of a contractual obligation, it is important for tenants to show that they took whatever reasonable steps were available to mitigate or prevent loss or damage – for example, that a bucket was placed under a leak, rather than simply allowing dampness to rot the floorboards and carpets. If a tenant delayed giving notice of disrepair or unfitness to the landlord (in a case where the landlord's liability was conditional on knowledge of the defect) so that the eventual damage was greater than it would otherwise have been, that tenant may see a reduction in damages on account of the failure to mitigate the loss.[70]

68 *Rookes v Barnard (No 1)* [1964] AC 1129, [1964] 2 WLR 269, HL.

69 See *Sampson v Wilson* (1994) 26 HLR 486, Ch, below at para 7.80.

70 *Minchburn v Peck* (1988) 20 HLR 392, CA.

7.59 It is a question of fact whether the tenant has failed to mitigate loss so as to reduce any damages that would otherwise be awarded. However, there is no failure to mitigate simply because the party in breach can suggest that other measures less burdensome to the party in breach might have been taken; the tenant's conduct is not to be 'weighed in nice scales at the insistence of the party whose breach of contract has occasioned the difficulty'.[71] In particular, a tenant is not be to be prejudiced if he or she is financially unable to mitigate.[72]

7.60 Refusal to permit access is a common allegation and can be treated as a failure to mitigate loss or, more commonly, as an action which entirely suspends the landlord's liability.[73] Any unreasonable behaviour which results in substantial delay in the completion of remedial works or additional costs may also constitute a failure to mitigate and result in a reduction in the damages payable.[74] In *English Churches Housing Group v Shine*,[75] the tenant was held to have failed to mitigate his loss because he refused to move to alternative accommodation in breach of an undertaking and injunctions. The Court of Appeal reduced the damages awarded for the period in question and assessed the damages payable by taking the lower figure of either: 1) discounting the rent by 75 per cent; or 2) assessing the time in which the works would have been completed if the tenant had co-operated and awarding damages for the shorter period.

7.61 However, in cases where landlords have patently neglected to repair property or keep it fit, the duty to mitigate does not impose an obligation on tenants to do the work themselves.[76] Nor are tenants to be penalised for any refusal (other than an unreasonable one) to move to alternative accommodation.[77] However, tenants can be expected to take reasonable measures, such as blocking up the source of draughts, moving furniture away from leaks or temporarily covering broken window glazing.

71 *Banco de Portugal v Waterlow and Sons Ltd* [1932] AC 452, per Lord McMillan at 506.

72 *Dodd Properties (Kent) Ltd v Canterbury CC* [1980] 1 WLR 433, [1980] 1 All ER 928, CA.

73 *Granada Theatres Ltd v Freehold Investment (Leytonstone) Ltd* [1959] Ch 592, [1959] 1 WLR 570, CA; *Empson v Forde* [1990] 1 EGLR 131, CA.

74 *English Churches Housing Group v Shine* [2004] EWCA Civ 434, [2004] HLR 42.

75 [2004] EWCA Civ 434, [2004] HLR 42.

76 *Sturolson & Co v Mauroux* (1988) 20 HLR 332, CA.

77 *Lubren v Lambeth LBC* (1988) 20 HLR 165, CA; *English Churches Housing Group v Shine* [2004] EWCA Civ 434, [2004] HLR 42.

Contributory negligence

7.62 Where a tenant's claim arises in *tort*, damages will be reduced if the court finds that the tenant was partly responsible for his or her losses: Law Reform (Contributory Negligence) Act 1945. In *Lips v Older*[78] where a tenant fell over the wall leading up to the front door of the premises and into the basement area below, damages were reduced by two-thirds because he was drunk and carrying a heavy load which caused him to lose his balance. Similarly, in *Sykes v Harry*,[79] damages were reduced by 80 per cent because of a failure to notify the landlord of the patent defects to the gas fire of which they were aware.

7.63 A similar reduction will be applied where there is a breach of contract, but the contractual liability duplicates an independent tort liability. There can be no reduction for contributory negligence where there is solely a breach of contract, but the same result may be achieved by reliance on a failure to mitigate (see paras 7.58–7.61) or absence of causation (see para 7.4).

Interest

7.64 The courts have a wide discretion to determine whether interest is to be awarded on compensation, the period of interest and the rate of interest.

7.65 As it is not unknown for disrepair cases to take months or years before the stage is reached for assessment of damages, advisers should ensure than any award for a retrospective period carries with it interest assessed under County Courts Act 1984 s69.

7.66 Interest should also be claimed on special damages from the date of loss. Despite the reduction in interest rates, such interest continues to be awarded at eight per cent, the judgment debt rate which has existed since April 1993, although the actual rate is at the court's discretion.[80]

7.67 Under CPR 36.17, where the judgment is more advantageous to the tenant than any offer they made under Part 36, the court can

78 [2004] EWHC 1686 (QB).

79 [2001] EWCA Civ 167, [2001] 3 WLR 62.

80 Judgment Debts (Rate of Interest) Order 1993 SI No 564.

order interest at a rate not exceeding ten per cent above base rate on the sums awarded and the costs.

Compensation cases

7.68 The notes below are of disrepair cases and they are arranged by reference to the level of court, in chronological order, save in respect of the county court decisions where the cases have also been arranged by type of defect. Figures given for the amount of damages awarded require adjusting for inflation (see para 7.45). Where the issue is one of compensation for fitness for habitation, these notes may provide a useful guide. However, the assessment in any particular case will always depend on the extent of the defects together with the level of distress and inconvenience experienced.

Court of Appeal decisions

7.69 ***Minchburn v Peck* (1988) 20 HLR 392**

A long leaseholder suffered two years of water penetration as a result of defective roof slates and three to four years of cracks to the party walls, which spoilt the decorations. There was no requirement that a tenant give notice in a long lease, but there was the possibility that the landlord would have carried out the works earlier if notice had been given. The Court of Appeal reduced the award of general damages for discomfort and dampness from £800 to £700 to make allowance for this.

7.70 ***Lubren v Lambeth LBC* (1988) 20 HLR 165**

Five years of cold and damp as a result of unspecified disrepair, which meant that the premises deteriorated from a reasonable condition at the outset to being 'appalling', resulted in an award of £4,000 to a tenant who had two adult sons. In the last two years the hot water and heating system worked intermittently and caused significant additional inconvenience. £500 was also awarded for the 14 months when the tenant was in alternative accommodation, waiting for remedial works to be completed, when the landlord had undertaken that the works would only take three months.

7.71 ***Chiodi v De Marney* (1989) 21 HLR 6**

A flat suffered from water penetration, collapsed ceilings, rotten windows, frequent electrical problems and periods with no hot water supply. The tenant's arthritis was exacerbated and she suffered colds and flu. The tenant was awarded general damages for inconvenience and distress at the rate of £30 per week for three and a half years (£5,460), even though the rent was only £8 per week. Special damages of £4,657 and damages for injury to health of £1,500 were awarded. The Court of Appeal described the award as being 'at least at the very top of any appropriate range of any monetary awards for such a case' but declined to interfere.

7.72 ***Davies v Peterson*** **(1989) 21 HLR 63**

One of the bedrooms and the living room in a house were uninhabitable because of damp for a period of at least 12 months. An award of £250 for discomfort, anxiety and inconvenience was appealed by the tenant. Russell LJ stated that in 1989 'the sum of £250 must . . . be regarded, when awarded by way of compensation for inconvenience, anxiety and discomfort, as little more than nominal'. This was not a case in which nominal damages were appropriate and the award of general damages was increased from £250 to £1,000. Russell LJ continued: 'It is plain that in this day and age the courts are prepared to award substantial sums to tenants who are the victims of defaulting landlords where disrepair occurs.'

7.73 ***Brent LBC v Carmel*** **(1995) 28 HLR 203**

From 1981 there were problems of water penetration and inadequate central heating in the winter; the tenant's teenage boy and girl had to share her bedroom as their bedroom became uninhabitable. The condition of the home became progressively worse, and from 1986 onwards was appalling and intolerable. £1,000 per annum was awarded from 1981 to 1986, and thereafter £1,500 per annum. In addition, damages for loss of value of the premises assessed at 30 per cent of the rent for period 1986 to 1987 and 50 per cent from 1988 to 1993. Special damages totalling £19,320 were also awarded, with interest at 13.5 per cent from 1986 to trial. The Court of Appeal refused the council's application for leave to appeal, on the basis that the award was 'not wrong in principle or manifestly excessive'.

7.74 ***Wallace v Manchester CC*** **(1998) 30 HLR 1111**

The tenant complained that her house was in disrepair: an external wall had partially collapsed, the windows were rotten and the house suffered from a constant infestation of rats. The judge awarded

£3,500 general damages on the basis of a global award to compensate the tenant for her distress and inconvenience. On the tenant's appeal it was held that 'assuming but without deciding' that there was a tariff of £1,000 to £2,750 per annum, the award of £3,500 for approximately three years of disrepair did not fall outside it. (This is assessed as a little under 50 per cent of the annualised rent in *English Churches Housing Group v Shine* (see para 7.76) at para 103.)

7.75 ***Long v Southwark LBC*** **[2002] EWCA Civ 403, [2002] HLR 56**

The tenant's flat was next to a large paladin bin into which a rubbish chute emptied. The tenant complained of noise, smells and maggot infestations around the bin from 1993 to 2001. Damages of £13,500 were awarded on the basis of £2,500 per annum for the period from 1993 to 1995 and at the rate of £1,500 for the next five and a half years.

7.76 ***English Churches Housing Group v Shine*** **[2004] EWCA Civ 434, [2004] HLR 42**

The tenant, acting in person, brought a claim for severe damp and dry rot in his basement flat, which was defended on the basis of his refusal of access. In the course of the proceedings the tenant was ordered to vacate the premises but failed to do so until February 2003 despite a number of further injunction orders against him. The remedial works to the premises were finally completed in June 2003. The trial judge awarded £19,000 for a seven-year period covering approximately May 1996 to June 2003 including £16,000 for the four years immediately before the hearing, when the tenant had refused to move to alternative accommodation.

On the landlord's appeal against the award of £16,000 for 1999 to 2003, the Court of Appeal found that the award was manifestly excessive. The judge had given no explanation of how he had arrived at it and he had failed to check it against the rent. The Court of Appeal reduced the award to £8,000, awarding 75 per cent of the rent for 1999 to 2001, when the tenant was living in very poor conditions without a bathroom and a gas supply (although this was partly because he had turned it off himself), but giving a very substantial discount for 2001 to 2003 for the tenant's failure to mitigate his loss. It assessed the damages payable for 2001 to 2003 by taking the lower figure of i) discounting the rent by 75 per cent or ii) assessing the period in which the works would have been completed if Mr Shine had cooperated, which it judged to be nine months.

7.77 ***Earle v Charalambous* [2006] EWCA Civ 1090, [2007] HLR 8**

A long leaseholder suffered with damp and water penetration to his top floor flat from January 2000 until September 2004. By December 2002 the kitchen ceiling had partially collapsed and the tenant had to move out. The trial judge awarded damages of £20,000 from January 2000 to December 2002, when the tenant was in occupation, and £10,000 for December 2002 to September 2004, when the tenant was staying with his parents. On appeal, the Court of Appeal held that the award in respect of the first period was not supported by adequate reasoning and was excessive when viewed against the tenant's own claim. The award was reduced to £13,500 but the award in respect of the second period was upheld as it was just under half the rental value.

7.78 ***Grand v Gill* [2011] EWCA Civ 554, [2011] HLR 37**

The tenant of a flat claimed damages for a defective boiler and extensive condensation dampness and mould growth which were largely due to design defects. The damp was so bad that the tenant's daughter had to move from the second bedroom into the living room. The trial judge awarded damages of £5,600 on the basis of an award of:

- £1,750 for the 30 weeks when there was no heating;
- £2,900 for the remainder of the three years when there was inadequate heating;
- £600 for the contribution the defective heating had made to the damp and mould; the judge having found that if the landlord had been liable for all the damp and mould he would have awarded £2,000 per annum making a total award of £6,000 in this regard; and
- £350 for breach of the covenant of quiet enjoyment.

The tenant appealed on the basis that the judge was wrong to apply a 90 per cent discount to the damages caused by the damp as the landlord was 100 per cent liable for the damaged plaster. The Court of Appeal found that the landlord was liable for the damaged plasterwork. The court assessed the plaster damage as representing £750 of the £6,000 that the judge would have awarded for the dampness and therefore substituted for the judge's award of £600 the figure of £1,275, made up of £750 for the plaster and £525 for the contribution that the defective heating made to the damp (ie ten per cent of £5,250 (£6,000–£750). The overall damages award therefore increased from £5,600 to £6,275 with the award for the damaged plaster amounting to £250 per annum.

7.79 ***Moorjani v Durban Estates Ltd*** **[2015] EWCA Civ 1252, [2016] HLR 6**

The long leaseholder of a mansion block in London claimed damages for the disrepair caused to his flat by a serious leak from the flat above in 2005. The damage was repaired by the contractors employed by the landlord's agents, but the works were inadequate due to their poor quality and an omission to do all that was required. In 2006, there was a second less serious but persistent leak from the flat above. HHJ May awarded no damages in respect of the period from 2005 to 2008, as the lessee had not been living in flat for reasons unconnected with the disrepair. From 2008 until 2011, she awarded damages of £1,500 in respect of the loss of amenity attributable to the shabby common parts. Mr Moorjani appealed the refusal to award any damages from 2005 to 2008 and asserted that the award from 2008 to 2011 was too low.

On appeal, the trial judge's award of damages was set aside and the Court of Appeal substituted its own award on the basis that it would have be a waste of time and money to remit it to the county court for redetermination, having accepted that the lessee could be awarded damages for loss of amenity even when he was not in occupation of the flat.

The Court of Appeal did not interfere with the trial judge's award of damages in respect of the disrepair to the common parts during the period when the lessee was living in the flat. It considered that the assessment of general damages for losses of amenity attributable to a failure to repair common parts does not lend itself to scientific analysis. As the judge had identified £1,500 as a provisional global award for general damages for a three-year period and then cross-checked it by reference to a notional reduction of rent, which resulted in an award of 1–2 per cent, there was no basis for suggesting that it was wrong in principle. The most that could be said was that her cross-check revealed a very low percentage notional reduction which, had the Court of Appeal been considering the matter afresh, might have suggested that the provisional figure was too low.

The Court of Appeal would have awarded five per cent of a notional rent of £550 per week for the year 2005/6 if the lessee had been in occupation, but since he was not in occupation the sum was reduced by half so that the lessee was awarded 2.5 per cent of the notional rental value for the period from 2005 to 2006 and from 2007 until the lessee resumed occupation of the flat.

For the period from April 2006 until the completion of the repairs in 2007, when the amenity value of the lessee's interest was impaired by the state of the common parts and by the disrepair to the flat itself, namely warped doors due to flood damage and repairs being required to the master bedroom to put right flood damage which occurred in 2005 (which was essentially decorative) the Court of Appeal quantified the award at 20 per cent of the notional rent, which it reduced by 50 per cent due to the lessee's non occupation resulting in an award of ten per cent of the rent, namely £2,574.

High Court decisions

7.80 ***Sampson v Wilson* (1994) 26 HLR 486, QBD**

The dwelling was in substantial disrepair. The absentee landlord and his agents carried out works of repair deliberately in such a manner as to make matters worse and drive out the tenants. Since the works were carried out without permission or exceeding any permission, there was a trespass in addition to a breach of contract, thereby permitting an award of exemplary damages to be made. The judge awarded the full amount of rent to each tenant, namely £25 and £24 per week and made an award of exemplary damages of £2,000.

7.81 ***Arnold v Greenwich LBC* [1998] 2 CLY 3618, May 1998 *Legal Action* 30**

£8,750 was awarded for almost six years of modest condensation damp and mould, smells from the refuse storage area and noise from the communal rubbish chute.

County court decisions

Cracking and subsidence

7.82 ***Rayson v Sanctuary Housing Association Ltd*, March 1996 *Legal Action* 15**

The tenant moved into a newly completed house in 1979 and began to notice structural cracking. By 1983 the cracking was pronounced, internal door frames distorted and by 1991 the cracks 3–5mm wide in places. £4,750 was awarded for the worst two years of severe, unsightly and worrying structural cracking.

7.83 ***Pierce v Westminster CC*, July 2001 *Legal Action* 27, *Housing Law Casebook* 7th edn, para R18.74**

A tenant's three-bedroomed house developed cracks owing to subsidence, with the worst being 12mm wide. Daylight could be seen around the lounge window. The trial judge awarded general damages at annual rates of between £500 and £1,000 for a seven-year period, producing a total award of £5,450.

7.84 ***Gorman and Lane v Lambeth LBC*, December 2009 *Legal Action* 23**

A long leaseholder of a one-bedroom flat which suffered from cracking due to subsidence from 1994. No effective work was undertaken and eventually the flat was sold at a substantial undervalue to a developer for £85,000. A claim was issued seeking £100,000 for loss of profit on the sale of the property, £22,000 general damages, £1,500 special damages and interest of £25,000. The claim settled at the door of the court for £120,000.

7.85 ***Thomson v Southwark LBC*, December 2015 *Legal Action* 41, *Housing Law Casebook* 7th edn, para R18.88**

From 2009 a tenant, in a block of flats, complained about water penetration from the property upstairs and from the exterior, ill-fitting, draughty windows with defective putties, an intermittently blocked kitchen sink and substandard workmanship following plumbing repairs in her bathroom. Subsequently, in 2013, the building and the tenant's property started to suffer from subsidence, resulting in cracking, falling plaster and uneven floors. In August 2015 the claimant's expert noted a significant deterioration of the condition of both the property and the building in comparison to his first inspection in June 2013.

A default judgment was entered against the defendant. DDJ Sofaer awarded the tenant general damages amounting to 20 per cent reduction in rental value for the period from 1 January 2009 to 23 June 2013, amounting to £4,659.59. For the period from 30 June 2013 to 30 September 2015 the court awarded the tenant 40 per cent reduction in rental value, amounting to £5,521.25, making a total of £10,180.84. Applying the uplift of ten per cent, the award for general damages was £11,198.92. The court also awarded the tenant £225 in special damages for curtains and bedding damaged by water ingress, making a total award of £11,423.92.

Damp and other defects

7.86 ***Vergara v Lambeth LBC and Hyde Southbank Homes*, August 2002 *Legal Action* 30, *Housing Law Casebook* 7th edn, para R18.93**

The case was described by the judge as the worst case of disrepair and nuisance he had ever tried. Water had penetrated various rooms of a three-bedroomed flat, windows were in disrepair, the hot water supply to the kitchen and bathroom failed on several occasions and the gas heater was not serviced. When the rest of the street was decanted, the claimant was left in occupation and the properties were allowed to fall into a state of dereliction, with rubbish accumulation, squatting and blocked drains. By 1999 there were vermin infestations, particularly by rats. The trial judge awarded £2,500 per annum for the first two years, £3,500 per annum for the next two years and £4,500 per annum for the final two years. He assessed damages for six months' inconvenience in temporary accommodation at £1,500.

7.87 ***Thornton and Jarrett v Birmingham CC*, November 2004 *Legal Action* 27, *Housing Law Casebook* 7th edn, para R18.89**

Ms Thornton complained of severe dampness affecting her home, which she occupied with her two children aged nine and 11, due to rising dampness, penetrating dampness from a fractured drain and condensation, from June 1998 to October 1998. She also complained that in carrying out a modernisation plan including the installation of UPVC windows, a new kitchen and bathroom from October 1998 to March 1999, the council took too long and interfered with her everyday life so as to constitute a breach of the covenant of quiet enjoyment. The premises were much improved from March 1999 but some defects remained. HHJ McKenna rejected a claim that it was reasonable to delay all repairs until the modernisation programme began in October 1998, and found that the works should have been undertaken by the end of July 1998. He accepted that the works were very noisy, dirty and disruptive, with Ms Thornton confined to one bedroom for over three months. Damages of £3,000 were awarded for August 1998 to March 1999; damages of £1,000 per annum were awarded for the period from March 1999 to trial, amounting to a total award of £7,667 plus special damages of £280. (The award for August 1998 to March 1999 amounts to an annual award of £4,500.)

7.88 ***Shefford v Nofax Enterprises*, December 2006 *Legal Action* 24, *Housing Law Casebook* 4th edn para P11.53**

The environmental health department had served notices prohibiting use of two basement rooms in a flat. The landlord let the flat to three joint tenants on the basis that they would use the basement rooms as bedrooms. All the bedrooms were damp and whole flat smelled of damp. Damages of £2,750 were awarded for a four-month period, based on the fact that the tenants had bargained for a three-bedroom flat and had got one bedroom and even that was in disrepair. This equated to 50 per cent of the rent of £1,300 per month.

7.89 ***Arabhalvaei v Rezaeipoor*, December 2007 *Legal Action* 30, *Housing Law Casebook* 7th edn, para S6.19**

In a possession claim for rent arrears, a Rent Act protected tenant of a one-bedroomed flat, which the tenant shared with his wife, counter-claimed damages for disrepair at the property and for harassment from his landlord. The disrepair included penetrating damp, cracks to various internal walls and a leaking toilet and sink. In addition, the heating system was out of order at various times over the period in question, with the result that the property was without heating and hot water. Judgment was entered for the tenant in respect of a claim for seven years and nine months. The trial judge awarded the tenant a total of £188,526.21 in damages, including:

- £22,500 in respect of the disrepair, which represented 50 per cent of the rental value of £455 per calendar month over the period in question;
- special damages of £4,926.68 in respect of works done by the tenant in default of the landlord, heating, cleaning and damages to belongings;
- interest at six per cent for three-and-a-half years which was approximately the mid-point of the damages claim, amounting to £5,759.60 in respect of the disrepair damages.

7.90 ***Ngoma v Dhillon*, December 2013 *Legal Action* 15, *Housing Law Casebook* 7th edn, para R18.69**

The claimant was the assured shorthold tenant of a two-storey, three-bedroom house which she rented from the defendant between February 2006 and February 2012. She lived at the premises with her three children. The rent was £550 per month. She brought a claim in respect of disrepair throughout the period of the tenancy, namely:

- penetrating dampness to large front bedroom and rear bedroom causing dampness and mould growth caused by defects to the building fabric (including perished brickwork and mortar);
- breakdown in the seal to the double glazing unit in the larger front bedroom;
- rising dampness to front living room with evidence of damp to rear living room;
- damp and mould growth in kitchen aggravated by leaks from bathroom above;

- leaks from the seals around the bath and taps and various other defects to sanitary fittings;
- degraded seal and leak from sink to kitchen unit below;
- various structural cracks;
- incomplete drainage work so that garden could not be used (from November 2010), leading to a foul odour.

The claimant contended that as a result the property had been cold, damp and smelly and incapable of receiving decoration in places. The property was unsightly and the claimant was concerned about possible structural movement. She suffered the inconvenience of having to mop up leaks and was worried about the health of her children.

HHJ McKenna accepted the claimant's evidence in full and awarded her general damages of £27,720 (70 per cent of the contractual rent over the relevant period) together with interest in the sum of £1,663.20 making a total of £29,383.20.

7.91 ***Asghar v Barnet LBC and Minoan Investments Ltd*, December 2013 *Legal Action* 15, *Housing Law Casebook* 7th edn, para R18.30**

The claimant was a non-secure tenant of a one-bedroomed flat let to him by the council who had leased the property from the freehold owner. The claimant sought damages for the damp condition he had suffered at the flat from March 2007 until he was rehoused in August 2010. He also made a claim for psychiatric injury namely that his depression and panic disorder which he had suffered historically had been triggered by the disrepair. Conditions deteriorated between 2007 and 2009 with no practical offer of rehousing until June 2009. By this time the claimant was ill and his depression continued long after September 2009.

HHJ Faber awarded damages from March 2007 until the end of October 2009 when she held that the council had made a reasonable offer of accommodation. She discounted an earlier offer of alternative accommodation on the basis that it was reasonable for the claimant to refuse to move there as the front door had been kicked in. She awarded damages at 35 per cent of the rent of £386.04 per week amounting to £16,745.82 over 130 weeks.

The judge also awarded damages for the psychiatric illness finding that the damp conditions were the main, although not the only cause, given that the claimant had other issues in the spring of 2009 which also contributed to the onset of the renewed illness. She held that the case fell within the moderate Judicial College bracket, although it was difficult to decide where without a prognosis, Given that the claimant was still suffering in January 2012 from the attack brought on largely by the council's breach of contract she held that the appropriate figure was £10,000 discounted by 20 per cent to £8,000 for the other causal issues. The total award of damages was therefore £24,745.82.

7.92 ***Thomas v AJ Bradburn (acting as receiver for Adelphi Properties Ltd)*, December 2014 *Legal Action* 27, *Housing Law Casebook* 7th edn, para R18.87**

The claimant was the tenant of a two-bedroom mid-terrace house from 5 November 2007. His rent was £85 per week until April 2009, when it went up to £95 per week. From the outset, the claimant experienced problems with the hot water system and the storage heaters. Central heating was installed in March 2008, but that did not work properly until May 2011. From late 2008 the roof leaked, and by late 2009 the problem had worsened to the extent that the claimant's bedroom ceiling collapsed. The claimant had to sleep downstairs for a period of a year because of the leaks and dampness and state of his bedroom ceiling. The claimant had a pre-existing diagnosis of asthma which he complained had been aggravated by the condition of the property.

District Judge Moss found that the landlord liable and made the following awards of damages:

- £750 for the defective storage heaters and faulty hot water system for the period November 2007 to the end of March 2008 (equating to around 40 per cent of the rent for that period);
- £3,750 for the intermittently functioning heating and hot water system from November 2008 to May 2011 (equating to approximately 30 per cent of the rent for that two-and-a-half year period);
- £1,500 for the disrepair to the roof and the associated state of the ceilings upstairs and of the damp from late 2008 to late 2009 (equating to approximately 30 per cent of the rent for that year);
- £2,500 for the leaks and dampness between the end of 2009 until the end of 2010 when the position worsened significantly and Mr Thomas had to sleep downstairs and was unable to use the upstairs of the property (equating to approximately 50 per cent of the rent for that year).

Therefore, between the end of 2008 and the end of 2009, Mr Thomas received, in total, a notional reduction in rent of approximately 60 per cent. For the period from the end of 2009 to the end of 2010 he received, in total, a notional reduction in rent of approximately 80 per cent.

Further, Mr Thomas was awarded £850 for the aggravation of his asthma by the conditions of the property, the aggravation being to the extent of 20 per cent.

7.93 ***Clark v Affinity Sutton Homes Ltd*, December 2014 *Legal Action* 27, *Housing Law Casebook* 7th edn, para R18.38**

The claimant was a tenant of a one-bedroom flat from 29 November 2004 until 10 February 2014 when he was decanted. The claimant suffered from poor health, namely a chronic lung condition since 2006, rheumatoid arthritis since 2007 and also had bladder cancer. A default judgment was obtained and the claimant sought damages for rising dampness from January 2007. Remedial works were carried out in 2008 and again in January 2013.

Deputy District Judge Gillman awarded damages for the period April 2007 to 31 August 2008 at 30 per cent of the rent actually due, and for the period from January 2012 to 10 February 2014 at 45 per cent of the rent due. The judge made no award for the period from September 2008 to January 2012, finding that on the balance of probabilities it was unlikely that there were any significant problems in this period. There were no complaints logged during this period and not a single email, although there had been extensive email correspondence in 2007 and again in 2012/13.

The award in respect of general damages was therefore £6,779.88, which was uplifted by ten per cent in accordance with *Simmons v Castle*[81] to give a total general damages award of £7,457.86. The judge also awarded £2,189.75 for special damages, having discounted the figures claimed by 25 per cent for depreciation, save in respect of the carpet which he allowed in full as it would be difficult if not impossible to purchase second hand carpets. The judge also awarded £20 per week for the use of a dehumidifier 24 hours a day for eight weeks (having received details of average running costs) and £5 per week for additional heating costs for 183 weeks in the six years claimed. The total award for special damages was therefore £3,742.60 making a total award of £11,200.46.

7.94 ***DR v Southwark LBC*, December 2015 *Legal Action* 41, *Housing Law Casebook* 7th edn, para R18.42**

The tenant of a two-bedroom flat bought a claim for disrepair including for historic penetrating damp to the bathroom wall and condensation which caused saturated plaster to the external wall in the

81 [2012] EWCA Civ 1288, [2013] 1 WLR 1239.

bathroom. After calcium carbide testing established that the core of the wall was dry, the tenant conceded that the majority of damp was due to condensation, but the council was found liable for the damp plaster in the bathroom. At first instance, District Judge Desai awarded damages of 20 per cent of the rent for a three-year period (approximately £3,000), having found that the claim included a claim for personal injuries as it was pleaded that the tenant suffered from considerable distress and anxiety with reference to depression and threats to the health and safety of the tenant. The council appealed to the circuit judge, who upheld the finding on liability, but reduced the award of damages to £1 per day or £365 per annum.

7.95 ***KS v Southwark LBC*, March 2017 *Legal Action* 33**

The tenant lived with his partner and child in a two-bedroom flat on the fifth floor of a block of flats. There were recurrent leaks into the flat over a period of seven years. The leaks affected the bathroom, passage-way and separate WC, causing severe damp, mould and significant plaster damage. The expert deemed the bathroom as unfit for use.

Other pleaded disrepair consisted of defective double-glazing (in one room); a loose bath panel; a defective extractor fan; regular problems with the lights (including a five-month period without a working light in the WC); the loss of wall tiles in the bathroom due to the damp plaster behind; and intermittent hot water and heating problems.

The defendant's defence was struck out, but there was a contested assessment of damages. The judge awarded the following in general damages:

- Period 1: December 2009 to July 2012 – 35 per cent of rent.
- Period 2: August 2012–December 2015, when the dampness was most severe – 50 per cent of rent.
- Period 3: January 2016 to August 2016, when the leak had stopped but some damp/mould remained – 20 per cent of rent.

Despite a lack of supporting evidence, the judge awarded £5,000 in special damages where £17,270 was claimed. The totals awarded, including interest, were £15,428.46 for general damages and £5,758.90 special damages.

7.96 ***Southwark LBC v Jalim and Jalim*, March 2018 *Legal Action* 37**

The tenants lived in a three-bedroom flat on the third floor of a five-storey block. In proceedings for possession based on rent arrears, they counterclaimed for disrepair consisting of penetrating damp to the front door and the WC; a leaking bath; damp and mould growth throughout; inoperative extractor fans for five years; a broken extractor fan pull cord for two years; defective window seals causing fogging and condensation; a loose light fitting; and the poor state of flooring.

District Judge Zimmels entered judgment on the counterclaim in default of any defence to it (with the possession claim stayed pending the assessment of damages). He awarded general damages at 25 per cent of the rent, plus the *Simmons v Castle*[82] ten per cent uplift, over the full length of the tenancy of seven-and-a-half years, amounting to £11,000. Special damages of £1,981 unsupported by documentary evidence, so District Judge Swan discounted them to £1,250. Interest was also awarded. The rent arrears were set off against the amount awarded.

Defective heating

7.97 ***Sarmad v Okello*, November 2004 *Legal Action* 29, *Housing Law Casebook* 7th edn, para R18.78**

The tenant complained of disrepair throughout the tenancy from November 1999 to November 2002. The supply of heating and hot water was intermittent for the first three years, and in 2002 the heating broke down altogether. In addition, there was water penetration to the bathroom and hallway and, from April 2002, to the bedroom. From 2001, there was an infestation of rats from the take-away on the ground floor. The trial judge found conditions intolerable and awarded £14,250 damages as follows:

- £2,000 pa from February 1999 to February 2002 for the intermittent heating and hot water supply;
- £1,750 pa from February 2002 to November 2002 for intermittent hot water and heating supply;
- £1,500 pa from February 1999 to February 2001 for all the other defects;
- £2,000 pa from February 2001 to November 2002 for the rat infestation.

7.98 ***Ferguson v Jones*, December 2008 *Legal Action* 32, *Housing Law Casebook* 7th edn, para R18.45**

The tenant resided at the premises with her husband (until he passed away) and her six-year-old daughter. From the commencement of the tenancy and for a period of 17 months, there was no heating or hot water throughout the property because the emergency gas services had declared the heating system to be dangerous and disconnected

82 [2012] EWCA Civ 1288, [2013] 1 WLR 1239.

it. The cooker was also disconnected. There was no other significant disrepair. Although the tenant had bought two heaters, these were insufficient to keep the tenant and her daughter warm. The trial judge held that the tenant was entitled to damages for inconvenience at the highest rate and, adopting a global approach, awarded damages at £2,700 per annum. An award of £4,000 was made for the total 17-month period. Special damages were awarded at £1,181.68. This included the cost of buying warm meals and two heaters.

7.99 ***Fakhari v Newman*, January 2011 *Legal Action* 19, *Housing Law Casebook* 7th edn, para R18.44**

The tenant rented a property from his landlord from May 2008 at a rent of £984 per month. There were problems with the boiler from the outset. In December 2008 the boiler broke down completely, leaving the tenant without heating and hot water until 17 June 2009 when hot water (but not heating) was restored. The property was also draughty because of defective windows that leaked during periods of heavy rain. The landlords harassed the tenant and claimed possession. On the tenant's counterclaim he was awarded £9,250 for disrepair, namely:

- 25 per cent of the rent from May 2008 to December 2008;
- 75 per cent of the rent between December 2008 and June 2009; and
- 43 per cent of the rent from June 2009 onwards.

The tenant also recovered damages for the harassment and failure to protect his deposit.

7.100 ***Shazad v Khan*, January 2011 *Legal Action* 20, *Housing Law Casebook* 7th edn, para R18.80**

The tenant lived with his wife and five children in a three-bedroomed house which he rented for £4,200 per annum. He brought a claim for disrepair from 2005. Two bedrooms suffered from water penetration, with one unusable throughout the year and the second only usable in the summer months. There had also been water penetration from the front entrance door when it rained, since 2008. The boiler had not worked properly since 2005 and would cut out unexpectedly so that there had only been intermittent heating and hot water.

Damages of 40 per cent of the rent were awarded for the disrepair to the bedroom and front entrance door for a period of four years and seven months (£7,700). Damages were awarded separately for the inconvenience in respect of the intermittent heating and hot water at £2,000 per annum. (Comment: as a global award this amounted to over 75 per cent of the rent.)

Defective lifts

7.101 ***Walker v Lambeth LBC*, September 1992 *Legal Action* 21, *Housing Law Casebook* 4th edn, para P11.62**

For 18 months one of two lifts was out of operation and the other was subject to frequent breakdowns. The tenant had a young child and was pregnant for nine months out of the 18. She was occasionally trapped in the lift and frequently had to use the stairs to the 15th floor. Damages of £3,750 were awarded.

Other/combined defects

7.102 ***Murray v Kelly*, December 2008 *Legal Action* 31, *Housing Law Casebook* 7th edn, para R18.67**

The tenant counterclaimed for damages for disrepair for the following defects:

- low water pressure to the shower from August 1998 to February 2007;
- lack of heating from January to March 2000;
- leak from shower from May 2005 to February 2007;
- no hot water for three weeks in early 2005;
- leak from wash-hand basin from late 2007 to February 2007;
- leak from washing machine from early 2006 to 2007.

The tenant's rent had been £630 per month for most of the tenancy. He sought damages of £10,359 calculated as follows:

- August 1998 to February 2007 for defective shower, eight-and-a-half years at ten per cent of the rent = £6,426;
- January 2000 to March 2000 for lack of heating at 50 per cent of the rent = £945;
- 2005 for lack of hot water for three weeks, leak from wash hand basin, leak from shower at 15 per cent of the rent = £1,134;
- 2006 ongoing leak from shower, plus leak from washing machine causing leak to bedroom, kitchen and hallway at 25 per cent of the rent = £1,890.

The trial judge awarded £9,000 general damages, having found that 25 per cent diminution in value for the leaks was a bit excessive and that the damages should be lowered slightly because the landlord had attempted repairs although these had been ineffectual. She also awarded interest of £225, making a total claim award of £9,225.

7.103 ***Frederick & Simpson v Frame*, January 2012 *Legal Action* 38**

In a possession claim for rent arrears, the assured shorthold tenant of one room in a shared house, let at a rent of £130 per week counterclaimed in respect of the disrepair she suffered throughout the tenancy which began in November 2009 until the date of trial in June 2011. DJ Dabezies found the landlords liable and awarded damages on the basis of a diminution in the value of the rent throughout the tenancy as follows:

- 15 per cent for a mouse infestation largely to the common parts;
- 30 per cent for a lack of hot water;
- 15 per cent for the lack of heating to the common parts;
- five per cent for other miscellaneous defects.

He awarded a total of 65 per cent of the rent throughout the tenancy amounting to £7,417 and £131 in interest.

7.104 ***Southwark LBC v Munu and Munu*, December 2013 *Legal Action* 14**

The defendants counterclaimed in possession proceedings for disrepair and negligence. HHJ Matheson QC dismissed a number of defects on the basis that they did not amount to disrepair in law, but found the council liable for a loose wash hand basin in the bathroom which had no functioning cold water supply, ill-fitting and draughty windows in two bedrooms, the failure to fix properly panels and kickboards following installation of a new kitchen, a non-operative bathroom extractor fan, a disconnected flush pipe in one of the toilets at the property and backsurges of sewage into the ground floor toilet and other parts of the ground floor as a result of a defective external drain. The backsurges occurred repeatedly over a period of approximately 18 months. The judge also found the defendants to have been uncooperative and to have refused access on occasions, but awarded them £1,250 for the various defects at the property. He also made a separate award of £2,000 for the backsurges. These were a significant and very unpleasant intervention to the defendants' home and their peace and quiet enjoyment. A further £3,000 was awarded for special damages and £500 to the defendants' three children.

7.105 ***Hammersmith & Fulham LBC v Millani-Kalkhorani*, December 2013 *Legal Action* 15, *Housing Law Casebook* 7th edn, para R18.49**

In possession proceedings for rent arrears, the defendant counterclaimed for disrepair. She complained that since May 2005 there had been problems with a blockage in the pipe taking waste from her bathroom, resulting in the toilet and wash hand basin being blocked. The toilet had leaked into the kitchen below which made the electricity in the kitchen short-circuit so that the tenant was often without power. The toilet was replaced twice in December 2005 and January 2009 but the problems continued. During 2009, things were more or less alright, but through the year 2010 there were further problems with the water, the toilet and the boiler. A new boiler was installed in June 2010, but even that did not work until July 2010. The boiler installation involved 15 visits, and it was still not satisfactory at trial. There were also missing banisters, defective windows and a defective front entrance door.

HHJ Copley adopted a 'broad brush' approach to the counterclaim. He accepted that works had been undertaken from time to time, but considered it clear that the works were not carried out in a proper fashion or in a reasonable time. Since the extent of the disrepair had varied the judge decided to look at it in the round. He awarded £2,500 per annum for the 3.5 years from mid-2005 to December 2008/January 2009 amounting to £8,750. Although the defendant was not complaining in 2009, there was disrepair, and she was entitled to a sum awarded at £750 for that year. He awarded a further £1,000 per annum for 2010, 2011 and 2012, resulting in a total award of £12,500 plus remedial works and costs.

7.106 ***Read v Notting Hill Housing Trust*, December 2013 *Legal Action* 16, *Housing Law Casebook* 7th edn, para R18.77**

The assured shorthold tenant of a ground floor two-bedroom flat complained about rising damp, a defective boiler which produced only intermittent hot water and rats getting into the property through holes in the floorboards. One of the tenant's two children refused to continue living in the flat because of the rats, and had to go to live with her grandmother. The rent of the property was £289 per week. The landlord eventually offered the tenant alternative accommodation, but this was over a year after the rat problem was first reported to them.

District Judge Davies awarded damages on a 'broad brush' basis and considered that the rat infestation was by far the most serious aspect caused by the disrepair, especially as the rats entered the flat. She awarded damages at the rate of 80 per cent of the contractual rent for the period commencing 28 days after notification of the rat problem until a reasonable offer of accommodation was made to the tenant. This period was 60 weeks, resulting in damages of £13,872. For the period after the tenant had refused what the judge held to be a reasonable offer of accommodation, she awarded damages at the rate of 20 per cent of the contractual rent until the termination of the tenancy amounting to £953, amounting to a total general damages award of £14,825 plus interest of £940.

The claimant had also beaten her own Part 36 offer both one made before 1 April 2013 and one made after that date. She was therefore also awarded an extra ten per cent on her award amounting to £1,661 plus further interest pursuant to Part 36 amounting to £130.

7.107 ***Bitan v Holme*, December 2014 *Legal Action* 28, *Housing Law Casebook* 7th edn, para R18.35**

The tenant of a two-bedroomed house counterclaimed for harassment and disrepair in a possession action, where the claim for possession was struck out. The tenant complained of water leaking from the bathroom into her dining room, draughts through a hole in the exterior wall and a defective window. The ceiling to the dining room began to perish and the tenant became anxious about her family's safety. An award of £5,873.22 was made for 23-and-a-half months of disrepair made up of 40 per cent diminution in value of the monthly rent of £550 plus an uplift of ten per cent in accordance with *Simmons v Castle*.[83] An order for specific performance was also made.

7.108 ***Whittingdon v Uddin*, December 2014 *Legal Action* 28, *Housing Law Casebook* 7th edn, para R18.99**

The tenant brought a claim for damages for breach of the covenant of quiet enjoyment, harassment and disrepair against his landlord. For a period of three years the premises suffered from defective windows throughout, water penetration in the bedroom, some internal leaks in the kitchen and WC and some external disrepair. The landlord failed to carry out any repairs despite repeated complaints.

District Judge Sterlini awarded £10,650 for disrepair. This comprised:

- £1,800, being a 100 per cent reduction in the rent for a six-week period in November and December 2013 when the claimant had to move out because the premises were uninhabitable; and
- a global award of £7,500 to reflect the other items of disrepair over a period of three years (including a 17 per cent reduction in rent during this period).

He also awarded £1,000 for defective chattels that were provided under the terms of the tenancy agreement and that were broken but

83 [2012] EWCA Civ 1288, [2013] 1 WLR 1239.

not repaired/replaced and £350 for the cost of plumbing repairs paid for by the tenant.

7.109 ***McLoughlin v Tower Hamlets LBC*, December 2015 *Legal Action* 41, *Housing Law Casebook* 7th edn, para R18.66**

The tenant of a two up, two down cottage complained of rotting windows, a defective boiler and damp to the kitchen and two bedrooms from 2007. In addition the claimant suffered a gas leak in 2013 reportedly caused by the damp corroding a copper pipe.

District Judge Rand made an award of damages as follows:

- 30 per cent reduction in rent for the damp and defective windows, making a total award of £16,359 including the ten per cent *Simmons v Castle*[84] uplift;
- a £1,000 one-off payment for the gas leak;
- £750 in respect of special damages which was two-thirds of the estimated replacement cost, even though the tenant had no receipts as the claim was not inflated.

The claimant beat her Part 36 offer and was awarded costs on an indemnity basis.

7.110 ***Williamson v Khan*, December 2015 *Legal Action* 41, *Housing Law Casebook* 7th edn, para R18.100**

The tenant of a one-bedroom flat sought damages for disrepair throughout her tenancy, namely:

- no hot water between February 2004 and October 2007 and January 2011 and April 2013;
- inadequate and defective heating throughout the tenancy;
- rising and penetrating damp;
- leaks from the kitchen waste pipe, bathroom basin and defective rainwater goods;
- infestation of rats due to defects in the structure;
- perished and defective plasterwork;
- holes in the floorboards;
- external brickworks, rendering and boundary wall in disrepair;
- damaged paving; and
- drainage problems resulting in offensive odours in the property.

HHJ Lopez upheld the claimant case in full and awarded diminution in value of 80 per cent of the rent for a period of ten-and-a-half years

84 [2012] EWCA Civ 1288, [2013] 1 WLR 1239.

(having refused an application to plead limitation at the start of the trial) together with a ten per cent uplift in accordance with *Simmons v Castle*.[85]

7.111 ***Kwegan and Kwegan v Industrial Dwellings Society*, March 2017 *Legal Action* 32**

After a finding on appeal that electric gates and an entry-phone system were an integral part of the common entrance to the tenants' property and, therefore, fell within the landlord's contractual repairing obligations, an award of eight per cent diminution in rent was made for the date the gates stopped working. The award was increased by ten per cent on the basis that *Simmons v Castle*[86] was of universal application, even if damages had been calculated on the basis of diminution in rent.

7.112 ***Southwark LBC v Barrett*, March 2017 *Legal Action* 32**

In a defence to a claim for possession based on rent arrears, the tenant counterclaimed for disrepair consisting of a blocked exterior rainwater drain, missing internal trickle vent covers, disrepair to both the bathroom and kitchen extractor fans, a defective smoke alarm, blistered décor from historic water penetration, damage to two internal doors, and defects to the heating and hot water system. There was damp and mould growth in the property that the joint expert opined was caused, in part, by the blocked rainwater drain and defective extractor fans. Southwark failed to file a defence to the counterclaim and was barred from defending.

At trial, District Judge Desai awarded damages fixed at 30 per cent of rent, together with a ten per cent *Simmons v Castle*[87] uplift. Special damages were claimed in the sum of £3,774, which were reduced to £1,520.

7.113 ***Bokhari v Belgrave*, March 2018 *Legal Action* 36**

The tenant was a single mother of two adult daughters. Mr Bokhari granted her an assured shorthold tenancy on 27 June 2004 at a monthly rent of £850. On 21 November 2014, he issued a claim for possession on the ground of rent arrears. Ms Belgrave counterclaimed for breaches of repairing covenants and of the tenancy

85 [2012] EWCA Civ 1288, [2013] 1 WLR 1239.

86 [2012] EWCA Civ 1288, [2013] 1 WLR 1239.

87 [2012] EWCA Civ 1288, [2013] 1 WLR 1239.

deposit provisions. The claim was struck out and judgment was given on the counterclaim.

Expert reports identified disrepair as an ill-fitting window, water penetration from the shower, inadequate ventilation and mould growth due to condensation. There had also been a defective boiler for four months in 2012–13 and defective kitchen appliances. The period of loss ran from the commencement of the tenancy to the date of trial.

General damages were awarded at a rate of 15 per cent of the rent and uplifted by ten per cent (*Simmons v Castle*[88]), resulting in a figure of £21,318. Special damages were awarded in the sum of £1,222.06, reduced to one-third of the claim to take account of that element caused by non-actionable condensation damp.

Asthma

7.114 In addition to the cases below, reference should also be made to the Judicial College guidelines,[89] which suggests damages of up to £4,520 (including ten per cent uplift) for mild asthma, bronchitis, colds and chest problems (usually resulting from unfit housing or similar exposure, particularly in cases of young children) treated by a general practitioner and resolving within a few months.

7.115 ***Bygraves v Southwark LBC* (1990) CLY 1640**

£5,000 to a child, who was five years old at the time of the award, for material exacerbation of very severe asthma since birth. £5,000 for future pain and suffering.

7.116 ***McCaffrey v Lambeth LBC*, August 1994 *Legal Action* 18; *Housing Law Casebook* 6th edn para P17.54**

This involved:

- £600 pa to a young girl who suffered upper respiratory tract infections and asthma over four-and-a-half years, including nine full-blown attacks but no hospital treatment, mainly suffering from wheezing and shortness of breath.
- £450 pa to a young girl who suffered a large number of colds over five-and-a-half years and developed asthma, requiring treatment from her GP on a number of occasions.

88 [2012] EWCA Civ 1288, [2013] 1 WLR 1239.

89 *Judicial College Guidelines for the Assessment of General Damages in Personal Injury Cases* 14th edn, OUP, 2017.

- £400 pa to a young girl who suffered intermittently from chest problems and wheeziness sometimes requiring antibiotics.

7.117 ***Stone and Stone (a minor) v Redair Mersey Agencies*, May 1997 *Legal Action* 18, *Housing Law Casebook* 6th edn, para P17.75**

£2,000 for a six-year-old girl who had suffered four years of constant chest infections and mild asthma exacerbated by damp and draughts.

7.118 ***Alienus v Tower Hamlets LBC* [1998] 1 CL 312, *Housing Law Casebook* 4th edn, para P11.12**

£11,000 to a child who contracted and suffered acute asthma for seven years.

7.119 ***Conroy v Hire Token Ltd*, February 2002 *Legal Action* 22, *Housing Law Casebook* 7th edn, para R18.40**

£650 each to two children aged two and four, who had both suffered from coughs and colds over a six-month period as a result of severe mould growth at their home. Neither child sought medical attention, nor was there a diagnosis of asthma.

7.120 ***C (a child) and L (a child) v Empire Estates* [2002] 6 QR 13, Kemp & Kemp paras K2–008 and K2–010**

Damages were:

- £8,500 to a four-year-old child who contracted asthma and suffered exacerbation of coughing. The condition was so bad that he had to take steroids daily as well as using inhalers frequently.
- £1,750 to a six-year-old child who already had asthma, which became worse after living in damp conditions for eight months. A causal link was established because there had been a clear improvement in the child's state of health when they moved to drier premises in 2002.

7.121 ***Rushton and others v Southwark LBC*, December 2006 *Legal Action* 24**

In this case:

- £5,500 was awarded to a child who developed breathing problems and pneumonia eight weeks after moving into the property and was admitted to hospital for two weeks. Diagnosis of asthma made. The damp conditions had exacerbated but not caused the asthma. Prognosis was good.
- £10,000 was awarded to a second child, who had worse symptoms. Admitted to hospital at eight months, followed by further asthma

attacks, sometimes requiring hospital admission. Prone to respiratory infections and repeated antibiotic treatment resulted in removal of enamel from one of front teeth. Asthma had been exacerbated by the damp. Prognosis that some risk of future illness, but condition improved since leaving property.

7.122 ***Smyth v Farnworth*, December 2009 *Legal Action* 23, *Housing Law Casebook* 7th edn, para R18.82**

In this case:

- £5,000 was awarded to the tenant for the fact that her depression had been exacerbated by the state of the property (namely water penetration to a conservatory throughout a tenancy and a defective boiler for a five-month period) and threats (over a five-week period) which had had an effect for a period of just over two years.
- £3,500 was awarded to her son for exacerbation of asthma for a two-year period, based on the basis of the lower award in *C (a child) and L (a child) v Empire Estates* (see para 7.120).

7.123 ***Thomas v AJ Bradburn (acting as receiver for Adelphi Properties Ltd)*, December 2014 *Legal Action* 27, *Housing Law Casebook* 7th edn, para R18.87**

Mr Thomas was awarded £850 for the aggravation of his asthma by the conditions of the property, the aggravation being to the extent of 20 per cent.

Infestations[90]

7.124 ***Clark v Wandsworth LBC*, June 1994 *Legal Action* 15, *Housing Law Casebook* 7th edn, para R18.30**

£3,500 per annum for a flat heavily infested with cockroaches.

7.125 ***McGuigan v Southwark LBC*, March 1996 *Legal Action* 14, *Housing Law Casebook* 4th edn para P11.46**

Awards ranging from between £1,000 pa to £3,500 pa for light to very severe cockroach infestations, including £3,000 for a severe one-year ant infestation, with some cockroaches.

7.126 ***Dadd v Christian Action (Enfield) Housing Association*, December 1994 *Legal Action* 18**

£2,090 per annum for a rat infestation with some other disrepair.

90 See 'Pest and vermin infestation' at para 2.226.

7.127 ***London & Quadrant Housing Trust v Riemy*, December 2008 Legal Action 31, *Housing Law Casebook* 7th edn, para R18.61**

£300 per annum for a mouse infestation which the judge found to be de minimis.

7.128 ***Harwood Properties Ltd v Remuinan*, January 2012 *Legal Action* 38**

Twenty per cent of the rent awarded for a six-month rat infestation of £768 which the judge considered to be more distressing then the other problems for which 20 per cent of the rent was also awarded.

7.129 ***Bernard v Meisuria*, January 2011 *Legal Action* 20, *Housing Law Casebook* 7th edn, para R18.33**

The tenant of a five-bedroom house who lived with his disabled wife and five children brought a claim for a rat infestation from 2005 until March 2009 when he moved out of the premises and other more minor items of disrepair, After a contested trial, the judge found that the infestation had emanated from the drains which were in disrepair. He awarded damages of £20,000 in respect of the rat infestation to include the special damages claim, having found that that a property which was infested with rats had little rentable value. He awarded a further £1,250 in respect of the other disrepair plus indemnity costs and interest on the damages and costs at one per cent over the minimum lending rate from 24 December 2007 as the tenant had beaten a Part 36 offer made on 3 December 2007. The total damages award was £22,290.

7.130 ***Ojo and Ojo v Hackney LBC*, Clerkenwell and Shoreditch CC, 4 November 2015**

Secure tenants of a two-storey maisonette in a block of 50 flats who became leaseholders in 1995, experienced an infestation of mice from 2007 until early 2014. The experts for each party agreed that the mice had gained access to the premises via vertical ducts which passed through the kitchen and bathroom, and which contained various drains and pipes from more than one property. The ducts were retained by the defendant as freeholder.

From 2007, the defendant had carried out block treatment works, putting down poison. The mice continued to be a persistent problem for the claimants until early 2014, when the claimants had installed a new kitchen and had sealed up holes.

DJ Manners found that the presence of mice in the premises for such a long period of time, and at the level described, amounted to a nuisance. The defendant did not create the nuisance, but its block treatment programme had not been an adequate response. The experts were agreed that the duct should have been proofed against mice. She noted that the claimants were leaseholders, rather than tenants, and they had the ability to mouse-proof their home by filling in holes from the inside. She also found that the general cleanliness and repair to the maisonette had not been of a high standard and that grease on the walls and kitchen floor would have encouraged the mice. She declined the invitation to assess damages by attributing an artificial rental value to the premises. She awarded an overall amount of £2,500 per annum, reduced by 50 per cent to reflect the fact that the claimants failed to carry out any internal proofing until 2013/2014. She did not make an order specifying works, given that the problems appeared to have been sorted out.

7.131 **Further cases**

Awards were also made for rats in *Vergara v Lambeth LBC* (see para 7.86), *Sarmad v Okello* (see para 7.97), *Frederick & Simpson v Frame* (see para 7.103), *Read v Notting Hill Housing Trust* (see para 7.106), and *Williamson v Khan* (see para 7.110).

APPENDICES

APPENDIX A

Legislation[1]

1 © Crown Copyright. Legislation is reproduced, as amended, up to date to 1 April 2019.

DEFECTIVE PREMISES ACT 1972 ss1–4

Duty to build dwellings properly

1 (1) A person taking on work for or in connection with the provision of a dwelling (whether the dwelling is provided by the erection or by the conversion or enlargement of a building) owes a duty–

(a) if the dwelling is provided to the order of any person, to that person; and

(b) without prejudice to paragraph (a) above, to every person who acquires an interest (whether legal or equitable) in the dwelling;

to see that the work which he takes on is done in a workmanlike or, as the case may be, professional manner, with proper materials and so that as regards that work the dwelling will be fit for habitation when completed.

(2) A person who takes on any such work for another on terms that he is to do it in accordance with instructions given by or on behalf of that other shall, to the extent to which he does it properly in accordance with those instructions, be treated for the purposes of this section as discharging the duty imposed on him by subsection (1) above except where he owes a duty to that other to warn him of any defects in the instructions and fails to discharge that duty.

(3) A person shall not be treated for the purposes of subsection (2) above as having given instructions for the doing of work merely because he has agreed to the work being done in a specified manner, with specified materials or to a specified design.

(4) A person who–

(a) in the course of a business which consists of or includes providing or arranging for the provision of dwellings or installations in dwellings; or

(b) in the exercise of a power of making such provision or arrangements conferred by or by virtue of any enactment;

arranges for another to take on work for or in connection with the provision of a dwelling shall be treated for the purposes of this section as included among the persons who have taken on the work.

(5) Any cause of action in respect of a breach of the duty imposed by this section shall be deemed, for the purposes of the Limitation Act 1939, the Law Reform (Limitation of Actions, etc) Act 1954 and the Limitation Act 1963, to have accrued at the time when the dwelling was completed, but if after that time a person who has done work for or in connection with the provision of the dwelling does further work to rectify the work he has already done, any such cause of action in respect of that further work shall be deemed for those purposes to have accrued at the time when the further work was finished.

Cases excluded from the remedy under section 1

2 (1) Where–

(a) in connection with the provision of a dwelling or its first sale or letting for habitation any rights in respect of defects in the state of the dwelling are conferred by an approved scheme to which this section applies on a person having or acquiring an interest in the dwelling; and

(b) it is stated in a document of a type approved for the purposes of this section that the requirements as to design or construction imposed by or under the scheme have, or appear to have, been substantially complied with in relation to the dwelling;

no action shall be brought by any person having or acquiring an interest in the dwelling for breach of the duty imposed by section 1 above in relation to the dwelling.

(2) A scheme to which this section applies–

(a) may consist of any number of documents and any number of agreements or other transactions between any number of persons; but

(b) must confer, by virtue of agreements entered into with persons having or acquiring an interest in the dwellings to which the scheme applies, rights on such persons in respect of defects in the state of the dwellings.

(3) In this section 'approved' means approved by the Secretary of State, and the power of the Secretary of State to approve a scheme or document for the purposes of this section shall be exercisable by order, except that any requirements as to construction or design imposed under a scheme to which this section applies may be approved by him without making any order or, if he thinks fit, by order.

(4) The Secretary of State–

(a) may approve a scheme or document for the purposes of this section with or without limiting the duration of his approval; and

(b) may by order revoke or vary a previous order under this section or, without such an order, revoke or vary a previous approval under this section given otherwise than by order.

(5) The production of a document purporting to be a copy of an approval given by the Secretary of State otherwise than by order and certified by an officer of the Secretary of State to be a true copy of the approval shall be conclusive evidence of the approval, and without proof of the handwriting or official position of the person purporting to sign the certificate.

(6) The power to make an order under this section shall be exercisable by statutory instrument which shall be subject to annulment in pursuance of a resolution by either House of Parliament.

(7) Where an interest in a dwelling is compulsorily acquired–

(a) no action shall be brought by the acquiring authority for breach of the duty imposed by section 1 above in respect of the dwelling; and

(b) if any work for or in connection with the provision of the dwelling was done otherwise than in the course of a business by the person in occupation of the dwelling at the time of the compulsory acquisition, the acquiring authority and not that person shall be treated as the person who took on the work and accordingly as owing that duty.

Duty of care with respect to work done on premises not abated by disposal of premises

3 (1) Where work of construction, repair, maintenance or demolition or any other work is done on or in relation to premises, any duty of care owed, because of the doing of the work, to persons who might reasonably be expected to be affected by defects in the state of the premises created by the doing of the work shall not be abated by the subsequent disposal of the premises by the person who owed the duty.

(2) This section does not apply–

(a) in the case of premises which are let, where the relevant tenancy of the premises commenced, or the relevant tenancy agreement of the premises was entered into, before the commencement of this Act;

(b) in the case of premises disposed of in any other way, when the disposal of the premises was completed, or a contract for their disposal was entered into, before the commencement of this Act; or

(c) in either case, where the relevant transaction disposing of the premises is entered into in pursuance of an enforceable option by which the consideration for the disposal was fixed before the commencement of this Act.

Landlord's duty of care in virtue of obligation or right to repair premises demised

4 (1) Where premises are let under a tenancy which puts on the landlord an obligation to the tenant for the maintenance or repair of the premises, the landlord owes to all persons who might reasonably be expected to be affected by defects in the state of the premises a duty to take such care as is reasonable in all the circumstances to see that they are reasonably safe from personal injury or from damage to their property caused by a relevant defect.

(2) The said duty is owed if the landlord knows (whether as the result of being notified by the tenant or otherwise) or if he ought in all the circumstances to have known of the relevant defect.

(3) In this section 'relevant defect' means a defect in the state of the premises existing at or after the material time and arising from, or continuing because of, an act or omission by the landlord which constitutes or would if he had had notice of the defect, have constituted a failure by him to carry out his obligation to the tenant for the maintenance or repair of the premises; and for the purposes of the foregoing provision 'the material time' means–

(a) where the tenancy commenced before this Act, the commencement of this Act; and

(b) in all other cases, the earliest of the following times, that is to say–

(i) the time when the tenancy commences;

(ii) the time when the tenancy agreement is entered into;

(iii) the time when possession is taken of the premises in contemplation of the letting.

(4) Where premises are let under a tenancy which expressly or impliedly gives the landlord the right to enter the premises to carry out any description of maintenance or repair of the premises, then, as from the time when he first is, or by notice or otherwise can put himself, in a position to exercise the right and so long as he is or can put himself in that position, he shall be treated for the purposes of subsections (1) to (3) above (but for no other purpose) as if he were under an obligation to the tenant for that description of maintenance or repair of the premises; but the landlord shall not owe the tenant any duty by virtue of this subsection in respect of any defect in the state of the premises arising from, or continuing because of, a failure to carry out an obligation expressly imposed on the tenant by the tenancy.

(5) For the purposes of this section obligations imposed or rights given by any enactment in virtue of a tenancy shall be treated as imposed or given by the tenancy.

(6) This section applies to a right of occupation given by contract or any enactment and not amounting to a tenancy as if the right were a tenancy, and 'tenancy' and cognate expressions shall be construed accordingly.

BUILDING ACT 1984 ss76–79

DEFECTIVE PREMISES, DEMOLITION ETC

Defective premises

76 (1) If it appears to a local authority that–

(a) any premises are in such a state (in this section referred to as a 'defective state') as to be prejudicial to health or a nuisance, and

(b) unreasonable delay in remedying the defective state would be occasioned by following the procedure prescribed by section 80 of the Environmental Protection Act 1990,

the local authority may serve on the person on whom it would have been appropriate to serve an abatement notice under the said section 80 (if the local authority had proceeded under that section) a notice stating that the local authority intend to remedy the defective state and specifying the defects that they intend to remedy.

(2) Subject to subsection (3) below, the local authority may, after the expiration of nine days after service of a notice under subsection (1) above, execute such works as may be necessary to remedy the defective state, and recover the expenses reasonably incurred in so doing from the person on whom the notice was served.

(3) If, within seven days after service of a notice under subsection (1) above, the person on whom the notice was served serves a counter-notice that he intends to remedy the defects specified in the first-mentioned notice, the local authority shall take no action in pursuance of the first-mentioned notice unless the person who served the counter-notice–

(a) fails within what seems to the local authority a reasonable time to begin to execute works to remedy the said defects, or

(b) having begun to execute such works fails to make such progress towards their completion as seems to the local authority reasonable.

(4) In proceedings to recover expenses under subsection (2) above, the court–

(a) shall inquire whether the local authority were justified in concluding that the premises were in a defective state, or that unreasonable delay in remedy-ing the defective state would have been occasioned by following the procedure prescribed by section 80 of the Environmental Protection Act 1990, and

(b) if the defendant proves that he served a counter-notice under subsection (3) above, shall inquire whether the defendant failed to begin the works to remedy the defects within a reasonable time, or failed to make reasonable progress towards their completion,

and if the court determines that–

(i) the local authority were not justified in either of the conclusions mentioned in paragraph (a) of this subsection, or

(ii) there was no failure under paragraph (b) of this subsection,

the local authority shall not recover the expenses or any part of them.

(5) Subject to subsection (4) above, in proceedings to recover expenses under subsection (2) above, the court may–

(a) inquire whether the said expenses ought to be borne wholly or in part by some person other than the defendant in the proceedings, and

(b) make such order concerning the expenses or their apportionment as appears to the court to be just,

but the court shall not order the expenses or any part of them to be borne by a person other than the defendant in the proceedings unless the court is satisfied that that other person has had due notice of the proceedings and an opportunity of being heard.

(6) A local authority shall not serve a notice under subsection (1) above, or proceed with the execution of works in accordance with a notice so served, if the execution of the works would, to their knowledge, be in contravention of a building preservation order under section 29 of the Town and Country Planning Act 1947.

(7) The power conferred on a local authority by subsection (1) above may be exercised notwithstanding that the local authority might instead have proceeded under Part VI of the Housing Act 1985 (repair notices).

Dangerous building

77 (1) If it appears to a local authority that a building or structure, or part of a building or structure, is in such a condition, or is used to carry such loads, as to be dangerous, the authority may apply to a magistrates' court, and the court may–

(a) where danger arises from the condition of the building or structure, make an order requiring the owner thereof–

(i) to execute such work as may be necessary to obviate the danger or,

(ii) if he so elects, to demolish the building or structure, or any dangerous part of it, and remove any rubbish resulting from the demolition, or

(b) where danger arises from overloading of the building or structure, make an order restricting its use until a magistrates' court, being satisfied that any necessary works have been executed, withdraws or modifies the restriction.

(2) If the person on whom an order is made under subsection (1)(a) above fails to comply with the order within the time specified, the local authority may–

(a) execute the order in such manner as they think fit, and

(b) recover the expenses reasonably incurred by them in doing so from the person in default,

and, without prejudice to the right of the authority to exercise those powers, the person is liable on summary conviction to a fine not exceeding level 1 on the standard scale.

(3) This section has effect subject to the provisions of the Planning (Listed Buildings and Conservation Areas) Act 1990 relating to listed buildings, buildings subject to building preservation notices and buildings in conservation areas.

Dangerous building – emergency measures

78 (1) If it appears to a local authority that–

(a) a building or structure, or part of a building or structure, is in such a state, or is used to carry such loads, as to be dangerous, and

(b) immediate action should be taken to remove the danger,

they may take such steps as may be necessary for that purpose.

(2) Before exercising their powers under this section, the local authority shall, if it is reasonably practicable to do so, give notice of their intention to the owner and occupier of the building, or of the premises on which the structure is situated.

(3) Subject to this section, the local authority may recover from the owner the expenses reasonably incurred by them under this section.

(4) So far as expenses incurred by the local authority under this section consist of expenses of fencing off the building or structure, or arranging for it to be watched, the expenses shall not be recoverable in respect of any period–

(a) after the danger has been removed by other steps under this section, or

(b) after an order made under section 77(1) above for the purpose of its removal has been complied with or has been executed as mentioned in subsection (2) of that section.

(5) In proceedings to recover expenses under this section, the court shall inquire whether the local authority might reasonably have proceeded instead under section 77(1) above, and, if the court determines that the local authority might reasonably have proceeded instead under that subsection, the local authority shall not recover the expenses or any part of them.

(6) Subject to subsection (5) above, in proceedings to recover expenses under this section, the court may–

(a) inquire whether the expenses ought to be borne wholly or in part by some person other than the defendant in the proceedings, and

(b) make such order concerning the expenses or their apportionment as appears to the court to be just,

but the court shall not order the expenses or any part of them to be borne by any person other than the defendant in the proceedings unless it is satisfied that that other person has had due notice of the proceedings and an opportunity of being heard.

(7) Where in consequence of the exercise of the powers conferred by this section the owner or occupier of any premises sustains damage, but section 106(1) below does not apply because the owner or occupier has been in default–

(a) the owner or occupier may apply to a magistrates' court to determine whether the local authority were justified in exercising their powers under this section so as to occasion the damage sustained, and

(b) if the court determines that the local authority were not so justified, the owner or occupier is entitled to compensation, and section 106(2) and (3) below applies in relation to any dispute as regards compensation arising under this subsection.

(8) The proper officer of a local authority may, as an officer of the local authority, exercise the powers conferred on the local authority by subsection (1) above.

(9) This section does not apply to premises forming part of a mine or quarry within the meaning of the Mines and Quarries Act 1954.

Ruinous and dilapidated buildings and neglected sites

79 (1) If it appears to a local authority that a building or structure is by reason of its ruinous or dilapidated condition seriously detrimental to the amenities of the neighbourhood, the local authority may by notice require the owner thereof–

(a) to execute such works of repair or restoration, or

(b) if he so elects, to take such steps for demolishing the building or structure, or any part thereof, and removing any rubbish or other material resulting from or exposed by the demolition,

as may be necessary in the interests of amenity.

(2) If it appears to a local authority that–

(a) rubbish or other material resulting from, or exposed by, the demolition or collapse of a building or structure is lying on the site or on any adjoining land, and
(b) by reason thereof the site or land is in such a condition as to be seriously detrimental to the amenities of the neighbourhood,

the local authority may by notice require the owner of the site or land to take steps for removing the rubbish or material as may be necessary in the interests of amenity.

(3) Sections 99 and 102 below apply in relation to a notice given under subsection (1) or (2) above, subject to the following modifications–
(a) section 99(1) requires the notice to indicate the nature of the works of repair or restoration and that of the works of demolition and removal of rubbish or material, and
(b) section 99(2) authorises the local authority to execute, subject to that subsection, at their election either the works of repair or restoration or the works of demolition and removal of rubbish or material.

(4) This section does not apply to an advertisement as defined in section 336(1) of the Town and Country Planning Act 1990.

(5) This section has effect subject to the provisions of the Planning (Listed Buildings and Conservation Areas) Act 1990 relating to listed buildings, buildings subject to building preservation notices and buildings in conservation areas.

LANDLORD AND TENANT ACT 1985 ss8–17

Implied terms as to fitness for human habitation: Wales[1]

8 (1) In a contract to which this section applies for the letting of a house in Wales[2] for human habitation there is implied, notwithstanding any stipulation to the contrary–

(a) a condition that the house is fit for human habitation at the commencement of the tenancy, and

(b) an undertaking that the house will be kept by the landlord fit for human habitation during the tenancy.

(2) . . .[3]

(3) This section applies to a contract if–

(a) the rent does not exceed the figure applicable in accordance with the subsection (4), and

(b) the letting is not on such terms as to the tenant's responsibility as are mentioned in subsection (5).

(4) The rent limit for the application of this section is shown by the following Table, by reference to the date of making of the contract and the situation of the premises:

Date of making of contract	*Rent limit*
Before 31st July 1923.	In London: £40. Elsewhere: £26 or £16 (see Note 1).
On or after 31st July 1923 and before 6th July 1957.	In London: £40. Elsewhere: £26.
On or after 6th July 1957.	In London: £80. Elsewhere: £52.

NOTES

1. The applicable figure for contracts made before 31st July 1923 is £26 in the case of premises situated in a borough or urban district which at the date of the contract had according to the last published census a population of 50,000 or more. In the case of a house situated elsewhere, the figure is £16.

2. The references to 'London' are, in relation to contracts made before 1st April 1965, to the administrative county of London and, in relation to contracts made on or after that date, to Greater London exclusive of the outer London boroughs.

1 Words ': Wales' inserted by the Homes (Fitness for Human Habitation) Act 2018 s1(1), (2)(a). In force 20 March 2019: Homes (Fitness for Human Habitation) Act 2018 s2(2).

2 Words 'in Wales' inserted by the Homes (Fitness for Human Habitation) Act 2018, s1(1), (2)(b). In force 20 March 2019: Homes (Fitness for Human Habitation) Act 2018 s2(2).

3 Subs (2) repealed by the Protection of Freedoms Act 2012 ss39(2), 115(2), Sch 2, Pt 3, para 12(1), Sch 10, Pt 2.

(5) This section does not apply where a house is let for a term of three years or more (the lease not being determinable at the option of either party before the expiration of three years) upon terms that the tenant puts the premises into a condition reasonably fit for human habitation.

(6) In this section 'house' includes–
   (a) a part of a house, and
   (b) any yard, garden, outhouses and appurtenances belonging to the house or usually enjoyed with it.

9 Application of section 8 to certain houses occupied by agricultural workers

(1) Where under the contract of employment of a worker employed in agriculture the provision of a house for his occupation forms part of his remuneration and the provisions of section 8 (implied terms as to fitness for human habitation) are inapplicable by reason only of the house not being let to him–
   (a) there are implied as part of the contract of employment, notwithstanding any stipulation to the contrary, the like condition and undertaking as would be implied under that section if the house were so let, and
   (b) the provisions of that section apply accordingly, with the substitution of 'employer' for 'landlord' and such other modifications as may be necessary.

(2) This section does not affect any obligation of a person other than the employer to repair a house to which this section applies, or any remedy for enforcing such an obligation.

(3) In this section 'house' includes–
   (a) a part of a house, and
   (b) any yard, garden, outhouses and appurtenances belonging to the house or usually enjoyed with it.

9A Fitness for human habitation of dwellings in England[4]

(1) In a lease to which this section applies of a dwelling in England (see section 9B), there is implied a covenant by the lessor that the dwelling–
   (a) is fit for human habitation at the time the lease is granted or otherwise created or, if later, at the beginning of the term of the lease, and
   (b) will remain fit for human habitation during the term of the lease.

(2) The implied covenant is not to be taken as requiring the lessor–
   (a) to carry out works or repairs for which the lessee is liable by virtue of–
      (i) the duty of the lessee to use the premises in a tenant-like manner, or
      (ii) an express covenant of the lessee of substantially the same effect as that duty;
   (b) to rebuild or reinstate the dwelling in the case of destruction or damage by fire, storm, flood or other inevitable accident;
   (c) to keep in repair or maintain anything which the lessee is entitled to remove from the dwelling;

4 Section 9A inserted by the Homes (Fitness for Human Habitation) Act 2018 s1(1), (3). In force 20 March 2019: Homes (Fitness for Human Habitation) Act 2018 s2(2).

(d) to carry out works or repairs which, if carried out, would put the lessor in breach of any obligation imposed by any enactment (whenever passed or made);

(e) to carry out works or repairs requiring the consent of a superior landlord or other third party in circumstances where consent has not been obtained following reasonable endeavours to obtain it.

(3) The implied covenant is also not to be taken as imposing on the lessor any liability in respect of the dwelling being unfit for human habitation if the unfitness is wholly or mainly attributable to–

(a) the lessee's own breach of covenant, or

(b) disrepair which the lessor is not obliged to make good because of an exclusion or modification under section 12 (power of county court to authorise exclusions or modifications in leases in respect of repairing obligations under section 11).

(4) Any provision of a lease or of any agreement relating to a lease (whether made before or after the grant or creation of the lease) is void to the extent that it purports–

(a) to exclude or limit the obligations of the lessor under the implied covenant, or

(b) to authorise any forfeiture or impose on the lessee any penalty, disability or obligation in the event of the lessee enforcing or relying upon those obligations.

(5) Where in any proceedings before a court it is alleged that a lessor is in breach of an obligation under the implied covenant, the court may order specific performance of the obligation (regardless of any equitable rule restricting the scope of that remedy).

(6) Where a lease to which this section applies of a dwelling in England forms part only of a building, the implied covenant has effect as if the reference to the dwelling in subsection (1) included a reference to any common parts of the building in which the lessor has an estate or interest.

(7) In a lease to which this section applies of a dwelling in England, there is also implied a covenant by the lessee that the lessor, or a person authorised in writing by the lessor, may enter the dwelling for the purpose of viewing its condition and state of repair.

(8) The covenant implied by subsection (7) requires entry to the dwelling to be permitted–

(a) only at reasonable times of the day, and

(b) only if at least 24 hours' notice in writing has been given to the occupier of the dwelling.

(9) In this section–

'common parts' has the meaning given by section 60(1) of the Landlord and Tenant Act 1987;

'lease' does not include a mortgage term;

'lessee' means the person for the time being entitled to the term of a lease;

'lessor' means the person for the time being entitled to the reversion expectant on a lease.

9B Leases to which section 9A applies[5]

(1) Section 9A applies to a lease under which a dwelling is let wholly or mainly for human habitation if either of the following applies–
  (a) the lease is for a term of less than 7 years, or
  (b) the lease is of a kind mentioned in subsection (1A) or (1AB) of section 13 (leases to which section 11 applies: secure, assured or introductory tenancies for fixed term of 7 years or more).

This is subject as follows.

(2) Section 9A does not apply to any lease of a kind mentioned in section 14 (exceptions for leases to which section 11 applies).

(3) Except as mentioned in subsections (4), (5) and (6), section 9A does not apply to a lease granted–
  (a) before the commencement date, or
  (b) on or after that date in pursuance of an agreement entered into, or an order of a court made, before the commencement date.

(4) Section 9A applies to a periodic or secure tenancy that is in existence on the commencement date, but in the case of any such tenancy the covenant implied by that section has effect in the following way–
  (a) subsection (1)(a) of that section has effect as if the reference to the later of the times there mentioned were a reference to the time that begins at the end of the period of 12 months beginning with the commencement date, and
  (b) subsection (1)(b) of that section has effect only in respect of times falling after the end of that 12 month period.

(5) Section 9A applies to a periodic or secure tenancy that comes into existence after the commencement date on expiry of a term of a lease granted before that date.

(6) Section 9A applies to a lease for a fixed term which–
  (a) is granted or renewed before the commencement date, and
  (b) is renewed for a further fixed term on or after that date,

and for this purpose the renewal on or after the commencement date is to be treated as a grant of the lease on or after that date.

(7) For the purposes of subsection (1) it is immaterial–
  (a) whether the dwelling is to be occupied under the lease or under an inferior lease derived out of it, or
  (b) that the lease also demises other property (which may consist of or include one or more other dwellings).

(8) In determining for the purposes of subsection (1)(a) whether a lease is for a term of less than 7 years–
  (a) any part of the term falling before the grant or creation is to be ignored and the lease is to be treated as a lease for a term commencing with the grant or creation;
  (b) a lease which is determinable at the option of the lessor before the expiry of 7 years from the commencement of the term is to be treated as a lease for a term of less than 7 years;
  (c) a lease (other than one to which paragraph (b) applies) is not to be treated as a lease for a term of less than 7 years if it confers on the lessee an option

5 Section 9B inserted by the Homes (Fitness for Human Habitation) Act 2018 s1(1), (3). In force 20 March 2019: Homes (Fitness for Human Habitation) Act 2018 s2(2).

for renewal for a term which, together with the original term, amounts to 7 years or more.

(9) In this section–

'the commencement date' means the date on which the Homes (Fitness for Human Habitation) Act 2018 comes into force;

'lease', 'lessee' and 'lessor' have the same meanings as in section 9A;

'secure tenancy' has the meaning given by section 79 of the Housing Act 1985.

9C Application of section 9A to certain dwellings occupied by agricultural workers[6]

(1) This section applies where under a contract of employment of a worker employed in agriculture–

(a) the provision of a dwelling for the worker's occupation forms part of the worker's remuneration, and

(b) the provisions of section 9A (implied term as to fitness for human habitation of dwellings in England) are inapplicable by reason only of the dwelling not being let to the worker.

(2) There is implied as part of the contract of employment (in spite of any stipulation to the contrary) a term having the same effect as the covenant that would be implied by section 9A if the dwelling were let by a lease to which that section applies.

(3) The provisions of section 9A apply accordingly–

(a) with the substitution of 'employer' and 'employee' for 'lessor' and 'lessee', and

(b) with such other modifications as may be necessary.

(4) This section does not affect–

(a) any obligation of a person other than the employer to repair a dwelling to which the covenant implied by section 9A applies by virtue of this section, or

(b) any remedy for enforcing such an obligation.

10 Fitness for human habitation

(1)[7] In determining for the purposes of this Act whether a house or dwelling is unfit for human habitation, regard shall be had to its condition in respect of the following matters–

repair,
stability,
freedom from damp,
internal arrangement,
natural lighting,
ventilation,
water supply,
drainage and sanitary conveniences,

6 Section 9C inserted by the Homes (Fitness for Human Habitation) Act 2018 s1(1), (3). In force 20 March 2019: Homes (Fitness for Human Habitation) Act 2018 s2(2).

7 Section 10(1) numbered and amended by the Homes (Fitness for Human Habitation) Act 2018 s1(1), (4): words 'or dwelling' and 'in relation to a dwelling in England, any prescribed hazard' added.

facilities for preparation and cooking of food and for the disposal of waste water;
in relation to a dwelling in England, any prescribed hazard;
and the house or dwelling shall be regarded as unfit for human habitation if, and only if, it is so far defective in one or more of those matters that it is not reasonably suitable for occupation in that condition.

(2) In subsection (1) 'prescribed hazard' means any matter or circumstance amounting to a hazard for the time being prescribed in regulations made by the Secretary of State under section 2 of the Housing Act 2004.

(3) The definition of 'hazard' in section 2(1) of the Housing Act 2004 applies for the purposes of subsection (2) as though the reference to a potential occupier were omitted.[8]

REPAIRING OBLIGATIONS

Repairing obligations in short leases

11 (1) In a lease to which this section applies (as to which, see sections 13 and 14) there is implied a covenant by the lessor–

(a) to keep in repair the structure and exterior of the dwelling-house (including drains, gutters and external pipes),

(b) to keep in repair and proper working order the installations in the dwelling-house for the supply of water, gas and electricity and for sanitation (including basins, sinks, baths and sanitary conveniences, but not other fixtures, fittings and appliances for making use of the supply of water, gas or electricity), and

(c) to keep in repair and proper working order the installations in the dwelling-house for space heating and heating water.

(1A) If a lease to which this section applies is a lease of a dwelling-house which forms part only of a building, then, subject to subsection (1B), the covenant implied by subsection (1) shall have effect as if–

(a) the reference in paragraph (a) of that subsection to the dwelling-house included a reference to any part of the building in which the lessor has an estate or interest; and

(b) any reference in paragraphs (b) and (c) of that subsection to an installation in the dwelling-house included a reference to an installation which, directly or indirectly, serves the dwelling-house and which either–

(i) forms part of any part of a building in which the lessor has an estate or interest; or

(ii) is owned by the lessor or under his control.[9]

(1B) Nothing in subsection (1A) shall be construed as requiring the lessor to carry out any works or repairs unless the disrepair (or failure to maintain in working order) is such as to affect the lessee's enjoyment of the dwelling-house or of any common parts, as defined in section 60(1) of the Landlord and Tenant Act 1987, which the lessee, as such, is entitled to use.[10]

8 Subss (2), (3) inserted by the Homes (Fitness for Human Habitation) Act 2018 s1(1), (3). In force 20 March 2019: Homes (Fitness for Human Habitation) Act 2018 s2(2).

9 Section 11(1A) added by HA 1988 s116.

10 Section 11(1B) added by HA 1988 s116.

(2) The covenant implied by subsection (1) ('the lessor's repairing covenant') shall not be construed as requiring the lessor–
(a) to carry out works or repairs for which the lessee is liable by virtue of his duty to use the premises in a tenant-like manner, or would be so liable but for an express covenant on his part,
(b) to rebuild or reinstate the premises in the case of destruction or damage by fire, or by tempest, flood or other inevitable accident, or
(c) to keep in repair or maintain anything which the lessee is entitled to remove from the dwelling-house.

(3) In determining the standard of repair required by the lessor's repairing covenant, regard shall be had to the age, character and the dwelling-house and the locality in which it is situated.

(3A) In any case where–
(a) the lessor's repairing covenant has effect as mentioned in subsection (1A), and
(b) in order to comply with the covenant the lessor needs to carry out works or repairs otherwise than in, or to an installation in, the dwelling-house, and
(c) the lessor does not have a sufficient right in the part of the building or the installation concerned to enable him to carry out the required works or repairs,

then, in any proceedings relating to a failure to comply with the lessor's repairing covenant, so far as it requires the lessor to carry out the works or repairs in question, it shall be a defence for the lessor to prove that he used all reasonable endeavours to obtain, but was unable to obtain, such rights as would be adequate to enable him to carry out the works or repairs.[11]

(4) A covenant by the lessee for the repair of the premises is of no effect so far as it relates to the matters mentioned in subsection (1)(a) to (c), except so far as it imposes on the lessee any of the requirements mentioned in subsection (2) (a) or (c).

(5) The reference in subsection (4) to a covenant by the lessee for the repair of the premises includes a covenant–
(a) to put in repair or deliver up in repair,
(b) to paint, point or render,
(c) to pay money in lieu of repairs by the lessee, or
(d) to pay money on account of repairs by the lessor.

(6) In a case in which the lessor's repairing covenant is implied there is also implied a covenant by the lessee that the lessor, or any person authorised by him in writing, may at reasonable times of the day and on giving 24 hours' notice in writing to the occupier, enter the premises comprised in the lease for the purpose of viewing their condition and state of repair.

Restriction on contracting out of s11

12 (1) A covenant or agreement, whether contained in a lease to which section 11 applies or in an agreement collateral to such a lease, is void in so far as it purports–

11 Section 11(3A) added by HA 1988 s116.

(a) to exclude or limit the obligations of the lessor or the immunities of the lessee under that section, or
(b) to authorise any forfeiture or impose on the lessee any penalty, disability or obligation in the event of his enforcing or relying upon those obligations or immunities,

unless the inclusion of the provision was authorised by the county court.

(2) The county court may, by order made with the consent of the parties, authorise the inclusion in a lease, or in an agreement collateral to a lease, of -provisions excluding or modifying in relation to the lease, the provisions of section 11 with respect to the repairing obligations of the parties if it appears to the court that it is reasonable to do so, having regard to all the circumstances of the case, including the other terms and conditions of the lease.

13 Leases to which s11 applies: general rule

(1) Section 11 (repairing obligations) applies to a lease of a dwelling-house granted on or after 24th October 1961 for a term of less than seven years.

(1A) Section 11 also applies to a lease of a dwelling-house in England granted on or after the day on which section 166 of the Localism Act 2011 came into force which is–

(a) a secure tenancy for a fixed term of seven years or more granted by a person within section 80(1) of the Housing Act 1985 (secure tenancies: the landlord condition), or
(b) an assured tenancy for a fixed term of seven years or more that–
  (i) is not a shared ownership lease, and
  (ii) is granted by a private registered provider of social housing.[12]

(1B) In subsection (1A)–

'assured tenancy' has the same meaning as in Part 1 of the Housing Act 1988;

'secure tenancy' has the meaning given by section 79 of the Housing Act 1985; and

'shared ownership lease' means a lease–

(a) granted on payment of a premium calculated by reference to a percentage of the value of the dwelling-house or of the cost of providing it, or
(b) under which the lessee (or the lessee's personal representatives) will or may be entitled to a sum calculated by reference, directly or indirectly, to the value of the dwelling-house.[13]

(2) In determining whether a lease is one to which section 11 applies–

(a) any part of the term which falls before the grant shall be left out of account and the lease shall be treated as a lease for a term commencing with the grant,
(b) a lease which is determinable at the option of the lessor before the expiration of seven years from the commencement of the term shall be treated as a lease for a term of less than seven years, and
(c) a lease (other than a lease to which paragraph (b) applies) shall not be treated as a lease for a term of less than seven years if it confers on the

12 Inserted by Localism Act 2011 s166.
13 Inserted by Localism Act 2011 s166.

lessee an option for renewal for a term which, together with the original term, amounts to seven years or more.

(3) This section has effect subject to–

section 14 (leases to which section 11 applies: exceptions), and

section 32(2) (provisions not applying to tenancies within Part II of the Landlord and Tenant Act 1954).

Leases to which s11 applies: exceptions

14 (1) Section 11 (repairing obligations) does not apply to a new lease granted to an existing tenant, or to a former tenant still in possession, if the previous lease was not a lease to which section 11 applied (and, in the case of a lease granted before 24th October 1961, would not have been if it had been granted on or after that date).

(2) In subsection (1)–

'existing tenant' means a person who is when, or immediately before, the new lease is granted, the lessee under another lease of the dwelling-house;

'former tenant still in possession' means a person who–

(a) was the lessee under another lease of the dwelling-house which terminated at some time before the new lease was granted, and

(b) between the termination of that other lease and the grant of the new lease was continuously in possession of the dwelling-house or of the rents and profits of the dwelling-house; and

'the previous lease' means the other lease referred to in the above definitions.

(3) Section 11 does not apply to a lease of a dwelling-house which is a tenancy of an agricultural holding within the meaning of the Agricultural Holdings Act 1986 and in relation to which that Act applies or to a farm business tenancy within the meaning of the Agricultural Tenancies Act 1995.

(4) Section 11 does not apply to a lease granted on or after 3rd October 1980 to–

a local authority,

a National Park authority

a new town corporation,

an urban development corporation,

a mayoral development,[14]

the Development Board for Rural Wales,

a non-profit registered provider of social housing,[15]

a registered social landlord,

a co-operative housing association, or

an educational institution or other body specified, or of a class specified, by regulations under section 8 of the Rent Act 1977 or paragraph 8 of Schedule 1 to the Housing Act 1988 (bodies making student lettings)

14 Inserted by the Localism Act 2011 s222.

15 Inserted by the Housing and Regeneration Act 2008 (Consequential Provisions) Order 2010 SI No 866.

a housing action trust established under Part III of the Housing Act 1988.

(5) Section 11 does not apply to a lease granted on or after 3rd October 1980 to–
(a) Her Majesty in right of the Crown (unless the lease is under the management of the Crown Estate Commissioners), or
(b) a government department or a person holding in trust for Her Majesty for the purposes of a government department.

Jurisdiction of county court

15 The county court has jurisdiction to make a declaration that section 11 (repairing obligations) applies, or does not apply, to a lease–
(a) whatever the net annual value of the property in question, and
(b) notwithstanding that no other relief is sought than a declaration.

Meaning of 'lease' and related expressions

16 In sections 11 to 15 (repairing obligations in short leases)–
(a) 'lease' does not include a mortgage term;
(b) 'lease of a dwelling-house' means a lease by which a building or part of a building is let wholly or mainly as a private residence, and 'dwelling-house' means that building or part of a building;
(c) 'lessee' and 'lessor' mean, respectively, the person for the time being en-titled to the term of a lease and to the reversion expectant on it.

Specific performance of landlord's repairing obligations

17 (1) In proceedings in which a tenant of a dwelling alleges a breach on the part of his landlord of a repairing covenant relating to any part of the premises in which the dwelling is comprised, the court may order specific performance of the covenant whether or not the breach relates to a part of the premises let to the tenant and notwithstanding any equitable rule restricting the scope of the remedy, whether on the basis of a lack of mutuality or otherwise.

(2) In this section–
(a) 'tenant' includes a statutory tenant,
(b) in relation to a statutory tenant the reference to the premises let to him is to the premises of which he is a statutory tenant,
(c) 'landlord', in relation to a tenant, includes any person against whom the tenant has a right to enforce a repairing covenant, and
(d) 'repairing covenant' means a covenant to repair, maintain, renew, construct or replace any property.

ENVIRONMENTAL PROTECTION ACT 1990 ss79–82

PART III: STATUTORY NUISANCES AND CLEAN AIR

Statutory nuisances

Statutory nuisances and inspections therefor

79 (1) Subject to subsections (1ZA) to (6A) below, the following matters constitute 'statutory nuisances' for the purposes of this Part, that is to say–

(a) any premises in such a state as to be prejudicial to health or a nuisance;

(b) smoke emitted from premises so as to be prejudicial to health or a nuisance;

(c) fumes or gases emitted from premises so as to be prejudicial to health or a nuisance;

(d) any dust, steam, smell or other effluvia arising on industrial, trade or business premises and being prejudicial to health or a nuisance;

(e) any accumulation or deposit which is prejudicial to health or a nuisance;

(f) any animal kept in such a place or manner as to be prejudicial to health or a nuisance;

(fa) any insects emanating from relevant industrial, trade or business premises and being prejudicial to health or a nuisance;

(fb) artificial light emitted from premises so as to be prejudicial to health or a nuisance;

(g) noise emitted from premises so as to be prejudicial to health or a nuisance;

(ga) noise that is prejudicial to health or a nuisance and is emitted from or caused by a vehicle, machinery or equipment in a street or in Scotland, road;

(h) any other matter declared by any enactment to be a statutory nuisance;

and it shall be the duty of every local authority to cause its area to be inspected from time to time to detect any statutory nuisances which ought to be dealt with under section 80 below or sections 80 and 80A below and, where a complaint of a statutory nuisance is made to it by a person living within its area, to take such steps as are reasonably practicable to investigate the complaint.

(1A) No matter shall constitute a statutory nuisance to the extent that it consists of, or is caused by, any land being in a contaminated state.

(1B) Land is in a 'contaminated state' for the purposes of subsection (1A) above if, and only if, it is in such a condition, by reason of substances in, on or under the land, that–

(a) significant harm is being caused or there is a significant possibility of such harm being caused; or

(b) significant pollution of the water environment is being caused or there is a significant possibility of such pollution being caused;

and in this subsection 'harm', 'pollution' in relation to the water environment, 'substance' and 'the water environment' have the same meanings as in Part IIA of this Act.

(2) Subsection (1)(b), (fb), (fba) and (g) above do not apply in relation to premises (or, in respect of paragraph (fba)(ii) above, a stationary object located on premises)–
   (a) occupied on behalf of the Crown for naval, military or air force purposes or for the purposes of the department of the Secretary of State having responsibility for defence, or
   (b) occupied by or for the purposes of a visiting force;
   and 'visiting force' means any such body, contingent or detachment of the forces of any country as is a visiting force for the purposes of any of the provisions of the Visiting Forces Act 1952.

(3) Subsection (1)(b) above does not apply to–
   (i) smoke emitted from a chimney of a private dwelling within a smoke control area,
   (ii) dark smoke emitted from a chimney of a building or a chimney serving the furnace of a boiler or industrial plant attached to a building or for the time being fixed to or installed on any land,
   (iii) smoke emitted from a railway locomotive steam engine, or
   (iv) dark smoke emitted otherwise than as mentioned above from industrial or trade premises.

(4) Subsection (1)(c) above does not apply in relation to premises other than private dwellings.

(5) Subsection (1)(d) above does not apply to steam emitted from a railway locomotive engine.

(5A) Subsection (1)(fa) does not apply to insects that are wild animals included in Schedule 5 to the Wildlife and Countryside Act 1981 (animals which are protected), unless they are included in respect of section 9(5) of that Act only.

(5B) Subsection (1)(fb) does not apply to artificial light emitted from–
   (a) an airport;
   (b) harbour premises;
   (c) railway premises, not being relevant separate railway premises;
   (d) tramway premises;
   (e) a bus station and any associated facilities;
   (f) a public service vehicle operating centre;
   (g) a goods vehicle operating centre;
   (h) a lighthouse;
   (i) a prison.

(5BA) Subsection (1)(fba) above does not apply to artificial light emitted from a lighthouse (within the meaning of Part 8 of the Merchant Shipping Act 1995).

(6) Subsection (1)(g) above does not apply to noise caused by aircraft other than model aircraft.

(6A) Subsection (1)(ga) above does not apply to noise made–
   (a) by traffic,
   (b) by any naval, military or air force of the Crown or by a visiting force (as defined in subsection (2) above), or
   (c) by a political demonstration or a demonstration supporting or opposing a cause or campaign.

(7) In this Part–

'airport' has the meaning given by section 95 of the Transport Act 2000;

'appropriate person' means–

(a) in relation to England, the Secretary of State;

(b) in relation to Wales, the National Assembly for Wales;

'associated facilities', in relation to a bus station, has the meaning given by section 83 of the Transport Act 1985;

'bus station' has the meaning given by section 83 of the Transport Act 1985;

'chimney' includes structures and openings of any kind from or through which smoke may be emitted;

'dust' does not include dust emitted from a chimney as an ingredient of smoke;

'equipment' includes a musical instrument;

'fumes' means any airborne solid matter smaller than dust;

'gas' includes vapour and moisture precipitated from vapour;

'goods vehicle operating centre', in relation to vehicles used under an operator's licence, means a place which is specified in the licence as an operating centre for those vehicles, and for the purposes of this definition 'operating centre' and 'operator's licence' have the same meaning as in the Goods Vehicles (Licensing of Operators) Act 1995;

'harbour premises' means premises which form part of a harbour area and which are occupied wholly or mainly for the purposes of harbour operations, and for the purposes of this definition 'harbour area' and 'harbour operations' have the same meaning as in Part 3 of the Aviation and Maritime Security Act 1990;

'industrial, trade or business premises' means premises used for any industrial, trade or business purposes or premises not so used on which matter is burnt in connection with any industrial, trade or business process, and premises are used for industrial purposes where they are used for the purposes of any treatment or process as well as where they are used for the purposes of manufacturing;

'lighthouse' has the same meaning as in Part 8 of the Merchant Shipping Act 1995;

'local authority' means–

(a) in Greater London, a London borough council, the Common Council of the City of London and, as respects the Temples, the Sub–Treasurer of the Inner Temple and the Under-Treasurer of the -Middle Temple respectively;

(b) in England outside Greater London, a district council;

(bb) in Wales, a county council or county borough council;

(c) the Council of the Isles of Scilly; and

(d) in Scotland, a district or islands council or a council constituted under section 2 of the Local Government etc (Scotland) Act 1994;

'noise' includes vibration;

'person responsible'–

(a) in relation to a statutory nuisance, means the person to whose act, default or sufferance the nuisance is attributable;

(b) in relation to a vehicle, includes the person in whose name the -vehicle is for the time being registered under the Vehicle Excise and -Registration Act 1994 and any other person who is for the time being the driver of the vehicle;
(c) in relation to machinery or equipment, includes any person who is for the time being the operator of the machinery or equipment;

'prejudicial to health' means injurious, or likely to cause injury, to health;

'premises' includes land (subject to subsection (5AB) above) and, subject to subsection (12) and, in relation to England and Wales section 81A(9) below, any vessel;

'prison' includes a young offender institution;

'private dwelling' means any building, or part of a building, used or intended to be used, as a dwelling;

'public service vehicle operating centre', in relation to public service vehicles used under a PSV operator's licence, means a place which is an operating centre of those vehicles, and for the purposes of this definition 'operating centre', 'PSV operator's licence' and 'public service vehicle' have the same meaning as in the Public Passenger Vehicles Act 1981;

'railway premises' means any premises which fall within the definition of 'light maintenance depot', 'network', 'station' or 'track' in section 83 of the Railways Act 1993;

'relevant separate railway premises' has the meaning given by subsection (7A);

'road' has the same meaning as in Part IV of the New Roads and Street Works Act 1991;

'smoke' includes soot, ash, grit and gritty particles emitted in smoke;

'street' means a highway and any other road, footway, square or court that is for the time being open to the public;

'tramway premises' means any premises which, in relation to a tramway, are the equivalent of the premises which, in relation to a railway, fall within the definition of 'light maintenance depot', 'network', 'station' or 'track' in section 83 of the Railways Act 1993;

and any expressions used in this section and in the Clean Air Act 1993 have the same meaning in this section as in that Act and section 3 of the Clean Air Act 1993 shall apply for the interpretation of the expression 'dark smoke' and the operation of this Part in relation to it.

(7A) Railway premises are relevant separate railway premises if–
(a) they are situated within–
(i) premises used as a museum or other place of cultural, scientific or historical interest, or
(ii) premises used for the purposes of a funfair or other entertainment, recreation or amusement, and
(b) they are not associated with any other railway premises.

(7B) For the purposes of subsection (7A)–

(a) a network situated as described in subsection (7A)(a) is associated with other railway premises if it is connected to another network (not being a network situated as described in subsection (7A)(a));
(b) track that is situated as described in subsection (7A)(a) but is not part of a network is associated with other railway premises if it is connected to track that forms part of a network (not being a network situated as described in subsection (7A)(a));
(c) a station or light maintenance depot situated as described in subsection (7A)(a) is associated with other railway premises if it is used in connection with the provision of railway services other than services provided wholly within the premises where it is situated.

In this subsection 'light maintenance depot', 'network', 'railway services', 'station' and 'track' have the same meaning as in Part 1 of the Railways Act 1993.

(7C) In this Part 'relevant industrial, trade or business premises' means premises that are industrial, trade or business premises as defined in subsection (7), but excluding–
(a) land used as arable, grazing, meadow or pasture land,
(b) land used as osier land, reed beds or woodland,
(c) land used for market gardens, nursery grounds or orchards,
(d) land forming part of an agricultural unit, not being land falling within any of paragraphs (a) to (c), where the land is of a description prescribed by regulations made by the appropriate person, and
(e) land included in a site of special scientific interest (as defined in section 52(1) of the Wildlife and Countryside Act 1981),

and excluding land covered by, and the waters of, any river or watercourse, that is neither a sewer nor a drain, or any lake or pond.

(7D) For the purposes of subsection (7C)–
'agricultural' has the same meaning as in section 109 of the Agriculture Act 1947;
'agricultural unit' means land which is occupied as a unit for agricultural purposes;
'drain' has the same meaning as in the Water Resources Act 1991;
'lake or pond' has the same meaning as in section 104 of that Act;
'sewer' has the same meaning as in that Act.

(8) Where, by an order under section 2 of the Public Health (Control of Disease) Act 1984, a port health authority has been constituted for any port health district, the port health authority shall have by virtue of this subsection, as respects its district, the functions conferred or imposed by this Part in relation to statutory nuisances other than a nuisance falling within paragraph (fb), (g) or (ga) of subsection (1) above and no such order shall be made assigning those functions; and 'local authority' and 'area' shall be construed accordingly.

(9) In this Part 'best practicable means' is to be interpreted by reference to the following provisions–
(a) 'practicable' means reasonably practicable having regard among other things to local conditions and circumstances, to the current state of technical knowledge and to the financial implications;

(b) the means to be employed include the design, installation, maintenance and manner and periods of operation of plant and machinery, and the design, construction and maintenance of buildings and structures;
(c) the test is to apply only so far as compatible with any duty imposed by law;
(d) the test is to apply only so far as compatible with safety and safe working conditions, and with the exigencies of any emergency or unforeseeable circumstances;

and, in circumstances where a code of practice under section 71 of the Control of Pollution Act 1974 (noise minimisation) is applicable, regard shall also be had to guidance given in it.

(10) A local authority shall not without the consent of the Secretary of State institute summary proceedings under this Part in respect of a nuisance falling within paragraph (b), (d), (e), (fb) or (g) and, in relation to Scotland, paragraph (ga), of subsection (1) above if proceedings in respect thereof might be instituted under regulations under section 2 of the Pollution Prevention and Control Act 1999 . . .[16]

(11) The area of a local authority which includes part of the seashore shall also include for the purposes of this Part the territorial sea lying seawards from that part of the shore; and subject to subsection (12) and, in relation to England and Wales, section 81A below, this Part shall have effect, in relation to any area included in the area of a local authority by virtue of this subsection–
(a) as if references to premises and the occupier of premises included respectively a vessel and the master of a vessel; and
(b) with such other modifications, if any, as are prescribed in regulations made by the Secretary of State.

(12) A vessel powered by steam reciprocating machinery is not a vessel to which this Part of this Act applies.

Summary proceedings for statutory nuisances

80 (1) Subject to subsection (2A) where a local authority is satisfied that a statutory nuisance exists, or is likely to occur or recur, in the area of the authority, the local authority shall serve a notice ('an abatement notice') imposing all or any of the following requirements–
(a) requiring the abatement of the nuisance or prohibiting or restricting its occurrence or recurrence;
(b) requiring the execution of such works, and the taking of such other steps, as may be necessary for any of those purposes,

and the notice shall specify the time or times within which the requirements of the notice are to be complied with.

(2) Subject to section 80A(1) below, the abatement notice shall be served–
(a) except in a case falling within paragraph (b) or (c) below, on the person responsible for the nuisance;
(b) where the nuisance arises from any defect of a structural character, on the owner of the premises;
(c) where the person responsible for the nuisance cannot be found or the nuisance has not yet occurred, on the owner or occupier of the premises.

16 Words in EPA 1990 s79(10) to be repealed by the Pollution Prevention and Control Act 1999 from a date to be appointed.

(2A) Where a local authority is satisfied that a statutory nuisance falling within paragraph (g) of section 79(1) above exists, or is likely to occur or recur, in the area of the authority, the authority shall–

(a) serve an abatement notice in respect of the nuisance in accordance with subsections (1) and (2) above; or

(b) take such other steps as it thinks appropriate for the purpose of persuading the appropriate person to abate the nuisance or prohibit or restrict its occurrence or recurrence.

(2B) If a local authority has taken steps under subsection (2A)(b) above and either of the conditions in subsection (2C) below is satisfied, the authority shall serve an abatement notice in respect of the nuisance.

(2C) The conditions are–

(a) that the authority is satisfied at any time before the end of the relevant period that the steps taken will not be successful in persuading the appropriate person to abate the nuisance or prohibit or restrict its occurrence or recurrence;

(b) that the authority is satisfied at the end of the relevant period that the nuisance continues to exist, or continues to be likely to occur or recur, in the area of the authority.

(2D) The relevant period is the period of seven days starting with the day on which the authority was first satisfied that the nuisance existed, or was likely to occur or recur.

(2E) The appropriate person is the person on whom the authority would otherwise be required under subsection (2A)(a) above to serve an abatement notice in respect of the nuisance.

(3) A person served with an abatement notice may appeal against the notice to a magistrates' court or in Scotland, the sheriff within the period of twenty-one days beginning with the date on which he was served with the notice.

(4) If a person on whom an abatement notice is served, without reasonable excuse, contravenes or fails to comply with any requirement or prohibition imposed by the notice, he shall be guilty of an offence.

(5) Except in a case falling within subsection (6) below, a person who commits an offence under subsection (4) above shall be liable on summary conviction to a fine not exceeding level 5 on the standard scale together with a further fine of an amount equal to one-tenth of that level for each day on which the offence continues after the conviction.

(6) A person who commits an offence under subsection (4) above on industrial, trade or business premises shall be liable on summary conviction to a fine not exceeding £20,000.

(7) Subject to subsection (8) below, in any proceedings for an offence under subsection (4) above in respect of a statutory nuisance it shall be a defence to prove that the best practicable means were used to prevent, or to counteract the effects of, the nuisance.

(8) The defence under subsection (7) above is not available–

(a) in the case of a nuisance falling within paragraph (a), (d), (e), (f), (fa) or (g) of section 79(1) above except where the nuisance arises on industrial, trade or business premises;

(aza) in the case of a nuisance falling within paragraph (fb) of section 79(1) above except where–

(i) the artificial light is emitted from industrial, trade or business premises, or

(ii) the artificial light (not being light to which sub-paragraph (i) applies) is emitted by lights used for the purpose only of illuminating an outdoor relevant sports facility;

(aa) in the case of a nuisance falling within paragraph (ga) of section 79(1) above except where the noise is emitted from or caused by a vehicle, machinery or equipment being used for industrial, trade or business purposes;

(b) in the case of a nuisance falling within paragraph (b) of section 79(1) above except where the smoke is emitted from a chimney; and

(c) in the case of a nuisance falling within paragraph (c) or (h) of section 79(1) above.

(8A) For the purposes of subsection (8)(aza) a relevant sports facility is an area, with or without structures, that is used when participating in a relevant sport, but does not include such an area comprised in domestic premises.

(8B) For the purposes of subsection (8A) 'relevant sport' means a sport that is designated for those purposes by order made by the Secretary of State, in relation to England, or the National Assembly for Wales, in relation to Wales. A sport may be so designated by reference to its appearing in a list maintained by a body specified in the order.

(8C) In subsection (8A) 'domestic premises' means–

(a) premises used wholly or mainly as a private dwelling, or

(b) land or other premises belonging to, or enjoyed with, premises so used.

(9) In proceedings for an offence under subsection (4) above in respect of a statutory nuisance falling within paragraph (g) or (ga) of section 79(1) above where the offence consists in contravening requirements imposed by virtue of subsection (1)(a) above it shall be a defence to prove–

(a) that the alleged offence was covered by a notice served under section 60 or a consent given under section 61 or 65 of the Control of Pollution Act 1974 (construction sites, etc); or

(b) where the alleged offence was committed at a time when the premises were subject to a notice under section 66 of that Act (noise reduction notice), that the level of noise emitted from the premises at that time was not such as to a constitute a contravention of the notice under that section; or

(c) where the alleged offence was committed at a time when the premises were not subject to a notice under section 66 of that Act, and when a level fixed under section 67 of that Act (new buildings liable to abatement order) applied to the premises, that the level of noise emitted from the premises at that time did not exceed that level.

(10) Paragraphs (b) and (c) of subsection (9) above apply whether or not the relevant notice was subject to appeal at the time when the offence was alleged to have been committed.

Abatement notice in respect of noise in the street

80A(1) In the case of a statutory nuisance within section 79(1)(ga) above that–

(a) has not yet occurred, or

(b) arises from noise emitted from or caused by an unattended vehicle or unattended machinery or equipment, the abatement notice shall be served in accordance with subsection (2) below.

(2) The notice shall be served–

(a) where the person responsible for the vehicle, machinery or equipment can be found, on that person;

(b) where that person cannot be found or where the local authority determines that this paragraph should apply, by fixing the notice to the vehicle, machinery or equipment.

(3) Where–

(a) an abatement notice is served in accordance with subsection (2)(b) above by virtue of a determination of the local authority, and

(b) the person responsible for the vehicle, machinery or equipment can be found and served with a copy of the notice within an hour of the notice being fixed to the vehicle, machinery or equipment,

a copy of the notice shall be served on that person accordingly.

(4) Where an abatement notice is served in accordance with subsection (2)(b) above by virtue of a determination of the local authority, the notice shall state that, if a copy of the notice is subsequently served under subsection (3) above, the time specified in the notice as the time within which its requirements are to be complied with is extended by such further period as is specified in the notice.

(5) Where an abatement notice is served in accordance with subsection (2)(b) above, the person responsible for the vehicle, machinery or equipment may appeal against the notice under section 80(3) above as if he had been served with the notice on the date on which it was fixed to the vehicle, machinery or equipment.

(6) Section 80(4) above shall apply in relation to a person on whom a copy of an abatement notice is served under subsection (3) above as if the copy were the notice itself.

(7) A person who removes or interferes with a notice fixed to a vehicle, machinery or equipment in accordance with subsection (2)(b) above shall be guilty of an offence, unless he is the person responsible for the vehicle, machinery or equipment or he does so with the authority of that person.

(8) A person who commits an offence under subsection (7) above shall be liable on summary conviction to a fine not exceeding level 3 on the standard scale.

Supplementary provisions

81 (1) Subject to subsection (1A) below, where more than one person is responsible for a statutory nuisance section 80 above shall apply to each of those persons whether or not what any one of them is responsible for would by itself amount to a nuisance.

(1A) In relation to a statutory nuisance within section 79(1)(ga) above for which more than one person is responsible (whether or not what any one of those persons is responsible for would by itself amount to such a nuisance), section 80(2)(a) above shall apply with the substitution of 'any one of the persons' for 'the person'.

(1B) In relation to a statutory nuisance within section 79(1)(ga) above caused by noise emitted from or caused by an unattended vehicle or unattended machinery or equipment for which more than one person is responsible,

section 80A above shall apply with the substitution–
(a) in subsection (2)(a), of 'any of the persons' for 'the person' and of 'one such person' for 'that person',
(b) in subsection (2)(b), of 'such a person' for 'that person',
(c) in subsection (3), of 'any of the persons' for 'the person' and of 'one such person' for 'that person',
(d) in subsection (5), of 'any person' for 'the person', and
(e) in subsection (7), of 'a person' for 'the person' and of 'such a person' for 'that person'.

(2) Where a statutory nuisance which exists or has occurred within the area of a local authority, or which has affected any part of that area, appears to the local authority to be wholly or partly caused by some act or default committed or taking place outside the area, the local authority may act under section 80 above as if the act or default were wholly within that area, except that any appeal shall be heard by a magistrates' court or in Scotland, the sheriff having jurisdiction where the act or default is alleged to have taken place.

(3) Where an abatement notice has not been complied with, the local authority may, whether or not–
(a) proceedings have been taken for an offence under section 80(4); or
(b) a fixed penalty notice has been given under section 80(4A) in respect of that offence (regardless of whether the fixed penalty notice is accepted),
abate the nuisance and do whatever may be necessary in execution of the abatement notice.

(4) Any expenses reasonably incurred by a local authority in abating, or preventing the recurrence of, a statutory nuisance under subsection (3) above may be recovered by them from the person by whose act or default the nuisance was caused and, if that person is the owner of the premises, from any person who is for the time being the owner thereof; and the court or sheriff may apportion the expenses between persons by whose acts or defaults the nuisance is caused in such manner as the court consider or sheriff considers fair and reasonable.

(5) If a local authority is of opinion that proceedings for an offence under section 80(4) above would afford an inadequate remedy in the case of any statutory nuisance, they may, subject to subsection (6) below, take proceedings in the High Court or, in Scotland, in any court of competent jurisdiction for the purpose of securing the abatement, prohibition or restriction of the nuisance, and the proceedings shall be maintainable notwithstanding the local authority have suffered no damage from the nuisance.

(6) In any proceedings under subsection (5) above in respect of a nuisance falling within paragraph (g) or (ga) of section 79(1) above, it shall be a defence to prove that the noise was authorised by a notice under section 60 or a consent under section 61 (construction sites) of the Control of Pollution Act 1974.

(7) The further supplementary provisions in Schedule 3 to this Act shall have effect.

Expenses recoverable from owner to be a charge on premises

81A(1) Where any expenses are recoverable under section 81(4) above from a person who is the owner of the premises there mentioned and the local authority serves a notice on him under this section–

(a) the expenses shall carry interest, at such reasonable rate as the local authority may determine, from the date of service of the notice until the whole amount is paid, and

(b) subject to the following provisions of this section, the expenses and accrued interest shall be a charge on the premises.

(2) A notice served under this section shall–

(a) specify the amount of the expenses that the local authority claims is recoverable,

(b) state the effect of subsection (1) above and the rate of interest determined by the local authority under that subsection, and

(c) state the effect of subsections (4) to (6) below.

(3) On the date on which a local authority serves a notice on a person under this section the authority shall also serve a copy of the notice on every other person who, to the knowledge of the authority, has an interest in the premises capable of being affected by the charge.

(4) Subject to any order under subsection (7)(b) or (c) below, the amount of any expenses specified in a notice under this section and the accrued interest shall be a charge on the premises–

(a) as from the end of the period of twenty-one days beginning with the date of service of the notice, or

(b) where an appeal is brought under subsection (6) below, as from the final determination of the appeal,

until the expenses and interest are recovered.

(5) For the purposes of subsection (4) above, the withdrawal of an appeal has the same effect as a final determination of the appeal.

(6) A person served with a notice or copy of a notice under this section may appeal against the notice to the county court within the period of twenty-one days beginning with the date of service.

(7) On such an appeal the court may–

(a) confirm the notice without modification,

(b) order that the notice is to have effect with the substitution of a different amount for the amount originally specified in it, or

(c) order that the notice is to be of no effect.

(8) A local authority shall, for the purpose of enforcing a charge under this section, have all the same powers and remedies under the Law of Property Act 1925, and otherwise, as if it were a mortgagee by deed having powers of sale and lease, of accepting surrenders of leases and of appointing a receiver.

(9) In this section–

'owner', in relation to any premises, means a person (other than a mortgagee not in possession) who, whether in his own right or as trustee for any other person, is entitled to receive the rack rent of the premises or, where the premises are not let at a rack rent, would be so entitled if they were so let, and

'premises' does not include a vessel.

(10) This section does not apply to Scotland.

Payment of expenses by instalments

81B(1) Where any expenses are a charge on premises under section 81A above, the local authority may by order declare the expenses to be payable with interest by instalments within the specified period, until the whole amount is paid.

(2) In subsection (1) above–

'interest' means interest at the rate determined by the authority under section 81A (1) above, and

'the specified period' means such period of thirty years or less from the date of service of the notice under section 81A above as is specified in the order.

(3) Subject to subsection (5) below, the instalments and interest, or any part of them, may be recovered from the owner or occupier for the time being of the premises.

(4) Any sums recovered from an occupier may be deducted by him from the rent of the premises.

(5) An occupier shall not be required to pay at any one time any sum greater than the aggregate of–

(a) the amount that was due from him on account of rent at the date on which he was served with a demand from the local authority together with a notice requiring him not to pay rent to his landlord without deducting the sum demanded, and

(b) the amount that has become due from him on account of rent since that date.

(6) This section does not apply to Scotland.

Summary proceedings by persons aggrieved by statutory nuisances

82 (1) A magistrates' court may act under this section on a complaint or, in Scotland, the sheriff may act under this section on a summary application, made by any person on the ground that he is aggrieved by the existence of a statutory nuisance.

(2) If the magistrates' court or, in Scotland, the sheriff is satisfied that the alleged nuisance exists, or that although abated it is likely to recur on the same premises or, in the case of a nuisance within section 79(1)(ga) above, in the same street or, in Scotland, road, the court or the sheriff shall make an order for either or both of the following purposes–

(a) requiring the defendant or, in Scotland, defender to abate the nuisance, within a time specified in the order, and to execute any works necessary for that purpose;

(b) prohibiting a recurrence of the nuisance, and requiring the defendant or defender, within a time specified in the order, to execute any works necessary to prevent the recurrence;

and, in England and Wales, may also impose on the defendant a fine not exceeding level 5 on the standard scale.

(3) If the magistrates' court or the sheriff is satisfied that the alleged nuisance exists and is such as, in the opinion of the court or of the sheriff, to render premises unfit for human habitation, an order under subsection (2) above may prohibit the use of the premises for human habitation until the premises are, to the satisfaction of the court or of the sheriff, rendered fit for that purpose.

(4) Proceedings for an order under subsection (2) above shall be brought–

(a) except in a case falling within paragraph (b), (c) or (d) below, against the person responsible for the nuisance;

(b) where the nuisance arises from any defect of a structural character, against the owner of the premises;
(c) where the person responsible for the nuisance cannot be found, against the owner or occupier of the premises.
(d) in the case of a statutory nuisance within section 79(1)(ga) above caused by noise emitted from or caused by an unattended vehicle or unattended machinery or equipment, against the person responsible for the vehicle, machinery or equipment.

(5) Subject to subsection (5A) below, where more than one person is responsible for a statutory nuisance, subsections (1) to (4) above shall apply to each of those persons whether or not what any one of them is responsible for would by itself amount to a nuisance.

(5A) In relation to a statutory nuisance within section 79(1)(ga) above for which more than one person is responsible (whether or not what any one of those persons is responsible for would by itself amount to such a nuisance), subsection (4)(a) above shall apply with the substitution of 'each person responsible for the nuisance who can be found' for 'the person responsible for the nuisance'.

(5B) In relation to a statutory nuisance within section 79(1)(ga) above caused by noise emitted from or caused by an unattended vehicle or unattended machinery or equipment for which more than one person is responsible, subsection (4)(d) above shall apply with the substitution of 'any person' for 'the person'.

(6) Before instituting proceedings for an order under subsection (2) above against any person, the person aggrieved by the nuisance shall give to that person such notice in writing of his intention to bring the proceedings as is applicable to proceedings in respect of a nuisance of that description and the notice shall specify the matter complained of.

(7) The notice of the bringing of proceedings in respect of a statutory nuisance required by subsection (6) above which is applicable is–
(a) in the case of a nuisance falling within paragraph (g) or (ga) of section 79(1) above, not less than three days' notice; and
(b) in the case of a nuisance of any other description, not less than twenty-one days' notice;

but the Secretary of State may, by order, provide that this subsection shall have effect as if such period as is specified in the order were the minimum period of notice applicable to any description of statutory nuisance specified in the order.

(8) A person who, without reasonable excuse, contravenes any requirement or prohibition imposed by an order under subsection (2) above shall be guilty of an offence and liable on summary conviction to a fine not exceeding level 5 on the standard scale together with a further fine of an amount equal to one-tenth of that level for each day on which the offence continues after the conviction.

(9) Subject to subsection (10) below, in any proceedings for an offence under subsection (8) above in respect of a statutory nuisance it shall be a defence to prove that the best practicable means were used to prevent, or to counteract the effects of, the nuisance.

(10) The defence under subsection (9) above is not available–

(a) in the case of a nuisance falling within paragraph (a), (d), (e), (f), (fa) or (g) of section 79(1) above except where the nuisance arises on industrial, trade or business premises;

(aa) in the case of a nuisance falling within paragraph (ga) of section 79(1) above except where the noise is emitted from or caused by a vehicle, machinery or equipment being used for industrial, trade or business purposes;

(b) in the case of a nuisance falling within paragraph (b) of section 79(1) above except where the smoke is emitted from a chimney;

(c) in the case of a nuisance falling within paragraph (c) or (h) of section 79(1) above; and

(d) in the case of a nuisance which is such as to render the premises unfit for human habitation.

(10A) For the purposes of subsection (10)(aza) 'relevant sports facility' has the same meaning as it has for the purposes of section 80(8)(aza).

(11) If a person is convicted of an offence under subsection (8) above, a magistrates' court or the sheriff may, after giving the local authority in whose area the nuisance has occurred an opportunity of being heard, direct the authority to do anything which the person convicted was required to do by the order to which the conviction relates.

(12) Where on the hearing of proceedings for an order under subsection (2) above it is proved that the alleged nuisance existed at the date of the making of the complaint or summary application, then, whether or not at the date of the hearing it still exists or is likely to recur, the court or the sheriff shall order the defendant or defender (or defendants or defenders in such proportions as appears fair and reasonable) to pay to the person bringing the proceedings such amount as the court or the sheriff considers reasonably sufficient to compensate him for any expenses properly incurred by him in the proceedings.

(13) If it appears to the magistrates' court or to the sheriff that neither the person responsible for the nuisance nor the owner or occupier of the premises or (as the case may be) the person responsible for the vehicle, machinery or equipment can be found the court or the sheriff may, after giving the local authority in whose area the nuisance has occurred an opportunity of being heard, direct the authority to do anything which the court or the sheriff would have ordered that person to do.

HOUSING ACT 2004 s4

Inspections by local housing authorities to see whether category 1 or 2 hazards exist

4 (1) If a local housing authority consider–
  (a) as a result of any matters of which they have become aware in carrying out their duty under section 3, or
  (b) for any other reason,
 that it would be appropriate for any residential premises in their district to be inspected with a view to determining whether any category 1 or 2 hazard exists on those premises, the authority must arrange for such an inspection to be carried out.

(2) If an official complaint about the condition of any residential premises in the district of a local housing authority is made to the proper officer of the authority, and the circumstances complained of indicate–
  (a) that any category 1 or category 2 hazard may exist on those premises, or
  (b) that an area in the district should be dealt with as a clearance area,
 the proper officer must inspect the premises or area.

(3) In this section 'an official complaint' means a complaint in writing made by–
  (a) a justice of the peace having jurisdiction in any part of the district, or
  (b) the parish or community council for a parish or community within the district.

(4) An inspection of any premises under subsection (1) or (2)–
  (a) is to be carried out in accordance with regulations made by the appropriate national authority; and
  (b) is to extend to so much of the premises as the local housing authority or proper officer (as the case may be) consider appropriate in the circumstances having regard to any applicable provisions of the regulations.

(5) Regulations under subsection (4) may in particular make provision about–
  (a) the manner in which, and the extent to which, premises are to be inspected under subsection (1) or (2), and
  (b) the manner in which the assessment of hazards is to be carried out.

(6) Where an inspection under subsection (2) has been carried out and the proper officer of a local housing authority is of the opinion–
  (a) that a category 1 or 2 hazard exists on any residential premises in the authority's district, or
  (b) that an area in their district should be dealt with as a clearance area,
 the officer must, without delay, make a report in writing to the authority which sets out his opinion together with the facts of the case.

(7) The authority must consider any report made to them under subsection (6) as soon as possible.

APPENDIX B

Pre-Action Protocol for Housing Disrepair Cases[1]

1 INTRODUCTION

1.1 This Protocol applies to residential property situated in England and Wales. It relates to claims by tenants and others in respect of housing disrepair. Before using the Protocol tenants should ensure that their landlord is aware of the disrepair. The Protocol is intended for those cases where, despite the landlords knowledge of the disrepair, the matter remains unresolved.

1.2 This Protocol describes the conduct the court will normally expect prospective parties in a housing disrepair claim to follow prior to the start of proceedings. It is intended to encourage the exchange of information between parties at an early stage and to provide a clear framework within which parties in a housing disrepair claim can attempt to achieve an early and appropriate resolution of the issues.

1.3 If a claim proceeds to litigation, the court will expect all parties to have complied with the Protocol as far as possible. The court has power to order parties who have unreasonably failed to comply with the Protocol to pay costs or to be subject to other sanctions.

2 AIMS

2.1 The aims of this Protocol are to–

(a) avoid unnecessary litigation;

(b) promote the speedy and appropriate carrying out of any repairs which are the landlords responsibility;

(c) ensure that tenants receive any compensation to which they are entitled as speedily as possible;

(d) promote good pre-litigation practice, including the early exchange of information and to give guidance about the instruction of experts; and

(e) keep the costs of resolving disputes down.

1 © Crown Copyright. The Protocol can be found on the procedure rules section of www.justice.gov.uk. Readers should refer to the online version of the Protocol which is being redrafted to incorporate changes introduced by the Homes (Fitness for Human Habitation) Act 2018.

3 THE SCOPE OF THE PROTOCOL

3.1 A disrepair claim is a civil claim arising from the condition of residential premises and may include a related personal injury claim (see 3.5 below). Although most claims are brought by a tenant against their landlord, this Protocol is not limited to such claims. It covers claims by any person with a disrepair claim including tenants, lessees and members of the tenant's family. The use of the word "tenant in this Protocol is intended to cover all such people.

3.2 The types of claim which this Protocol is intended to cover include those brought under section 11 of the Landlord and Tenant Act 1985, section 4 of the Defective Premises Act 1972, common law nuisance and negligence, and those brought under the express terms of a tenancy agreement or lease. It does not cover claims brought under section 82 of the Environmental Protection Act 1990 (which are heard in the Magistrates' Court).

3.3 This Protocol does not cover disrepair claims which originate as counter-claims or set-offs in other proceedings i.e. where the tenant is seeking to have the compensation due for disrepair set against money claimed by the landlord (typically in a possession claim for rent arrears). In such cases the landlord and tenant will still be expected to act reasonably in exchanging information and trying to settle the case at an early stage.

3.4 The Protocol should be followed in all cases, whatever the value of the damages claim.

3.5 Housing disrepair claims may contain a personal injury element. If the personal injury claim requires expert evidence other than a General Practitioners letter, the Personal Injury Protocol should be followed for that element of the disrepair claim. If the personal injury claim is of a minor nature and will only be evidenced by a General Practitioners letter, it is not necessary to follow the Personal Injury Protocol. If the disrepair claim is urgent, it would be reasonable to pursue separate disrepair and personal injury claims, which could then be case managed together or consolidated at a later date.

THE PROTOCOL

4 *Alternative dispute resolution*

4.1 The parties should consider whether some form of alternative dispute resolution procedure would be more suitable than litigation and if so, try to agree which form to use. Both the landlord and the tenant may be required by the court to provide evidence that alternative means of resolving their dispute were considered.

The courts take the view that litigation should be a last resort, and that claims should not be issued while a settlement is still actively being explored. Parties should be aware that the court will take into account the extent of the parties compliance with this Protocol when making orders about who should pay costs.

4.2 Options for resolving a dispute include the following–

(a) mediation: information about mediation can be found at http://www.civilmediation.org/contact.php

(b) for council tenants–

Local authority repairs, complaints and/or arbitration procedures.

The Right to Repair Scheme. The scheme is only suitable for small, urgent repairs of less than £250 in value. Information and leaflets about the scheme in England can be obtained from the Department for Communities and Local Government, Eland House, Bressenden Place, London SW1E 5DU, tel: 0303 444 0000, https://www.gov.uk/repair-council-property.

Information about the scheme in Wales can be obtained from the National Assembly for Wales, Cardiff Bay, Cardiff, CF99 1NA, tel: 0845 010 5500, http://www.assemblywales.org/index.htm.

In England, the Housing Ombudsman Service, 81 Aldwych, London WC2B 4HN, tel: 0300 111 3000, http://www.housing-ombudsman.org.uk/.

In Wales the Public Services Ombudsman for Wales, tel: 0300 790 0203, http://www.ombudsman-wales.org.uk.

(c) for housing association tenants and for tenants of qualifying private landlords–

Any complaints procedure operated by the landlord.

In England, the Housing Ombudsman Service, 81 Aldwych, London. WC2B 4HN, tel: 0300 111 3000, http://www.housing-ombudsman.org.uk/.

In Wales, the National Assembly for Wales, Cardiff Bay, Cardiff, CF99 1NA, tel: 0845 010 5500, http://www.assemblywales.org/index.htm.

Information about repair rights generally is available free of charge from the following web pages: http://england.shelter.org.uk/get_advice/repairs_and_bad_conditions and http://www.communitylegaladvice.org.uk/en/legalhelp/leaflet04_1.jsp.

The former Department for Transport, Local Government and the Regions issued Good Practice Guidance on Housing Disrepair Legal Obligations in January 2002. Copies of the Guidance (ISBN 185112523X) can be obtained from Communities and Local Government Publications, PO Box 236, Wetherby LS23 7NB, tel: 0300 123 1124, fax: 0300 123 1125, textphone: 0870 1207 405, e-mail:product@communities.gsi.gov.uk. (free to download from the Communities and Local Government website at http://www.communities.gov.uk/publications/housing/deliveringhousingadaptations2).

A summary, Housing Research Summary No. 154, is available free on the Communities and Local Government website at the following link http://www.communities.gov.uk/archived/publications/housing/housingdisrepair. The Communities and Local Government website http://www.communities.gov.uk is a general source of information for landlords and tenants.

5 Tenant's Letter of Claim

5.1 It is recognised that disrepair cases can range from straightforward to highly complex, and that it is not always possible to obtain detailed information at an early stage. In order to avoid unnecessary delay and to ensure that notice of the claim is given to the landlord at the earliest possible opportunity, particularly where repairs are urgent, it may be appropriate for the tenant to send a letter notifying the landlord of the claim before a detailed Letter of Claim is sent.

5.2 The tenant should send to the landlord a Letter of Claim at the earliest reasonable opportunity. A specimen Letter of Claim is at Annex A. The letter may be suitably adapted as appropriate. The Letter of Claim should contain the following details–

(a) the tenant's name, the address of the property, the tenant's address if different, the tenant's telephone number and when access is available;
(b) details of the defects, including any defects outstanding, in the form of a schedule, if appropriate (See Annex C for a specimen schedule which can be used to inform the landlord of the disrepair);
(c) history of the defects, including any attempts to rectify them;
(d) details of any notification previously given to the landlord of the need for repair or information as to why the tenant believes that the landlord has knowledge of the need for repair;
(e) the effect of the defects on the tenant (including any personal injury claim by the tenant);
(f) the identities of all other persons who plan to make a personal injury claim and brief details of their personal injury claims;
(g) the details of any special damages (see the form at Annex D);
(h) the proposed expert (see paragraph 7);
(i) the proposed letter of instruction to the expert (see Annex B); and
(j) relevant documents disclosed by the tenant.

5.3 The Letter of Claim should also request disclosure from the landlord of all documents relevant to the disrepair including–

(a) a copy of the tenancy agreement including the tenancy conditions;
(b) the tenancy file;
(c) any documents relating to notice of disrepair given, including copies of any notes of meetings and oral discussions;
(d) any inspection reports or documents relating to works required to the property; and
(e) any computerised records.

5.4 Documents relating to rent arrears or other tenancy issues will not normally be relevant. Nothing in the Protocol restricts the right of the tenant to look personally at their file or to request a copy of the whole file. Neither is the landlord prevented from sending to the tenant a copy of the whole file, should the landlord wish.

5.5 A copy of the Protocol should be sent to the landlord if the tenant has reason to believe that the landlord will not have access to the Protocol e.g. because the landlord is an individual or small organisation. If in doubt, a copy should be sent.

6 Landlord's response

6.1 Where a landlord is not an individual, a person should be designated to act as a point of contact for the tenant (and their solicitor, if one is involved). The designated persons name and contact details should be sent to the tenant and their solicitor as soon as possible after the landlord receives the Letter of Claim from the tenant.

6.2 The landlord should normally reply to the Letter of Claim within 20 working days of receipt. Receipt is deemed to have taken place two days after the date of the letter. The landlord's response should include at least the following–

(a) copies of all relevant records or documents requested by the tenant; and
(b) a response to the tenant's proposals for instructing an expert including–
  i. whether or not the proposed single joint expert is agreed;
  ii. whether the letter of instruction is agreed;
  iii. if the single joint expert is agreed but with separate instructions, a copy of the letter of instruction; and
  iv. if the appointment of a single joint expert is not agreed, whether the landlord agrees to a joint inspection.

6.3 The landlord must also provide a response dealing with the issues set out below, as appropriate. This can be provided either within the response to the Letter of Claim or within 20 working days of receipt of the report of the single joint expert or receipt of the experts agreed schedule following a joint inspection–
(a) whether liability is admitted and, if so, in respect of which defects;
(b) if liability is disputed in respect of some or all of the defects, the reasons for this;
(c) any point which the landlord wishes to make regarding lack of notice of the disrepair or any difficulty in gaining access;
(d) a full schedule of intended works, including anticipated start and completion dates and a timetable for the works;
(e) any offer of compensation; and
(f) any offer in respect of costs.

6.4 Failure to respond within 20 working days of receipt of the Letter of Claim or at all, is a breach of the Protocol (see paragraph 1.3) and the tenant is then free to issue proceedings.

6.5 The Letter of Claim and the landlords response are not intended to have the same status as a statement of case in court proceedings. Matters may come to light subsequently which mean that the case of one or both parties may be presented differently in court proceedings. Parties should not seek to take advantage of such discrepancies provided that there was no intention to mislead.

7 Experts

7.1 *General*

(a) Parties are reminded that the Civil Procedure Rules provide that expert evidence should be restricted to that which is necessary and that the courts permission is required to use an experts report. The court may limit the amount of experts fees and expenses recoverable from another party.
(b) When instructing an expert, the parties must have regard to CPR Practice Direction 35 and the Guidance for the Instruction of Experts in Civil Claims 2014 at http:www.judiciary.gov.uk.
(c) In some cases it might not be necessary to instruct an expert to provide evidence of disrepair, for example, if the only issue relates to the level of any damages claimed. It may be advisable for tenants to take photographs or video footage of any defects before and after works.
(d) The expert should be instructed to report on all items of disrepair which the landlord ought reasonably to know about, or which the expert

ought reasonably to report on. The expert should be asked to provide a schedule of works, an estimate of the costs of repair, and to list any urgent works.

7.2 *Single joint expert*

(a) If the landlord does not raise an objection to the proposed expert or letter of instruction within 20 working days of receipt of the Letter of Claim, the expert should be instructed as a single joint expert, using the tenant's proposed letter of instruction. (See Annex B for a specimen letter of instruction to an expert.)

(b) Alternatively, if the parties cannot agree joint instructions, the landlord and tenant should send their own separate instructions to the single joint expert. If sending separate instructions, the landlord should send the tenant a copy of the landlord's letter of instruction with their response to the Letter of Claim.

7.3 *Joint inspection*

(a) If it is not possible to reach agreement to instruct a single joint expert, even with separate instructions, the parties should attempt to arrange a joint inspection, meaning an inspection by different experts instructed by each party to take place at the same time. If the landlord wishes their own expert to attend a joint inspection, they should inform both the tenant's expert and the tenant's solicitor.

(b) Should a case come before the court, it will be for the court to decide whether the parties have acted reasonably in instructing separate experts and whether the costs of more than one expert should be recoverable.

7.4 *Time limits*

(a) Whether a single joint expert or a joint inspection is used, the property should be inspected within 20 working days of the date that the landlord responds to the tenant's Letter of Claim.

(b) If a single joint expert is instructed, a copy of the experts report should be sent to both the landlord and the tenant within 10 working days of the inspection. Either party can ask relevant questions of the expert who should send the answers to both parties.

(c) If there is a joint inspection, the experts should produce an agreed schedule of works detailing–

  i. the defects and required works which are agreed and a timetable for the agreed works

  ii. the areas of disagreement and the reasons for disagreement.

(d) The agreed schedule should be sent to both the landlord and the tenant within 10 working days of the joint inspection.

Urgent cases

7.5 The Protocol does not prevent a tenant from instructing an expert at an earlier stage if this is considered necessary for reasons of urgency. Appropriate cases may include–

(a) where the tenant reasonably considers that there is a significant risk to health and safety;

(b) where the tenant is seeking an interim injunction;
(c) where it is necessary to preserve evidence.

Access

7.6 Tenants must allow the landlord reasonable access for inspection and repair in accordance with the tenancy agreement. The landlord should give reasonable notice of the need for access, except in the case of an emergency. The landlord must give access to common parts as appropriate, for example, for the inspection of a shared heating system. If the tenant is no longer in occupation of the premises the landlord should take all reasonable steps to give access to the tenant for the purpose of an inspection.

7.7 *Expert's fees*

(a) Experts terms of appointment should be agreed at the outset, including the basis of charging and time for delivery of the report.
(b) If a single joint expert is instructed, each party will pay one half of the cost of the report. If a joint inspection is carried out, each party will pay the full cost of the report from their own expert.

7.8 Information about independent experts can be obtained from–

(a) The Chartered Institute of Environmental Health, Chadwick Court, 15 Hatfields, London, SE1 8DJ, tel: 020 7928 6006, http://www.cieh.org/about_us.html. Ask for a copy of the Consultants and Trainers Directory;
(b) The Expert Witness Directory http://www.sweetandmaxwell.co.uk/our-businesses/directories.aspx.
(c) The Royal Institution of Chartered Surveyors, 12 Great George Street, Parliament Square, London, SW1P 3AD, tel: 024 7686 8555, http://www.ricsfirms.com/Ask for a copy of the relevant regional directory.

Taking stock

8 Where the procedure set out in this Protocol has not resolved the dispute between the landlord and the tenant, they should undertake a review of their respective positions to see if proceedings can be avoided and, at the least, to narrow the issues between them.

9 *Time limits*

(a) The time scales given in the Protocol are long stops and every attempt should be made to comply with the Protocol as soon as possible. If parties are able to comply earlier than the time scales provided, they should do so.
(b) Time limits in the Protocol may be changed by agreement. However, it should always be borne in mind that the court will expect an explanation as to why the Protocol has not been followed or has been varied and breaches of the Protocol may lead to costs or other orders being made by the court.

10 *Limitation period*

(a) There are statutory time limits for starting proceedings (the limitation period). If a tenant starts a claim after the limitation period applicable to that type of claim has expired, the landlord will be entitled to use that as a defence to the claim. In cases where the limitation period is about to expire, the tenant should ask the landlord to agree not to rely on a limitation defence, so that the parties can comply with the Protocol.

(b) If proceedings have to be started before the parties have complied with the Protocol, they should apply to the court for an order to stay (i.e. suspend) the proceedings until the steps under the Protocol have been completed.

Costs

11 If the tenant's claim is settled without litigation on terms which justify bringing it, the landlord will pay the tenant's reasonable costs. The Statement of Costs Form N260 available on the HMCTS website can be used to inform the landlord of the costs of the claim.

ANNEXES

12 The following documents are annexed to this pre-action protocol–

[. . .]

ANNEX A – LETTER OF CLAIM

(a) *Letter from solicitor*
To Landlord

Dear Sirs,
RE: TENANT'S NAME AND ADDRESS OF PROPERTY
We are instructed by your above named tenant. (Where the tenant is legally aided or a party to a conditional fee agreement entered into before 1 April 2013 insert a sentence stating how their case is being funded.) We are using the Housing Disrepair Protocol. We enclose a copy of the Protocol for your information.*

Repairs

Your tenant complains of the following defects at the property (set out nature of defects).

We enclose a schedule which sets out the disrepair in each room.*

The history of the disrepair is as follows: (set out history of defects)

You received notice of the defects as follows: (list details of notice relied on).

The defects at the property are causing (set out the effects of the disrepair on the client and their family, including any personal injury element. Specify if there will be any additional claimants).

Please arrange to inspect the property as soon as possible. Access will be available on the following dates and times: (list dates and times as appropriate)

Please confirm whether you intend to carry out repairs at this stage or whether you wish to wait until the property has been inspected by the expert(s) as set out below.

If you intend to carry out repairs at this stage, please set out a full schedule of intended works including anticipated start and completion dates and a timetable for the works

Disclosure

Please also provide within 20 working days of this letter the following:

All relevant records or documents including:

(i) a copy of the tenancy agreement including the tenancy conditions
(ii) the tenancy file
(iii) documents relating to notice of disrepair given, including copies of any notes of meetings and oral discussions
(iv) inspection reports or documents relating to works required to the property.
(iv) computerised records

We enclose a signed authority from our client for you to release this information to us.

We also enclose copies of the following relevant documents from our client:

Expert

If agreement is not reached about the carrying out of repairs within 20 working days of this letter, we propose that the parties agree to jointly instruct a single joint expert (insert experts name and address) to carry out an inspection of the property and provide a report. We enclose a copy of their CV, plus a draft letter of instruction.

Please let us know if you agree to his/her appointment. If you object, please let us know your reasons within 20 working days.

If you do not object to the expert being instructed as a single joint expert, but wish to provide your own instructions, you should send those directly to (insert experts name) within 20 working days of this letter. Please send us a copy of your letter of instruction. If you do not agree to a single joint expert, we will instruct (insert experts name) to inspect the property in any event. In those circumstances, if you wish to instruct your expert to attend at the same time, please let us and (insert experts name) know within 20 working days.

Claim

We take the view that you are in breach of your repairing obligations. Please provide us with your proposals for compensation. (Alternatively, set out suggestions for general damages i.e. £x for x years).

Our client also requires compensation for special damages, and we attach a schedule of the special damages claimed.*

Yours faithfully,

* Delete as appropriate

ANNEX A: LETTER OF CLAIM

(b) *Letter from tenant*

To Landlord

Dear Sirs,

RE: YOUR NAME AND ADDRESS OF PROPERTY

I write regarding disrepair at the above address. I am using the Housing Disrepair Protocol.

I enclose a copy of the Protocol for your information. *

Repairs

The following defects exist at the property (set out nature of defects).

I enclose a schedule which sets out the disrepair in each room.*

The history of the disrepair is as follows: (set out history of defects)

You received notice of the defects as follows: (list details of notice relied on).

The defects at the property are causing (set out the effects of the disrepair on you and your family, including any personal injury element. Specify if there will be any additional claimants).

Please arrange to inspect the property as soon as possible. Access will be available on the following dates and times: (list dates and times as appropriate)

Please confirm whether you intend to carry out repairs at this stage or whether you wish to wait until the property has been inspected by the expert(s) as set out below.

If you intend to carry out repairs at this stage, please set out a full schedule of intended works including anticipated start and completion dates and a timetable for the works.

Disclosure

Please also provide within 20 working days of this letter the following:

All relevant records or documents including:

(i) a copy of the tenancy agreement including the tenancy conditions;
(ii) the tenancy file;
(iii) documents relating to notice of disrepair given, including copies of any notes of meetings and oral discussions;
(iv) inspection reports or documents relating to works required to the property;
(iv) computerised records.

I enclose copies of the following relevant documents:

Expert

If agreement is not reached about the carrying out of repairs within 20 working days of this letter, I propose that we jointly instruct a single joint expert (insert experts name and address) to carry out an inspection of the property and provide a report. I enclose a copy of their CV, plus a draft letter of instruction. Please let me know if you agree to his/her appointment. If you object, please let me know your reasons within 20 working days.

If you do not object to the expert being instructed as a single joint expert, but wish to provide your own instructions, you should send those directly to (insert experts name) within 20 working days of this letter. Please send me a copy of your letter of instruction. If you do not agree to a single joint expert, I will instruct (insert experts name) to inspect the property in any event. In those circumstances, if you wish to instruct your expert to attend at the same time, please let me and (insert experts name) know within 20 working days.

Claim

I take the view that you are in breach of your repairing obligations. Please provide me with your proposals for compensation. (Alternatively, set out suggestions for general damages i.e. £x for x years). I also require compensation for special damages, and I attach a schedule of the special damages claimed.*

Yours faithfully,

* Delete as appropriate

ANNEX B: LETTER OF INSTRUCTION TO EXPERT

(a) *Letter from solicitor*

Dear

RE: TENANT'S NAME AND ADDRESS OF PROPERTY

We act for the above named in connection with a housing disrepair claim at the above property.

We are using the Housing Disrepair Protocol.

We enclose a copy of the Protocol for your information.*

Please carry out an inspection of the above property by (date)** and provide a report covering the following points:

(a) whether you agree that the defects are as claimed;
(b) whether any of the defects is structural;
(c) the cause of the defect(s);
(d) the age, character and prospective life of the property;
(e) a schedule of works;
(f) an estimate of the costs of repair.

Access will be available on the following dates and times: (list dates and times as appropriate).

You are instructed as a single joint expert / The landlord is (landlords name and details) / The landlord will be providing you with their own instructions direct / The landlord will contact you to confirm that their expert will attend at the same time as you to carry out a joint inspection.*

Please provide the report within 14 days of the inspection. Please contact us immediately if there are any works which require an interim injunction.

If the case proceeds to court, the report may be used in evidence. Please ensure that the report complies with Civil Procedure Rules Practice Direction 35.3 and the Guidance for the Instruction of Experts in Civil Claims 2014 at http:www.judiciary.gov.uk.

If you do not have a copy please let us know.

Insert details as to cost and payment

Yours sincerely,

* Delete as appropriate
** The date to be inserted should be 20 working days from the date of the letter

ANNEX B: LETTER OF INSTRUCTION TO EXPERT

(b) *Letter from tenant*

Dear

RE: YOUR NAME AND ADDRESS OF PROPERTY

I am currently in dispute with my landlord about disrepair at the above property. I am using the Housing Disrepair Protocol.

I enclose a copy of the Protocol for your information.*

Please carry out an inspection of the above property by (date)** and provide a report covering the following points:

(a) whether you agree that the defects are as claimed;
(b) whether any of the defects is structural;
(c) the cause of the defect(s);
(d) the age, character and prospective life of the property;
(e) a schedule of works;
(f) an estimate of the costs of repair.

Access will be available on the following dates and times: (list dates and times as appropriate)

You are instructed as a single joint expert / The landlord is (landlords name and details) / The landlord will be providing you with their own instructions direct / The landlord will contact you to confirm that their expert will attend at the same time as you to carry out a joint inspection.*

Please provide the report within 14 days of the inspection. Please contact me immediately if there are any works which require an interim injunction.

If the case proceeds to court, the report may be used in evidence. Please ensure that the report complies with Civil Procedure Rules Practice Direction 35.3 and the Guidance for the Instruction of Experts in Civil Claims 2014 at http:www.judiciary.gov.uk. If you do not have a copy please let me know.

Insert details as to cost and payment

Yours sincerely,

* Delete as appropriate

** The date to be inserted should be 20 working days from the date of the letter

ANNEX C: HOUSING DISREPAIR PROTOCOL–SCHEDULE OF DISREPAIR

Schedule
Disrepair Protocol

TENANT

	Item Number	Room (tick where appropriate	Disrepair (identify briefly)	Notice given (How was the landlord made aware of the problem)	Inconvenience suffered (How has the disrepair affected you)
Exterior of premises, roof and access Comment: Entrance, hall and storage Comment: Living room (s) Comment: Kitchen Comment: Bathroom Comment: Bedroom 1 Comment: Bedroom 2 Comment: Bedroom 3 Comment: Other Comment					

ANNEX D: HOUSING DISREPAIR PROTOCOL–SPECIAL DAMAGES FORM

	ITEM	DATE PURCHASED	WHERE PURCHASED	PRICE	RECEIPTS – YES/NO	HOW DAMAGED
1						
2						
3						
4						
5						
6						
7						
8						
9						
10						

APPENDIX C

Precedents

Introduction

This appendix contains precedent documentation for a routine case about housing conditions in which the tenant:

(1) brings a claim for damages in the county court (see chapter 3); or

(2) brings proceedings in the magistrates' court under the Environmental Protection Act (EPA) 1990 s82 (see chapter 6); or

(3) asks for an official complaint to be made under the Housing Act (HA) 2004.

It is assumed that, before launching the proceedings, the tenant's advisers have taken the preliminary steps recommended in this book.

The facts

Anna Tennant lives with her five-year-old son in a two-bedroom flat on the fourth (top) floor of a purpose-built council block. She has been the tenant for five years. Throughout the tenancy the flat has been damp. There are damp patches on the ceilings of the small bedroom and kitchen and rain-water penetration around the windows. The bathroom and kitchen walls are covered with black mould and the flat suffers from a cockroach infestation. There are other defects. Her rent is £160 per week and all but the water rates element is paid by housing benefit.

She has complained frequently to the council's housing officer, reported the defects at the neighbourhood housing office and seen her councillor, but only limited (and largely 'botched') remedial work has been undertaken.

There are alleged rent arrears of £750.

With her son in declining health, Anna turns to the Rainbow Community Law Centre for help.

As Anna's tenancy is already in existence at the date that Landlord and Tenant Act 1985 s9A came into force, no claim can be made under that provision until 20 March 2020. However, the relevant amendments which might be made are stated in parentheses in the appropriate parts of the precedents, were she to bring this claim after that date. An amendment is also included for a new tenancy beginning from 20 March 2019.

County court proceedings (see chapter 3)

1 QUESTIONNAIRE CHECKLIST

INFORMATION AND DOCUMENTS NEEDED FROM YOU[1] FOR YOUR CLAIM

1 Defects

For each defect please let us[2] know:

- ☐ The precise nature of each defect (eg, water penetration)
- ☐ Location (eg, in the lounge)
- ☐ The date when you first noticed this
- ☐ Details of any remedial works done by you including the date and cost
- ☐ Any remedial works done by your landlord including the date and whether these were effective

2 Complaints to your landlord

For each defect we need to know:

- ☐ When this was first reported to your landlord
- ☐ Who reported this (eg, you, member of your family, social worker etc)
- ☐ To whom you reported this (eg, housing officer, surveyor) and how this was done (eg, by telephone, letter or by visiting your housing office)
- ☐ Similar details in respect of subsequent complaints to your landlord
- ☐ Details of any visits by your landlord including the dates and person who visited

3 The effects of the defects on you and your family

We need to know how you and your family were affected by the defects which will include, for example:

- ☐ The nature of the inconvenience or discomfort resulting from the defect (eg, unable to use the lounge for six months, ashamed to invite friends and relatives around etc)
- ☐ The effect on the physical health of you and your family
- ☐ The effect on the mental health of you and your family

4 Financial loss

You may have suffered financial loss as a result of the defects which include:

- Increased heating costs, in which case please let us know:
  - ☐ Type of heating used
  - ☐ Rooms affected
  - ☐ Period of claim

1 ie, the tenant.

2 ie, the tenant's adviser.

   - ☐ Cost in previous comparative period (eg, previous winter when there were no defects)
   - ☐ Copies of all bills for the period of claim and previous comparative period
- Specific items damaged, eg, furniture, carpets, clothes, etc. Please fill in the attached list.
- Redecoration costs – please let us know:
   - ☐ Which rooms were affected
   - ☐ Date of redecoration costs (with receipts if possible)
- Any other financial losses and expenses such as increased telephone bills, travel, cleaning expenses, costs of eating out of the home. Where possible please provide receipts or bills.

5 Documents

Please provide all documents that you have in your possession relating to your case. These may include:

☐ Any letters or notes concerning arrangements before the tenancy commenced.
☐ The original signed tenancy agreement.
☐ Any documents handed to you with the tenancy agreement.
☐ Any notices of rent increase.
☐ Any notices concerning housing benefit.
☐ Any Notices to Quit or Notices of Intention to Seek Possession.
☐ Old and current rent books.
☐ Any copy rent accounts or rent statements.
☐ Any receipts relating to costs incurred by you as a result of the condition of your home.
☐ All letters, texts, emails and notes sent by you or received by you in connection with the tenancy since you have been a tenant.
☐ Correspondence with Councillors and/or MPs, if these relate to the tenancy.
☐ Gas, electricity bills, etc.
☐ Diaries and notes that you have kept of dealings with your landlord.
☐ Any other relevant documents.

2 LETTER OF CLAIM

To Landlord

Dear Sir or Madam,

Anna Tennant, 17 Tower House, Moors Estate,
Anytown North Neighbourhood Office

We are instructed by your above named tenant. We are using the Housing Disrepair Protocol [and the tenant is being funded with legal aid].[2] [We enclose a copy of the Protocol for your information].[3]

Defects

Your tenant complains of the following defects at the property:
[*set out nature of defects, eg:*

- *perished wall plaster and mould growth in the kitchen;*
- *wet patches on the ceilings of the small bedroom and kitchen;*
- *mould growth on the walls of the bathroom and kitchen, caused or exacerbated by water penetration;*
- *rainwater penetration around the kitchen windows; and*
- *the flat suffers from a cockroach infestation.]*

[We enclose a schedule which sets out the defects in each room].[4]

If you intend to carry out remedial works at this stage, please set out a full schedule of intended works including anticipated start and completion dates and a timetable for the works.

History of the defects [*eg*

- *the leaks around the kitchen windows have been present since our client's tenancy began in 2014;*
- *there has been a problem with mould growth in the bathroom and kitchen since the winter of 2016;*
- *the stains on the ceilings of the small bedroom and kitchen first appeared in March 2016 but have become much worse in 2019; and*
- *there have been intermittent cockroach infestations since 2014 but the most recent infestation started in about November 2018.]*

Your knowledge of the defects*:*

[list details of notice relied on eg:

- *since March 2014 Ms Tennant has complained frequently by telephone to your housing office on numerous occasions;*

2 Omit if appropriate (there is no need to give details of CFA funding if the CFA was signed after 1 April 2015).

3 Omit if the landlord is likely to be well familiar with the protocol.

4 Optional but this can be in the format used in annex C of the disrepair protocol. See appendix B.

- *the property has been inspected by your officers Ms Jane Grant in about March 2018 and Mrs Pamela Griffiths in late June 2018;*
- *in or about August 2018 your technical officer visited the premises and carried out an inspection;*
- *in about September 2018 our client reported the problems to counsellor Timothy Thorogood; and*
- *in October 2018 our client brought a jar full of cockroaches into your Anytown North neighbourhood housing office and left it on the counter, she apologises for her behaviour which was a result of her desperation.]*

Inspection

Please arrange to inspect the property as soon as possible. Access can be arranged directly with our client on telephone number: [number].

Please confirm whether you intend to carry out works at this stage or whether you wish to wait until the property has been inspected by the expert(s) as set out below.

Expert

If agreement is not reached about the carrying out of works within 20 working days of this letter, we propose that the parties agree to jointly instruct a single joint expert to carry out an inspection of the property and provide a report. We propose:

Maria Expert MIEH
Experts EHC Ltd
Robertsbridge Road
Anytown AT24 3PL

We enclose a copy of her CV, plus a draft letter of instruction.

Please let us know if you agree to her appointment. If you object, please let us know your reasons within 20 working days.

If you do not object to Ms Expert being instructed as a single joint expert, but wish to provide your own instructions, you should send those directly to Ms Expert within 20 working days of this letter. Please send us a copy of your letter of instruction. If you do not agree to a single joint expert, we will instruct Ms Expert to inspect the property in any event. In those circumstances, if you wish to instruct your own expert to attend at the same time, please let us and Ms Expert know within 20 working days.

Disclosure

Please provide within 20 working days of the date of this letter the following:

All relevant records or documents including:

(i) a copy of the tenancy agreement including the current tenancy conditions;
(ii) the tenancy file;
(iii) documents relating to notice of defects given, including copies of any notes of meetings and oral discussions;

(iv) inspection reports or documents relating to works required to the property; and
(iv) computerised records.

We enclose a signed authority from our client for you to release this information to us.

We also enclose copies of the following relevant documents from our client: *(eg:*
(i) prints of text messages requesting repairs;
(ii) a copy of a letter sent to you by our client's MP;
(ii) photos taken a year ago;
(iii) photos taken last month; and
(iii) any other relevant documents).

Claim

(set out the effects of the defects on the tenant and their family, including any personal injury element. Specify if there will be any additional claimants, eg

Since March 2015 there has been a pervading smell of dampness throughout the flat. Ms Tennant has cleaned mould off the walls regularly in cold weather, only to see it return within a matter of days. Her decorations in the kitchen, bedroom and bathroom have been spoiled. She has suffered distress which has been worsened by lack of response to her complaints. The cockroach infestation has terrified her and she has not prepared food in the flat since November 2018. She claims additional heating costs, the cost of eating ready meals and the cost of additional cleaning materials.)

We take the view that you are in breach of your repairing obligations. Please provide us with your proposals for compensation. *(Alternatively, set out suggestions for general damages, ie £x for x years).*

[Our client also requires compensation for special damages, and we attach a schedule of the special damages claimed].[5]

Yours faithfully,

5 Delete if inappropriate.

3 CHRONOLOGY[6]

Anna Tennant – 17 Towers House, Moors Estate, Anytown
Entries in ordinary font relate to documents produced by Ms Tennant.

Entries in italics relate to entries produced by Anytown District Council (DC), as part of pre-action disclosure.

Date	*Event*	*Source and Comment*
09.01.14	Start of tenancy, Anna Tennant (AT) and Anytown DC (DC))	Tenancy file
Early 2015	AT notices dampness on ceiling in small bedroom, reports it to DC, reports gap above living room window frame	
01.03.15	Approx date: AT complains of cock-roach infestation	
09.12.15	*Computer entry: tenant complaining of damp and insects*	*Maintenance file*
2016	Ineffective works to kitchen window	
22.11.16	*Arrears letter DC to AT – arrears £280.86*	*Tenancy file*
01.02.18	Approx date: inspection by housing officer (Ms Grant)	
31.05.18	Approx date: inspection by housing officer (Mrs Griffiths)	
29.07.18	Technical officer from DC calls and inspects. Tells AT he suspects roof leaks.	
15.11.18	Inspection by Ms Expert	
29.11.18	Ms Expert's report sent to DC	

6 A chronology will not be necessary in every case.

4 LIST OF ITEMS DAMAGED OR DESTROYED BY DISREPAIR OR DEFECTS

No.	Quantity	Description	Nature of damage	Approx. date of damage	Date bought	Price paid £	Do you have the original receipt?	Cost to replace it today £	Do you have a written estimate?
1.									
2.									
3.									
4.									
5.									
6.									
7.									
8.									
9.									
10.									
11.									
12.									
13.									
14.									
etc									

5 PARTICULARS OF CLAIM

Note: the part in italics should be omitted if there is no infestation. The parts in parentheses are only relevant to unfitness claims for new tenancies from 20 March 2019, and for existing tenancies after 20 March 2020.

In County Court at Anytown Case No: 9AT04723

BETWEEN

ANNA TENNANT Claimant

and

ANYTOWN DISTRICT COUNCIL Defendant

PARTICULARS OF CLAIM

1. In or about January 2014 the Claimant was granted a secure tenancy of 17 Tower House, Moors Estate, Anytown ('the premises') by the Defendant.
2. The premises consist of a two-bedroom flat on the fourth floor of a block of flats. *Surrounding the parts of the premises demised to the Claimant are service ducts, common parts and other parts of the structure and exterior of the block which constitute land retained by the Defendant.*
3. The premises have at all material times been occupied by the Claimant and her son Jeremy who was born on 3 December 2013. The current rent is £160 per week.
4. The Claimant has at all material times been entitled to the benefit of:
   a) Express repairing obligations. A copy of the relevant terms of the tenancy agreement is filed with these Particulars.
   b) A term implied by section 11 of the Landlord and Tenant Act 1985.
   c) A term implied by section 11A of the Landlord and Tenant Act 1985.
   d) An implied term that the Defendant would give the Claimant quiet enjoyment of the premises.
   e) An implied term that the Defendant would ensure that the parts retained in its possession and control remain reasonably safe and do not cause damage to the Claimant or the flat.
   f) An implied term that the Defendant would carry out works of repair or improvement in a proper manner and with proper materials.
   g) An implied term that the Defendant would make good and would redecorate on completing all work done further to its obligations and duties.
5. [In addition, section 9A of the Landlord and Tenant Act 1985 has implied a term into the tenancy agreement that the premises are fit for human habitation.]
   [Alternatively, for a new tenancy – In addition, section 9A of the Landlord and Tenant Act 1985 implies a term into the tenancy agreement that the premises were fit for human habitation at the beginning of the term and remain so throughout the tenancy.]
6. Further, section 4 of the Defective Premises Act 1972 has imposed a duty on the Defendant to take such care as is reasonable in all the circumstances to ensure that the Claimant and her family should be reasonably safe from personal injury or from damage to their property due to the defective state of the premises.

7. The Defendant has throughout the period of the tenancy been in breach of the terms, duties and obligations set out above. [As a result of these breaches, the premises are unfit for human habitation].

Particulars

i) From the outset of the tenancy there has been a half-inch gap above the window frame of the main window in the kitchen which has allowed water penetration. A repair was carried out in approximately May 2016 but within 24 hours the window had dropped again and the gap reappeared.

ii) The wallplaster to the external kitchen wall immediately below the window is cracked and since in or about November 2015 has crumbled and flaked upon contact. Black mould spots have been present on that wall since December 2015.

iii) Since early 2015 there has been penetrating damp to both the kitchen and small bedroom due to defects to the roof above. Damp patches (approximately two feet in diameter) formed on the ceilings in the small bedroom and kitchen. They are intermittently wet and dry and have discoloured the ceiling paper. Plaster in these areas is cracked and since December 2018 rainwater has dripped from the cracks whenever it rains.

iv) In or about April 2015 a crack developed around the window frame of the window in the main bedroom. The plaster around this window is loose and crumbling.

vi) The inner sills to both the kitchen and living room windows are rotted by reason of the accumulation of water upon them.

vii) From the outset of the tenancy, the pull-cord switch to the bathroom ceiling light has operated intermittently and the electrical socket provided in the hallway of the premises emits a spark when used

viii) The parapet wall to the walkway balcony immediately opposite the front door of the premises has throughout the tenancy had three of its upper row of bricks missing.

ix) The window glazing to the common stairwell providing access to the premises has been broken on two occasions. In 2016, the Defendant replaced the same after a delay of eight months. In 2017, after the glass was again broken, the Defendant replaced the same after six months.

x) In or about September 2016 a patch of damp began to develop on the wall of the premises immediately above the front door as a result of overflows from the roof guttering above.

[xi) Since about December 2014 the premises have been infested with cockroaches]

xii) Further details of these and other defects are given in the report that is appended hereto as schedule 1, prepared by Ms Expert following an inspection on 15 November 2018.

8. *Further, since about December 2014 the premises have been infested with cockroaches which come from parts retained by the Defendant and by reason of which the Defendant has caused a nuisance. No effective steps have been taken by the Defendant to eradicate the infestation either from the Claimant's flat or from the common parts.*
9. *The Defendant also owes the Claimant a duty of care to take reasonable steps to abate a nuisance that entered the premises from the parts retained by it and from the parts demised by it over which it had control.*
10. *Furthermore, in its treatment of the cockroaches the Defendant breached its common law duty of care by reason of the following:*

Particulars

The Defendant:

i) failed to carry out a survey of the block of flats in order to ascertain the full extent and origin of the infestation;

ii) failed to treat properly the parts retained by it;

iii) failed to treat properly the parts demised by it but under its control;

iv) failed to take any or any adequate steps to prevent/control the spread of cockroaches through the parts of the premises retained by the Defendant and from there into the demised premises;

v) failed to monitor after each treatment the extent of any remaining or new infestation; and

vi) failed to treat properly or at all any remaining or new infestation after each treatment.

11. The matters complained of in paragraph 7 and 8 above are known to the Defendant.

Particulars of knowledge

i) On occasions too numerous to particularise (but no less frequently than six times each year throughout the tenancy) the Claimant has reported the defects *and cockroaches* by telephone and in person to the Defendant at its Anytown North Neighbourhood Housing Office.

ii) On occasions too numerous to particularise Housing Officers, workmen and other persons employed by the Defendant have visited the premises for the purpose of inspection and to carry out works.

iii) Without prejudice to the generality of the foregoing, the Claimant has been visited at the premises by two successive Housing Officers (Ms Grant and Mrs Griffiths) in or about February 2018 and May 2018 respectively and both were shown the defects in the premises at the dates of their visits.

iv) In or about July 2018 a technical officer in the employ of the Defendant visited the premises and inspected the state thereof.

v) In or about August 2018 the Claimant reported the aforementioned defects *and cockroaches* to Timothy Thorogood who is a councillor for the Defendant.

vi) On 2 September 2018 the Claimant's solicitor sent a letter to the Defendant notifying it of the defects. This was the letter of claim as required by the CPR disrepair protocol. The Claimant's solicitors subsequently sent the Defendant a copy of the inspection report annexed hereto as schedule 1 on the 29 November 2018.

12. By reason of the aforementioned breaches of terms, obligations and duties the Claimant has suffered loss, damage, distress and inconvenience.

Particulars of inconvenience and distress

i) For the duration of the tenancy, the premises have been damp and unsightly and each winter have carried a pervading smell of dampness. The penetrating damp has caused and/or exacerbated a problem with condensation to the premises.

ii) The Claimant is forced to clean mould from the walls regularly, only to see it return within days.

iii) The Claimant's decorations, carpets and soft furnishings have been ruined by dampness and/or mould growth.

iv) Clothing kept in the premises by the Claimant and her son has to be repeatedly washed and/or replaced as a result of permeation by damp odour and the effect of mould.

v) The Claimant is embarrassed and ashamed about the appearance of the premises. The Claimant is frustrated by the failure of the Defendant to remedy the defects and in particular by the ineffectiveness of the works which have been undertaken.

[(vi) As a result of the dampness and mould growth the premises are a risk to the health and safety of the Claimant and her household.]

vii) *From the winter of 2014/15, and during each successive winter, the premises have been infested with cockroaches most particularly in the kitchen area which has caused additional stress and inconvenience to the Claimant and caused her to incur additional expenditure through the cost of eating out.*

Particulars of special damages

Schedule 1

[insert expert's report here]

See attached Schedule 2

13. The Claimant claims interest pursuant to the provisions of section 69 of the County Courts Act 1984 at such rate as the court may think fit.

AND THE CLAIMANT CLAIMS

i) An order for specific performance requiring the Defendant to remedy the defects [and unfitness];

ii) An injunction requiring the Defendant to take all steps necessary to discharge its statutory duty of care under section 4 of the Defective Premises Act 1972;

iii) *An injunction requiring the Defendant to take all steps necessary to eradicate the cockroach infestation from the premises and the building;*

iv) That the cost of repairs is more than £1,000;

v) Damages exceeding £10,000 but not more than £25,000;

vi) Interest on damages as provided by statute;

vii) Costs.

I ANNA TENNANT believe that the facts stated in these Particulars of Claim are true.[7]

Signed .... Dated ....

Name of signatory ....

Dated the .... day of .... 20...

Rainbow Community Law Centre

Rainbow High Street

Anytown

Solicitors for the Claimant

Tennant v Anytown Claim No. 9AT 04723

7 This wording assumes that Anna signs the statement of truth.

SCHEDULE 2

i) For six weeks in early 2018 the Claimant was forced by conditions in the premises to leave and stay with her mother. She paid her mother £40 weekly for expenses during that stay.

ii) The Claimant has expended additional monies which she estimates at £150 per year since 2014 on heating and £3 per week on cleaning materials as a result of the dampness of, *and cockroaches at,* the premises.

iii) The Claimant has expended additional monies on eating out which she estimates at £50 per week since November 2018.

6 DEFENCE AND COUNTERCLAIM

If the Council issues possession proceedings based on the alleged rent arrears, Anna can counterclaim for damages for the condition of the premises. This precedent assumes that the council has set out its particulars of claim on the current N119 court form.

In the County Court at Anytown Case No: 9AT05106

BETWEEN

ANYTOWN DISTRICT COUNCIL Claimant

and

ANNA TENNANT Defendant

DEFENCE AND COUNTERCLAIM

1. The Defendant denies that the Claimant has a right to possession as alleged in paragraph 1 of the Particulars of Claim but admits paragraphs 2 and 3 of the Particulars of Claim.
2. The Defendant does not admit paragraph 4 of the Particulars of Claim and requires the Claimant to prove the existence and extent of the arrears that it is claiming.
3. The Defendant claims the protection of section 84 of the Housing Act 1985 and asserts that in all the circumstances it would not be reasonable to make a possession order. The Defendant asserts that if arrears of rent have accrued, these arrears are due to the failure of the Claimant to pay and/or credit the rent account with housing benefit that is due to her.
4. In particular:
   i) The Claimant has failed to pay the Defendant her full housing benefit entitlement between February 2018 and April 2018 even though she completed a claim form in respect of the said period and has been eligible for maximum housing benefit throughout the period.
   ii) The Claimant has failed to pay any housing benefit from April 2018 to June 2018 even though the Defendant was entitled, had lodged her claim and dealt with all enquiries raised by the Claimant.
5. The Defendant cannot recall whether she received all the letters that the Claimant alleges were sent. Other than that, the Defendant admits paragraphs 5 and 6 of the Particulars of Claim.[8]

8 This assumes that Anna confirms that she has received a valid notice of seeking possession.

6. The Defendant asserts that in all the circumstances it would not be reasonable for an order for possession to be made and relies upon the matters pleaded above and also on the following facts and matters:
   i) The Defendant has been the Claimant's tenant since January 2014. She lives in the flat with her son Jeremy, who was born on 3 December 2013. Since her son was born the Defendant has been unable to work and she is currently dependent upon income support.
   ii) If the Defendant loses her home she will have nowhere else to live.
   iii) The Defendant is not well. She has uterine fibroids and as a result she is severely anaemic. This makes her constantly exhausted.
7. Further and alternatively, the Defendant is entitled to set off the sums counterclaimed herein in diminution or extinction of the arrears claimed.

COUNTERCLAIM

8. The Defendant repeats the defence set out above.
9. [From here on insert paragraphs 1–13 as per the Particulars of Claim on pages 372–376].[9]

AND THE DEFENDANT COUNTERCLAIMS:

i) An order for specific performance requiring the Claimant to remedy the defects and unfitness;
ii) An injunction requiring the Claimant to take all steps necessary to discharge its statutory duty of care under section 4 of the Defective Premises Act 1972;
iii) An injunction requiring the Claimant to take all steps necessary to eradicate the cockroach infestation from the premises and the building.
iv) That the cost of repairs is more than £1,000;
v) Damages of more than £10,000 but not more than £25,000;
vi) Interest on damages as provided by statute; and
vii) Costs.

Statement of truth

I ANNA TENNANT believe that the facts stated in this defence and counterclaim are true.[10]

Signed .... Dated ....

Name of signatory ....

Dated the .... day of .... 20...

Rainbow Community Law Centre
Rainbow High Street
Anytown
Solicitors for the Defendant

9 But reverse 'claimant' for 'defendant' in each paragraph.

10 This wording assumes that Anna signs the statement of truth.

7 APPLICATION FOR INJUNCTION (FORM N16A)

Click here to reset form | Click here to print form

Application for Injunction (General Form)

Name of court County Court at Anytown	Claim No. 9AT04723
Claimant's Name and Ref. Anna Tennant (02/1010/Ten)	
Defendant's Name and Ref. Anytown District Council (LED/HD/A8/23792)	
Fee Account no.	

Notes on completion

Tick which boxes apply and specify the legislation where appropriate

(1) Enter the full name of the person making the application

(2) Enter the full name of the person the injunction is to be directed to

(3) Set out any proposed orders requiring acts to be done. Delete if no mandatory order is sought.

(4) Set out here the proposed terms of the injunction order (if the defendant is a limited company delete the wording in brackets and insert 'whether by its servants, agents, officers or otherwise').

(5) Set out here any further terms asked for including provision for costs

(6) Enter the names of all persons who have sworn affidavits or signed statements in support of this application

(7) Enter the names and addresses of all persons upon whom it is intended to serve this application

(8) Enter the full name and address for service and delete as required

☐ By application in pending proceedings

☐ Under Statutory provision

☐ This application is made under Part 8 of the Civil Procedure Rules

Seal

This application raises issues under the Human Rights Act 1998 ☐ Yes ☑ No

The Claimant[(1)]

applies to the court for an injunction order in the following terms:

The Defendant[(2)] Anytown District Council

must[(3)] carry out repair work as listed in the attached draft order on or before 18 March 2019 at premises known as 17 Tower House, Moors Estate, Anytown

The Defendant

be forbidden (whether by himself or by instructing or encouraging or permitting any other person)[(4)]

And that[(5)]

The grounds of this application are set out in the written evidence

of[(6)] Anna Tennant (signed) on 15/2/19

This written evidence is served with this application.

This application is to be served upon[(7)]

The principal solicitor, Anytown District Council, Council Offices, Anytown, Any County

This application is filed by[(8)]

(the Solicitors for) the Claimant

whose address for service is

Rainbow High Street, Anytown, Any County

Signed Dated

* Name and address of the person application is directed to

To*

of

This section to be completed by the court

This application will be heard by the (District) Judge

at

on the day of 20 at o'clock

If you do not attend at the time shown the court may make an injunction order in your absence

If you do not fully understand this application you should go to a Solicitor, Legal Advice Centre or a Citizens' Advice Bureau

The court office at

is open between 10am and 4pm Mon - Fri. When corresponding with the court, please address all forms and letters to the Court Manager and quote the claim number.

N16A General form of application for injunction (05.14)

8 DRAFT MANDATORY ORDER

This can be used for an interim or final injunction and/or specific performance.

Before His Honour Judge Right sitting at Anytown County Court on ....

UPON HEARING ....

UPON READING the Claimant's evidence dated 15 February 2019

AND UPON the Claimant undertaking by her solicitor to abide by any order that this Court may make for the payment of damages in case this Court shall hereafter find that the Defendant has sustained any loss or damage by reason of this Order[11]

IT IS ORDERED THAT within 14 days of service of this order the Defendant shall carry out the following work at the premises known as: 17 Tower House, Moors Estate, Anytown:

a) repair the roof immediately above the premises to prevent the ingress of rainwater;
b) seal the gaps and cracks around the windows to the main bedroom of the premises; and
c) provide to the solicitors for the Claimant a written report from a qualified electrical engineer setting out any work needed to the electrical system in the premises together with a proposed timescale for that work.

IT IS FURTHER ORDERED that the Defendant should pay the costs of and incidental to this hearing in any event.

PENAL NOTICE

Any officer of the Defendant disobeying this order may be held to be in contempt of court and may be liable to be committed to prison.

Dated ....

Judge Right

11 It is hoped that the judge will not require this undertaking. See para 3.133.

9 TOMLIN ORDER

Order

In the	**COUNTY COURT AT ANYTOWN**
Claim No.	9AT 04723
Claimant (including ref)	ANNA TENNANT (re: 02/0921/ten)
Defendant(s) (including ref)	ANYTOWN DISTRICT COUNCIL (ref: LS/HD/AB/33354)
Date	15 September 2019

Before Judge ....

Upon the parties agreeing terms, and by consent

IT IS ORDERED THAT:

1. All further proceedings in this claim shall be stayed upon the terms in the attached Schedule, except for the purpose of carrying such terms into effect.
2. The Claimant has permission to apply to the Court if the Defendant does not give effect to the terms set out in the Schedule.
3. The Defendant shall by 4 pm on 13 October 2019 pay to the Claimant's solicitors the sum of £10,000 on account of the Claimant's costs of the action.[12]
4. The Defendant shall pay the Claimant's costs as agreed or as assessed by the Court at a detailed assessment hearing.
5. There be a detailed assessment of the Claimant's publicly funded costs.

We hereby consent to an order in the above terms:

....	....
Rainbow Law Centre	The Principal Solicitor
Rainbow High Street	Anytown District Council
Anytown	Council Offices
Anycounty	Anytown
Tel:........................	Tel:........................
Fax:........................	Fax:........................
Ref: 02/0921/ten	Ref:. LS/HD/AB/33354
Solicitor for the Claimant	Solicitor for the Defendant

Tennant v Anytown Claim No. 9AT 04723

12 This is a useful way of obtaining some of the costs before a lengthy wait for a detailed assessment.

SCHEDULE

1. The Defendant shall pay the Claimant the sum of £14,500, by 4 pm on 13 October 2019 in full and final satisfaction of all claims arising in these proceedings.
2. In the event of late payment, the Defendant will pay interest on the sum of £14,500 or any part remaining due at the applicable interest rate for unpaid County Court judgments.
3. The Defendant shall by 10 November 2019 complete the roofing works as referred to in the report dated 29 November 2018 of Ms Expert, the joint expert.
4. The said roofing work will be completed to the satisfaction of the joint expert whose reasonable further charges the Defendant shall pay.

Dated ....

Signed	Signed ....
Solicitor for the Claimant	Solicitor for the Defendant
Date	Date ....

Environmental Protection Act 1990 proceedings

10 NOTICE OF INTENDED PROCEEDINGS

The Clerk	Date:	27 January 2019
Anytown District Council	Our ref:	
Council Offices, Anytown	Your ref:	

Dear Sir or Madam

Anna Tennant, 17 Tower House, Moors Estate, Anytown

We act for the above tenant.

We enclose a copy of an environmental health officer's report. You will see that the expert concludes that the state of the premises is such that they are prejudicial to the health of our client. Full particulars of the matters complained of are given in the report.

This letter is notice, given under section 82(6) of the Environmental Protection Act 1990, of our client's intention to bring proceedings against your local authority in its capacity as owner and landlord and as the person responsible for the statutory nuisance.

Our client requires you to abate the statutory nuisance and to carry out any works necessary to prevent it from recurring. Unless this is done within 21 days she will start her prosecution without further notice to you.

Please confirm safe receipt of this letter.

Yours faithfully,

Rainbow Law Centre

Copies to: The Borough Solicitor
The Moors Estate Neighbourhood Office

11 INITIAL INFORMATION UNDER PART 7 OF THE CRIMINAL PROCEDURE RULES[13]

INFORMATION
(Magistrates' Courts Act 1980 s1)

.... Anytown **Magistrates' Court** (Code)

Date:[14] ....

Accused: ....The Anytown District Council ....

Address: .. Council Offices, Anytown, postcode ....
....

Alleged offence: (short particulars and statute) ....

That on this day a statutory nuisance as defined by section 79(1)(a) of the Environmental Protection Act 1990 exists at 17 Tower House, Moors Estate, Anytown and continues to exist and that the statutory nuisance (particulars of which are given in the attached statement) is the responsibility of the Anytown District Council and in so far as it results from structural defects is its responsibility as owner.

The information of: Anna Tennant, being a person aggrieved for the purposes of section 82 of the said Act.

Address: 17 Tower House, Moors Estate, Anytown

whose **address for service** of these proceedings is:[15]

c/o Rainbow Community Law Centre, Rainbow High Street, Anytown

Telephone No: 0275 125689 (ask for Ms Lewis, the informant's solicitor)

who (upon oath) states that the accused committed the offence of which particulars are given above.

Taken (and sworn) before me,
.... **Justice of the Peace**
.... **(Justices' Clerk)**

13 This is a prescribed form which can be accessed at www.justice.gov.uk.

14 Leave date blank, for magistrates' clerk to complete.

15 If the court can be persuaded to send all correspondence about the prosecution directly to the adviser's office it considerably simplifies matters.

12 STATEMENT IN SUPPORT OF INFORMATION

STATEMENT OF WITNESS
(Criminal Procedure Rules r16.2, Criminal Justice Act 1967 s9))

STATEMENT OF Anna Tennant
Age of witness (if over 18, enter 'over 18'): over 18 This statement (consisting of pages) **is true to the best of my knowledge and belief and I make it knowing that, if it is tendered in evidence, I shall be liable to prosecution if I have wilfully stated in it anything which I know to be false, or do not believe to be true.**

1. My name is Anna Tennant. I am currently unemployed.
2. I live at 17 Tower House, Moors Estate, Anytown. I live there with my son Jeremy (date of birth 3 December 2013).
3. My home is a two-bedroom flat on the fourth floor of small block. I rent it from Anytown District Council; they own my flat and they own and control the block. My tenancy began in January 2014 and I moved in at about that time.
4. About two months, after I had moved in a damp patch appeared on the ceiling in Jeremy's bedroom. I noticed that it was about a metre square and that it got wet after rain and then it dried out again. In about March 2015 I noticed a similar patch had developed on the kitchen ceiling.
5. The patches have discoloured the ceiling wallpaper and since about December 2018 water has dripped from the patches whenever it rains heavily.
6. Black mould spots started to form on the kitchen wall in about December 2016.
7. There have been several cockroach infestations of Tower House whilst I have been living there. The most recent one started in about December 2014 and is the worst one yet. Cockroaches come out of the service ducts in the kitchen and crawl all over the walls, floors and work surfaces every night.
8. I have complained to my landlords about the mould and the cockroaches by telephone and by going into their office at least six times a year since December 2014.
9. Two housing officers (Ms Grant and Mrs Griffiths) have visited me. Ms Grant visited in about February 2018 and Mrs Griffiths visited in May 2018. I showed both of them the mould, the wet patches and some dead cockroaches.
10. In about July 2018 a technical officer employed by my landlords visited and inspected.
11. I consulted solicitors in 2018 and they instructed Ms Expert, an Environmental Health Consultant to report on the conditions in my home. She inspected and I am now shown her report as exhibit 'AT 1'. I have read the report and I agree with what it says.
12. Ms Expert says that the roof of block is leaking which is causing the damp in the bedroom and kitchen. She says that this has caused the moisture levels to rise in the flat and this has caused the mould growth.

He says in his report that the cockroaches are getting in along the pipes that bring water to the whole block.

13. I am now shown 'AT 2' a letter dated 27 January 2019 that my solicitor sent to my landlords giving them 21 days in which to remedy the problems. Their acknowledgement is also attached.
14. No work has been carried out since Ms Expert inspected and, if anything, the conditions are a bit worse than when she saw my flat. There are more cockroaches and the damp smell is worse.
15. The cockroaches and mould make me feel sick. On one occasion I had invited a friend round and a cockroach ran across the floor whilst she was standing with me in the kitchen. This made me feel very dirty and ashamed and I have not invited anyone to visit since.
16. My son's room is very small so we cannot move the bed out of the way when rain water drips in. I try to protect his bed by covering it with plastic bags but sometimes it is soaked and he has to sleep on the settee. I used to spend hours each week washing the mould off with bleach but it always came back within a matter of days and the bleach started to damage the walls so I had to stop. I try to keep my kitchen extremely clean so that there is nothing for cockroaches to eat. I wash all the kitchen surfaces down with bleach every night but they are still there.
17. I accuse my landlords of being responsible for premises that are a statutory nuisance as defined by section 79(1)(a) of the Environmental Protection Act 1990. I rely of the facts set out in the attached report of Ms Expert, the Environmental Health Officer.
18. I am therefore a person aggrieved for the purposes of section 82 of the Environmental Protection Act 1990
19. The premises have been in the condition set out in Ms Expert's report since the late summer of 2018. They are prejudicial to health today.
20. The notice required under section 82(6) of the Environmental Protection Act 1990 was given as described above. No effective work has been carried since then or at all.
21. The council has therefore had 21 days clear notice of my intentions and in spite of this the defects have not been remedied and my home remains prejudicial to my health.
22. In the circumstances, I request that the court grant me a summons against the accused.

Signed: .... (witness)
Date: ....
(***To be completed if applicable***: .... being unable to read the above statement I, ...of ...., read it to him/her before he/she signed it.
Signed: .... **Date**: ....)

13 FURTHER INFORMATION UNDER PART 7 OF THE CRIMINAL PROCEDURE RULES[16]

INFORMATION
(Magistrates' Courts Act 1980 s1)

.... Anytown **Magistrates' Court** (Code)
Date:[17] ....
Accused: ....The Anytown District Council ....
Address: .. Council Offices, Anytown, postcode ....
....
Alleged offence: (short particulars and statute) ....
That contrary to section 82(8) of the Environmental Protection Act 1990 you have without reasonable excuse failed to comply with an order made by this court on 10 April 2019 requiring you to abate a statutory nuisance at 17 Tower House, Moors Estate, Anytown

The information of: Anna Tennant, being a person aggrieved for the purposes of section 82(1) of the said Act.

Address: 17 Tower House, Moors Estate, Anytown

whose **address for service** of these proceedings is:[18]
c/o Rainbow Community Law Centre, Rainbow High Street, Anytown
Telephone No: 0275 125689 (ask for Ms Lewis, the informant's solicitor)

who (upon oath) states that the accused committed the offence of which particulars are given above.

Taken (and sworn) before me,
.... **Justice of the Peace**
.... **(Justices' Clerk)**

16 This is a prescribed form which can be accessed at www.justice.gov.uk.

17 Leave date blank, for magistrates' clerk to complete.

18 If the court can be persuaded to send all correspondence about the prosecution directly to the adviser's office it considerably simplifies matters.

14 STATEMENT IN SUPPORT OF FURTHER INFORMATION

STATEMENT OF WITNESS
(Criminal Procedure Rules r16.2 Criminal Justice Act 1967 s9))

STATEMENT OF Anna Tennant
Age of witness (if over 18, enter 'over 18'): over 18 This statement (consisting of one page) **is true to the best of my knowledge and belief and I make it knowing that, if it is tendered in evidence, I shall be liable to prosecution if I have wilfully stated in it anything which I know to be false, or do not believe to be true.**

1. My name is Anna Tennant. I am currently unemployed.
2. I live at 17 Tower House, Moors Estate, Anytown. I live there with my son Jeremy (date of birth 3 December 2013).
3. My home is a two-bedroom flat on the fourth floor of small block. I rent it from Anytown District Council; they own my flat and they own and control the block. I am therefore a person aggrieved for the purposes of section 82 of the Environmental Protection Act 1990
4. On 10 April 2019 this court made a Nuisance Order under section 82(2) of the Environmental Protection Act 1990 compelling the accused to carry out works at my home by 10 June 2019.
5. The accused failed to comply with the court order within the period prescribed by that order. As at 13 June 2019 none of the prescribed work had started.
6. In the circumstances, I request that the court grant me a summons against the accused under section 82(8) of the Environmental Protection Act 1990.

Signed: .... **(witness)**

Date: ....
(***To be completed if applicable***: .... being unable to read the above statement I, ...of ...., read it to him/her before he/she signed it.

Signed: .... **Date**: ....)

Official complaint under Housing Act 2004 s4 (see chapter 4)

15 DRAFT REQUEST FOR A COMPLAINT TO BE MADE

To: Mr John Smith, a Justice of the Peace for the Anytown Area
*Or: Ms Jenny Brown, clerk to the Anytown Parish (or Community) Council**

Our client Anna Tennant complains that the property occupied by her at 17 Tower House, Moors Estate, Anytown, being residential premises within the district of the Anytown District Council, is in such poor condition that an inspection of it should be made by the District Council so that it may determine whether the condition is a hazard and, if so, exercise its powers (and carry out any duties) given by the Housing Act 2004 Part 1.

Our client asks that you consider the documents and photographs enclosed.

She asks that if you/*your council** agree that these conditions merit a visit and inspection of the premises by an Environmental Health Officer employed by the District Council that you do cause complaint to be made to the said District Council in writing as provided by Housing Act 2004 section 4(3) requiring them to carry out an inspection of the said premises and to make such report, if any, as may be required by section 4(6). A form is supplied for your signature. We shall be pleased to submit it to the District Council if you would prefer us to do so. We also enclose, for your assistance, a copy of section 4.

Dated this 28th day of March 2019

Rainbow Community Law Centre
Rainbow High Street
Anytown
Solicitors for the Complainant

* delete as appropriate

16 DRAFT OFFICIAL COMPLAINT

To: The Proper Officer and the Senior Environmental Health Officer of the Anytown District Council, Anytown.

OFFICIAL COMPLAINT: HOUSING ACT 2004 s4(3)

I, John Smith being an appointed Justice of the Peace for the area of Anytown

Or: I, Jenny Brown, the clerk to – and on behalf of – the Anytown Parish/ Community Council

do hereby make official complaint to you in the terms of section 4(3) Housing Act 2004 that the condition of the residential premises at 17 Tower House, Moors Estate, within the area of your District Council, calls for an inspection to be made by your Council pursuant to that section so that it may be considered whether a hazard is present and what action (if any) should be taken.

Dated this 29th day of March 2019

Signed ....

APPENDIX D

Technical information: understanding experts' reports

A lawyer's guide written by Mel Cairns MCIEH

Walls and brickwork

Main types of dampness

Rising damp – ground water moving up walls by capillary action into buildings

Penetrating damp – water entering the building as a result of rain or snow ingress

Condensation damp – atmospheric moisture condensing out on cold surfaces

Traumatic damp – caused by leaks/floods

Construction moisture – damp caused by building work: wet trades, plaster, mortar, paint etc

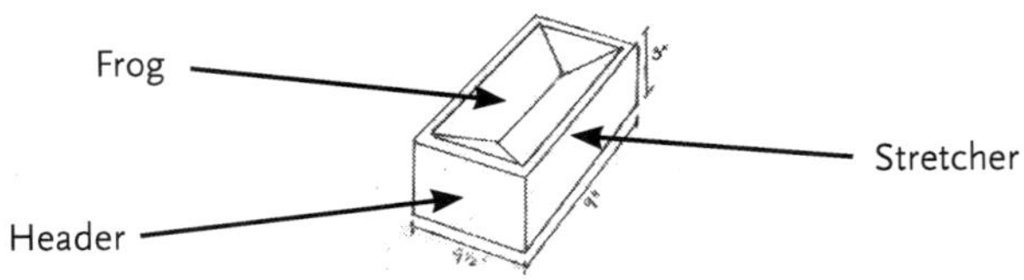

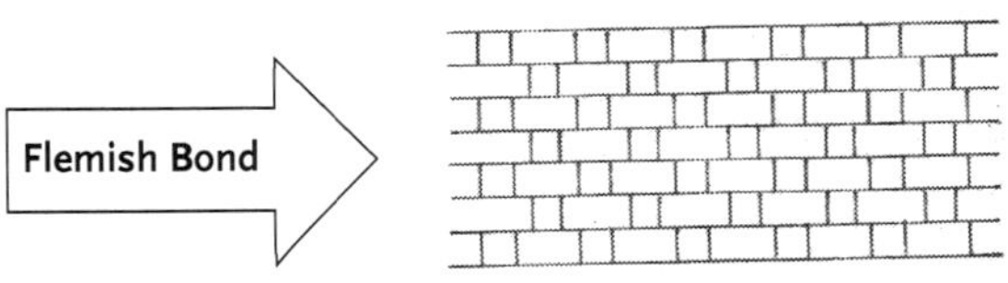

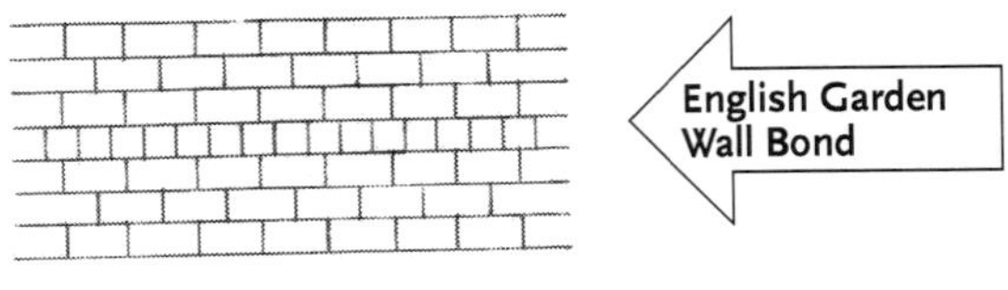

Terms used in relation to walls

Cavity wall – a wall formed of two layers of brick with a space between them, as a precaution against penetrating damp; common in buildings since the 1940s

Cold bridge – cold spot: especially at corners or concrete lintels/framing

Damp proof course – a horizontal barrier in a wall designed to prevent rising damp – in solid floors the barrier is termed a damp-proof membrane

Efflorescence – soluble salts collecting as white crystals on the face of bricks

Engineering bricks – dense/hard bricks (sometimes used as a damp-proof course)

Footings – foundations (in older properties sometimes formed of stepped courses of bricks)

Hygroscopic salts – salts that form on contaminated building materials which absorb or attract moisture from the air

Perpend – vertical mortar joint/end face of brick or stone

Plinth – base of the wall/column (often rendered)

Quoin – corner junction of brick walls

Render – a first layer of plaster or cement on a wall

Solid brick wall – external wall built of one layer, usually 9" thick; common in pre-1940s buildings

Sleeper wall – wall supporting floor joists (contains gaps for ventilation and so sometimes called a 'honeycomb' wall)

Stucco – render coating usually painted

Stud partition – plasterboard on timber frame

Systems building – non-traditional/prefabrication

Wall ties – metal straps linking inner and outer leaves of cavity wall

Weephole – omitting mortar joints at intervals above a damp-proof course to permit a cavity wall to drain

Roofs

Terms used in relation to roofs

Dished or settled roof – sagging of roof slope; often as a result of recovering with heavier concrete tiles without additional strengthening

Fire break wall – party wall continued up through roof space to prevent spread of fire in linked properties

Firring pieces – angled timber to support boarding and provide a self-draining slope on flat roofs

Flaunching – cement render embedding chimney pots

Nail fatigue – corrosion of slate fixings allowing slates to slip

Verge – edge of roof

Wall plate – timber along the top of a wall carrying rafters or joists

Pitched roof

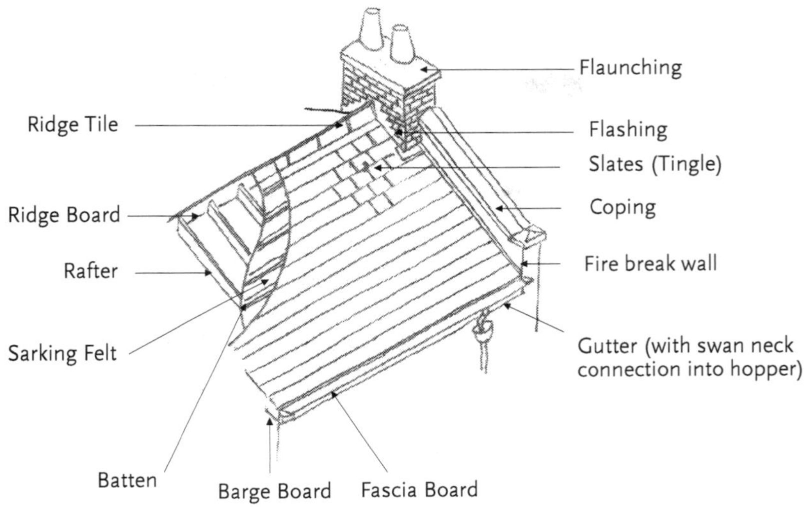

Loft

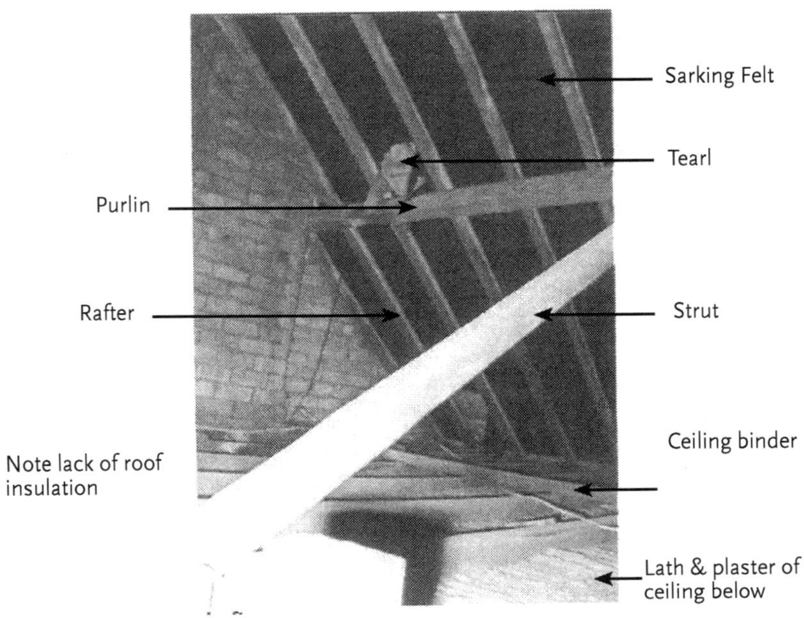

Windows

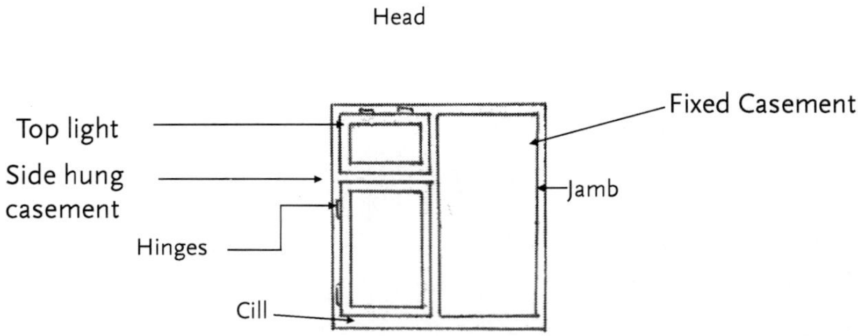

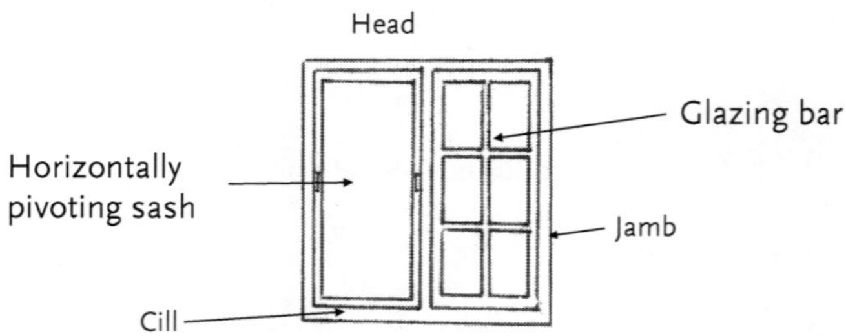

Terms used in relation to windows

Borrowed light – glazed panel in interior wall to introduce daylight from adjoining room

Crittall – steel framed windows

Espagnolette bolts – several bolts locking a door or window from a single handle/lock

Friction hinge – holds window ajar

Hopper window – small toplights or fanlight hinged on bottom edge

Spring action spiral/spring tape balances – modern versions of double hung sash replacing pulleys, cords and weights

Throating – drip details on underside edge of cills to prevent rain tracking back

Transom – horizontal rail in a window frame

Trickle vent – small adjustable vent in window head to provide background ventilation

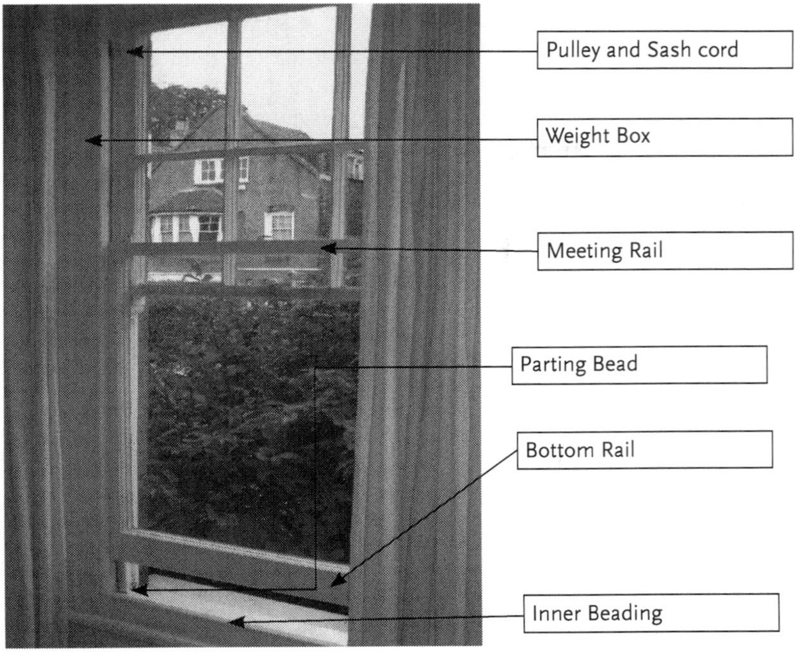

Services

Terms used in relation to heating and hot water

Balanced flue – combustion gas and air supply sealed from room (ie, from/to exterior via dual flue)

Combi (combination) boiler – heats the radiators and the domestic hot water in one box; does not need a hot water tank

Cylinder stat – thermostat on hot water cylinder

Lockshield valve – valve on radiator used on installation to balance (set up) the flow of water in the system

Randall programmer – dated electro mechanical timer/programmer for central heating and hot water

Terms used in relation to electrics

Consumer unit – meter, main switch and cut-out (fuse/circuit breaker)

Junction box – covers ends of joints to conductors

Spur – socket outlet from ring main (fused/illuminated versions)

Terms used in relation to drainage:

Bolt down or double seal cover – second cover for a manhole inside a dwelling to prevent odours and flooding from backing up into the dwelling

Cone joint – flexible joint connecting WC flush pipe to back of WC

Inspection chambers – manhole allowing access to section of drain; particularly where two or more drains meet

Rodding eye – point in pipe length where drain rods can be introduced (bolted on in cast iron pipes)

Soil stack – takes sewage to drain system; top section continues above roof to vent methane

Other technical terms

Bressemer [Breastsummer] – large heavy lintel – usually timber (older housing/shop fronts)

Dry riser – duct rising in block of flats to which the fire brigade can connect water supplies for hoses on landings

Floating floor – independent noise reducing overlay on an existing floor

French drain – shingle filled trench.

Garshey – waste disposal grinder in sink waste pipes

Half a person – child under 10 years of age in the statutory overcrowding standard

Scarf joint – angled joint in wood.

Sempatap – thin foam sheet with fibreglass on one side applied like wallpaper for insulation

Soffit – underside of stairs, arch, beam, window head etc

Splay – angle (e.g. cut brick, side wall of bay etc)

Sponge effect – potential for furnishings etc to take up water vapour temporarily

Tingle – a clip to temporarily secure loose slates

Upside down roof – Thermal insulation laid over (usually existing) flat roof

U-value – thermal transmittance co-efficient – an indication of the thermal insulation value of an element (eg the external walls) – limit specified by Building Regulations

Experts' equipment

Boroscope – allows examination of cavity walls and other voids

Carbide meter – on-site test for free moisture in walls

Current tester – detects current in wiring

Fibre optic viewer – allows examination of cavity walls and other voids

Data loggers/thermohygrometers – sample temperature and humidity data

Martindale – electric socket tester

Protimeter/damp meters – conductance/search mode/deep wall probes – provides an indication of the relative dampness of an element

Abbreviations

ABE – Association of Building Engineers
AFD – automatic fire detector
BA '84 – Building Act 1984
BBA – British Board of Agrément
BRE – Building Research Establishment
BREDEM – BRE Domestic Energy Model
BPA – British Pest Control Association
BWPDA – British Wood Preserving & Damp Proofing Association
Cat 1 – Category 1 hazard under HHSRS
Cat 2 – Category 2 hazard under HHSRS
CDM – Construction (Design & Management) Regulations
CI – cast iron
CO2 – Fire extinguisher using carbon dioxide (kitchen situations)
CIEH – Chartered Institute of Environmental Health
CIOB – Chartered Institute of Building
CIOP – Chartered Institute of Plumbing
Combi – combined heat and hot water boiler
CORGI – Council of Registered Gas Installers
COSHH – Control of Substances Hazardous to Health Regulations
CP – call point (fire alarm) or Code of Practice
CP12 – Landlords' statutory annual gas certificate under the Gas Safety (Installation & Use) Regulations
DPA – Defective Premises Act
dhs – double hung sash window
DHS – Decent Homes Standard
dpc – damp-proof course (in walls)
dpm – damp-proof membrane (in solid floors)
EDMO – Empty Dwelling Management Order
EHO – environmental health officer
EL – Emergency Lighting Unit (fire plans)
EPA – Environmental Protection Act 1990
EPO – Emergency Prohibition Order (HA 2004)
ERA – Emergency Remedial Action (HA 2004)
FED – front entrance door
FB – fire blanket (fire plans) or Fire Brigade
FFT(RP) – First-tier Tribunal (Residential Property)
FMO – Final Management Order (HA 2004)
GS(I&U)R – Gas Safety (Installation and Use) Regulations
HA – Housing Act (+ date)
HAN – Hazard Awareness Notice (HA 2004 Part 1)
HASWA – Health and Safety at Work Act 1974

HD – heat detector (fire plans)
HHSRS – Housing Health and Safety Rating System (HA 2004 Part 1)
HIP – home information pack
HMO – house in multiple occupation
HSE – Health and Safety Executive
H20 – water type fire extinguisher (fire plans)
IC – inspection chamber
IEE – Institute of Electrical Engineers (now part of the IET)
IET – Institution of Engineering and Technology
IMO – Interim Management Order (HA 2004)
IN – Improvement Notice (HA 2004 Part 1)
IP – indicator panel (fire plans)
IVS – intervening ventilated space
LD (1 of 3) – grades of fire detection systems
MDHS – method for determination of hazardous substances
MO – Management Order (HA 2004)
NHER – National Home Energy Rating Scheme
OT – occupational therapist
Part P – Electrical Safety Requirements (Building Regulations)
PO – Prohibition Order (HA 2004 Part 1)
PDPA49 – Prevention of Damage by Pests Act 1949
QS – quantity surveyor
RICS – Royal Institution of Chartered Surveyors
RIDDOR – reporting of injuries, disease and dangerous occurrences
RRO – Rent Repayment Order (HA 2004)
RWDP – rain-water down pipe
SA – smoke alarm (fire plans)
SAP – standard assessment procedure (energy label)
SD – smoke detector (fire plans)
S/C – self-closer
S/F – supply and fit (specifications)
Sika – tanking and waterproofing
SVP – soil vent pipe
TCRV – thermostatically controlled radiator valves
VOCs – volatile organic compounds (HHSRS)
WME – wood moisture equivalent (indicator of dampness in materials other than wood)
WWP – waste water preventer (flushing cistern)

Sources of information

Oxford Dictionary of Contruction Surveying and Civil Engineering, Oxford University Press, 2012

Index